The European Union and its Order:
The Legal Theory of European Integration

𝔅

The European Union and its Order: The Legal Theory of European Integration

Zenon Bańkowski
and
Andrew Scott

BLACKWELL
Publishers

Copyright © Zenon Bańkowski and Andrew Scott

First published 2000

ISBN: 0-631-21504-2 pbk

Blackwell Publishers Ltd
108 Cowley Road
Oxford OX4 1JF, UK

Blackwell Publishers Inc
350 Main Street
Malden, Massachusetts 02148, USA

British Library Cataloguing in Publication Data has been applied for

Library of Congress Cataloging in Publication Data has been applied for

Typeset by Polestar
Printed and bound in Great Britain
By MPG Books, Bodmin, Cornwall

This book is printed on acid-free paper

CONTENTS

Preface

Zenon Bańkowski and Andrew Scott

The papers in this volume stem from a research seminar series funded by the ESRC and convened by Zenon Bańkowski and Andrew Scott. The aim of the seminar series was to clarify legal theoretical questions raised by the demise of the sovereign state within the context of the European Union and to elaborate a theoretical framework within which these questions were to be raised. The first five chapters in the volume were previously published in December 1998 as a Special Issue of the *European Law Journal* (Volume 4, Issue 4). However, this volume additionally contains a further five chapters not previously published, written by colleagues who also participated in the seminar series. We are delighted to have the opportunity here of presenting this work, an opportunity that *ELJ* space constraints prevented. Needless to say we thank the authors of these additional chapters in particular for their patience in seeing their work published.

The fundamental starting point in our collective thinking on legal theory in the context of the European Union was the rather obvious observation that the development of the European Union has brought within it the development of a new legal order. It is an order that challenges traditional thinking about law. It decouples law and state. By so doing it raises profound questions concerning the structure and legitimacy of an emerging normative order which does not depend upon the existence of a sovereign state. The European Union is a rapidly developing legal regime involving a judiciary of diverse legal developments and traditions. Fundamental principles in legal development are illuminated by the process and principles that shape the normative legal order. Driving this process is the objective of creating a transnational free market. But the impact of the unfolding economic legal order extends beyond the strictly economic arena. Consequently, the ECJ has started the process of creating what is effectively a constitutional structure for the European Union; however, this is a structure whose legitimacy as a polity cannot be taken for granted. Scholars of European integration and of the role of the ECJ in this process have demonstrated the way in which the Court has in the past established the framework within which the EU has evolved. Although previously, the ECJ was, in large measure, unimpeded in this, this is now no longer the case. This constitutional-isation process is now more public and contested. One of the reasons for this is because of the pace at which the EU's legal order has outstripped its polity.

The interaction between forms of polity, democratic legitimacy and the building of a pan European normative legal order can only be properly theorised within an interdisciplinary context. Legal developments and theorising about European law need to be located within the appropriate political and economic context. This is particularly pertinent to the European situation in which legal theory has had to abandon the notion of a fixed and immutable coincidence between law and the sovereign state. For in the European Union, national sovereignty in its absolute sense is no longer tenable. How, then, can a legal order that embraces legal pluralism be created.

The ten papers in this volume each—in its own way—seek to develop these themes by focusing on the way that entities like the EU force us to look at law in a polycentric way; on the way different normative systems interact and interlock; on the relations between normative and territorial space. In particular the focus will be on the way national identities not based on the nation state can be fostered, while at the same time constructing a European identity. Following on from that they will consider what that vision of unity means for democracy and 'European Integration' and how this comes to terms with a transnational free market. Unsurprisingly, a recurring theme throughout the volume is 'citizenship', and this is addressed explicitly in two of the later contributions in the volume.

Lindahl and Van Roermund look at the foregoing and try to show what it means to understand the EU as an autonomous order but not a political unity. Part of the problem for them is the idea of a representational substitutionism—for there to be an autonomous order it must represent and refer to a pre-existing political unity—the view of the German Constitutional Court in the *Brunner* decision. For them the EU is already a political community but not a nation state. One can view the legal order as the institutional instantiation of the common good of the European peoples. But that is not a linear relation but a reflexive one. The political community is created in the interaction always changing and developing between the two. This in turn creates other institutions all of which develop the idea of the political community and recursively feed back upon each other. In doing that they also explain why the notion of a common economic market is an important but not determinative part of the process. This notion of the immanence of the community, always in the process of becoming is further developed in the next paper.

Zenon Bańkowski and Emilios Christodoulidis try and produce a general conceptual scheme for understanding the interlocking and intertwined normative schemes and identities and the mode of their articulation. They describe the EU in a way that decouples law and state, that gets away from debates as to the ultimate site of sovereignty in the EU and seeks instead to conceptualise the EU as an entity of interlocking normative spheres with no particular one being privileged. The EU is to be found in the continuous process of negotiation and renegotiation, which does not have a single reference point or end in view. The whole system and its identity emerges in the clash of these systems. This way of looking at it has the consequence that it tries to see as normal the system's mode of existence, which for many legal theorists would be seen as a system in crisis. European identity then is something that is essentially contested in a systemic way and the metaphor of an ongoing journey without a destination shows how this can be an ongoing process, a continuing negotiation without end; how the identity is always contested with no fixed definition. The use of systems theory to make more precise what the contestability of Europe is, since the theory is about how different systems interact, with none being particularly privileged. At the same time, they do not want to suggest that this contestability is arbitrary, that there are no signposts on the journey and so they start by looking at something like signposts—the ideals with which the whole process began.

Neil Walker deals with this articulation in more concrete detail, especially in regard to sovereignty, and explores what these mechanisms mean for integration and the new European polity. For him, the growing challenge to the principle of uniformity within EU law, now marked by the endorsement of differential participation across all three Pillars in the Treaty of Amsterdam, means that politically, flexible arrangements appear indispensable to accommodate conflicting preferences over the rate and direction of integration. Analyses of the EU have typically addressed a configuration of authority involving a relationship between two fixed units—the fifteen Member States and the EU itself (a 'binocular' vision). A two-dimensional analysis is no longer appropriate. Instead, there are various different 'Europes', their breadth and depth dependent upon arrangements specific to the policy field, and embedded in a complex of relations with one another and with the Member States. He develops a multi-dimensional approach, interpreting sovereignty as a series of (competing) plausible claims to ultimate legal authority within a polity. The way he does this is by assessing the political dynamics of differentiated integration and looking at the associated difficulties. Finally, he assesses the political and constitutional prospects for the new Europe and questions whether the political dynamics driving differentiated integration provide a hospitable climate for the successful treatment of the problems associated with multi-dimensionality.

In her paper Jo Shaw examines the 'membership element' in EY citizenship. She criticises conventional approaches which see membership in terms of formally defined rules which can be derived from the key Treaty sources. She argues that what she thinks of as a 'relational' approach to citizenship is more important. This involves keeping the notion in flux and seeing it as an emergent property of the complex interactions at the various boundaries. In this it links in with the notion of 'inter-locking normative spheres' that was developed in the seminar and takes up the themes of Bańkowski's and Christodoulidis', and Walker's papers. In looking at citizenship in that context she looks in more detail at the mechanisms of and the results at the interfaces between different spheres. In looking at case studies 'at the boundaries' in respect of non-economic migrants, sex equality and the status of affirmative action, and sexual orientation she shows how the articulations change the idea of citizenship and membership both in the specific cases and in general. In particular, within these interactions, she shows how the notion of equality relates to and is transformed in the concept of citizenship.

Michelle Everson shows how traditional views (as exemplified in the Brunner decision of the Bundesverfassungsgericht) fail to meet the demands of the new polity and its transnational single market. She shows how that decision, though ostensibly limiting the supremacy of European law and subjecting its further evolution to the normative values encapsulated in the German Constitution may be argued to be indicative of two legal/constitutional problems. First, the failing normativity of a body of European law which is no longer merely concerned with the neutral codification of a private sphere of European economic activity, and now plays a far greater part in the substantive and thus public/political process of market regulation. And secondly, the inability of traditional constitutional thought normatively to capture and structure an uncertain, pluralistic and open-ended process of European polity-building. Following on from this, she seeks to identify a new normative basis for European law; urging European lawyers to consider their law as a new and novel constitutional order, dedicated to ensuring that the on-going process of European polity-building is founded on civic and deliberative debate between varied and still-evolving national, Community and even private interests.

Daniel Wincott takes up this challenge. He deals with how traditional statist views misdiagnose the problems of democracy and 'the democratic deficit' within the EU. He argues that the 'statist' character of most notions provide a misleading view of the democratic qualities of existing states, and an impossible standard for the European Union. He, however, sounds a note of caution and argues that even in more sophisticated 'post-statist' attempts to recaste themselves as 'new constitutionalist' literature, the analyses retain their conventionality and that there may therefore still be a problem of the EU perverting democracy. For him, the new constitutionalist work does not succeed in neutralising the 'democratic critique' fully. He tries to rescue the democratic accountability in EU integration work from its statist entanglements. He does this by emphasising the role of actors in positions of state power, rather than reified 'states' as well as the consequent potential for fragmentation of state governments. He makes a pessimistic normative assessment about the possibility of changing the EU's current political architecture so as to make it adequately democratic.

Caitríona Carter and Andrew Scott look at how this normative dimension is missing and is needed in debates on European integration. They consider the notion of 'Europeanisation' from the perspective of the public policy aspect of European integration. 'Europeanisation' is generally interpreted as describing the (positive) process whereby Member State public policies, and policy processes, are adapted as a consequence of public policy activism on the part of the European Union. They identify, and discuss, three 'levels' at which this discourse can, and should, be engaged—the systemic, the policy, and the individual. They suggest that only by considering these three elements together will we be able to develop a paradigm (and not a theory) within which to study the process of integration. By so doing, they highlight the normative political element hitherto absent from the Europeanisation debate and suggest that, in the absence of this normative element, the legitimation crisis which forms a central aspect in the perceived crisis of European integration, cannot properly be understood.

Carole Lyons engages the question of EU citizenship, a concept which she regards being—at one and the same time—a statement of inclusiveness and empowerment capable of propelling the Union forward to a new era of social legitimacy *and* an expression of symbolism which is devoid of substantive content and which may deepen rather than alleviate the legitimacy crisis facing the Union. As presented in the Treaty, and as interpreted by the ECJ through the relevant case law, Lyons regards EU citizenship is a restrictive and functional notion. However, in the central part of her paper, Lyons engages the discussion of citizenship at three levels—judicial citizenship, constitutional citizenship and participatory citizenship—arguing that a wider analysis of each element would produce an interpretation of the possibilities of EU citizenship which extend significantly beyond that which currently is recognised. Indeed, looking outside the immediate context of the EU, she points both to historical and contemporary instances where both an understanding and judicial interpretation of citizenship has been a primary force for social inclusion. In looking to the future, Lyons concludes that the challenge for the EU is to energise for its citizens what EU citizenship is, and what it means.

The paper by Richard Bellamy and Dario Castiglione represents a fundamental questioning of many of the standard analyses of the European Union as an emerging polity. They argue that any remedy to the current malaise surrounding the EU as a democratic system must begin from a recognition of the nature of the global forces currently shaping the nature of liberal democracy, and responsible for a general dysfunction within that arrangement at the level of the nation state. Only by so-doing can a EU-wide arrangement emerge which addresses the weaknesses in the current practice—weaknesses that have produced both inequitable and sub-optimal EU measures. Their contribution draws extensively on the neo-republican tradition in politics.

In the final essay, Ian Ward provides a review of themes appertaining to identity and democracy in the new Europe through a lens informed predominantly by a post-modernist critique of the development of late twentieth century social order. Ward's critique of the European Union owes much to the crises themes which characterise the analysis of contemporary social thinkers such as Jurgen Habermas and Jacques Derrida. Accordingly, for Ward the crisis of legitimacy which confronts the EU is rooted fundamentally in the crisis of liberal constitutionalism as a governance framework which is no longer capable of representing the aspirations and needs of an increasingly diverse society. The postmodern politics is one where multiple identities compete for expression and within which the link between the attainment of material prosperity on the one hand and the legitimacy of the governing order on the other hand has been severed. The old politics cannot deliver in general, and with respect to the construction of an integrated European Union in particular. Ward closes his essay with a review of alternative approaches to resolving the constitutional crisis of the EU, a review which demonstrates the volume of intellectual energy which is being expended as social, legal and political theorists seek out new perspectives on the fundamental question of governance and legitimacy in a new social order.

Taken as a whole, these papers are both descriptive and normative in purpose. They aim to respond to the challenge which an entity such as the European Union poses for legal theory and legal scholarship generally. In trying to reconceptualise the EU, they also illustrate the advantages of such a multi-dimensional approach. In both respects they raise challenging questions and propose stimulating answers. No one, let alone the authors represented here, would pretend that this work is the end of the story. But at least they indicate some of the main paths which should be cleared and developed if we are to achieve a more theoretically adequate, and indeed more realistically constructive, conception of the EU and the role of different institutions in European integration.

The papers in this volume are significant in the European debate for another important reason. They demonstrate without any doubt the tremendous theoretical gains which can be made if research councils and other funding agencies, either national or EU or both, seek seriously to support innovative legal scholarship. As exemplified here, such scholarship draws on law together with other social sciences, and it seeks to identify, analyse and reconceptualise the basic assumptions and presuppositions underlying previous work on European legal integration and on the functioning of the EU itself. In this respect these papers are a tribute to the role of the United Kingdom Economic and Social Research Council (ESRC) in fostering excellent research and writing on European integration and on European law.

1

Law Without a State?
On Representing the Common Market

Hans Lindahl and Bert van Roermund

Can the European Community be an autonomous legal order if the EC is not a political unity? If not, in what sense, if any, is the EC a political unity? As evidenced by the Maastricht judgement of the German Federal Constitutional Court, the key to these questions is the concept of political representation. For the BVerfG underpins its critique of the alleged autonomy of Community law with a conceptual argument: a legal order is autonomous only if it represents a pre-given political unity. Suggesting that the BVerfG relies on a form of metaphysical dualism, this paper develops an account of political representation that shows why the EC, in its present configuration, is already a political community under a political constitution.

I Legal Unity Without Political Unity?

In its well-known *Les Verts* judgement of 1983, the ECJ ruled that 'the European Economic Community is a Community based on the rule of law, inasmuch as neither its Member States nor its institutions can avoid a review of the question whether the measures adopted by them are in conformity with the basic constitutional charter, the Treaty'.[1] By calling the EC Treaty a constitutional charter, the ECJ indicates that the treaty fulfils the function apposite to a constitution in general, namely apportioning powers horizontally between the EC's institutions, and vertically between the EC's institutions and its Member States.[2] The Court justifies the constitutionalisation of the Community treaties by reference to the aim of economic integration. As set out in articles 2 and 3 of the EC Treaty, economic integration can only be accomplished in the framework of an autonomous legal order uniformly interpreted and applied throughout all Member States. Whence the so-called teleological interpretation of Community law: who wills the end, wills the means.

In this context, the phrasing of the *Les Verts* judgement neatly illustrates the most innovative yet most perplexing development in Community law: is it possible to call the Community treaty a constitution if the EC is not a *political* community? Note that the judgement refers to the EC as a community based on the rule of law, but refrains

---

[1] Case 294/83: *Parti écologiste 'Les Verts' v. European Parliament,* ECR (1986), at 1365.
[2] The constitutionalisation of the Community treaties ensures that the EC remains the flywheel of European integration, even though the TEU broadens the scope of the integration process, and the recent Amsterdam Treaty introduces the possibility of differentiated integration.

from qualifying it as a political community. In its first opinion concerning the European Economic Area, the ECJ confirms this distinction, asserting that 'the EEC Treaty, albeit concluded in the form of an international agreement, none the less constitutes the constitutional charter of a Community based on the rule of law. As the Court of Justice has consistently held, the Community treaties established a new legal order . . .'.[3] In the same vein of thinking, R. Barents and L.J. Brinkhorst remark that the autonomy of Community law 'does not rest on determinate meta-juridical conceptions about European unity, federal structures or something of the sort. On the contrary, the ECJ understands its mandate as a call to interpret Community law in view of the far-reaching integration objectives set out in articles 2 and 3 of the Community Treaty'.[4] In another context, T. Koopmans, a former justice of the ECJ, has succinctly formulated the implication of the Court's position as follows: 'We are moving toward a law without a state'.[5]

Not unexpectedly, the ECJ's move to distinguish between a legal and political concept of constitution has met with resistance, most forcefully in the Maastricht judgement of the German Federal Constitutional Court. The Bundesverfassungs-gericht's challenge to the doctrine of the ECJ is radical because it concerns the very concept of legal and political unity. In effect, by calling popular sovereignty a 'principle of imputation' (*Zurechnungsprinzip*),[6] the Federal Court reminds us that in democracy all normative relations must be referred to the sovereign people. This apparent truism is the point of departure for a sharp challenge to the autonomy of Community law. This challenge can be resumed as follows: (1) either the EC is a political community or it is not an independent legal order. In effect, the constitu-tional distribution and limitation of powers implies that these powers represent a *single*, highest power, to which all normative relations can be imputed. In democracy, the highest power is the sovereign people. In other words, constitutionalism—limited government operating under the rule of law—presupposes political unity. (2) There is no sovereign European people that could be represented by the institutions of the EC. There are only sovereign European peoples (in the plural). Notice that the preamble of the EC Treaty, later taken up in article A of the TEU, refers to 'an ever closer union among the peoples of Europe'. In contrast with, say, the American constitution, the Treaty does not begin by declaring 'We, the European people . . .'. Consequently, and although the Maastricht judgement falls short of reaching this particular conclusion, the European Parliament is strictly speaking not a parliament at all: it does not represent the people because there is no European people to be represented. As there is no sovereign European people that could be the ground of the European legal order, the bearers of this order are the peoples of the member states. (3) By implication, the EC is an 'association of states', not an independent political and legal order with its own constitution.

A fundamental question this reasoning raises is, of course, what characterises the people as the 'bearer' of a democratic legal order. In other words, what constitutes the people as a *political* unity? The Federal Court conceives political unity as 'what binds

---

[3] Opinion 1/91, ECR (1991), at I-6102.

[4] R. Barents and L.J. Brinkhorst, *Grondlijnen van Europees recht* (Alphen aan den Rijn, The Netherlands: Samsom H.D. Tjeenk Willink, 1996), at 242.

[5] T. Koopmans, 'Federalism: The Wrong Debate' in *Common Market Law Review* 29 (1992), at 1051.

[6] Extracts from *Brunner et. al. v. The European Union Treaty* in *Common Market Law Review* 31 (1994), at 252. The complete translation of the judgment is published in CMLR 1 (1994), at 57ff.

the people together (to a greater or lesser degree of homogeneity) spiritually, socially and politically' (*op. cit.,* at 257). Here is the snag. By contending that the legal order represents a pre-given existential unity, the Federal Court lapses into a form of representationalism. The ambiguity of this criterion of political unity can best be illustrated by showing that homogeneity has also been used as an argument *in favour* of the existing substantial unity of Europe. In the recent discussion as to whether Turkey should be admitted to the EU, Wilfried Martens summarised the standpoint of various European Christian Democratic parties as follows:

> 'European integration can only succeed if our peoples become conscious of their common identity. They must show adhesion to the great objective of a Union based on a common civilisation project for the coming century. The scope of our efforts is broader than the realisation of a free-trade zone (sic!) with merely economic interests. The European project is essentially political; it implies adhesion to common values'.[7]

According to Martens, respect for democratic institutions and the values embodied in the Judeo-Christian 'cultural heritage' determine European political identity. Para-doxically, Martens' view mirrors the substantialism of the Maastricht judgement, yet draws the opposite conclusion: Europe is relatively homogeneous and, as such, can be the bearer of an autonomous legal order. In both cases, the homogeneity thesis becomes the instrument of a politics of exclusion.

The critics of the Maastricht judgement decry the 'relative homogeneity' of the *Staatsvolk* as the criterion of political unity. Habermas, for instance, argues that 'What unites a nation of citizens as opposed to a *Volksnation* is not some primordial substrate but rather an intersubjectively shared context of possible understand-ing . . .'.[8] Habermas justifiably rejects a representationalistic conception of political unity. But it is doubtful whether his appeal to the normative idea of a 'common political culture' suffices to grasp the representational logic at the heart of any concept of political power. Indeed, the Federal Court is right in arguing that all powers within the community present themselves as conditioned or grounded, i.e. as the repre-sentatives of a 'highest' or sovereign power. Accordingly, the problem with the BVerfG's reasoning does not lie in positing the people as the ground of a democratic legal order; the problem resides in the substantialistic concept of ground endorsed by the Federal Court. Again, the BVerfG's reasoning is not flawed because it argues that political power represents the sovereign; its reasoning is flawed because it involves a substantialistic concept of representation. From this perspective, Habermas' appeal to a 'common political culture' does not provide us with an alternative view that could obviate the Federal Court's representationalism, while accounting for the represent-ational character of political power. 'Constitutional patriotism' is at best a *conditio sine qua non,* but certainly not the *conditio per quam* of a European political union.

In short, while the BVerfG and Habermas correctly argue against the ECJ that securing the autonomy of Community law implies the political unity of the EC, neither view adequately grasps the representational logic germane to political unity. In contrast with the Federal Court and Habermas, the ECJ's teleological interpretation of

---

[7] Wilfried Martens, 'Als Turkije EU-lid wordt, mislukt de Europese integratie', published in the 20 March 1997 number of the leading Dutch newspaper *NRC-Handelsblad.*

[8] Jürgen Habermas, 'Remarks on Dieter Grimm's "Does Europe Need a Constitution?"' in *European Law Journal* 3 (1995), at 305. See also J. Weiler's critique of the Maastricht judgement in the same number of *ELJ*.

Community law does seem to be on the right (institutional) track. In effect, the ECJ determined the representational logic of Community law by positing the common market as its purpose. Yet, precisely because realising a common market spearheads *economic* integration, the ECJ has hesitated to conclude that the European legal order is a political community, not merely a 'Community under the rule of law'. The ECJ's hesitation points to a deeper level of what we take to be the BVerfG's challenge: by emphasising that a democratic legal order represents the *people,* the German Federal Court purports to rescue the specificity of the political realm *vis-à-vis* economics. By subordinating legal integration to economic integration, the ECJ seems to reduce politics to economics, and the public to the private sphere. Notice that Martens evokes the same argument, albeit by asserting that the EU is essentially a political project, not 'merely' an economic union. This critique echoes Carl Schmitt's dictum, 'The political substance that belongs to democracy can certainly not be found in economics. Political homogeneity does not follow from economic equality . . .'.[9] Thus, the Maastricht judgement may be read as denying that economic integration could satisfy the conditions necessary for *political* representation, in the absence of which Community law can be neither autonomous nor legitimate. This criticism is far more radical than those views which point to the institutional shortcomings of law-making in the EC. Whereas such views argue that the European Parliament needs to be endowed with greater powers to transform it into the leading representative organ of the EC, the BVerfG contests the very possibility of political representation in the EC, regardless of the institutional arrangements which could bolster the European Parliament.

The forthcoming considerations contest the BVerfG's radical critique. In our view, the European legal order is *already* a political community, albeit not a nation state. Koopmans' expression, 'Law without a state', should be construed literally; a nation state is only *one* form of political unity, not political unity *tout court.* By the same token, the constitution of the nation state does not exhaust the possible modes of a political constitution. The task at hand consists, therefore, in providing a better account of the ECJ's teleological interpretation of Community law, an account that shows why the realisation of a common market instances the logic of political representation, making of the European legal order a political unity, and of the Community treaties a political constitution. In particular, it will be necessary to show that economic integration, as set out in article 2 of the EC Treaty, is a full blooded political project. Thus, two questions present themselves to our attention. First, what is political representation without representationalism? Second, how does the realisation of a common market instance political representation? These questions will be addressed in, respectively, §§2 and 3.

II Political Representation: The Institution of Representation

An analysis of political power and representation must begin with an analysis of the concept of institution, for political power and representation are first and foremost institutional phenomena. The institutional character of power finds its primordial cause in the fact that political power cannot be understood merely in terms of effectiveness, i.e. as the *de facto* capacity to demand and obtain obedience to commands. Political power always presents itself as conditioned or grounded power,

---

[9] Carl Schmitt, *The Crisis of Parliamentary Democracy,* trans. by Ellen Kennedy (Cambridge, Mass: The MIT Press, 1985), at 90.

thereby raising the claim to being *de jure* power. Precisely this *de jure* claim determines the institutional character of political power. Conversely, the subordination or conditioning of power yields the material for a preliminary characterisation of institutions in general, and political institutions in particular. For the concept of institution finds its most general framework in the relation between the condition and the conditioned, the ground and the grounded. Furthermore, this relation yields the key to the concept of representation as an institutional phenomenon. In its most general and abstract formulation, representation denotes the relation between the condition and the conditioned, the ground and the grounded. To be sure, this preliminary approximation to the concepts of institution, representation and political power is no more than the point of departure for a more concrete and detailed analysis. Section 2.1. fleshes out the relation between the condition and the conditioned in terms of the relation between the regulative and constitutive rules characteristic of institutions in general. Subsequently, section 2.2. focuses on the concept of political institution, outlining the representational logic of political power in a way that avoids representationalism.

A Constitutive and Regulative Rules

The distinction (and relation) between the 'condition' and the 'conditioned' is too massive and abstract to account for the specificity of institutions in general, and political institutions in particular. Institutions can best be characterised by reference to the distinction (and relation) between constitutive and regulative rules.[10]

To illustrate the meaning of these terms, and how they determine the concept of institution, let us consider an example far removed from the world of politics. Imagine someone making wild efforts to move forward on skates. We might say either that the person is not skating at all, or that he or she *is* skating, but skating very badly. In the first case, we suppose that some elements constitute the action of skating; in the second, we say that the skater falls short of certain regulative requirements which should be met if you want to skate well. Both the constitutive and the regulative elements can be framed as 'rules', 'criteria', 'norms' or (why not) 'principles'. We submit, moreover, that the constitutive rules depend on or are conditioned by the regulative criteria. They are simply default requirements of 'good skating', which depend on the purpose (or the joy) of skating, or in more casual parlance, on 'what skating is all about': gliding swiftly with a minimum of energy, or turning a maximum of energy into the highest velocity possible, mainly by letting Newtonian laws do all the work. An institution is a default reflexive setting, rather than a pattern, of meaningful behaviour in a social group. This is the only reason why

---

[10] We respectfully acknowledge that our account of this rather received distinction derives from a not so received reading of L. L. Fuller's *The Morality of Law* (New Haven: Yale University Press, 1969), at 15 ff., and N. MacCormick's and O. Weinberger's *An Institutional Theory of Law. New Approaches to Legal Positivism* (Dordrecht: Reidel, 1986). In particular, we are aware of the fact that the latter criticise the Searlian version of this distinction: 'Particularly unsatisfactory is the Searlian distinction between constitutive and regulative rules' (*op. cit.,* at 23). We take it that the emphasis is on 'Searlian', as there are several versions of this distinction. Our version does not accept, as a definition, the idea that 'constitutive rules constitute an activity the existence of which is logically dependent on the rules', for reasons similar to those offered by MacCormick and Weinberger. Our account comes close, we believe, to (especially) MacCormick's argument to the effect that rules creating institutions specificy 'ordinarily necessary' or 'presumptively necessary' conditions of validity (*ibid.,* at 69). This is why we speak of 'default setting'.

we are justified in saying that someone crawling on the ice 'is not skating at all'. These constitutive rules define a more or less standardised practice, but only because such a default setting is possible, and only as long as these constitutive rules preserve their inner connection with regulative rules. Preserving this connection means that who obeys the constitutive rules implicitly acknowledges the normative force of the regulative dimension. Such an acknowledgement can take on a variety of forms: an aspiration to 'perform better', a willingness to concede that others 'skate better', an agreement to organise races of a specific design, or an inclination to adjust the default setting of constitutive rules in a certain way. In general, however, it is self-contradictory to engage in an institutional practice without recognising the inner connection between 'doing the right things' (as governed by constitutive rules) and 'doing these things right' (as governed by the regulative rules).[11] Often, but not always, the 'things' in question are more or less shared *purposes,* so that in institutional practices 'meaningful' behaviour boils down to purposive behaviour. The setting itself is always purposive to the extent that it is a second order operation on behaviour acknowledged as meaningful or purposive.

A central feature of institutions is that these can be nested within other institutions, or if you will, that institutions are recursive. This means that the constitutive rules of one institutional practice can function as the regulative rules of another (nested) institutional practice. While 'good skating' can grow into an institutional practice (which may show regional differences), skating contests can be designed as nested institutions, with subordinate institutions under them (ice dancing, speed skating, the latter divided into short track and long track, each of these with their own different distances). Or, to take another example, monogamous marriage can be seen as nested within the more general institution of marriage (sharing at least some purposes and characteristics with it), while the institution of wedding anniversaries is nested within (as far as we know) monogamous marriage in certain communities. Recursiveness implies that institutions stand in hierarchical relationships: the nested institution is subordinated to the nesting institution, which can itself be nested in yet a higher order institution. Notice that there is no *a priori* limit to the recursiveness of institutions; the degree of nesting or hierarchisation of institutions within institutions depends on the character of the institutional practice itself.

Importantly, the relation between regulative and constitutive rules yields the key to institutional representation. Most simply, constitutive rules represent regulative rules. But what defines this relation as representational? We want to emphasise three points here:

---

[11] The distinction, a cliché in the contemporary consultancy idiom, reflects nevertheless the profound insight of Rawls' classic distinction between 'justifying a practice and justifying a particular action falling under it' (J. Rawls, 'Two Concepts of Rules' in *The Philosophical Review* 64 (1995), at 3). Two caveats are called for at this point. First, not every practice can be institutionalised at even a minimum level. A notable example is art. As there is no default setting for creating art, we do not say: He or she 'created a work of art, but it is bad art'. Of course we do say, on the other hand, that he or she 'wrote a novel, but it is a bad novel'. That is because 'the' novel has come to be defined by a set of certain default (though by no means exhaustive or unalterable) characteristics of genre. Second, games are by definition highly institutionalised practices, often governed by explicit constitutive rules of the canonical form 'Doing *x* counts as doing *y* in context *C*'. Frequently, the force of regulative rules is obliterated by their highly conventional, elaborate and massive default setting. But this should not tempt us into thinking that there is no connection with regulative rules, nor make us believe that all institutionalised practices are like games. In this sense, the vocabulary of 'language games' can be highly misleading.

(1) Notice, to begin with, that we have defined constitutive rules as a *default* reflexive setting of regulative rules. This implies, obviously, that such settings can be changed, yet also that each of the default settings counts as a setting of the *same* regulative rule. Accordingly, regulative rules are related to constitutive rules as the general to the particular. In other words, constitutive rules concretise or instance regulative rules, that is to say, give these a content. 'Assigning a content to a regulative rule' is the basic structure of institutional representation.

(2) Note, however, that the act of assigning is, according to our definition, *reflexive;* that is to say, its object refers back to its subject. To put it another way: what counts as 'the same' is determined from the perspective of those involved in or committed to (re-) creating the institution. It does not necessarily hold from the point of view of a third person who undertakes to understand, to analyse and to criticise the institution. Thus, the latter may point out that a certain default setting *i* does not (no longer, not yet) instance the regulative rule *I* to which it claims to assign a content. Conversely, the participants may point out that the outsider has the wrong understanding of *i* with respect to *I.* In the political context, this means that political agents will be engaged in the logic of representation by a practical cognitive attitude different from those who, from a philosophical point of view, study how these agents are engaged in the logic of representation. The difference in cognitive attitude accounts for the possibility of mutual criticism between participants and philosophers, and, thus, for overlapping consensus in the Rawlsian sense. But, in contradistinction to Rawls, we want to stress that the possibility of critical, reflective exchange is itself something which can only be part of the philosophical cognitive attitude, not the political one as such. As far as the political attitude is concerned, it will be reflexive rather than reflective. That is to say, it will tend to back up its self-referential logic by self-legitimation.

(3) Two further features of this characterisation of representation are crucial for our discussion. They both pertain to *setting,* the third element of our definition. First, the relation between the particular and the general, between constitutive rules and regulative rules, is a *two-way* relation. While the constitutive rule can only be understood as an instance or representative of the regulative rule, i.e. as 'governed' by the regulative rule, on the other hand the regulative rule must be presented in, i.e. 'commanded' by, the constitutive rule. To put it another way, 'grounding' or 'conditioning' the constitutive rule in the regulative rule does not only consist in *deriving* the former from the latter; it also consists in *positing* the content of the regulative rule by means of its default setting. Precisely for this reason the constitutive rule is a default *setting* of a regulative rule. Representation encompasses both aspects of this operation, namely 'deriving' and 'presenting'. Although the presentative character of representation is only striking when we change the default setting of a regulative rule, it is no less at work in those cases in which the default setting remains unchanged.

Second, the relation between constitutive and regulative rules is *dynamic.* In effect, a peculiar 'dialectic' lies at the heart of institutions. On the one hand, a default setting effects a *closure* of the regulative rule; the setting restricts the relatively 'open' or undetermined regulative rule. Notice that this closure is not merely a shortcoming of institutions, but the condition of possibility of what we call 'order'. A constant openness to alternatives, to criticism or to heterodoxy would frustrate the setting in both directions. A certain form of orthodoxy is implicit in the representational structure of institutions. On the other hand, the limitation brought about by a default setting is provisional, as suggested by the notion of default setting, which implies the *openness* or 'pro-jectiveness' of institutions. Otherwise, the institution could not hope to survive over even a relatively short period of time. For the environment of an institutional practice can and often does call into question the default setting of a regulative rule. Experience presents institutional practices with 'anomalies', with situations that cannot be addressed within the limited framework provided by the extant default setting. Integrating these new situations into the institutional practice requires reformulating the default setting of the regulative rule, or to put it otherwise, giving it a new content (hence, closing it anew). An institution, we could say, is incidentally opened to closures, but permanently closed to openness. This dynamic is of essential importance, because it yields the key to representation without representationalism: as a default setting of purposive behaviour, an institution is always 'unfinished'. The unfinished character of institutions, as implied in the relation between constitutive and regulative rules, stands in sharp contrast to the institutional immobility implied in representationalism.

B   Representation and Political Power

We can now turn to consider how politics instances the general definition of institutions as default reflexive settings of purposive behaviour. In particular, the task at hand consists in reconstructing the concept of political power in a way that, in line with the Bundesverfassungsgericht's reasoning, recognises the representational logic of power, yet obviates the Federal Court's representationalism.

The BVerfG supports its argument for the representational logic of political power with a largely implicit theory about the concept of legal order in general, and democratic legal order in particular. Its gist is the following: A legal order may confer power on various organs. These organs, operating jointly or separately, give rise to a manifold of normative relations. The totality of the normative relations composing a legal order (including the constitution) must be referred to a ground whence this totality appears as a unity. The ground of a legal order is not itself a legal norm; it is the purpose whence a manifold of relations can appear as a purposive unity, namely 'the common good'. In democracy, the common good is 'the people', in the sense that norms are enacted and enforced 'for the sake of' the people. Moreover, the definite article 'the' of 'the people' evokes the identity of a political community, the closure in the absence of which a legal order can be neither autonomous nor legitimate. Not only does democracy subordinate all normative relations to the people, but the reference to this purpose makes it possible to view this manifold of relations as a single legal order. Finally, 'referring' the norms of a legal order to the people means that, in democracy, conditioned powers represent the sovereign people.

We submit that the Court's reasoning is correct up to this point. The theory goes wrong, however, the moment the Court interprets the legal order as reproducing a pre-given political identity or 'existential sameness' (*existentieller Gemeinsamkeit*). Notice that the Court's concept of representation is dualistic: the people must *already* be a unity, prior to all legal normativity. By implication, a polity is *two* orders, not one: an existential order and a legal order, where the latter reproduces the former. The sovereign people is not merely the common good toward which the legal order is oriented; the homogeneity thesis implies that the content of the common good is fixed in advance, thereby condemning political identity to immobility.

The concept of institution as the default reflexive setting of purposive behaviour suggests that the Federal Court is correct in stressing the representational logic of power, while incorrect in conflating representation with substantialism. Let us discuss each of these aspects in greater detail, parallel to the three points of the previous subsection.

(1) The BVerfG's basic insight is, first, that a legal order, including the powers it institutes, represents a purpose and, second, that the purpose of a legal order is not itself a norm of positive law. If, as noted above, legal norms are always default settings of purposive behaviour, then, from the cognitive perspective of practical commitment, there is ultimately a purpose that unifies all (nested) institutions into a single legal order or institution. This purpose is not a norm of positive law, i.e. a constitutive rule; it is the regulative rule of the legal order as a whole: the 'common good'. All institutions composing the 'substantive law' of a legal order, such as family, commercial, environmental and penal law (in turn, each of these institutions is characterised by a variable degree of recursiveness), are default settings of, or *represent,* the common good, i.e. they give it a definite content. This is why Kelsen could say that, at the end of the day, all law is public law.

(2) But—and this is what the BVerfG's reasoning obliterates—legal orders are also characterised by the fact that default setting, as an operation, is itself a recursive institution. This implies that the purpose of a legal order cannot be set without reference to its 'highest' (legislative) power or authority: the sovereign. The sovereign is not, therefore, a political actor; it denotes the purpose unifying a manifold of normative relations. If we define the constitution of a legal order as the (constitutive) rule which empowers the organs of the legal order to produce norms, then constitutional empowerment is a default setting of the 'highest' power. This insight returns us to the '*Faktum*' noted earlier, namely, that political power raises the claim to being conditioned or grounded power, i.e. power *de jure.* Political power is an institutional phenomenon because what we have called the 'representational logic' of power instances the representational relation between constitutive and regulative rules characteristic of institutions in general. Again, the institutional character of political power means that power unfolds a representational logic: the *pouvoir constitué* is such by virtue of representing the *pouvoir constituant,* the sovereign.

Three cardinal features of political power emerge from the foregoing analysis. First, the highest power of a legal order—viz. God or the people—is 'absent' from political reality; only subordinate or limited powers may be present in the community. Power brings *three* elements into play: the prince issues commands to the polity's subjects, but commands on behalf of God; parliament issues commands to the polity's subjects, but commands on behalf of the people. Thus, representing the sovereign is not merely one property amongst others pertaining to political power; it *defines* power. Second, the representational structure of political power is purposive. No only are actions commanded 'on behalf of' the sovereign, but such actions are commanded 'for the sake of' the sovereign. In other words, political power represents the sovereign because the laws it enacts and enforces claim orientation toward the common good in the first place. The binding claim of laws resides, therefore, in the capacity of the latter to reveal action as oriented toward the realisation of the common good. This claim can of course be contested by political actors in society; but political opposition contests the representativeness of the powers that be, not the representational structure of political power as such. Third, the representational structure of political power provides the key to the concept of *political unity.* The sovereign is the foundation of a community because it functions as the unifying reference point—the purpose—of a manifold of normative relations. In other words, a manifold of normative relations appears as a unity because these relations are held to represent the sovereign.[12]

(3) Finally, let us look into the intricate relationship between 'deriving' and 'positing' hidden in the notion of 'setting'. If the concept of institution corroborates the BVerfG's insight about the representational structure of political power, it also rejects the Federal Court's representationalism. Indeed, the concept of political representation sketched out in the foregoing paragraph implies, first, that the relation between the legal order and its purpose is a *two-way* relation. The setting of constitutive rules—norm production—requires both showing that these constitutive rules depend on the common good and positing the common good in the constitutive rule, i.e. assigning the common good a content. To be legitimate, legal norms must appear as a particularisation of the common good, but we cannot apprehend the common good otherwise than in the multiple particularisations which it obtains in the ongoing process of norm-production. Thus, the enactment of norms in a legal system unfolds the dynamic of 'deriving' and 'positing' characteristic of representation in general. Importantly, although the legitimacy of legal norms implies that the values protected by law represent the identity of a political community, the identity of the polity is grasped in the values postulated and protected by the legal order. In other words, although a legal order must always represent the political identity of a community, this does not mean that political identity is merely a pre-established set of values which is subsequently captured in a legal order. An institutional concept of representation implies that representing political identity is also assigning an identity to a polity.

Second, the institutional concept of political representation suggests that the relation between a legal order and its purpose is *dynamic*. It is a truism that politics is an incessant process of reformulating the common good, i.e. readjusting its default settings. A legal order must be oriented toward the realisation of the common good but, at the same time, the common good must always be given a content, thus *limited,* by legal institutions. See here an instance of the operation of closure which characterises all institutional practices. The counterpart to institutional closure is incidental openness. Once and again, experience confronts politics with new situations which resist integration into the common good, as concretised by the positive legal order. Such situations call into question the values positivised in the law as determinant of the identity of a political community. In the face of such questioning, the option of a politics of exclusion can and often is pursued by recurring to a substantialistic conception of representation. A politics of integration, on the other

---

[12] Although Claude Lefort approaches political power from the point of view of its 'symbolic' dimension, his analyses coincide in decisive aspects with the view propounded in this paper. Lefort's basic insight concerning the symbolic dimension of political power is summarised in the following passage: 'The fact that [society] is organised as *one* despite (or because of) its multiple divisions, and that it is organised as *the same* in all its multiple dimensions, implies a reference to a place from which it can be seen, read and named. This symbolic pole proves to be power, even before we examine it in its empirical determinations... Power makes a gesture towards an outside (*un dehors*), whence [society] defines itself. Whatever its form, [political power] always refers to the same enigma: that of an internal-external articulation, of a division which institutes a common space, of a break which simultaneously establishes relations, of a movement of the externalisation of the social which goes hand in hand with its internalisation' (Claude Lefort, *Democracy and Political Theory,* trans. by David Macey (Oxford: Polity Press, 1988), at 225). We submit that the relation between the 'inside' and 'outside' of a political community instances the basic representational logic of institutions, a structure which we have described as the relation between constitutive and regulative rules.

hand, recognises the need to constantly reformulate the common good by re-negotiating the default setting of the community's legal norms. See here the openness of a polity. To put it another way, the logic of political representation implies that the relation between legal order and political identity is and must remain unfinished.

III The Politics of Economic Integration

The foregoing section outlines a concept of political representation that circumvents the representationalism of the Maastricht judgement. We can now turn to consider how this conceptual framework impinges on the BVerfG's challenge to the autonomy of Community law. This challenge has two related parts. The first, addressed in §3.1, is the thesis that there is no European people that could be the bearer of an autonomous European legal order. The second, addressed in §3.2, pertains to the question whether economic integration can satisfy the conditions necessary for political unity.

A   A Monistic Concept of Political Unity

The ECJ summarises the central argument of its famous *Van Gend & Loos* judgement as follows: 'The objective of the EEC Treaty, which is to establish a Common Market, the functioning of which is of direct concern to interested parties in the Community, implies that this Treaty is more than an agreement which merely creates mutual obligations between the contracting states'.[13] To be sure, the Single European Act (and the TEU) later introduced the notion of an 'internal market', but, as the ECJ itself has noted, this notion does not imply a break with the common market. Additionally, although the TEU broadens the scope of the EC to include Economic and Monetary Union, EMU (and the 'common policies and activities') is not an end in itself; it is a condition for the realisation of the common market. The modifications and additions introduced by the Union Treaty confirm that the EC remains firmly oriented toward the realisation of a common market.

A fundamental difficulty arising from the ECJ's teleological interpretation of Community law is, as we have noted, that by making of an autonomous legal order the condition for attaining a common market, the ECJ hoped to avoid the problem of political unity. The Maastricht judgement correctly argues that the distinction between an autonomous legal order and political unity is specious. Having shown that the distinction is untenable, the BVerfG can then invert the ECJ's reasoning: 'The Union Treaty . . . establishes an association of States for the purpose of realising an ever closer union of the peoples of Europe (organised as States) and not a state based on the people of one European nation . . .'.[14] Not only does the EC not meet (for the time being) the homogeneity criterion advocated by the Federal Court, but the EC is not the result of a decision by a European people to organise itself as a political unity. As Dieter Grimm, a justice of the BVerfG, puts it, 'The European public power is not one that derives from the people, but one mediated through States. Since the Treaties thus have not an internal but an external reference point, they are also not the expression of a society's self-determination as to the form and objectives of its political unity'.[15] This

---

[13] Case 26/62: *Van Gend & Loos,* ECR (1963), at 12.

[14] *Brunner et. al. v. The European Union Treaty,* at 258. The English version incorrectly translates *Staatenverbund* as 'federation of states'.

[15] Dieter Grimm, 'Does Europe Need a Constitution?', *European Law Journal* 1 (1995) 3, at 291.

second argument in fact repeats the Federal Court's thesis concerning the absence of a European people. For it only makes sense to deny that the treaties ratifying the *acquis communautair* partake of what Grimm calls the 'internal reference point' if ratification presupposes a European people existing prior to and independently of Community law. Certainly, the BVerfG does not exclude the possibility that a European people could emerge at some time in the (distant) future. But by denying that there is already a European people, the Federal Court effectively denies that the European legal order is a political community under a political constitution and, consequently, that Community law is autonomous.

Let us consider this objection from the perspective of the account of political representation developed in §2.2. Crucially, the Federal Court's argument presupposes that a legal order is autonomous if and only if it represents a pre-given political ('existential') unity. In other words, it views political unity as existing prior to and independently of legal unity. In short, the BVerfG's argument against the autonomy of Community law is dualistic in nature.

A non-representationalistic approach to the concept of political representation exposes this dualism as false: rather than two orders, a polity is a *single* order.[16] To put it another way, a polity is the *relation* between a legal order and its purpose, not the composition of two independent terms. As implied in the representational relation between constitutive and regulative rules, the purpose of a legal order does not enjoy an existence separate to the legal order itself. To be sure, the very notion of *default* setting indicates the need to distinguish between a legal order and its purpose. Nonetheless, regulative and constitutive rules can only be abstracted from their relation; neither term can be understood in isolation from the other. Hence, the Maastricht judgement's representationalism exemplifies the typical error of metaphysical thinking, which Ernst Cassirer, in another context, has characterised as 'sever[ing] . . . points of view that belong together, that are only determinate in relation to each other, thereby transforming the logically correlative into a reified opposition (*Dinglich-Gegensätzliches*)'.[17] In other words, the Maastricht judgement falls prey to representationalism because it views the distinction between the purpose of a legal order and the order itself as a *distinctio in re*. Concretely, the sovereign people is *not* the ('relatively homogeneous') electorate of a community. The sovereign people is the purpose of a democratic legal order—the common good—represented or concretised in the constitutive rules comprising a legal order (including the nested institution of elections).[18] Accordingly, although the concept of political representation requires distinguishing between a legal order and its purpose, this distinction is strictly a *distinctio rationis*. In contrast with the metaphysical dualism characteristic of the

---

[16] See Bert van Roermund, 'Jurisprudential Dilemmas of European Law' in *Law and Philosophy* 16 (1997), at 357 ff.

[17] Ernst Cassirer, *Substanzbegriff und Funktionsbegriff. Untersuchungen über die Grundfragen der Erkenntniskritik* (Darmstadt: Wissenschaftliche Buchgesellschaft, 1994), at 359.

[18] The metaphysical dualism of the Maastricht judgement (a dualism it shares, incidentally, with most interpretations of political power in democracy) already manifests itself when the Federal Court argues that 'In the act of voting the power of the state proceeds from the people' (*Brunner et. al.,* at 252). In effect, the electorate, as a numerical or aggregate concept of 'the people', presupposes the reference to the sovereign people as the ground of the unity of a manifold of power relations. For a justification of the distinction between the people as sovereign and as electorate, on the basis of an analysis of art. 20(2) of the German constitution, see Hans Lindahl, 'Sovereignty and Symbolization', *Rechtstheorie* 28 (1997) 3, at 347 ff.

Maastricht judgement, a non-representationalistic account of political representation enjoins a *monistic* concept of political unity.

These considerations cast the ECJ's teleological interpretation of Community law in a different light. Conceiving of the EC as a political unity does not require postulating the existence of a European people *prior* to the emergence of an autonomous Community legal order. Returning to the preamble of the EC Treaty, the possibility of an 'ever closer union among the peoples of Europe' requires a purpose whence these different peoples can appear as the participants of a single community: the realisation of a common market. In contrast with the German Federal Court's dualism, a non-representationalistic account of political representation suggests that there is *already* a European people as a political unity, in the sense of an effective legal order oriented toward the attainment of a common market. Again, the two terms of the teleological relation instituted by the ECJ are co-originary, rather than sequential: the regulative rule of a common market and the constitutive rules comprising Community law are simply the two aspects of the single political order called the European Community.

This insight impinges on Grimm's argument to the effect that the EC is not the result of an act of political self-determination by a European people. For it is not necessary to await a decision by all member states to become a single European state before we can speak about the EC as a political union. To the extent that the member states have accepted a European legal order as internally binding in view of attaining a common market, they have already entered a political union. In other words, the Community treaties, as they now stand, provide a default setting of the 'form and objectives of political unity'. The ongoing negotiation about such form and objectives is the very heart of EC politics. Thus, it would be a mistake to conceive economic 'integration' as a process that precedes and leads, if successful, to political unity. Economic integration is not the harbinger of European political unity; it is the continued process of re-negotiating the default settings of the purpose of Community law, or if you will, of the content of political identity. This process has no predetermined terminus because, as stated earlier, the relation between a legal order and its purpose is dynamic, unfinished. In this context, if the member states of the EC were to transfer all their remaining powers to a European polity, the effect of this decision would not be to *transform* the EC into a political unity; it would simply be to provide a *new* default setting of what Grimm calls 'the form and objectives of political unity'. Recognising that the EC is already a political unity does not mean, however, that the member states have ceased to be political communities, nor that sovereignty is 'divided' between the EC and its member states ('divided sovereignty' is a contradiction in terms). It means that the member states and the EC are sovereign from different points of view.[19]

B   The Common Market and the Common Good

Yet, even if one accepts a monistic interpretation of Community law, need we conclude that the EC is a *political* unity? This question confronts us with the second aspect of

---

[19] On the basis of an analysis of sovereignty which is roughly parallel to that expounded in this paper, Neil Walker observes that the introduction of differentiated integration by the Treaty of Amsterdam paves the way for the emergence of multiple political units, 'their breadth and depth dependent upon the integration arrangements specific to the policy field in question, and embedded in a complex network of relations with one another and with the various Member States' (Walker, 'Sovereignty and Differentiated Integration in the European Union', published in this volume).

the BVerfG's challenge: can the realisation of a common market meet the conditions necessary for political representation? Notice that we are neither raising nor answering the question about the institutional conditions necessary to assure the democratic legitimisation of Community law-making. The institutional shortcomings of the EC are clear, even if the modifications that would be required to meet these shortcomings are, contrary to what many think, less than perspicuous.[20] The challenge posed by the BVerfG is, conceptually speaking, prior to the question concerning the institutional ways and means of political representation in the EC: the BVerfG's question, as we understand it, is whether we can meaningfully speak about the common *market* as the common *good*. This question does not possess a merely theoretical interest; it is connected to the distortions of political representation associated with neo-corporatism, on the one hand, and with the instrumentalisation of politics urged by ordo-liberalism, on the other.

The foregoing analysis of the relation between regulative and constitutive rules, and of the recursiveness of (political) institutions, offers a way out of the problem posed by the BVerfG. Consider article 2 of the EC Treaty, which outlines the highest level of recursiveness or institutional nesting in Community law. In its present formulation, art. 2 states that

> 'The Community shall have as its task, by establishing a common market and an economic and monetary union and by implementing the common policies or activities referred to in Articles 3 and 3a, to promote throughout the Community a harmonious and balanced development of economic activities, sustainable and non-inflationary growth respecting the environment, a high degree of convergence of economic performance, a high level of employment and of social protection, the raising of the standard of living and quality of life, and economic and social cohesion and solidarity among Member States.'

We can distinguish three levels of nesting in this article. (1) At the highest level, the tasks enumerated in art. 2 concretise or represent the common good. In other words, they provide the idea of the common good, which is empty and indeterminate, with an initial content. To put it another way, objectives such as 'non-inflationary growth', 'high level of employment', 'economic and social cohesion' and 'solidarity' are *default settings* of the common good. Precisely because they are default settings (constitutive rules) of the common good, these tasks can be re-adjusted; as compared with the original default setting of article 2 of the EC Treaty, article G.b.2. of the TEU provides for a *new* default setting of the common good by broadening the scope of tasks to be fulfilled by the EC. (2) A further level of nesting concerns the relation between these objectives and the common market. In effect, the common market (including EMU and common policies and activities) concretises or particularises the objectives of the EC. Conversely, these objectives function as the regulative rules of the common market; they are the criteria which indicate what counts as a *good* market. A market functions well when it succeeds in achieving these criteria. (3) This brings us to the third level of institutional nesting in the EC: substantive Community law is the default setting of the good market. In other words, the legal rules structuring market behaviour determine what counts, for the time being, as a *good* market. By the same token, the criteria which determine the good market have a critical function with

---

[20] We have in mind here all too quick appeals to the *'trias politica'* of the nation state as the suitable model for the constitutional distribution and limitation of political power in the EC.

respect to substantive law. In effect, the bulk of Community law-making consists in the continuous process of adjusting this default setting, in view of bringing the common market, as an institutional practice, into unison with the idea of a good market.[21]

In short, article 2 of the EC Treaty effects a triple closure: (1) the tasks to be accomplished by the EC concretise the common good, (2) the idea of a good market concretises the tasks of the EC, and (3) substantive Community law concretises the good market.

The foregoing reconstruction of the purposiveness of Community law allows us to address the problem posed by the BVerfG. Notice, to begin with, that characterising the common market as a default setting of the common good in no way implies elevating the market into a false historical necessity. Future developments in the EC could lead to a fundamentally different default setting of the common good (although it is hard to imagine that such a massive adjustment could occur even in the medium term). But if, as we argue, the EC is already a political unity, then we must address the pressing problem raised by the Maastricht judgement: can we meaningfully speak about the common market as the good of a *political* community?

Implicitly, the Federal Court's objection turns on the traditional opposition between the economic and the political. In turn, this opposition rests on the assumption that economic activity, market exchange in particular, belongs purely to the private domain, whereas politics defines the public domain *par excellence*. The foregoing analysis of article 2 of the EC Treaty leads to another conclusion. As the institution of the common market implies that its constitutive rules preserve an inner connection with regulative rules, the market cannot be a purely private enterprise. Although market operation certainly concerns the exchange of private interests, creating and sustaining the common market as an institution is a matter of public interest. Indeed, the market is the most 'primitive' form of establishing the category of public interest in action. This sheds new light on the cited passage of *Van Gend & Loos.* When the ECJ argues that 'the functioning of [the Common Market] is of direct concern to interested parties in the Community', these parties are not only, and not even primarily, economic agents (especially undertakings); the regulative rules enumerated in art. 2 make clear that 'interested parties' to the functioning of the common market are *all* citizens in the EC. The citizen's interest is not only related to the legal concretisation of the good market, as defined by the criteria (tasks) enumerated in art. 2 of the EC Treaty; it also concerns the criteria themselves which define the market as a good. In other words, being an interested party to the functioning of the common market means taking an interest in the (default setting of the) common good. This interest is thoroughly political.[22] Determining what counts as a good market is no 'merely' economic decision; (re-)negotiating the constitutive and

---

[21] EC law on market competition points to yet a fourth level of institutional nesting. By stipulating that the activities of the Community shall include 'a system ensuring that competition in the internal market is not *distorted*' (our italics, HL & BvR), art. 3 (g) of the EC Treaty underscores that an inner connection between constitutive and regulative rules determines market competition as an institution. We submit that the core of EC law consists in arranging, adapting, applying and enforcing the default setting of competition, and which the ECJ has elaborated by reference to what it terms 'workable competition'.

[22] This conclusion should make clear that the concept of political representation endorsed by this paper in no way implies a theoretical legitimation of either neo-corporatism or ordo-liberalism. Although we cannot discuss these issues here, a non-representationalistic concept of political representation provides the point of departure for a critique of both strands of thinking.

regulative rules of the common market instances the process of *political* representation.

The fundamental problem posed by Community law is not that economic integration cannot meet the conditions necessary for political representation; it *can*. The problem is rather to design a form of democratic political representation sensitive to the economic focus of Community law.

2

The European Union as an Essentially Contested Project

Zenon Bańkowski and Emilios Christodoulidis

Κι αν πτωχικη την βρεις, η Ιθακη δεν σε γελασε.
Ετσι σοφος που εγινες, με τοση πειρα,
ηδη θα το καταλαβες οι Ιθακες τι σημαινουν.
Κ Π Καβαφης

I Introduction

The European Union, as has often been noted, presents a challenge for legal theory. This is because the EU does not lend itself to the old way of seeing sovereignty and law as closely connected. It gives, as Neil MacCormick points out, a 'binocular vision' that produces the debates as to whether sovereignty lies in Brussels or in Westminster.[1] Indeed if we must seek a single site of sovereignty, then we are inevitably led into that kind of dilemma; one that has no room for competing systems that need to be conceptualised as simultaneously valid over the same territory. The challenge that this represents has been detailed by MacCormick, and he and Bańkowski have propounded solutions which seek a theory that decouples law and state; one that can describe the EU as an entity of 'interlocking normative spheres' where no particular one is privileged.[2] The important point is the following. If we take the traditional ways of looking at it, such as Hart's, then what we see when we look at the EU is a legal system in crisis.[3] For we see different competing systems with not one of them apparently being able to gain ascendancy—there being nothing remotely like a rule of recognition or something equivalent. Even if we take a theory explicitly against such foundational rules like Dworkin's, we find that the law's integrity as a guiding ideal cannot cope with the uneasy co-existence or inter-locking of normative orders; not least because with the contestability over jurisdiction and competence the criterion of 'coherence' is left with no ground on which to build. So again, we have a system that is either in crisis or, worse still, we are left without the possibility of conceiving of it as a coherent practice, in other words for Dworkin, without the possibility of conceiving of it at all.[4]

---

[1] MacCormick, 'Beyond the Sovereign State'(1993) *MLR*, 1–18

[2] MacCormick, 'Democracy, Subsidiarity, and Citizenship in the 'European Commonwealth' in (1997) *Law and Philosophy*, 331–356; Bańkowski, 'Subsidiarity, Sovereignty and Self,' in K. Norr and T Oppermann (eds) *Subsidarität: Idee und Wirtlichkeit. Zur Reichweite eines Prinzips in Deutschland und Europa* (1977 J C B Mohr), at 23–39

[3] We would like to thank Claudio Michelon for valuable insights.

[4] Christodoulidis, 'The Suspect Intimacy between Law and Political Community: the case of *Law's Empire*' in (1994), *Archiv für Rechts und Sozialphilosphie* , 1–18

But it is impossible to leave it at that. The challenge is to find a way of describing the 'crisis' as something that is normal. To see crisis not as detrimental to the legal system but as something that underlies its mode of existence. It is here that we enlist the help of systems theory. The whole point of trying to describe the EU in terms of 'interlocking normative spheres' is to be able to see the whole system as a continuous process of negotiation and renegotiation; one that does not have to have one single reference point to make it either a stable state system or one that is approaching that end. For that would, as we shall see later, lead to a form of 'idolatry.' In some ways, the *Brunner*[5] decision of the German Constitutional Court illustrates this. Part of the decision there rested on the fact that there was no recognisable European *demos*. In the sense of wanting, as the Court did, to fix and define that *demos* or identity, they wanted to have one single reference point.[6] Our contention is that, in this example, too, the *demos* is itself constituted in the clash of different systems. There are no criteria to which we need to look to see if we have arrived at what counts as the *demos*—there is no destination we have to arrive at. The whole system and its identity emerges in the clash of these systems. Thus, we might say that there is no essence of European identity but rather that it is always essentially contested in a systemic way. And because this is an ongoing process, a continuing negotiation, we use the metaphor of a journey albeit, as we shall see, one without a destination. For that shows us how the identity is contested always with no fixed definition. By using systems theory, we want to make what it means for something to be essentially contested precise. This theory, since it is about how different systems interact, with none being particularly privileged, enables us to capture the essential contestability in the articulation of different systems. At the same time, we do not want to suggest that this contestability is arbitrary, that there are no signposts on the journey, and so we start by looking at something like signposts— the ideals with which the whole process began.

II   The Ideals of Union

Joseph Weiler[7] in a lecture delivered at Edinburgh University and in a subsequent paper, talked of the ideals of European integration after the War and after Maastricht.

There were three ideals which drove the process of European integration after the War: peace, prosperity and supranationalism. Peace was something more than 'peace and quiet'—it was something like a call for forgiveness after the war. Prosperity, too was something more than being rich—it involved self-sacrifice and the promise of dignity and self reliance. Finally, supra-nationalism. How did the developing Europe embody this? It was not, according to Weiler, a concept opposed to nationalism. Instead, it patrols the boundaries of nationalism and tries not to let it deteriorate as happened before the war.

What are the values of nationhood for Weiler? They are belongingness and originality. The former is important because it appeals to our sociality. It gives us a place and a social home. We belong because we are. 'Even though he sins he remains 'Israel.' Nationhood transcends family and tribe and calls for loyalty to those who are

---

[5] 2BvR 2134/92 and 2159'92 JZ 1993, 1100 cf [1994] CMLR 57

[6] For an excellent defence of the representation of the demos as ongoing, against essentialist representations, cf. Lindahl, 'Substance and Function: Two Concepts of Representation in the EU' in *Law & Philosophy* (forthcoming)

[7] Weiler, 'Fin de Siècle Europe,' in, R. Dehousse (ed) *Europe after Maastricht; An ever closer Union?'* (1994 Becks) 203–216.

not your blood connection. That loyalty is not to be given out of utilitarian self-interest. Originality is important because we have different potentialities and thus need different nations. For Weiler, the state is only there to help the nation. It abuses nationalism, territorially, by the idea that one should die, fighting for the symbols of the state, thus forgetting the nation and thinking that one state is somehow superior to another. Supranationalism prevents these abuses because it brings in solidarity. It modifies the liberal concept of international law. There, the state's relation to it is the same as, in classical liberal theory, the relation of the atomic individual to state law. States are treated as atomic individuals. Supranationalism redresses this. It lets us minimise nationality as the principal reference point for transnational culture. It also means states cannot keep foreigners, products and culture out. It enables the alien to be protected. States, therefore, have to be original in order to establish and maintain their identity.

All systems of ideals, Weiler goes on to say, have a propensity to move beyond the ideal and become corrupted and be corrupting. They become frozen and what he calls 'idolatry' comes into play. The ideal becomes a fixed corrupting idol. What then has happened to these ideals in the post Maastricht period? We still have the desire for peace but without the same bite. It no longer resonates with the Christian Doctrine of grace and forgiveness. It is just peace and quiet. Prosperity, too, is no longer so idealistic. Now, it is just the desire to have more. Supranationalism is also undermined. The European Union appropriates the symbols of state and thus undermines the nation. Whereas in the old way of looking at things we were to relate to each other as French, German, *etc*, we are now Europeans. We have a single state. It is for this that we are meant to live as Europeans. And that state abuses nationalism. The symbols of the state are taking over the nations. Perhaps we now see in Europe a suspicion of grand ideals?

Weiler's vision is grand and sweeping, resonant with religious and moral imagery. But if we look at it from the inside, as it were, then what do we see? What needs to be made clear here is the relation between these ideals and the notion of 'community' and 'the community.' It seems to us that we can understand these ideals as in some way describing what a community is. Here we do not mean it in the straightforward way of saying that community means bread and peace for all. The ideals say something not about what [the] community is meant to achieve but rather about things that try and explicate our deepest thought about community. That is why the ideals of peace, prosperity and supranationalism were described further by Weiler in perhaps unexpected ways. Prosperity was not bread but also the ability to live with justice, dignity and self reliance. Peace meant something more than a quiet life. It also had connotations of being 'at peace' with oneself and others and thus of forgiveness after the war. Supranationalism meant more than no nation state and one identity but the ability to have something like unity in difference. And it is precisely this point about how identity through difference can be brought about without exclusion, that we will be picking up later with the help of systems theory.

Weiler describes the freezing of these ideals at a particular point as idolatry. Another way of looking at it would be to employ Fuller's[8] distinction between the morality of duty and the morality of aspiration. For Fuller, the morality of aspiration is most plainly exemplified in Greek philosophy. For the Greeks, morality was not about right and wrong. It was about what was fitting conduct and what was not. If one

---

[8] L. L. Fuller, *The Morality of Law*, (1969 Yale University Press), chapter 2.

failed to realise one's capacities, one was condemned, not for not fulfilling one's duty, but rather for failure to live up to what one was. The morality of duty, as opposed to aspiration, starts from the bottom rung of the ladder. It says what you should not do rather than ask that you live up to something. We may, as did Adam Smith, use the analogy of grammar to make this point clearer. The rules of grammar are the essential rules without which one cannot write and make oneself understood. We need them to be able to make human communication possible. The rules of good writing or style, on the other hand,

> are loose, vague and indeterminate, and present us rather with a general idea of the perfection we ought to aim at, than afford us any certain and infallible directions of acquiring it[9]

Take an analogy with art. Here, it has been argued by some that nonfigurative painting can best be done by those who have been classically trained. True creativity then, it might be said, is derived from discipline. It is only then that your creativity allows you to start changing the rules of the discipline. Non-figurative art is not a matter of just slapping paint onto a canvas. The analogy of grammar and writing reinforces this point. It is only those who have mastered the rules of grammar who can then go on to write well and with style. It is only those who have got to this point that are able to play creatively with the rules of grammar. Writing, to continue the analogy, is not merely slapping words onto paper.

Where does duty end and aspiration start? That, of course is a matter of judgement and balance. For Fuller, it is important to acknowledge that you do not have to have an idea of excellence in order to know what your duties are. For what is appropriate as the *sine qua non* of a particular institution does not have to be known by reference to the best example. Thus, to take grammar as an analogy again, one can have it without having a notion of the finest style. We do not have to have the notion of a particular end in view to seek excellence or work out what our basic duties are to be. But what happens if we do not have at least some idea of the excellence of an institution, of what we should aspire to? We think that our duties are all that is necessary and that there is nothing more. The Pharisee who thinks that he is saved because he obeys all the commandments but does not love is the classic example.

We could then interpret Weiler in those terms. When he elaborates the ideals mentioned above, he is talking about the aspirational part of what it means to live in community. When he says that the ideals have become idolatrous, he is saying that they have become frozen, that we think that our duties are all that there is to it. Thus, we may think that communities should provide, bread, peace and quiet and a certain universality and nothing more. We look inward to our duties and not outward to the aspiration.

These same questions are raised from another angle by Ian Ward[10] in a review of Derrida's *The Other Heading: Reflections on Today's Europe*. According to Ward, what Derrida is saying is that, in trying to redefine itself, Europe is forgetting and ignoring its own cultural history. In Ward's view, Derrida claims that Europe sees itself as 'a universal defined by its internal differentness.' In this sense what was important about the idea of Europe was that it was pluralistic and heterogeneous. Not homogeneous. It is this which Europe is trying to deny and, in doing so, denying its own culture. For

---

[9] Quoted by Fuller, *op cit,* n 8, at 6
[10] Ward, ' In Search of European Identity,' in (1994) *MLR* 315

Derrida, the new European discourse is one of 'centralisation and the diminution of particularity through the appropriation of nationalism.' One might say that the force of capital and technology is championing homogeneity over difference.

In his introduction to *The Other Heading*, Michael Naas writes

> Derrida argues not only that Europe must be responsible for the other, but that its own identity is in fact constituted by the other. Rejecting the easy or programmatic solutions of either complete unification ('The new World Order') or total dispersion, Derrida argues for the necessity of working with and from the Enlightenment values of liberal democracy while at the same time recalling that these values are never enough to secure respect for the other. Derrida thus seeks a redefinition of European identity that includes respect for both universal values and difference.[11]

One can see how this resonates with Weiler. For what Derrida is pointing to is what Weiler calls idolatry. What has happened is that the state has taken over the nation; that we worship the single European state. We start moving away from the idea of different nations. The diversity goes away.

What happens then is that we act on a continuum of aspiration which gets shortened artificially by fixing that aspiration as a duty at one point on the continuum. Weiler's ideals can be viewed as something like the continuum of aspiration. The point about the ideal, like Fuller' view of aspiration, is that while there must be an idea of the fact that there is excellence, one must not think of it as some definite definable property. For once one does that, then one tends to forget that there is more to it than that and forgets to grow in excellence or aspiration. Aspiration is the horizon. And that neatly encapsulates Weiler's point about idolatry. Thus, when prosperity becomes merely seen as providing bread for everyone, then, when that is more or less achieved, we think we have have prosperity and worship that as our goal, whereas it is but a step, and a necessary step, towards the broader aspiration of prosperity.

The metaphor that is appropriate here then is that of the journey and we can turn the duty/aspiration distinction round in another way. The aspiration is the ideal but since there is no idea (actual) of excellence then it is the journey itself that is important and it is the ideal (aspiration) that gives us the hope of going on this journey where there is no apparent destination.

III   The Journey

What does it mean to go on a journey like this? Often the metaphor of a journey is one where some sort of ultimate destination is posited. The idea of Utopia as a blueprint, a worked out programme, lends credence to this for it is often put forward as the ideal society which we can arrive at. This, from Thomas More on, has been a substantial literary genre. But we can make a distinction here and we can see it when Peter Young[12] talks about the problem that the idea of Utopia poses for social science. For Utopias seem to be neither clearly theoretical nor empirical in nature. They are, he says following Zygmund Bauman, in a third category close to the idea of 'praxis' or knowledge for action. The implications of that are that it often appears as bad scholarship in the sense that it is slippery and elusive and arguments from Utopian

---

[11] Quoted by Ward, *ibid*, at 320.

[12] Young, 'The Importance of Utopias in Criminological Thinking,' in (1992) 32 *British Journal of Criminology,* 423–237.

positions slide from one thing to another. This is because they do not denote any particular theory—it is not, in fact, a theory at all. Instead, it is a grouping of ideas that we use not so much as a guide to our action but rather as something that informs and transforms our actions. What we mean here is that though Utopias are (in a way necessarily) other- and future-directed, it does not mean to say that they are a distance beacon at the end of a road to which we travel. Their looking at the future is important in the sense that they show how intimately they are connected with hope; with optimism for the future. They need imagination and faith. But, to use the metaphor of the journey again, this is not to say that we just have to pick out a road to the hoped for destination. It is the journey itself that is important. Our Utopia, our act of hopeful imagination, is one that transforms that journey for it makes the act of travel a Utopian activity in itself. We might say that part of our Utopia is constructing the road that we have to travel on. And as we do this, fired by the future directed hope that the actual destination does not have to be our paramount aim, the process of constructing the road becomes as important, if not more so. The point here is that the Utopian vision is something that through its future direction, works in the present. In transforming our activity now, the future dwells in the present. So we might say that the significance of the eschatological thinking of the early church is that the vision of the kingdom was so strong (it was imminent) that it transformed its practice which differed later when that hope was less strong. It is an active and enabling presence which transforms us and makes us the people we are here and now. In one sense, the journey becomes the destination. Now, there are clearly tensions here. For one might argue that the final destination is something that cannot be denied, otherwise the hope really goes. The journey cannot take over entirely. We will return to this in the context of the EU at the end of the paper. But the one important thing about vision that must not be lost sight of is that it gives sense to our activity in the here and now, and makes it hopeful and Utopian. And this is not only in the sense that we see it *sub specie aeternitatis* as worthwhile because it is leading somewhere but because it is valuable in itself. If our lives were to finish, we would not think them wasted because we have not arrived there; our lives are complete because of what we are doing and not because that is where we should end. Take Victor Serge.[13] Here was a man who took part in the Russian Revolution, fought in the Spanish Civil War, was a Communist, Trotskyist, Anarchist—his life was a catalogue of failures, in the positions he took and the sides he fought on. But he never thought that his life and activities were a waste, because the hope that transformed them gave them a point—brought the future into the present and made his life complete. This is beautifully captured by Cavafy in *Ithaca*:

> As you set out for Ithaka
> hope your road is a long one,
> full of adventure, full of discovery.
>
> Keep Ithaka always in your mind.
> Arriving there is what you're destined for.
> But don't hurry the journey at all.
> Better if it lasts for years,
> so you're old by the time you reach the island,
> wealthy with all you've gained on the way,
> not expecting Ithaka to make you rich.

---

[13] V. Serge, *Memoirs of a Revolutionary* , (1967 OUP 1967)

Ithaka gave you the marvellous journey.
Without her you wouldn't have set out.
She has nothing left to give you now.
And if you find her poor, Ithaka won't have fooled you.
Wise as you will have become, so full of experience,
you'll have understood by then what these Ithakas mean.

We suggest viewing the EU in terms of a journey such as this, viewing it, that is, as an essentially contested project. One which is a journey with no end, sustained by ideals which, if frozen, would terminate it. Already we encounter a paradox of identity: for who are our travellers? This is because community appears here as both foundation and aspiration. How can an entity that has not yet been defined—and must not at any stage be definitively delimited since that would spell self-limitation, closure and exclusion—enable us to make a communal journey? How can it become the name in which 'we' undertake our aspirational journey? The identification of the 'we' that undertake the journey is one that the journey itself will determine, reconfigure or undermine, since the journey will identify the 'we' and resist the fixing of 'our' closure. 'We Europeans,' is both the presupposition and the stake of the process of integration; 'we Europeans' is the name that we reserve for the subject of the undertaking as well as the name to which the undertaking aspires. It is precisely this dual nature as origin and *telos* of the undertaking that the notion of 'essential contestability' is intended to capture by allowing us to contest the meanings that we ascribe to that identity and in the process of that contestation realise it. The paper aims to show how this reflexivity works. We now turn more precisely to describe what we mean by essential contestability and examine the mechanisms of the operations of this essentially contested project.

III   Systemic Essential Contestability

A   Semantic Ambiguity

'Europe as an essentially contested project' is a phrase that consciously brings up W. B. Gallie's notion of the essentially contested concept, although our view of it will differ in some ways from his work. Gallie is well summarised by Hurley:

> essentially contested concepts [are] appraisive and applicable to objects of an internally complex character that may be described in various ways by altering one's views of the significance of their descriptions of their component features.[14]

The point for Gallie was to show how two people could disagree substantively about a certain concept and yet agree that some example could be a paradigm for the concept. Some concepts, such as democracy, are essentially contested. And even though we might have such radical disagreements over the term, we agree in some sense that we are talking about democracy. For the point, in your saying what democracy is, is to defend or attack a particular vision of it. Thus we have a substantive disagreement about democracy rather than one which is merely conceptual (disagreeing about the meaning of the word). Is Europe an essentially contested project in this sense? We think not, for when talking about European identity in this sense, this would imply in the last instance an essentialist view of the European project

---

[14] S.L. Hurley, *Natural Reasons*, (1989 OUP) at 46.

and this would be an example of the freezing and idolatry that we have talked about above. On the Gallie[15] view of it, to say that the notion of Europe and European identity will always be problematic, since its definition will always be essentially contested, assumes some identity that we agree on; otherwise we can have no argument, merely posturing. So, in a sense, we all know what European identity is. Our point is that essential contestability rests on application and not on semantic ambiguity. Thus, European identity is to be understood in the process of the renegotiation of different identities and it is in this process that we get what we can call Europe. It is in this process that we find the notion of essential contestability.

One way to make sense of the dilemma and 'unfold the paradox' of identity may be given by systems theory. This approach also allows us to retain essential contestability as pivotal to the project. If essential contestability matters in this context it is because it offers us a unique way to understand the mode in which a concept is contestable. Essential contestability is not linguistic ambiguity, it is not vagueness in use, it is, in any case, not something to be explained away. The European *demos* is something to be understood in the doing, not in its blueprint. The doing is contesting.

B   *Interlocking Systems and Misreading*

Systems theory in its autopoietic form is a radical theory of legal closure expressed in a sociological way. Law and other such systems exist in a world where they are each the background or environment of each other. They become increasingly isolated from each other as they become more and more self-referential. In an increasingly complex world, this is a way of reducing the problems, such as information overload and the like that come with complexity. One system can never directly penetrate another. Autopoiesis thus explains, in an interesting and useful way, why it is that systems such as law seem such closed worlds and why all attempts at fresh 'social scientific' input into the law fail. It helps us understand why regulation so often fails as social problems get translated into legal categories. The same goes for attempts to control other areas in society through law. The other systems just translate them into their own categories. This expresses a truth about the interaction of different normative systems in such a stark way (that of total and absolute closure), that it is difficult to understand how systems can influence each other at all, except in a blind and indeterminate way. But this would make such things as regulation impossible and this is plainly not the case. In trying to deal with this problem, autopoiesis has to develop a theory for understanding the articulation and communication between systems and yet keep the basic insight of non-communication. This gives us a principle of linkage with the idea of 'structural coupling' where systems become linked and then can influence each other in a blind way—'communication through mutual misunderstanding.' And it is this that can help us. For it is in the way in which different systems of meaning come together and interact that we can see how 'Europe' is created in the continual negotiation and renegotiation of differing identities and how it is that process which is Europe. To understand this, we will look both at the operations and observations of systems.

Systems theory with its commitment to problem-oriented functional analysis shows that the concept of the European community (the people) is, first of all, a functional

---

[15] Cf, B. B *Law, Language and Legal Determinacy*: (Clarendon Press 1993) pp 50–62 for a discussion of these issues.

term for purposes of integration. This gives us a specific purchase into essential contestability that has to do with function. Systems of meaning employ the concept of 'the people' to effect specific operations. The concept is functional because it allows particular articulations—structural couplings—of systems. What does this mean? It means that when systems employ concepts, the meaning of those concepts is aligned, in the last instance, to a specific code or 'guiding distinction' that is specific to a system. Thus legal systems work by understanding everything in terms of their legality or illegality whereas political systems understand everything ultimately in terms of votes. The one would see 'the people' in terms of the constitutional notion of 'popular sovereignty' *vis-à-vis* , say, a political reading of the term; of how popular, say, a certain view of 'the European people' would make those in power. There are, as a result no shared meanings across systems. And yet systems of meaning find themselves under constant pressure to communicate through these concepts in order to interact with their environments which are, as we saw, the other systems. These interactions or interlockings that coincide in time are called 'structural couplings.' They result in a series of mis-readings that may be 'constructive' for systems because they allow continuous adaptations, but are mis-readings nonetheless. For example, the legal system has a particular view of economics (as where the economically rational way of running London Transport was seen as a matter of making revenue meet costs)[16] and the economics systems has a particular view of law (as, for example, where crime becomes just another cost to be distributed in an economically efficient manner).[17] These misunderstandings can be constructive in that they drive each system to produce new communications and new solutions. But there is no direct input—neither system understands the other as the other would or recognises that its view of the other is not the other's view of itself.

The fact that these articulations can be nothing but mis-readings accounts for why communications can be nothing but essentially contested. The contestability is real because systems involve real communications. The contestability is essential: it cannot be resolved. And that is because systems theory is a theory of communication that relies on constructive misreadings, and not on the identity of significations (as, say, in Habermas). Because who would be the privileged observer that would arbitrate on the identity of significations? And how could discourse, however uncoerced, settle mis-readings that neither side conceives of as mis-readings? The European *demos* is forever caught up in the definition of systems that articulate around it by simultaneously claiming to undercut the privilege of its naming.

One might see trying to understand Europe in this way as fundamentally conservative; as the never-ending dance of solipsistic systems entrenched in their own world.[18] But nothing in this way of looking at it precludes the kind of openness to the future, and the riskiness that comes with seeing European identity as an essentially contested journey. The concept of the European *demos*, or public, is tied to functional imperatives of systems that need to tailor it to their own requirements, thus limiting it and reducing it. At the same time systems must be open to the environment because they need to attune their operations to external changes and in the process re-specify the meanings of concepts, even one such as the *demos* that is relatively entrenched.

---

[16] Cf, *Bromley London Borough Council* v *Greater London Council* [1982] 1 All E. R. 193–203

[17] An example would be how industrialists see fines for pollution as a tax

[18] Cf, Bańkowski, 'How Does it Feel to be on Your Own? The Person in the Sight of Autopoiesis' in (1994) *Ratio Juris.*

This re-negotiation is sustained by the systems' need to develop. It cannot be ignored or suspended. If social communication occurs as the polyphony of systems[19] that must interact to continue, concepts that are operative in many discourses are continuously re-embedded. In the process, the meaning of community is always postponed, always in the process of becoming. Note how complex the process is. It is not merely different social sub-systems like law, politics or the economy that make different sense of the concept and yet have to communicate about it and interlock through it. In each system the meaning of the term will be appropriated by a number of what Luhmann calls 'internal environments' or sub-systems. In politics, for example, the concept of the public receives a different treatment by the press and by public administration.[20] In law, it is thematised differently at different levels, *eg* national and European, but also even at one and the same level it is simultaneously the 'same and different'; 'the populace' is celebrated in constitutional terms as the bearer of sovereignty, merely colours 'public interest' elsewhere and disappears completely from, say, the law of industrial relations.

C Grenzstellen

There is one final way of looking at the interlocking of the spheres that we want to look at. Here we talk of the concept of 'border posts' that Gunther Teubner uses in his work[21] in the context of the learning process of the legal system, the complex interplay between the individual trial and the law's evolutionary mechanism. Legal 'learning' occurs in the trial in which a specific solution is given to a clash of expectations. The problem for Teubner is how this learning feeds into the dynamic of legal evolution. What Teubner is attempting to explain here is how expectations, competing at the interactional level of the trial, feed into the legal system to reshape its assumptions, *ie,* vary the expectations it will henceforth project. It is the individual interaction that makes social experimentation possible, says Teubner.[22] 'Social experimentation' as variation allows new impulses to be felt in law. The trial is where the claims for legal change are articulated. In this sense, the trial, itself an interaction system, is the negotiating or border post between the vast area of social demands and their sanctioning in law, *ie* their being vested the status of confirmed legal expectations. Teubner claims that it is through this negotiating process that legal evolution makes

---

[19] On the basis of the distinction system/environment, every subsystem perceives society and other subsystems as environment. This reflection is 'totalising' in the sense that each encoding makes sense of the whole of reality and claims exclusivity for that depiction—N. Luhmann, *Ecological Communication*. Cambridge (1986 Polity Press) chapter 16. The social is thus given a reality from every systemic perspective, and done so in incommensurable ways: subsystems do not join together into higher level systems—no ultimate (or meta) observer will resolve their differences—nor can they be conceived of as instances of a totality. This leaves society in the situation of being the totality of communications, yet its unity is forever undermined by the irreconcilabity of sub-systems which not only perceive reality in different ways but also perceive their differences in different ways. *Unitas multiplex*; a society that is at once unity (all communication as distinct from life and consciousness) and multiplicity. And, at the same time, in the current evolutionary phase of functional differentiation, a heterarchy; the multiplicity of descriptions of society cannot be co-ordinated hierarchically

[20] N. Luhmann, *Political Theory in the Welfare State* (1990 De Gruyter) chapter 2.

[21] G. Teubner, *Law as an Autopoietic System*. (1993 Blackwell).

[22] Also Heller: 'Litigation, when not simply a form of debt collection, is designed to upset legal practice, invoke the search for meaning in legal reason.' Heller, 'Accounting for Law' in Teubner (ed) *Autopoietic Law: A New Approach to Law and Society*. (1998 de Gruyter) 186 n 13.

sense and thus evolution must be understood as involving the 'interlocking of two communicative cycles,' that of the trial and that of the legal system proper. The trial is the way that individual disputes are sorted out and where the parties are satisfied in their dispute and clash of expectations. But, at the same time, the trial is the mechanism by which more general norms are fed into the legal system as a whole and they can then be used to help solve the next individual dispute that comes along in the trial. Thus the trial has a foot in at least two camps, the realm of individual disputes and the system of legal doctrine. Through it those two worlds interact and gain from each other. Legal doctrine is used to solve individual disputes and in those disputes being solved more rules are produced which then enter and change the system of legal doctrine. To put it in system terms, the legal system's mechanism of retention (the legal decision) 'bequeaths what has been learnt in the process of interaction.' Stabilisation, the final step, involves the play, in law, of all those mechanisms that 'enable insights gained in one trial to . . . become part of the memory of the law,' and thus allow its autopoiesis, when that memory furnishes new legal expectations to be tested, affirmed or disappointed in future legal episodes. Through the tripartite process, the insight gained in one trial, (a variation possibly), is 'skimmed off as normative surplus,' to establish (through retention and stabilisation) a principle for future selection in law.[23]

Thus one can see the trial and other such institutions as 'bridging institutions' or a form of border post which is the site of a common meeting ground which facilitates the transfer of information from one institution to another. Within the European Union one can see the ECJ performing this role. With reference to the essential contestability of the European identity we can see how the openness that we require for our concept can be premised on the operative closure of different interlocking systems, yet at the same time remain open because none of these systems can, at the general social level, become definitive of the aspiration. The essential contestability of our central concept develops in ways that both feed off and contest one another, while always remaining open to learning. Of course, meaning always comes with closure. But in a situation where closure is contingent, necessary for each system but contingent for the observer who can switch amongst systems, the closure of an identity as such is undercut.

IV   Inclusionary European Identity

We have implied that the construction of what it means to be Europe or have a European identity is a reflexive task. It is in the construction of that identity that one can say that Europe exists. This is useful, for it enables us to get away from the problems of exclusion. This was partly alluded to in Bańkowski and Scott,[24] where it was shown how Europe can enable sub-national groups to claim identity and representation without necessarily falling foul of the problem of excessive nationalistic demands. Thus, the slogan 'Scotland in Europe' as used by the Scottish National Party in the last election is able both to say that 'we are Scots because we are not English' while at the same time saying that 'we are like the English because we are Scots.' But here we can go further and say that since the identity is never fixed—being always in the process of becoming—the fact that we define our identity by exclusion from the

---

[23] *Op cit*, n 14.
[24] Bańkowski and Scott, 'The European Union?,' in R. Bellamy (ed) *Constitutionalism, Democracy and Sovereignty* (1996 Avebury Press), 77–95.

other does not ultimately exclude because there is no way of knowing where the next redefinition will go. It is precisely when a definition is taken as settling the matter once and for all that the journey is stopped because reflexivity ceases. And this is the condition that Weiler describes as idolatry.

Bert van Roermund argues that it is impossible to conceive of an identity that is particular yet not exclusionary. In many ways, this would be like trying to get the best of both worlds: accept a particular definition of self that must occur in the mirror of a significant other, yet not exclude that other. For him, it is inevitable that 'a whole can only be a whole by virtue of being limited, that is, to include some and exclude others.'[25]

We may be able to enlist systems-theory to counter this inevitablity. The argument would go somewhat like this. The whole as unmarked state allows no purchase into it. A whole needs at least one internal boundary if it is to be observed, and for this, we will have to sever the whole by drawing a distinction.[26] The unity of the whole as 'unmarked state' is violated, something is indicated that leaves something out. Note that no observation can be established before the first distinction is drawn. It is not possible to envisage the unmarked state before the initial distinction is drawn. Only by severing the whole can we see it, but then it is only in the terms in which we have severed it that we see it. It is in this sense that Luhmann says that the whole always necessarily eludes us. Because all knowledge of the whole is always already partial knowledge, dependant on the distinction we employed to observe it, that alone, through its form, allows us to see the unity; but with the distinction itself determining the shape of both self and other (indicated and nonindicated), the world that is over and above both is determined through the mark we inflict on it.

Now, this may well capture the gist of van Roermund's arguments about the dilemmas of 'irrepresentability' of the people in democratic politics, at least in one sense: that no representation can ensure self-transparency, but will inevitably involve substitution and partiality. Systems theory not only acknowledges but, in fact, begins from that irrepresentability of society to itself. How do we not get exclusion then? One way of conceptualising the slogan 'Scotland in Europe' is to take the Luhmann point that the system/environment distinction is itself internal to the system. Every observation of the world is a severing of the world. Just as there is no purchase into the unmarked state before the mark, there is no account of the world that precedes the system. Systems come about as distinctions are drawn, indications made and 're-entries' effected. We need to understand the concept at that, the most abstract level: the distinctive feature of the system is that it differentiates itself by establishing a boundary between internal and external, between what it is and what it is not, and conceives of the world as spanning them both. The way it achieves this is in terms of the operation outlined: a distinction is drawn, one side indicated, the distinction 're-entered' in the indicated side, because only from the inside is the distinction between inside/outside perceivable.

The operation of distinction-indication-re-entry allows the system to establish—and in time compound—a boundary between itself and the environment, to see itself and, as the non-indicated side re-enters, to see what in contra-distinction to itself the outside world is. Because establishing the self as self requires distinguishing it from something

---

[25] van Roermund, 'The Concept of Representation in Parliamentary Democracy' in (1996) 14 *Current Legal Theory,* 31–52.
[26] Cf, Derrida, *infra*

else. In order to define itself the system needs to reintroduce its other; this reintroduction takes the form of 're-entry.' The process resembles Lacan's 'mirror stage' in the development of the system; through re-entry, the system can observe itself-in-an-environment. Only thus does 'emerge the distinction for the system between the environment which it sees confronting it, and the world to which it belongs,'[27] enabling both self-observation and observation of the environment. Then, Luhmann can say that 'a system that re-introduces the system—environment difference into the system is capable of equating its boundaries with those of the world.'[28] Without the difference, the indication and the re-entry we would have no purchase point into the meaning of the entity. System boundaries have to be drawn, internal and external space designated, for anything to make any sense at all. [29]

So in calling myself and acting as a Scot I come up against others, the English for example. But the only way that I can make sense of myself (of indicating myself) is by making that distinction an internal one by bringing the 'other' into my space and making sense of it so that I can make sense of myself. In that sense, I do not exclude it for it becomes part of the way that I define myself. I become a European and more specifically a Scottish European for being European is part of my Scottish identity. The French, the English and others will do likewise. And as these distinctions multiply and I bring in other 'others' into my space (and they do as well), then I come to much more nuanced ideas of myself as Scottish which will not necessarily exclude but produce a great number of cross cutting distinctions.

All this is not to say that racism will be excluded merely to argue that this way of looking at it does not necessarily include it but preserves the openness and reflexivity that we have argued for. When the self/other distinction—as system/environment—is placed within an inclusive whole, that of the European people, this inclusive whole can be observed and defined without being delimited. It no longer relies on an external boundary; its sense comes from an internal distinction, or at least a distinction of self and other that it serves as horizon. A horizon is something not captured, represented or transcended but that which provides a context against which definitions become possible. This also fits neatly with our metaphor of the journey without a destination. If we think of what we, at any particular time, aim for as a horizon, then we can see it as never ending for the horizon always, when we get there, expands and opens up new possibilities. Nationhood now can be understood as the locus of originality because it can contribute something to an identity that spans both self and other. Or more accurately: an identity that does not extirpate that against which it defines itself—the 'internal environment'—but employs it to locate itself in a more inclusive context. A claim, say, of 'Us Scots, Europeans' is able to (a) to provide an identity which represents an identity in context (and there can be no other representation), (b) establish a 'mark,' a perspective on the context through which to conceive European-ness and (c) acknowledge other descriptions of what it means to be European, but also

---

[27] N. Luhmann, 'The Self-Thematization of Society,' included in (*idem*) *The Differentiation of Society*. (1975 Columbia University Press), 347.

[28] Luhmann, 'The Coding of the Legal System,' in G. Teubner & A. Febbrajo (eds): *State, Law, Economy as Autopoietic Systems*. (1986 Giuffré), at 21.

[29] '[A system] must be able to observe [its] operations as the drawing of a boundary, as the fencing in of what belongs to it and the shutting out of what does not. It must be able to distinguish between self-reference and external reference. The intrinsic value of intrinsic values—this is what constitutes the system: the system as boundary, as a form with two sides, as a distinction of system and environment.' (N. Luhmann, *Risk: A Sociological Theory*. Translated by R Barret (1991 de Gruyter) 224–5)

to consolidate a sense of belonging since now has 'emerge[d] the distinction for the system between the environment which it sees confronting it, and the world to which it belongs.'[30]

V   Conclusion

We have argued that the European project is something that poses a challenge for legal theory for it appears to be an entity that cannot adequately be captured by existing legal theory. At the same time, of course, our task has not been wholly descriptive. For our contention is that traditional theory would in fact mould the Union into a form which we think of as normatively damaging. The way we have sought to conceptualise it would be a way which we would want normatively to recommend as a way forward. In very general terms our contention has been to put forward a view of that the construction of what Europe means or what it means to have a European identity is a reflexive task; one that has to make sense of interlocking normative systems and identities that are not especially privileged, the one against the other; one that is essentially contested. Systems theory has been used to make more precise the kind of reflexive and eschatological view we want to propound and not to explain the EU in system theoretic terms. Otherwise 'We European citizens' is an *a priori*. It can, of course, be delimited and thus defined in the mirror of those who are not Europeans. But such limitations are forms of exclusion and they give political aspirations little leverage, and all too often a leverage we abhor. Otherwise than an exclusionary 'Euro-racism,' European citizenship is an *a priori* circumference of political space. We do not think that it has to be. Our suggestion for a reflexive politics could potentially turn the identification 'Europe' into a contested rather than a natural setting, and furthermore one where the mode of contestation is in turn contestable. Because solidarities that are significant enough to inform identities form locally and partially, cutting across other political identifications. Our Europe is a multiple Europe, but significantly one that hosts mutually undercutting and mutually denying identifications. And it is worrying to prioritise any of these to the exclusion of others in the name of community. Only as a site of political reflexivity, as an essentially contested community, can 'the European community' remain a political aspiration.

With one of the crises and challenges of the EU being enlargement towards the East, the image of border posts taken from systems theory is especially appropriate. For these institutions are, as we saw, ones that by being located on sites that are common to both systems are able to facilitate their interlocking and interaction. Those real border posts at the East of the EU in Germany stand on land that for centuries has been seen as both Polish and German.

---

[30] 'Luhmann 'The Coding of the Legal System,' *loc cit*, n 28

3

Sovereignty and Differentiated Integration in the European Union

Neil Walker

I Introduction

It is well-known that in recent years there has been a growing challenge to the principle of uniformity in the development of the law and the institutions of the European Union (EU).[1] The Treaty of Maastricht, with its opt-outs in respect of the Social Policy Protocol and the final stage of Economic and Monetary Union, and now the Treaty of Amsterdam, with its broader endorsement of differential participation by Member States in policy areas across the First, Second and Third Pillars, have built upon the more modest provisions in earlier European Treaties for a departure from the foundational Community norm of 'common rules for a common market.'[2] This trend towards differentiated integration presents pressing political and theoretical questions. The issues raised are urgent as a matter of practical politics because flexible arrangements now, and for the foreseeable future, appear indispensable to accommodate conflicting preferences over the proper rate and direction of development of the EU. The new theoretical challenge flows from the fact that differentiated integration is not easily accommodated within our existing frameworks for understanding transnational patterns of political authority. Most of the concepts which have been coined or adapted to help us make sense of the political structure of Western Europe in the age of the EU, terms such as intergovernmentalism, supranationalism, federalism, subsidiarity and consociationalism, have tended to be deployed with a view to illuminating a configuration of political authority which consists of a relationship between two fixed political units—the (fifteen) Member State(s) on the one hand, and the EU on the other. With the trend towards

---

[1] Overviews include, Ehlermann, 'How Flexible is Community Law? An Unusual Approach to the Concept of 'Two Speeds,'' (1984) 82 *Michigan Law Review* 1274; Harmsen, 'A European Union of Variable Geometry: Problems and Perspectives' (1994) 45 *Northern Ireland Legal Quarterly* 109; Ehlermann, 'Increased Differentiation or Stronger Uniformity,' in J. Winter *et al* (eds) *Reforming The Treaty on European Union* (1996 Asser Institute); Stubb, 'A Categorization of Differentiated Integration,' (1996) 34 *Journal of Common Market Studies* 283; A. Duff *Reforming The European Union* (1977 Federal Trust) chs. 1 and 8; M. Dewatripont, F. Giavazzi, J. von Hagen, I. Harden, T. Persson, G. Roland, H. Rosenthal, A. Sapir and G. Tabellini, *Flexible Integration, Towards a More Effective and Democratic Europe* (1995 Centre for Economic Policy Research); Usher, 'Variable Geometry or Concentric Circles: Patterns for the European Union' (1997) 46 *International and Comparative Law Quarterly* 243; Weatherill, 'On the Depth and Breadth of European Integration,' (1997) 17 *Oxford Journal of Legal Studies* 536; and for early analysis of the implications of the Treaty of Amsterdam for differentiated integration, cf, Edwards and Phillipart 'Flexibility and the Treaty of Amsterdam: Europe's New Byzantium,' *CELS Occasional Paper*, no 3, November 1997; Shaw 'The Treaty of Amsterdam: the challenges of flexibility and legitimacy' (1998) 4:1 *European Law Journal;* Tuytschaever *Differentiation in European Law* (1999 Hart); de Burca and Scott (eds) *The European Constitution: Between Uniformity and Flexibility* (2000 Hart).

[2] Weatherill, *loc cit,* n 1, 537.

differentiated integration, a two-dimensional analysis is no longer appropriate. Instead, we may envisage a number of different 'Europes,' their breadth and depth dependent upon the integration arrangements specific to the policy field in question, and embedded in a complex network of relations with one another and with the various Member States. In turn, we require a set of analytical tools that is adequate to this emerging multi-dimensional configuration of authority, a task which may involve a significant revision of the theoretical language honed to make sense of the two-dimensional Europe.

The central tool employed in this task below is the concept of sovereignty. At first sight, this might seem an unduly old-fashioned key with which to seek to unlock the mysteries of the new Europe. After all, the term was introduced into legal and political thought as a way of comprehending a one-dimensional pattern of state-centred authority. As we shall see, the concept of sovereignty already required significant extension and revision in order to come to terms with the two-dimensional Europe of fixed states and a fixed supranational entity, still less the multi-dimensional Europe of differentiated integration. Nonetheless, it is submitted, the concept of sovereignty has sufficient analytical scope to be capable of illuminating more or less complex configurations of authority. Indeed, it is this analytical scope which makes sovereignty so valuable for our purposes; precisely because it can provide a basis for meaningful comparison between political orders of different levels of complexity, it promises to reveal what is most importantly distinctive about the highly complex world of differentiated integration.

The argument proceeds in four sections. First, the theoretical framework is established. Sovereignty is an oft-used and highly contested concept, and thus the particular 'conception of the concept'[3] which is intended in the present context must be closely defined. In turn, the means by which the chosen conception of sovereignty is capable of illuminating a multi-dimensional configuration of authority is explained. Secondly, the political dynamics of differentiated integration are explored. What forces have encouraged it, and how deeply have they penetrated the constitutional structure of Western Europe? Thirdly, the difficulties and drawbacks associated with the type of multi-dimensionality, of which a developed pattern of differentiated integration in Europe is an instance, are assessed. This assessment will be situated in a comparative framework. The types of problems which might arise under the emerging multi-dimensional framework are compared to the problems which have typically arisen, and the way in which these have been addressed under the traditional two-dimensional framework within Europe. In the final section, the elements of the earlier discussion are drawn together in an attempt to assess the political and constitutional prospects for a Europe of differentiated integration. In particular, we consider whether or not the political dynamics which underpin the development of differentiated integration provide an hospitable climate for the successful treatment of the sorts of problems which arise under a multi-dimensional framework.

II Sovereignty in the New Constitutional Order

A *The Concept of Sovereignty*

In what follows, we define sovereignty in legal rather than political terms; as a threshold concept; as referring to the internal order of a polity rather than its external

---

[3] R. Dworkin, *Law's Empire* (1986 Fontana) 90–101.

relations; and as divisible, yet requiring finality of decision. Each of these character-istics builds towards a conception of sovereignty which has broad explanatory power, and which is appropriate to the analysis of multi-dimensional authority.

To begin with, our conception of sovereignty is concerned with ultimate legal authority rather than ultimate political power. Both legal and political conceptions of sovereignty have strong historical lineages, and, indeed, one influential current of thought associated both with Bentham[4] and with Austin's[5] command theory of law,[6] collapses political and legal elements into a single definition. For present purposes, however, it is important to distinguish between them,[7] and to assert the priority of the legal conception. Conceived of in political terms, sovereignty is a term which seeks to describe rather than to explain power relations. Political sovereignty is a *measure* of the capacity to command of a government elite, or in its popular variant, of the capacity of the wider community to ensure that its interests are secured.[8] In neither case is any attempt made to *account for* this ultimate political power. Thus political sovereignty is a term which lacks theoretical purchase. It is useful, at best, as a marker of a certain empirical state of affairs, but even this residual value is challenged by the circumstances of a multi-dimensional configuration of political authority. The defining characteristic of a multi-dimensional configuration of authority is the co-existence of different sources and centres of power. It refers to a heterarchical rather than a hierarchical political space. The search within such a space for a pattern of power relations which reflects an ultimate source of authority—or political sovereign—is, therefore, destined to prove inconclusive.

Of course, to demonstrate that the political conception of sovereignty is both theoretically empty and empirically redundant for the purposes of the present inquiry does not imply that a legal conception is any better equipped. To demonstrate that legal sovereignty is a more helpful device in explaining a complex configuration of political authority, we must introduce two distinctive characteristics of law. First, law is institutionally autonomous.[9] It provides an internally coherent system of rules—in Hartian terms, a 'structured set of primary and secondary rules'[10]—which allows it to be considered *apart from* the other levers and incidents of political power, as a discrete influence upon the overall authority structure. In the second place, law itself makes significant claims to authority.[11] It is a type of normative power which purports to be able to settle for practical purposes matters within the polity which are controversial and disputed.

To be properly equipped for the task of investigating multi-dimensionality, a conception of *legal* sovereignty which stresses the institutional autonomy and decision-making authority of its defining characteristic requires further refinement and qualification. To begin with, drawing upon the work of Steven Lee, legal

---

[4] Cf, in particular, J. Bentham *Of Laws in General* (Hart and Burns (eds)) (1970 Clarendon), chs 1,2,17, App A.

[5] J. Austin *The Province of Jurisprudence Determined* (1955 Weidenfeld and Nicholson), 155.

[6] For a useful overview, cf, J W Harris *Legal Philosophies* (2nd ed, 1997 Butterworths), ch 3.

[7] Cf,, for example, Lee, 'A Puzzle of Sovereignty' (1997) 27 *Californian Western International Law Journal* 241, 243–250; MacCormick, 'Sovereignty: Myth and Reality,' (1995) *Scottish Affairs* no 11 1.

[8] Lee, *loc cit,* n 7, 248–249.

[9] For a useful restatement of the distinct characteristics of law viewed from a positivist perspective, cf, MacCormick, 'The Concept of Law and 'The Concept of Law,''(1994) 14 *Oxford Journal of Legal Studies* 1.

[10] *Ibid* 10; for the original Hartian position, cf, H L A Hart *The Concept of Law* (2nd ed 1997 OUP) esp ch 5.

[11] McCormick, *loc cit,* n 9, 12–15.

sovereignty is defined as a 'threshold concept.' A threshold concept applies 'in an all-or-nothing fashion when certain variable background conditions... have reached a certain threshold of intensity.'[12] Negatively, this means that legal sovereignty should be defined neither as an absolute concept nor as a concept which may admit of degrees of applicability. The absolute version of legal sovereignty, although frequently espoused, is sociologically naive, insofar as it requires an unlimited legal authority, uniquely capable of resolving every dispute and commanding perfect obedience to its rule.[13] The absolute version, moreover, is particularly ill-suited to a multi-dimensional configuration of authority, which already presupposes different centres of power. Yet if the absolute version of sovereignty demands too much of any actually-existing legal system, to conceive of sovereignty in more-or-less terms asks too little. Sovereignty necessarily implies 'sovereignty over' a limited territory, and perhaps also a limited set of functions, and so tends to be shaped and restricted by boundaries of space and subject-matter. Within these boundaries, however, the nature of the authority claimed cannot be further restricted. The alternative, namely the idea of partial sovereignty, is surely an oxymoron, for if ultimate authority resides in a particular source, such authority, by definition, cannot be qualified by degree or condition.

The virtue of a threshold definition of sovereignty lies in the fact that it retains the sense of ultimate and categorical authority without imposing the impossible standards of absolutism. Arguably, there may be different ways in which to operationalise the threshold approach,[14] but for present purposes the most appropriate is through the idea of a *plausible claim* to ultimate legal authority identifying and grounding a particular legal order. As with Hart's 'minimum conditions... for the existence of a legal system,'[15] this combines subjective and objective factors. Subjectively, there has to be common assertion or acceptance by the key officials of the legal system in question—in particular its judges—that such a legal system exists and that it does so in accordance with certain fundamental and irreducible propositions or assumptions. Objectively, this set of beliefs and claims must be plausible, in that there is evidence of a high level of general obedience to the framework of laws which are valid according to the system's ultimate criteria of validity.

Next, legal sovereignty must be conceived of in internal, rather than, external terms. Traditionally, legal notions of sovereignty have operated within two quite distinct discourses—the discourse of constitutional law and the discourse of international law—with the former discourse treating sovereignty as authority *within* the state and the latter discourse treating sovereignty as the authority *of* the state in international relations. Some writers have treated internal and external sovereignty merely as different perspectives on the same phenomenon, following Austin's view that habitual obedience within the domestic social order and the absence of any external superior authority are two sides of a single (sovereign) coin.[16] However, this view does not withstand close scrutiny. To begin with, ultimate legal authority is differently identified and differently located in the two approaches. The source and agency(ies) of ultimate

---

[12] *Loc cit,* n 7 245.

[13] *Ibid,* 244–245.

[14] For example, Lee uses the test of a 'substantial preponderance of power' (246); however, this seems vulnerable to the criticism made earlier in the text of political conceptions of sovereignty in that it attributes theoretical significance to a characteristic which is defined by reference to a vague, quasi-empirical test.

[15] Hart *loc cit,* n 10, 116.

[16] Cf, Austin, *loc cit,* n 5; cf, also Lee *loc cit,* n 7, 247.

legal authority within the state are quite distinct from the source and agency (ies) of the ultimate legal authority of the state. For instance, the fact that external sovereignty tends to be exercised primarily through the agency of the executive branch of government implies nothing about the location of authority for the purposes of internal sovereignty. Secondly, the type of capacity described by the two types of sovereignty are, any case, very different. Ultimate authority in the external context means no more than that the independence of the state and its capacity to participate in international decision-making is unchallenged. Unlike internal sovereignty, external sovereignty does not also imply ultimate authority over the content and operation of the relevant legal order; rather, the international legal order is a product of negotiation between formally equal states.[17]

It is worth underlining the difference between internal and external authority because of the nature of the entity we are dealing with. The EU is a polity which transcends state boundaries. However, the empirical fact that the state is no longer the widest boundary of political authority does not alter the analytical point that internal sovereignty and external sovereignty are, in conceptual terms, no more than 'remote cousins.'[18] Rather than collapsing the conceptual distinction in response to the changing political order, we must recognise that the two legal conceptions of sovereignty continue to have quite separate functions in the analysis of that changing order. And having acknowledged this, it becomes clear that the internal conception has the more significant role to play in that analysis. After all, what is new about the multi-dimensional configuration of authority is precisely the emergence of new 'plausible claims' to ultimate legal authority *within* a particular political space, whether at the level of the EU or at the level of other variable groupings. To be sure, external sovereignty has its part to play, in that the new configuration is the product of the exercise of external sovereignty by Member States and, in some respects, will continue to be shaped by its exercise. However, this is merely to say that the operation of external sovereignty is part of the broader context within which the new configuration has evolved, whereas developments in internal sovereignty are intrinsic to the definition of the new configuration in multi-dimensional terms.

A final key characteristic of our definition of sovereignty is that it is divisible, but requires 'finality of decision.'[19] The idea of the indivisibility of sovereignty has historical roots in the personalization of sovereignty in the position of the absolute monarch of the 16th and 17th centuries. While the pattern of political authority has since altered, there remains an analytical case for indivisibility, in that ultimate legal authority arguably requires that it be monopolistically possessed by a single source. However, this is only persuasive if we conceive of the source and subject of sovereignty exclusively in *agency-based* terms. If sovereignty within a particular legal order is merely, and at root, a matter of the authority of agencies—whether these be the monarch, or the national legislature, or the European Council—then it can reside in only one such agency at any particular moment, otherwise it loses its defining status as ultimate and unchallengeable.

But an agency-based approach does not provide an exhaustive analysis of sovereignty. A full analysis of ultimate legal authority with regard to a legal system

---

[17] Cf,, for example, P Eleftheriadis 'Begging the Constitutional Question' (1998) 36 *Journal of Common Market Studies*.

[18] *Ibid.*

[19] P King 'Sovereignty' in D Miller (ed) *The Blackwell Encyclopaedia of Political Thought* (1987 Blackwell), 492, 495.

also requires an investigation of the underlying norms, practices and assumptions which grant authority to a particular agency or agencies. For example, where there is a written constitutional framework, one would have to include the complex of constitutional rules which allocates legal powers to different levels and organs of government. Further, whether or not there is a written constitutional framework, one would also have to include, at an even more fundamental level, both the background presuppositions or hypotheses relating to 'the unity of a manifold'[20] which render intelligible the very idea of a legal order, and, more concretely, the practices and propositions which ground and articulate the plausible claim that seeks to underpin the particular legal order in question and establish its basic criteria of identity and validity—what Hart terms the rule of recognition.[21]

In other words, if we take the analysis of sovereignty *qua* ultimate legal authority seriously, then it is arbitrary to draw a line under our search when we locate the most fundamental agency or agencies within the legal system; instead, we have to be prepared to dig deeper to discover the ultimate source of the claim to authority which purports to allocate powers to and between any such agencies. Only if we penetrate to this basic level and to the finality of decision that it claims to provide, and only if we can demonstrate that the practices, propositions or assumptions through which this claim is articulated underscore the division of fundamental legal authority between agencies, can we accept such a division of authority as consistent with the notion of legal sovereignty. If, on the other hand, we fail to locate any such fundamental practices, propositions or assumptions as underpinning a division of authority between agencies, or—even more crucially in the present context—if it appears that the fundamental practices, propositions or assumptions that underpin these different agencies and purport to allocate authority to them are rooted in different plausible claims about the existence of different legal orders, we cannot talk meaningfully about a sharing of sovereignty between these agencies.[22]

In summary, therefore, for the purposes of the present article sovereignty is characterised as a plausible claim to ultimate legal authority identifying and grounding a particular legal order, the articulation of which claim takes the form of fundamental practices, propositions or assumptions, which, *inter alia*, may allocate constituent legal authority to a particular agency or between particular agencies.

B *Sovereignty in a Multi-Dimensional Europe*

How does this characterisation of sovereignty help us to make sense of a multi-dimensional configuration of authority? It does so, first, and most generally, because a conception of sovereignty which is grounded in law, with its characteristics of institutional autonomy and authoritativeness, identifies a discrete and significant factor shaping the body politic; secondly, because the idea of a plausible claim to

---

[20] Hans Lindahl has developed a powerful critique of the classical view of sovereignty in a series of papers : 'Sovereignty and Symbolization (1997) 27 *Rechtstheorie* 3; 'Democracy and the Constitution of Society' (1998) 11 *Ratio Juris* 12; 'The Purposiveness of Law: Two Concepts of Representation in the European Union' 17 *Law and Philosophy* 481.

[21] Hart, *op cit,* n 10, 94–95.

[22] Accordingly, we should be wary of loose talk of sovereignty being shared between or pooled by different legal orders and their institutional representatives, when in fact none of the parties has recognized any *ultimate* legal authority—or sovereignty—other than its own. Nevertheless, the language of pooling and sharing is a staple of a certain type of political discourse associated with European integration.

ultimate legal authority admits of the possibility of the co-existence of a plurality of such plausible claims, potentially in competition with one another; and thirdly, as these different claims seek to identify and ground different legal orders and so are logically inextricable from these different putative legal orders, then the plurality allowed within the definition of sovereignty clearly refers not merely to different and rival underlying conceptions of a *single*, undisputed legal order within a particular political space, but to the underlying conceptions of *various*, and perhaps mutually disputed legal orders within a particular political space. In other words, our definition of sovereignty allows us to develop the idea that there may be a plurality of claims to legal sovereignty, and that these claims refer to a plurality of legal orders, each with their own architecture and fundamental 'sovereign' agencies. As we shall see, it is this idea of a plurality of legal orders within a single political space which goes to the heart of the idea of a multi-dimensional configuration of authority within the new Europe.

The notion of different legal orders operating within a single space is already present in analyses of Europe as a two-dimensional configuration of legal authority. Writers such as Bańkowski,[23] MacCormick,[24] Weiler[25] and Eleftheriadis[26] have, in very different ways, begun to develop a conception of the European legal order in which claims to ultimate legal authority are postulated at two different levels—the EU and the Member State, with neither intrinsically more plausible than the other. That is to say, rather than take sides in the enduring and unresolvable conflict over whether the ultimate authority within the European legal order may still be traced to the Member States and their national legal systems, or whether the EU instead constitutes a new, self-defining legal order,[27] this new pluralist position has sought to distance itself from the assumptions of both camps; and in so doing, advocates of the new position have concluded that there is no objective basis—no Archimedean point—

---

[23] Cf, *eg*, Bańkowski and Christodoloudis 'The European Union as an essentially contested project' (present volume); Bańkowski, 'Comment on Weiler' in S Bulmer and D Scott (eds) *Economic and Political Integration in Europe* (1994 Blackwell) 161; Bańkowski and Scott, 'The European Union?' in R Bellamy (ed) *Constitutionalism, Democracy and Sovereignty; American and European Perspectives* (1996 Avebury) 77.

[24] Cf, *eg*, 'Beyond the Sovereign State,' (1993) 56 *Modern Law Review* 1; 'Liberalism, Nationalism and the Post-sovereign State,' (1996) 64 *Political Studies* 553; 'The Maastricht-Urteil; sovereignty now' 1 *European Law Journal* (1995) 259.

[25] Weiler is a particularly interesting case. On the one hand, probably more than any other academic commentator he has been active in cultivating and effective in disseminating a pluralist perspective; cf, *eg*, his path-breaking article, 'The Transformation of Europe,' (1991) 100 *Yale Law Journal* 2403; cf, also 'The Reformation of European Constitutionalism,' (1997) 35 *Journal of Common Market Studies* 97. On the other hand, he has often defended the autonomy and authority of the EU legal order in a manner reminiscent of the *internal* discourse—the plausible claim to ultimate authority—developed in support of the European legal order by its key officials in the ECJ. Cf, in particular his reply to the powerfully-restated, state-centred view of the international legal order by Theodor Schilling, 'The Autonomy of the Community Legal Order: An Analysis of Possible Foundations' (1996) 37 *Harvard Journal of International Law* 389, in J H H Weiler and U R Halpern, 'The Autonomy of the Community Legal Order—Through the Looking Glass,' (1996) 37 *Harvard Journal of International Law* 411. Of course, there is no necessary inconsistency between these two positions.

[26] *Loc cit,* n 17; cf, also 'Aspects of European Constitutionalism,' (1996) 21 *European Law Review* 32.

[27] Notable recent debates between the two positions include the exchange between Weiler and Halpern and Schilling, *loc cit,* n 25 and the exchange between a State-centric Dieter Grimm and the more Euro-centric Joseph Weiler and Jurgen Habermas in Volume 1 of the *European Law Journal* in 1995, and reprinted in P Gowan and P Anderson (eds) *A Question of Europe?* Verso: London (1997): cf, Grimm 'Does Europe need a Constitution?' 239; J Habermas 'Reply to Grimm' 259; J H H Weiler, 'Demos, Telos, Ethos and the Maastricht Decision,' 265.

from which one claim can be viewed as more authentic than the other, or superior to the other within a single hierarchy of norms. Rather, the claims of the Member States and the claims of the EU to ultimate authority within the European legal order are equally plausible in their own terms and from their own perspective.

In a European Union characterised by a differentiated pattern of integration, the pluralist perspective may require to be further refined. As the two-dimensional configuration of authority begins to give way to a multi-dimensional configuration, the range of co-existing legal orders will broaden and the complexity of the organisation of the overall juridical space deepen. To explain this adequately, however, we must first concede that differentiated integration is still very much an *emergent* feature of the legal architecture of contemporary Europe. It is not yet possible to argue that alongside the plausible claims to sovereignty and ultimate legal authority made at the level of the individual states and the Europe of the Fifteen, there is a third level of equally plausible claims to sovereignty amongst other groupings of states entering into different collective arrangements in different functional areas. Indeed, there is no inevitable historical law which dictates that this multi-dimensional picture will ever be complete. Nevertheless, as argued in Section Two, the social and political dynamics of contemporary Europe reveal a strong tendency towards such a state of affairs.

Yet, even if it can be demonstrated that there is significant momentum behind the development of differentiated integration, some might remain sceptical about conceptualising such a shift as radically distinct from the classical two-dimensional order of the European Union. Would it not be more appropriate, it might be argued, to conceptualise the changing order merely as a mature and complex version of two-dimensionality rather than as a qualitatively distinct multi-dimensional order? It is submitted that such scepticism can be answered by demonstrating the strength of the *analytical* connection between differentiated integration and a multi-dimensional configuration of authority. And, in order to demonstrate this bond, it is necessary to look at the range of possible models through which the uniform structure of the EU may be varied, and to consider to what extent that model, or those models which conform most closely to the received version of differentiated integration, imply the development of a third level of claims to sovereignty.

As we shall see, there is no political consensus as to which model should be pursued, and, in practice, there is to be found a wide range of different forms of differentiation which cannot be subsumed under any single model. Equally, there is no firm consensus as to the way in which these different models may be categorised, nor, more especially, as to the labels to be attached to them.[28] Nevertheless, the following taxonomy attempts to specify, in a relatively uncontroversial manner, the main routes along which differentiation might progress, and the implications of the choice of route for the deep structure of constitutional authority in Europe.

C   Models of Differentiated Integration

It is possible to imagine a continuum ranging from a pole of common rules to one of extreme flexibility, with a number of intermediate positions. At the one extreme, we have the traditional model of *uniformity*. At the other extreme, there is the model of Europe *à la carte*. Between these two extremes, and in increasing order of flexibility,

---

[28] For a detailed inventory of the vocabulary associated with differentiated integration, cf, Stubb *loc cit,* n 1, 285.

there are three additional general types, *multi-speed* Europe; Europe of *concentric circles*; and Europe of *flexible integration*.

The two polar positions can be disposed of in fairly short order. Clearly, uniformity provides the paradigm case of a two-dimensional configuration of authority, and offers no prospect of a three-dimensional structure. Having said that, we must recognise that uniformity is an ideal type, and in practice the EU, like other actually existing legal orders, has never strictly conformed to its standards. From the beginning, the Treaties have contained provisions giving special treatment to certain Member States for certain purposes,[29] such as the Protocols to the original EEC Treaty on German Internal Trade and on Luxembourg Agriculture, as well as provisions which contain special rules for disadvantaged regions. Other provisions are identical for all Member States and regions, but allow differentiation in accordance with certain general conditions, such as the various safeguard clauses designed to protect national interests, or the principle of progressiveness as it applied during the transitional period towards the establishment of the common market. At the level of Community legislation too, there has long been in circulation a broad range of techniques for differentiating between Member States on the basis of both general and specific provisions.[30]

Further, it should be noted that just as these aspects of variability have always been inscribed in the basic framework of EC law, while remaining largely unacknowledged as instances of differentiated integration, so too the EU increasingly exhibits a 'structural variability'[31] whose affinity with the theme of differentiated integration—or 'jurisdictional variability'[32]—is also little recognised. The Three Pillar structure introduced by the Maastricht Treaty[33] endorses significant variation in the institutional framework for EU policy-making between matters falling under the central pillar of EC law and matters falling under the two flanking pillars of Justice and Home Affairs (JHA) and Common Foreign and Security Policy (CFSP). Of course, this type of variability is quite distinct in form from differentiated integration in that it preserves the integrity of the Fifteen as the unit of authority; indeed, the structural compromise over the development of European competence in foreign and home affairs, which effectively favours the Member States over the supranational institutions in the two flanking pillars, was arrived at precisely *in order to* safeguard the integrity of the Fifteen.[34] Yet there remains a link between the two types of variability in the sense that each is a response to the same set of stresses and strains upon the EU as a coherent unit of authority (see next section), and in the sense that each, in its own way, involves a departure from the ideal type of a uniform legal order.

If it is clear that the traditional system of European law, while not fully conforming to the ideal typical case of uniformity, involves no prospect of a third dimension of

---

[29] For analysis of the various traditional forms of flexibility, cf, Ehlermann, *loc cit*, n 1 'How Flexible is Community Law?,' 1279–1281.

[30] *Ibid*, 1281–1285.

[31] Harmsen, *loc cit*, n 1, 110;

[32] *Ibid*, 118.

[33] Titles V (CFSP) and VI (JHA)

[34] Cf, M den Boer, 'Justice and Home Affairs,' in H Wallace and W Wallace (eds) *Policy-making in the European Union* (1996 3rd ed OUP) 389; Forster and Wallace, 'Common Foreign and Security Policy,' in Wallace and Wallace (eds) 411; N Walker, 'European Policing and the Politics of Regulation,' in P Cullen and W Gilmore (eds) *Crime sans frontières: International and European Legal Approaches* (1998 David Hume Institute). Cf, also n 77 below and associated text.

political authority and no prospect of a third level of claims to sovereignty, it is equally clear that, at the other extreme, the model of Europe *à la carte* does offer such a prospect. Europe *à la carte* has been defined as that 'mode of differentiated integration whereby respective Member States are able to pick-and-choose, as from a menu, in which policy area they would like to participate, whilst at the same time holding only to a minimum number of common objectives.'[35] What is envisaged here is an open-ended arrangement whereby Member States are free to decide their own levels and patterns of integration in different areas without reference to other Member States and without deferring to the interests of the EU conceived of as an undifferentiated unit.

If Europe *à la carte* were to be capable of embracing a third dimension of authority and a third level of claims to sovereignty, certain strict conditions would have to be met. The arrangements between Member States, other than the unit of Fifteen, to develop the capacity to make and enforce legal measures in particular functional areas would have to be the subject of plausible claims to ultimate legal authority within such areas. These claims would be made by key legal officials within the new arrangements; they would take the form of a basic assumption or proposition to the effect that the new legal arrangements were autonomous and self-authorising; they would identify a key 'sovereign' agency—or agencies—within the new legal order; and there would be objective evidence of the plausibility of the claim, in the form of a pattern of obedience to rules consistent with the conception of the new legal order held by its sponsors.

In practice, the idea of Europe *à la carte* has commanded little support within the EU. Moreover, in its most widely circulated version, which was sponsored by John Major's British Conservative Government,[36] it fails to fulfil the conditions for a multi-dimensional structure. Under the British version, although detail is lacking, the clear intention was that the *à la carte* arrangements should be independent of the Fifteen. However, it is equally clear that, in line with the statist philosophy of its sponsors, these arrangements should not be independent of the legal authority of the individual states. They would remain intergovernmental arrangements, lacking the capacity to develop the institutional and 'interpretative autonomy'[37] without which the articulation of a plausible claim to ultimate legal authority is not possible.

If neither uniformity nor Europe *à la carte* provide options which are either practicable or likely to produce a three-dimensional structure, what of the three intermediate models? Multi-speed Europe has been defined as that 'mode of differentiated integration according to which the pursuit of common objectives is driven by a core group of Member States which are both able and willing to go further, the underlying assumption being that the others will follow later.'[38] This model has undoubted political significance. When differentiated integration was first seriously mooted as a template for the development of the European Union by the German Chancellor, Willy Brandt, in 1974 and by the Belgian Prime Minister, Leo Tindemans, in 1975, it was in the form of a multi-speed Europe. Further, many of the more ambitious experiments in differentiated integration in recent years have conformed to

---

[35] Stubb *loc cit*, n 1, 285.

[36] This position was first publicly adopted by Major in September 1994, and consistently supported by his Government thereafter until it lost power in the general election of May 1997; cf, Edwards and Philippart, *loc cit*, n 1, 7.

[37] Schilling, *loc cit*, n 25, 389

[38] Stubb, *loc cit*, n 1, 285

the structural demands of a multi-speed model. For example, Article 15 of the Single European Act of 1987 (which became Article 7C of the EC Treaty) permitted the Commission to take account of developmental differences in the various national economies to justify temporary derogations from particular rules designed to complete the internal market. Similarly, under the Maastricht Treaty on European Union of 1992, progress to stage three of Economic and Monetary Union, including adoption of the single currency, depends upon Member States being able to satisfy the Council that they have met certain economic convergence criteria,[39] thus raising the possibility of staggered progress towards fiscal integration.

It is clear, nevertheless, that multi-speed Europe holds out no direct prospect of a third level of claims to sovereignty. Under the multi-speed model, different purposes are not allowed, merely different timetables, decided upon by EU institutions. Neither those in the vanguard nor those in the rearguard can make a plausible claim to possess legal authority independent of that which resides in the EU as a whole. Indeed, the purpose of a multi-speed strategy is precisely to preserve the notion that there should be a common level of integration—an undifferentiated unit of Fifteen—even if some variation is required as a temporary expedient to achieve this end.

While the model of multi-speed Europe does not directly challenge the conception of Europe as a two-dimensional configuration of authority, as a political strategy it has gained only limited support. Rather, it has tended to provide a staging-post to other options which offer more serious prospects of a multi-dimensional configuration of authority. Multi-speed Europe has been criticised from the point of view of both the pace-setters and the laggards. From the perspective of the pace-setters, the proviso that uneven progress towards integration should only be tolerated as a means to the end of even standards, frustrates aspirations they might hold to form a permanent vanguard dedicated to achieving the highest possible level of integration amongst the most *communautaire* Member States. From the perspective of the laggards, their position in the slow lane of integration may attract the politically unattractive label of underdevelopment and immaturity. A related criticism of the multi-speed approach, which draws upon the dissatisfactions of both potential pace-setters and potential laggards, is that it makes an unduly rigid distinction between core and periphery and fails to acknowledge that Member States may wish to find their own level of integration on a sector-by-sector basis.[40]

In turn, these criticisms have laid the foundations for the development of the other two intermediate models. Europe of concentric circles 'admits to unattainable differences within the integrative structure by allowing permanent or irreversible separation between a hard core and less developed integrative units.'[41] In other words, it directly answers the criticism of multi-speed Europe made by the most impatient of the pace-setters by allowing them to forge ahead indefinitely, leaving those Member States less equipped for or less committed to integration to find a more shallow depth of common interests and concerted action.

A Europe of concentric circles clearly implies a multi-dimensional configuration of authority and a third level of claims to sovereignty. The idea of a permanent separation between core and periphery as regards certain policy areas, together with the traditional common structure for certain basic functions of the Union, suggests

---

[39] Art 109j (now Art 121) EC Treaty.
[40] Dewatripont *et al, op cit,* n 1, 55–56.
[41] Stubb *loc cit,* n 1, 285.

that alongside the original claim of the agencies of the sovereign state and the continuing claim to sovereignty made on behalf of the Union of Fifteen as regards its common baseline of functions, in the areas of separate and accelerated development new agencies would, in time, emerge to make their own distinctive claim to ultimate legal authority.

A proposal along these lines was developed by Karl Lamers of the CDU/CSU in 1994[42] and helped to stimulate the debate on differentiated integration in the lead-up to the Intergovernmental Conference of 1996–97.[43] Yet, despite its political attractiveness to those in the vanguard of integration, such a proposal was bound to provoke significant opposition. The dangers of marginalisation of those consigned to the outer circle(s) are even greater than in the case of the multi-speed model. Further, the concentric circles model shares with the multi-speed model an absence of discrimination on a sector-by-sector basis, leaving it open to the criticism of undue rigidity.[44]

In consequence, the outline of an alternative model which addresses these questions of discrimination and inflexibility while continuing to encourage initiatives in deeper integration within a structure which preserves the integrity of the Fifteen has begun to develop. This alternative lacks the clear definition of the others, and relatedly, it lacks a clear label. It is easier to define negatively, as the model—or range of models—which occupy the place on the uniformity/flexibility continuum between the rigid hierarchy of concentric circles and the protean permissiveness of Europe *à la carte*. Perhaps the most serious attempt to develop a model within this conceptual space is the 'flexible integration' of Dewatripont *et al*,[45] and so their label may be applied as an umbrella to cover all occupants of this space.

For Dewatripont *et al*, the key to flexible integration is a division between a substantial common base on the one hand, and, a set of open partnerships in particular policy sectors on the other.[46] The common base should include the direct regulation of the single market based upon the four freedoms of goods, services, people and capital together with other policy measures required to preserve a well-functioning single market.[47] Beyond that common base, however, variation is organised sector by sector rather than state by state, as in the concentric circles model. Further, within the basic outline of a model characterised by a common baseline and sectoral variation at the periphery, we can envisage a number of different nuances. The common baseline need not be defined at the particular point chosen by Dewatripont *et al*. Equally, various different conditions might attach to the open partnerships; for example, to preserve the integrity of the common baseline; or to protect the open partnerships themselves from interference;[48] or, re-introducing a territorial dimension to differentiation, to ensure that membership of open partnerships involving 'deep' integration was only open to states already participant in open partnerships involving 'shallow' integration. This last variant provided the basic structure of the proposal of

---

[42] K Lamers and W Schauble *Reflections on European Foreign Policy—Document by the CDU/CSU Group in the German Bundestag* (1994 CDU/CSU)

[43] Cf, Edwards and Phillipart, *loc cit*, n 1, 7–8; Duff, *loc cit*, n 1 14–21, 185–196.

[44] Dewatripont *et al, op cit*, n 1 56–58.

[45] *Ibid*, 58–77.

[46] *Ibid* 58–59.

[47] *Ibid* ch 4.

[48] Indeed, these are amongst the general principles governing closer co-operation laid down in the Amsterdam Treaty; see new Arts K15–17 (now Arts 43–45) TEU, as supplemented by new Art 5a (now Art 11) EC Treaty (First Pillar) and new Art K12 (now Art 40) TEU; for discussion, cf, Shaw *loc cit,* note 1; Edwards and Philippart *loc cit,* note 1, 13–24.

the then French prime minister, Edouard Balladur, in response to the German CDU proposal for concentric circles.[49] It resembles the concentric circles model in that it conceives of integration as a linear process in terms of which states are more or less advanced, but differs from it in allowing each state to decide its own stage of development rather than requiring them to join mutually exclusive clubs whose members adhere to the same level of integration across every sector.

While neither the original Balladur model nor any of its subsequent refinements to emerge from the French camp[50] were explicitly endorsed by the drafters of the Treaty of Amsterdam, support for the broad strategy of flexible integration has been implicit in a number of recent treaty amendments, becoming more pronounced after Amsterdam. The constitutional framework described by the treaties has remained wedded to the idea of a substantial common base—an inviolable *acquis communautaire*, but beyond this there has been a growing accommodation of the freedom of Member States to pick and choose their own level of integration across different sectors.

As early as the Single European Act of 1987, there is evidence of the new flexible arrangements. Thus, Article 100a(4) (now Art 95(4)) of the EC Treaty[51] allows Member States to opt out of single market harmonisation measures 'on grounds of major needs' relating to public morality, public policy, public security, public health, protection of the natural environment and the working environment, and a range of other public interest grounds.[52] The 1992 Treaty on European Union develops the theme of sectoral flexibility. Alongside the narrow 'case-by-case' flexibility exemplified by Article 100a(4) (now Art 95(4)), two other species of flexibility are introduced; 'predetermined flexibility,' where an area of flexibility is defined in advance; and 'enhanced co-operation,' where Member States are generally empowered to make their own additional co-operative arrangements over a broad policy spectrum.[53] Predetermined flexibility may be found in the British and Danish opt-outs in respect of the final stages of Economic and Monetary Union[54] and the British opt-out in respect of the Protocol on Social Policy,[55] while brief provision is made recognising general powers of enhanced co-operation in the general fields of justice and home affairs[56] and of common foreign and security policy.[57]

---

[49] Edwards and Philippart, *op cit*, n 1 8; Duff *loc cit*, n 1 20; Dewatripont *et al* n 1 56–58.

[50] Edwards and Philippart, *op cit*, n 1 20. The subsequent Franco-German initiative, in the form of the De Charette-Kinkel memorandum of October 1996 was an important further staging post on the way to the endorsement of flexibility in the Treaty of Amsterdam; cf, Duff, *loc cit*, 188–190.

[51] Added by Art 18 Single European Act.

[52] Art 36 (now Art 30) EC Treaty.

[53] The tripartite classification referred to here is based upon the scheme arising out of the pre-Amsterdam IGC negotiations and adopted by the second Dublin European Council in December 1996 (*The European Union Today and Tomorrow: Adapting the European Union for the Benefit of its Peoples and preparing it for the Future—A General Outline for a Draft Revision of the Treaties—Dublin II*, Conference of the Representatives of the Governments of the Member States, Brussels, 5 December 1996. CONF 2500/96), as further developed by Edwards and Philippart, *op cit*, n 1 10–34 and 66.

[54] Protocol on Certain provisions Relating to the United Kingdom of Great Britain and Northern Ireland; Protocol on Certain Provisions Relating to Denmark.

[55] Protocol on Social Policy; Agreement On Social Policy Concluded Between The Member States Of The European Community With The Exception Of The United Kingdom Of Great Britain And Northern Ireland.

[56] Art K7 (now Art 35) TEU.

[57] Art J4(5) (now Art 14(5)) TEU.

The Treaty of Amsterdam builds substantially upon these general enabling clauses, providing a full statement of the general principles of enhanced co-operation[58] and providing detailed conditions for its application in both the First[59] and Third[60] Pillars, (although in the Second Pillar enhanced co-operation is replaced by 'constructive abstention' on a case-by-case basis).[61] Further, enhanced co-operation is presented as a positive entitlement rather than a negative permission, and those Member States who opt for closer ties are now permitted to 'make use of the institutions, procedures and mechanisms'[62] of the EU. At the level of predetermined flexibility too, Amsterdam marks a significant advance. As the most developed instance of a trend towards the blurring of boundaries between the EU and other regional systems and initiatives,[63] the Schengen Agreements of 1985 and 1990 amongst those Member States who sought to take the initiative in abolishing internal border controls and in establishing compensatory security measures and institutions are incorporated into the EU Treaty.[64] Iceland and Norway, who are not members of the EU but who are associate members of Schengen, are recognised within the new arrangements as participants in the deliberations of the Justice and Home Affairs (European) Council insofar as they concern Schengen matters and as bound by its decisions;[65] conversely, Britain and Ireland, who are members of the EU but not members of Schengen, are not bound by 'Schengen law,'[66] nor, relatedly, by measures securing the abolition of internal border controls and free movement of persons within the EU,[67] from which principle they have been exempted.[68] Denmark, too, has negotiated an exemption, albeit more limited, from the provisions of Schengen.[69] Finally, the UK, Ireland and Denmark each retains the capacity to opt-in to specific measures within the relevant exempt categories on a case-by-case basis.[70]

If flexible integration is the inarticulate major premise of the EU's developing approach to differentiated integration, it remains unclear whether, and to what extent this will involve the development of a third level of claims to sovereignty in the various new open partnerships which have been established or may be established. The general principles of flexibility set out at Amsterdam seek to ensure that in the final analysis the new arrangements will remain subordinate to and integrated with the general rules and institutions of the Fifteen.[71] Against that, we should recognise that the two more recent and more ambitious treaty strategies for pursuing differentiated integration,

---

[58] New Arts K15–16 (now Arts 43–44) TEU.

[59] New Art 5a (now Art 11) EC Treaty.

[60] New Art K12 (now Art 40) TEU.

[61] New Art J13 (now Art 23) TEU.

[62] New Arts K15(1) (now Art 43(1)) TEU; 5a(1) (now Art 11(1)) EC Treaty; K12(1) (now Art 40(1)) TEU.

[63] Other examples include the EU's relationship with GATT/WTO and with the Council of Europe; se also text at ns below.

[64] Protocol Integrating the Schengen Acquis into the Framework of the European Union; cf, also, Walker, 'Justice and Home Affairs,' (1998) 47 *International and Comparative Law Quarterly* 236.

[65] Protocol Integrating the Schengen Acquis into the Framework of the European Union Art 6.

[66] Protocol Integrating the Schengen Acquis into the Framework of the European Union Arts 4–5.

[67] Protocol on the Position of the United Kingdom and Ireland.

[68] Protocol on the Application of Certain Aspects of Article 7a of the Treaty Establishing the European Community to the United Kingdom and to Ireland.

[69] Protocol on the Position of Denmark.

[70] Protocol Integrating the Schengen Acquis into the Framework of the European Union Arts 4–5.

[71] See in particular new Art K15(1) (now Art 43(1)) TEU; Art 5a (1)-(2) (now Art 11(1)–(2)) EC Treaty; Art K12(1)-(2) (now Art 40(1)–(2)) TEU; see also Shaw, *loc cit,* note 1.

namely predetermined flexibility and enhanced co-operation, facilitate the development of differentiated integration in a dynamic fashion, with the potential to alter radically the present configuration of authority within Europe.

As we have seen, the strategy of predetermined flexibility has been used to recognise and to 'integrate' a pre-existing regional organisation, namely Schengen, and could be so utilised again. Pre-existing organisations have their own institutional architecture, their own spheres of regulation and their own political culture, and may thus already have a developed sense of their own legal and political authority. Accordingly, it should not readily be assumed either that the political and legal framework within which they and the EU become mutually implicated will necessarily involve the subordination or loss of autonomy of the new centres of authority, or that these new centres of authority will defer to the individual states. As for the strategy of enhanced flexibility, it has an inherently open-ended quality which again questions the enduring supremacy of the traditional EU framework. Unlike the previous case, however, here the challenge is likely to come from within the Fifteen, with new partnerships gradually developing the institutional apparatus, regulatory scope and sense of political identity necessary to make plausible claims to independent legal authority. In both cases, there is a clear but incomplete trend towards the development of new sovereignties within Europe, and, for that reason, it is apt to describe multi-dimensionality as an emergent feature of the legal architecture of contemporary Europe.

III   Political Dynamics of Differentiated Integration

In this section, we look behind the legal forms of differentiation to investigate the political dynamics driving the emergence of a multi-dimensional configuration of authority. What factors have contributed to the trend towards multi-dimensionality, and what does an analysis of these factors and their inter-relationship tell us about the coherence, or otherwise, of the differentiation 'project'? Basically, we can identify three different political arenas in which forces contributing to differentiated integration have been generated.

A   Strategic Politics

First, there is the arena of strategic politics. Strategic politics are those within which states and other units of political authority (including the institutions of the EU and other transnational organisations) seek to advance their view of the proper allocation of political authority in a regional or global context, with particular reference to their own position within this wider allocation. In the context of the EU, the focus of strategic politics is upon the balance of power between the Member States and the EU, with a deeply integrated EU favoured by the more *communautaire* institutions of the EU itself (especially the Commission and the Parliament) and those Member States who believe that a strong 'supranational' organisation better protects or advances their own strategic interests, and a less deeply integrated EU favoured by those Member States who believe that a weaker 'intergovernmental' organisation better protects or advances their own strategic interests. From this angle, differentiated integration is but the latest theme in a structural debate, engaging the EU, its Member States and other associated states, in which the European polity is continuously renegotiated in a form which is acceptable from the strategic perspective of the various parties. The structural accommodations reached between the various parties reflect various different strategic dynamics,[72] two of which are of particular importance in the present context. First, an accommodation between the parties may reflect a compromise between distinct interests.[73] Secondly, such an accommodation may involve what Cass Sunstein describes as an 'incompletely theorized agreement'[74]—a formulation or set of arrangements, often negotiated in high constitutional or international law texts, whose underlying principle is unresolved between the parties and whose long-term consequences for different and contending strategic interests is uncertain, and, consequently, whose endorsement parties, with different and contending interests, are prepared to risk on the basis that it may be interpreted and developed to their long-term advantage.[75]

The perennial debate over the acceptability and scope of qualified majority voting as a means of decision-making within the Community is one example where each new Treaty settlement or political bargain[76] represents a fresh compromise between those who want to facilitate the process of EU policy-making across various sectors and those who are intent on preserving the national veto in matters where important state interests are at stake. The introduction of structural variability at Maastricht through the three pillar hybrid is another example of compromise between a more integrationist tendency which would seek to absorb new competences in foreign and home affairs into a single, cohesive framework, and a less integrationist tendency which would prefer to maintain co-operation in these two areas of sensitive state interests at arms-length from the EU's institutional and decision-making centre.[77] On the other hand, to the extent that they are influenced by the strategic interests of Member States and the EU institutions,[78] the successive accommodations reached in the continuing debate about the expansion of the EU and its institutional consequences offer an example of the politics of incomplete theorization and risk-taking rather than the politics of compromise on the part of pro-integrationist and anti-integrationist tendencies. Each accommodation is understood from conflicting positions of principle, with different long-term consequences projected. For pro-integrationist tendencies, it is calculated that a wider Europe will lead to a deeper Europe, as all parties to a wider Europe come to appreciate that a larger and more culturally diverse polity is operationally ineffective without a much greater emphasis upon majoritarian decision-making procedures. In contrast, anti-integrationist tendencies are apt to draw precisely the opposite conclusion from the same premise.

---

[72] On strategic interaction in international relations generally, cf, M Hollis and S Smith *Explaining and Understanding International Relations* (190 Clarendon) esp chs 6 and 8.

[73] Cf, A Kuflick, 'Morality and Compromise,' in J R Pennock and J Chapman (eds), *Compromise in Ethics, Law, and Politics* (1979 New York University Press) 38; M Benjamin, *Splitting the Difference: Compromise and Integrity in Ethics and Politics* (1990 Lawrence).

[74] C R Sunstein *Legal Reasoning and Political Conflict* (1996 OUP) esp ch 2.

[75] For a similar type of strategic analysis of decision-making in the EU context, cf, Moravcsik, 'A Liberal Governmentalist Approach to the EC,' in, S Bulmer and A Scott (eds) *op cit,* n 23 29, 66.

[76] For example, the Luxembourg Compromise; cf, Teasdale, 'The Life and Death of the Luxembourg Compromise,' (1993) 31 *Journal of Common Market Studies* 567. A more recent example is the Ioannina Compromise, agreed under the Greek presidency in March 1994, whereby new guidelines were developed regarding the appropriate size of the blocking minority when qualified majority voting applies in the Council in the context of the increase in size of the Union from twelve to fifteen members. Unlike the Luxembourg Compromise, the Ioannina Compromise was subsequently reduced to law in the form of a Council Decision ((OJ 1994C 105/1, amended by OJ 1995 C1/1).

[77] Cf, den Boer, *loc cit,* n 34; Forster and Wallace, *loc cit,* n 34; Walker, *loc cit,* n 34.

[78] These accommodation are also influenced by broader geo-political considerations.

On this view, a larger and more culturally diverse Europe should be less disposed than at present to trust its own institutions with the decision-making capacity to disregard minority state interests, and instead should settle for a more modest measure of integration.[79]

From the perspective of strategic politics differentiated integration presents a particularly complex case in that both compromise and risk-taking approaches underwrite its development. On the one hand, specific cases of differentiated integration may be viewed as trade-offs between the advocates of deeper integration and more sceptical voices. For example, the introduction of qualified majority voting as a means of accelerating the passage of measures to complete the internal market under the Single European Act[80] could only be negotiated by permitting state opt-outs on grounds of major needs. Similarly, the endorsement of Economic and Monetary Union at Maastricht, which like the commitment to complete the internal market at the previous Treaty negotiations was an important marker of the Union's integrationist ambitions in the key area of economic policy, could only be purchased at the price of granting opt-outs to British and Danish sceptics.

On the other hand, if we look beyond particular instances of variability and address differentiated integration as a holistic theme, then, as with the deepening and widening debate, the uncertainties surrounding the interpretation of the current structural tendency are so great and the contingencies bearing on the pattern of future development so large that different strategic actors may plausibly risk the endorsement of similar measures in pursuit of quite different ends. To recall our discussion of the various models of differentiated integration, flexible integration—the default definition applied to the current patchwork—is poised uneasily and unsteadily between multi-speed Europe and Europe of concentric circles on the one hand and Europe *à la carte* on the other. And while the first two alternatives are expedients to ensure that integrationist ambitions are not thwarted by the slower travellers, the third alternative endorses a more fragmented and less monolithic European polity. Therefore, as the debate in and around the 1996–97 IGC indicated, parties with quite different strategic visions could reasonably support the forms of 'flexibility' on the table in pursuit of their own ends.[81]

Furthermore, the propensity of strategic actors to gamble on the final shape of an immature and indistinct pattern of variability is reinforced by the fact that, as Edwards and Phillipart have argued, differentiated integration 'is a means of managing diversity when all other methods to bring about agreement have been tried and have failed.'[82] In other words, differentiated integration is not merely the latest form of structural accommodation between contending strategic actors in the EU, it is the *final option* in structural accommodation. It is the last throw of the dice in a polity whose growing breadth of competence and membership is not matched by a growing singularity of political purpose. For as long as all the parties want, on balance, to continue playing the integration game in accordance with the basic rules set down in the Treaty of Rome, then they have no choice but to speculate with the high-risk tactics of differentiated integration.

---

[79] Cf, J A McMahon, '12, 16, 20 or 24? The Future Shape of the European Union,' (1994) 45 *Northern Ireland Legal Quarterly* 134.

[80] See Art 100a(4) (now Art 95(4)) EC Treaty.

[81] Edwards and Philippart, *op cit,* n 1, 5–12.

[82] *Ibid,* at 36.

B Sectoral Politics

The arena of sectoral politics provides a second set of forces conducive to differentiated integration. By sectoral politics, we mean the competition and negotiation over the substantive preferences of state actors in particular policy sectors. The developing pattern of substantive policy-making connects with the growth of differentiated integration through the much-documented trend away from the state as the mainspring of economic and social power. As myriad versions of the globalization thesis have argued, the increasing political, economic and cultural interconnectedness of international society, largely driven by the power of private capital and mediated by factors such as the modern communications industry and information technology, has eroded the control which states previously exercised over their own territorial communities and restricted the extent to which they are able to wield influence on the international stage.[83] Faced with declining political capital and increasing demands from constituencies themselves affected by new social forces, states have conceded or even encouraged a reduction in their regulatory sphere in the form of delegations of power 'downward' to regional and local government, 'outward' to private centres of governance, and 'upward' to regional and global organisation.[84] Indeed, having relinquished their position as masters of public policy, states, despite frequent rhetorical claims to the contrary, have come to adopt a much more pragmatic approach to the identification of the appropriate level and site of decision-making authority within any policy sector.[85]

In one sense, this process benefits regional organisations, such as the EU, which have the leverage to deal more effectively with transnational social forces. In another sense, however, the pursuit of the sectorally appropriate site of decision-making threatens such regional organisations insofar as they demand rigid adherence to the same procedures and levels of collective action in each policy domain. In this respect, differentiated integration offers a degree of flexibility in the search for the most appropriate locus of regional decision-making. Opt-outs, enhanced co-operation and the various other forms of variability, allow many of the advantages of scale and co-ordination associated with regional decision-making in each policy sector without slavish adherence to a single decision-making template across all. For example, the Maastricht Protocol on Social Policy allowed those states which wanted enhanced protection of rights associated with the workplace to pool their authority; the staggered introduction of the third stage of EMU allows those states who so wish and who conform to certain criteria of economic health to trade control of some of the key tools of fiscal policy in return for the advantages of a common currency; the Schengen Agreement allows co-ordination between free movement policy and internal security policy on the part of those states which want the economic and social advantages of the former while minimising its perverse effects in terms of increases in crime and illegal cross-border trade in persons and goods. In all of these areas, sectoral policy imperatives have demanded the redrawing of the traditional contours of EU decision-making.

---

[83] Cf, Himsworth 'In a State No Longer: The End of Constitutionalism?' 639; D Held, *Democracy and the Global Order* (1995 Polity); G Mulgan *Politics in an Antipolitical Age* (1994 Polity).

[84] Harmsen, *loc cit,* n 1, 128.

[85] Marks, Hooghe and Blank, 'European Integration from the 1980s: State-Centric v. Multi-Level Governance,' (1996) 34 *Journal of Common Market Studies* 341.

C   Geopolitics

The arena of geopolitics offers a final set of influences conducive to differentiated integration. This refers to the broader, global context of international relations within which the Fifteen operate. The geopolitical arena both represents the backdrop against which the strategic and sectoral politics of the Fifteen are formulated leading to 'internal' differentiation, and provides the source of additional 'external' pressures towards differentiation.

As Harmsen argues, the end of Cold War bipolarity 'relativises'[86] the position of the EU within the European context. No longer is its regional superiority anchored in a world order defined by competing super-powers. Rather, the broader international scenario is more fluid, the opportunities to develop new patterns of regional and global power greater. In turn, this leads to more complex forms of co-operation and mutual adjustment between the EU and other international organisations as they jockey for position in the new order. For instance, the regional profile of the Council of Europe, with its flagship Convention of Human Rights (ECHR), has been raised by the extension of membership, on terms far more accessible than offered by the EU, to the post-Warsaw Pact states of Central and Eastern Europe.[87] This reflects the growing importance of the human rights discourse as a key form of 'symbolic capital'[88] in international relations, with a strong domestic human rights commitment increasingly perceived as a prerequisite of legitimate membership of the new international order.[89] In turn, this has contributed to a growing concern with the articulation and vindication of fundamental rights within the EU, culminating in an opinion by the Court of Justice in 1996 as to whether the Union has competence to accede to the ECHR.[90] The Court answered in the negative, but the fact that judicial consideration of the question was requested by the Council is indicative of the increasing significance of the strategic and ideological relationship between the two regional organisations.[91] Similarly, in the defence field, the end of the Cold War has increased the scope for an autonomous western European organisation, and the provision made under the Treaty of Amsterdam for enhanced co-operation between the EU and the Western European Union bears witness to the increasingly intricate links between these two entities.[92] Or to take a final example, the increasing dynamism of the GATT/WTO structure is, in part, a function of the recent demise of the command economy and the new global ascendancy of market structures and principles, and in turn this has led to a thickening web of interconnections between the EU and the WTO legal

---

[86] *Loc cit,* n 1, 127.

[87] Cf, Storey, 'Human Rights and the New Europe: Experience and Experiment,' (1995) 43 *Political Studies* 131.

[88] P Bourdieu, *Language and Symbolic Power* (1991 Polity).

[89] Cf, Boyle, 'Stock-Taking on Human Rights: The World Conference on Human Rights, Vienna 1993,' (1995) 63 *Political Studies* 79.

[90] Opinion 2/94 *Re the Accession of the Community to the European Human Rights Convention* [1996] 2 CMLR 265; cf, Beaumont, 'The European Community Cannot Accede to the European Convention on Human Rights, (1997) 1 *Edinburgh Law Review* 235; Toth, 'The European Union and Human Rights: The Way Forward,' (1997) 34 *Common Market La Review* 490.

[91] Storey *loc cit,* n 87.

[92] See new Title V, Art J7 (now Art 17) TEU; more generally, cf, B Laffan *Integration and Co-operation in Europe* (1992) Routledge: London 223–226.

orders.[93] While none of these developments implies any of the standard forms of internal differentiation discussed earlier, they nevertheless suggest possibilities for the co-existence of legal orders which are equally conducive to the emergence of a multi-dimensional configuration of political authority on a territorial canvas broader than that of the EU.

A more orthodox trend in multi-speed integration is suggested by another external process which has been accelerated by the end of the Cold War. Under the Agenda 2000 initiative which builds on the Europe Agreements involving the Central and Eastern European Countries,[94] former Communist states figure prominently in the new wave of candidates which aspire to membership of an enlarged Europe of as many as twenty six members by the early years of the next century. The elaborate institutional pathways associated with joining the EU range from the existence of satellite organisations such as EFTA and the EEA to customised pre-accession agreements and transitional arrangement for the early years of membership in the case of each candidate state. Taken together, these arrangements recognise the need for complex and varied trajectories of integration for each candidate state. And when, as presently, there are virtually as many candidates or associates as full members, then the management of differentiation at the margins of the EU ceases to be a regulatory footnote and becomes a mainstream issue of governance.

D   The Non-Project of Differentiated Integration

In accounting for the present level of differentiated integration, therefore, the combined influence of strategic politics, sectoral politics and geopolitics suggests a richly varied mix. Crucially, it also suggests a lack of coherence underpinning the whole enterprise of differentiation. The present pattern of differentiation is clearly not the outcome of a teleological process. It is not the product of any fixed purpose on the part of all actors or any dominant coalition of actors within the Union. Rather, it has evolved as a result of a series of strategic compromises and gambits, of policy-driven sectoral initiatives, and of accommodations of new geopolitical forces. Contingency, ambiguity and disagreement, rather than design, certainty and consensus, are key motifs in the composition of the new differentiated structure: contingency, rather than design, in that many of the strategic compromises, the sectoral arrangements and the external accommodations, which have given shape to the new structure, have done so in an unintended and unplanned fashion in response to situational exigencies; ambiguity rather than certainty, in that, insofar as broader structural blueprints emerge or are negotiated, they tend to lack theoretical anchorage and to be compatible with different long-term models of development; and disagreement, rather than consensus, in that, at least part of the attraction of structural ambiguity and incomplete theorization is that it masks fundamental differences in the long-term strategic vision of different key actors.

---

[93] Cf, in particular Opinion 1/94 [1994] ECR I-5267; for commentary, cf, J H H Weiler 'The Community Legal Order and the International Legal Context,' Unpublished Paper; Europa Institute, Edinburgh University, April 1998

[94] Cf, Harmsen, *loc cit* n 1 122–126; Sedelmeier and Wallace, 'Policies Towards Central and Eastern Europe,' in H Wallace and W Wallace (eds), *Policy-Making in the European Union* (3rd ed 1996 OUP) 353.

IV   Some Problems of Multi-Dimensionality

As an example of a putative multi-dimensional configuration of authority, what problems are likely to beset the EU? In the following analysis, which does no more than provide an indicative outline of the matters at issue, the sorts of difficulties associated with multi-dimensional Europe are highlighted by comparing and contrasting them with the sorts of difficulties associated with the Europe of one and two dimensions. These difficulties are divided into four categories: first, difficulties associated with the mutual recognition and management of the boundaries between different legal orders; secondly, difficulties associated with the efficacy of the overall political framework; thirdly, difficulties associated with the democratic accountability of the overall framework; and finally, difficulties associated with the overall social legitimacy of the resulting political order.

A   The Boundaries of Legal Order

In a one-dimensional international order where the building-blocks are the discrete centres of power known as states, the specification of jurisdictional boundaries between legal orders tend not to pose a problem. State legal systems typically lack plausible internal rivals in their claim to sovereignty within the state, while, provided the claims to ultimate legal authority made by other state legal orders are similarly restricted to their own territory—a situation which often did not prevail in and during the decline of the age of empire[95]—no difficulty arises of overlapping jurisdictional claims between different state legal systems.

   As suggested earlier, in a two-dimensional configuration of authority such as that presented by the co-existence of state legal orders and the legal order of the EU, boundary skirmishes may arise since rival claims to sovereignty are made at both levels of legal order. The state legal authorities continue to claim ultimate legal authority over all matters of domestic law, while the EU legal authorities claim ultimate legal authority over a broad and open-ended area of domestic law corresponding to their own interpretation of the jurisdictional limits of the EU as set out in its constitutive treaties. In these circumstances, there is enormous potential for demarcation disputes, and that this is largely avoided is, in part, a tribute to the sophistication of the various *bridging mechanisms* through which the different legal systems protect their own integrity while recognising and accommodating the norms, techniques, and legitimate sphere of competence of other legal systems.[96] For example, on this view, the Article 177 reference procedure is a means by which the substantive solution to a legal question arrived at by the Community authorities is authoritatively introduced into the framework for the resolution of disputes specific to the domestic

---

[95] On the constitutional boundary disputes which arose between the legal order of the UK and the emergent legal orders of its former colonies during the long decline of British empire, cf, K C Wheare, *The Constitutional Structure of the Commonwealth* (1960 Clarendon); G Marshall, *Constitutional Theory* (1971 Clarendon) ch 3.

[96] Within the conventional discourse of European law, the work of legal engineering through which the EU is co-ordinated with the various national legal orders tends to be described under the label of 'integration,' a term which arguably implies a greater degree of consensus and common ultimate purpose than exists between the various players on the European juridical stage; for criticism of this tendency, cf, Shaw, 'European Union Legal Studies in Crisis? Towards a New Dynamic,' (1996) 16 *Oxford Journal of Legal Studies* 321; for a particularly incisive, and healthily sceptical analysis of the range of bridging mechanisms, cf, S. Weatherill, *Law and Integration in the European Union*, (1995 Clarendon) chs 4 and 5.

legal order. This and other bridging mechanisms such as the doctrine of pre-emption,[97] or the technique of minimum harmonisation,[98] or, more tentatively, the developing jurisprudence of procedural harmonisation in the area of domestic court enforcement of Community rules,[99] seek to ensure that the terms of mutual accommodation between the two levels of legal order prevent the outbreak of argument in the border regions in the first place.

Yet, such bridging mechanisms are not foolproof, and, in particular, while they are most adept at resolving recurrent and predictable co-ordination problems between legal systems, they cannot prevent disputes arising over matters which directly challenge the fundamental capacity of each legal order to define the boundaries of its own competence. This was graphically illustrated in 1993 by the German Constitutional Court which, while confirming that the Maastricht Treaty did not breach domestic constitutional law, fired a warning shot to the effect that if a further transfer of authority was made to the European level under circumstances which violated the domestic constitutional commitment that political authority be exercised in accordance with democratic principles, then it would not hesitate to intervene.[100] This willingness to take unilateral action to ringfence the area of competence of the state legal order against possible encroachments by the Community resonates with the earlier attitude of the German Constitutional Court on the protection of constitutionally-guaranteed rights in the *Solange* cases,[101] and also finds a more recent echo in the approach of the French[102] and Danish[103] courts to the legality of the Maastricht Treaty.

Yet, just as these cases signal domestic refusal to defer to the Community over fundamental constitutional principles, the Court of Justice is no more constitutionally predisposed to accept the dictat of national courts in these matters. Accordingly, the cases raise, in acute form, the conceptual limits of old constitutionalism in a new political order. If both national and European levels are treated as fundamental and constitutive by their own key political and judicial officials, as in the classic tradition of the sovereign state within a one-dimensional order, then we are faced with a problem of *incommensurability* between different levels and paradigms of legal authority. In exceptional cases which concern fundamental principles, rival sources of authority may simply refuse to recognise and agree common jurisdictional boundaries or to provide a meta-procedure for resolving inter-systemic conflict.

Even with regard to the fundamental fault-lines between legal systems, however, it has been claimed that what is irresolvable in accordance with the logic of systems theory may be settled by reference to the strategic imperatives of game theory. Thus,

---

[97] Cf, S. Weatherill, *op cit*, n 96, 135–151.

[98] *Ibid*, at 151–157.

[99] Cf, M. Storme, *The Storme Report on the Approximation of Judiciary Law in the European Union* (1994 Report by Expert Group to European Commission); Himsworth, 'Things Fall Apart: The Harmonisation of Community Judicial Procedural Protection Revisited,' (1997) 22 *European Law Review* 291.

[100] *Brunner v The European Union Treaty* [1994] 1 CMLR 57, see also Everson, 'Beyond the Bundesverfassungsgericht,' in this volume.

[101] *Internationale Handelsgesellschaft (Solange I)* [1974] 2 CMLR 540; *Wunsche Handelsgesellschaft (Solange II)* [1987] 3 CMLR 265.

[102] Decision 92–308 DC du 9 avril 1992, Journal Official de la Republique Francaise du 11 avril 1992 5354.

[103] Case 272/94 *Carlsen v Prime Minister Rasmussen*; discussed in Obradovic, 'Repatriation of Powers in the European Community,' (1997) 34 *Common Market Law Review* 59. For the final stage of the litigation in the Danish Supreme Court, which upheld the Danish ratification of the TEU, cf, the judgment of 6th April 1998 (I 361/1997).

Weiler argues that if one applies the analogy of the Cold War and the logic of Mutual Assured Destruction (MAD) to the situation of the national and supranational authorities in a boundary dispute between legal orders, then neither side is likely to go further than merely threatening the use of its judicial 'nuclear weapon' to strike down a properly constituted rule of the other side, for fear of reprisals and the extremely hazardous consequences for all which would flow from this chain of activity.[104] On this view, even in the most fundamental dispute, each side will apply the 'rule of anticipated reactions'[105] to take a moderate approach and develop a more 'even conversation'[106] with the other, which results in a mutual adjustment of position rather than the total breakdown of boundary discipline. And, in defence of Weiler's view, it may be argued that this, in fact, is how the principals have behaved in EU-state boundary disputes to date, the belligerent rhetoric masking a willingness to compromise in the final instance.[107]

Now, it is clear that the methods used to regulate the relationship between legal orders under a two-dimensional configuration cannot guarantee success—neither the bridging mechanisms utilised to avoid boundary disputes nor the MAD logic used to address them. Bridging mechanisms may outlive their usefulness, as in the classical doctrine of pre-emption, which proved to be excessively rigid and a bar to innovation in the context of an expanding market;[108] they may place a tremendous onus on the judgement and political sensibilities of a small group of actors whose loyalty is owed to one of the legal orders to be accommodated, as with the ECJ's role in developing its preliminary reference jurisdiction;[109] or they may lack comprehensive development and systematic expression, as with the rules on harmonisation of domestic judicial enforcement.[110] Equally, the MAD logic invests heavily in the steady commitment of the parties to the ultimate desirability of peaceful co-existence, and indeed, Weiler's own scepticism about this has led him to suggest a Constitutional Council for the Community, modelled on the French example and staffed by representatives of both levels of the legal order, as a formal meta-procedure which would provide a more stable device for resolving conflict.[111]

For all that these are serious difficulties, it is also clear that the problems associated with boundary disputes would be compounded in the case of a three-dimensional configuration of authority of the type associated with a developed system of differentiated integration. To begin with, there would simply be more border territory, and more scope for boundary disputes. It might be argued that since, at least on some scenarios, differentiated arrangements would be confined to narrow sectors of activity, in comparison to the open-ended frontiers of the state and the traditional EU it would be easier to draw firm lines which all sides could respect. However, given that most

---

[104] Cf, 'The Reformation of European Constitutionalism,' *loc cit,* n 25 125–128; European Neo-Constitutionalism: In Search of Foundations for the European Constitutional Order,' (1996) 44 *Political Studies,* 517 531–532; cf, also Hollis and Smith, *op cit,* n 72 119–128.

[105] C J Friedrich, *Constitutional Government and Politics* (1937 Harper) 16–18.

[106] Weiler, 'The Reformation of European Constitutionalism,' *loc cit,* n 25, 126.

[107] *Ibid;* cf, also MacCormick, 'The Maastricht-Urteil: Sovereignty Now,' (1995) 1 *European Law Journal* 255 261.

[108] Cf, S. Weatherill, *op cit,* n 96, 147–149

[109] Cf, Weiler, 'Journey to an Unknown Destination: A Retrospective and Prospective of the European Court of Justice in the Arena of Political Integration,' (1994) 32 *Journal of Common Market Studies* 1–30.

[110] Cf, Himsworth, *loc cit,* n 99, 306–311.

[111] *Loc cit,* n 25 127.

demarcation lines would likely seek to separate out 'core' single market policies from other more 'peripheral' activities,[112] the difficulties would remain severe. Such is the social and political context within which Western European markets operate that the fashioning of the single market already takes into account various 'external' policy considerations—from environmental policy to security policy to various aspects of social welfare policy, which makes the subsequent separation of these matters for the purpose of deciding questions of the competence of new legal systems a complicated and somewhat artificial process.[113] Indeed, the history of functional 'spillover' and expansion within the EU, and the problems repeatedly encountered by the policy-making institutions and the Court in deciding the relevant Treaty base for the pursuit of policies associated with the single market is testimony to the dynamic relationship between the economic mainspring of the EU and wider social policies and political considerations.[114]

Accordingly, the fine-tuning of boundaries and the building of bridging mechanisms within a three-dimensional configuration would take place in objectively more difficult circumstances. Some preliminary indication of this has been given during Britain's short-lived opt-out of the Social Policy Protocol. As one commentator suggested, the process of discriminating between the various legal bases in the crowded policy space straddling internal market measures,[115] other Community measures dealing with health and safety in the workplace,[116] and the differentiated arrangements under the Social Policy Protocol, promised 'fearsome legal complexity.'[117] Further, the development of adequate bridging mechanisms presupposes forward regulatory planning and a willingness to devise and apply mechanisms in a spirit of mutual accommodation. Our analysis of the social and political conditions attendant upon differentiation suggests these qualities are likely to be in less plentiful supply than they have been within a two-dimensional Europe.

In suggesting that the day-to-day mutual articulation of legal orders would be less manageable, these considerations also imply that fundamental boundary disputes would be more likely to break out under a three-dimensional configuration of authority. Further, where these more frequent skirmishes arose, the strategic logic of MAD would provide less security against the complete breakdown of boundary discipline than under two-dimensional arrangements. As indicated, the deterrent logic of MAD presupposes that each party has a stake in peaceful co-existence, but there is no guarantee of this under the social and political conditions of multi-dimensionality. MAD also works most effectively where the actions of each party are transparent to the others, and where there is no possibility of parties building coalitions sufficiently powerful to encourage the belief that third party boundaries may be breached with impunity. In other words, the logic of deterrence is most effective in the context of the two-party game, and becomes dangerously blurred in the context of a multi-party game.

---

[112] Cf, Dewatripont *et al, op cit,* n 1 ch 4.

[113] Cf, Weatherill, *loc cit,* n 1, 544–546.

[114] Cf, *Commission v Council* Case C-300/89 [1991] ECR I-2867; and more generally, Weatherill, *loc cit,* n 96, 88–92.

[115] Art 100a EC Treaty.

[116] Art 118a EC Treaty

[117] Weatherill, *loc cit,* n 96 178; cf, C-84/94 *United Kingdom v Council* [1996] ECR I-5755.

B Political Efficacy

As noted in the previous section, there is an influential line of argument to the effect that the traditional model of the sovereign state is becoming increasingly inadequate as a societal steering mechanism. This is so partly because the growing inter-penetration of private and public spheres of governance makes the state a more complex entity to regulate, and partly because the primary forces within society are increasingly resistant to regulation at state level.[118] Regulation within a two-dimensional or multi-dimensional context confronts a different set of problems of political efficacy. The availability of political leverage at supranational level addresses some of the difficulties of regulating transnational social forces and trends, and, as we have seen, the flexibility to develop separate initiatives within particular policy sectors may further enhance regulatory capacity. However, the prior problem of constituting and regulating an effective European polity becomes more profound as we move from a one-dimensional to a two-dimensional and, finally, to a three-dimensional configuration of authority.

In particular, regulating the multi-layered polity of the EU raises various problems of institutional co-ordination. EU institutions and national institutions have evolved to meet the needs of their different political systems and have been nurtured within different political cultures. Questions of trust, mutual understanding and technical co-ordination, therefore, are more acutely posed with regard to inter-systemic institutional relationships between the EU and the Member State than with regard to intra-systemic institutional relationships. For instance, despite the fact that they often have concurrent interests in monitoring executive power, the relationship between national parliaments and the European Parliament remains undeveloped.[119] Further, national executives and parliaments tend to have an uneven relationship with the European Commission, with levels of trust and co-ordination variable over time and between sectors.[120] To take a final example, while the powerful role of the Court of Justice in giving constitutional depth to integration from the 1960s onwards has been widely acknowledged,[121] in recent years national executives and parliaments have come increasingly to challenge the legitimacy of an activist role for the court, and indeed it is less insulated from political criticism than many national courts which wear more easily the cloak of judicial neutrality.[122]

Problems of trust and mutual understanding and co-ordination are bound to be exacerbated in a three-dimensional structure. Existing initiatives in differentiated integration have involved the reconstitution of the Council of Ministers to reflect the states participating,[123] although the institutional structure has not yet been varied or

---

[118] Cf, Habermas, *loc cit*, n 27.

[119] Although in recent years a number of initiatives have been taken to improve this relationship; cf, the 'Declaration on the Role of National Parliaments in the European Union' and the 'Declaration on the Conference of the Parliaments' attached to the TEU; cf, generally, Corbett, 'Representing the People,' in A Duff, J Pinder and R Pryce (eds), *Maastricht and Beyond: Building the European Union* (1994 Routledge) 207.

[120] Cf, Fitsmaurice 'The European Commission,' in Duff, Pinder and Pryce (eds) *op cit*, n 119, 179.

[121] Cf, Alter, 'The European Court's Political Power,' (1996) 19 *West European Politics* 458.

[122] Cf, Weiler *loc cit*, n 109; Gibson and Caldiera, 'Changes in the Legitimacy of the European Court of Justice: A Post-Maastricht Analysis,' (1998) 28 *British Journal of Political Science* 63.

[123] For example, under the Social Protocol and in the third stage of economic and monetary union; and, in relation to the new procedures under the Treaty of Amsterdam, cf, new Arts K16(1) and K12(2), TEU; cf, more generally, Usher *loc cit*, n 1 266–272.

fragmented in any other respect. For its part, externally-driven differentiation promises even greater proliferation of institutions, and greater cultural distance between the various parts of the institutional complex.

The increased institutional fragmentation involved in the movement from a two-dimensional to a three-dimensional structure also undermines political efficacy to the extent that it creates a tendency to treat participation in any particular sector in isolation. Where, for example, as will be possible under the Treaty of Amsterdam, differently constituted groups develop policy in mainstream areas of community law, in the area of EMU, and in justice and home affairs, there is less scope for beneficial trade-offs between governments across policy areas and for the level of concerted action thereby made possible.[124]

C   Democratic Accountability

The greater technical complexity of the work of representative institutions, the increase in executive power at the expense of legislatures; a rising tide of public disillusionment and apathy in 'an antipolitical age'[125]; these are familiar criticisms made of the condition of democracy within the state.[126] Does the development of governmental institutions at EU level and through other differentiated arrangements exacerbate or alleviate these problems?

On the one hand, the development of democratic institutions at European level may provide a system of interest representation which is more pluralist in form— recognising a wide variety of functional and territorial constituencies, and thus satisfying the demands of a more complex and heterogeneous polity. The shift away from the cultural community of the nation state as the sole anchor of democratic politics might also provide more scope to protect and nurture the democratic voice of national and international minorities.[127]

On the one hand, the structure of representative government may be even more opaque and less well-understood within the multi-level European polity, and, given the particularly low level of support for the European Parliament,[128] may be even more concentrated within the executive arm. Relatedly, the electorate may feel less affinity with European-level institutions than with the institutions of states, which are pitched at a level which is more likely to correspond to their sense of an appropriate *demos*. These problems of transparency and affinity are likely to be exacerbated under a multi-dimensional system, further weakening the bonds of popular responsiveness and accountability.

If there are certain intrinsic difficulties involved in democracy taking root within a complex configuration of authority, these problems are exacerbated by inter-institutional conflict. The so-called 'democratic deficit' of the European Parliament may be, in large part, about its low visibility and remoteness, but it is also, notwith-standing recent improvements, about the restricted scope of its legislative, executive-

---

[124] Dewatripont *et al, op cit,* n 1 53.

[125] Mulgan, *loc cit,* n 83.

[126] Cf, Habermas, *loc cit,* n 27.

[127] Cf, Weiler, 'The Reformation of European Constitutionalism,' *loc cit,* n 25, 112–122.

[128] For analysis of recent trends, cf, Shephard, 'The European Parliament: Laying the Foundations for Awareness and Support,' (1997) 50 *Parliamentary Affairs* 438.

monitoring and budgetary powers.[129] In the final analysis, its modest constitutional status is a consequence of a strategic rivalry of a kind which is more likely to take place between, rather than within, political orders. Nationalist champions of the state are jealous of the growing authority of the EU, and perceive any extensions of its powers—including the powers of its more democratically-responsive institutions such as the Parliament—in zero-sum terms, as a direct threat to the authority of the state.[130] Equally, some criticisms of the adequacy of state-centred democratic channels from a pro-European perspective owe as much to impatience with a nation state-based traditionalism as to objective appraisal of their democratic responsiveness. In either case, democracy may be relegated to a side-issue in a larger struggle between different institutional orders, and may even become its casualty. Again, it is not difficult to conclude that with the development of new legal and political orders within a multi-dimensional framework, the scope for such rivalry is increased, as is the potential damage to the democratic framework as a whole.

D   Social Legitimacy

The most important, but also the most imponderable, quality of a particular configuration of political authority is its overall social legitimacy. To what extent does the multi-dimensional polity command popular support, or at least acquiescence? Partly, this is a function of our answers to the first three questions. A polity which is capable of resolving difficulties associated with the management of the boundaries between legal orders, which can overcome problems of inter-institutional co-ordin-ation and of political efficacy more generally, and which maximises its democratic credentials, is likely to enhance its public acceptability. However, other factors contribute to the legitimacy of a polity.[131] Some, such as the capacity of the policy choices made within that polity to articulate the value preferences of the citizenry or to deliver them material benefits, are common to all political systems,[132] and whether or not popular policy choices are made does not depend upon whether the polity is or is not configured in multi-dimensional terms. Other factors are more closely tied to the nature of the polity, in particular the constitutional discourse or meta-constitutional discourse associated with a polity, and so it is worth pausing to consider whether and under what circumstances the constitutional discourse associated with a multi-dimensional polity may help to foster its legitimacy.

In part, this again connects back to the questions of boundary management, political efficacy and democratic accountability, since the answers to these questions may (or may not) be found in certain concrete structural norms associated with the constitutional order. These are the norms which concern the decision-making

---

[129] For discussion of recent expansion of the powers of the Parliament, cf, S Weatherill and P Beaumont *EC Law* (2nd ed 1995 Penguin) ch 4.. While it may be the case that the legal powers of the European Parliament may now equal or even exceed these of national Parliaments, criticisms of its overall authority within the European institutional system still find their mark. The Parliament remains the only European institution directly elected at the European level, and so the measure of its authority tends to be treated as the measure of the democratic credentials of the EU as a whole. On the basis of this exacting test, the Parliament is still found wanting by many.

[130] For discussion in the context of the Third Pillar, cf, Walker, 'The Accountability of European Police Institutions,' (1993) 1 *European Journal on Criminal Policy and Research* 34.

[131] Cf, *eg* D Beetham *The Legitimation of Power (1991)* Macmillan: London Part II.

[132] Cf, N Walker 'European Constitutionalism and European Integration,' (1996) *Public Law* 266, 271–275.

apparatus of the political order, including the internal workings of the various institutions and the rules of hierarchy and/or co-ordination which govern their inter-relationship.[133] At a more fundamental level, however, constitutional or meta-constitutional discourse is also where the basic principle of structural design of the polity is capable of being developed and articulated. This is the point at which constitutionalism connects most closely with the social legitimacy of the political order, since the basic design principle may not only provide an important generative mechanism shaping the concrete structural norms discussed above, but also serve a key symbolic function in providing an authenticating language of self-identification and a reflexive language of self-understanding for the emergent political order.

The significance of this potential application of constitutional discourse may be highlighted by considering the effects of its absence. Within the one-dimensional constitutional polity the authenticating principles of structural design typically concerned ideas such as federalism, the separation of powers, the protection of fundamental rights, and—so heavily understood so as to be rarely the subject of explicit appraisal—the idea of sovereign statehood itself.[134] Within more complex political orders, some of these ideas may remain relevant, but must be augmented by design principles specifically tailored to the particular configuration of authority. This has proved a difficult and controversial enough task within the two-dimensional European order,[135] and it is hard to escape the conclusion that the problem of constitutional design will appear even more formidable in a context, such as differentiated integration, which is even more remote from the one-dimensional, statist context within which the very idea of constitutional law originated and was for long domiciled.

In this regard it is instructive to remind ourselves that the terminology associated with differentiated integration within the official constitutional discourse of the EU has a distinctly pragmatic flavour. The preoccupation with shape and velocity reflects an instrumental attitude towards differentiated integration, its exponents treating it as a vehicle in pursuit of some other political objective rather than a political form which can be defended in its own right and must be justified to all constituencies regulated by it. As discussed earlier,[136] the incompletely theorized quality of the language of differentiated integration is partly a function of the interests of the strategic players in masking disagreement, but we should also recognise it as a sign of the impoverished status of constitutional thinking within a multi-dimensional framework. And whatever the balance of explanation between an instrumentally-based unwillingness to develop a more comprehensive constitutional discourse and an inability to develop an adequate constitutional dialogue in the uncharted terrain of a multi-dimensional configuration of authority, the resulting mechanical approach is unlikely to provide a powerful symbolic flagship for the new order or to set its sponsors on a demanding voyage of self-understanding.

---

[133] *Ibid* 275–276; Kay, 'Substance and Structure as Constitutional Protections: Centennial Comparisons,' (1989) *Public Law* 428.

[134] Cf, Walker, *loc cit,* n 132 275–276, 289–290.

[135] Cf, MacCormick, 'Democracy, Subsidiarity and Citizenship in the Context of the European Union,' (1997) 16 *Law and Philosophy*; Bellamy and Castiglione, ' The Normative Challenge of a European Polity: Cosmopolitan and Communitarian Models Compared, Criticised and Combined,' (1997) 16 *Law and Philosophy*.

[136] Cf, n 74 above..

V Conclusion

The emergent framework of differentiated integration faces many difficulties concerning its capacity to manage boundaries between legal orders, its political efficacy, its democratic credentials and its capacity for self-legitimation. This does not mean, however, that it should be viewed in apocalyptic terms, as a development which threatens to destroy the present configuration of authority and all the virtues associated with it, yet which is incapable of providing a broadly acceptable alternative template for the organisation of legal and political authority.

To begin with, we should recall that, while not itself the subject of an explicit design, differential integration is the structural outgrowth of a number of initiatives which do express the preferences of political actors, whether in terms of strategic politics, sectoral politics, or geopolitical imperatives. The main political players might not have willed the end, but they have willed the means, and this must be borne in mind when evaluating the new order. Secondly, it should not be assumed that a multi-dimensional order is unique in facing problems of boundary management, political efficacy, democratic accountability and social legitimacy. As the earlier discussion indicated, these problems have become increasingly pressing in the context of one-dimensional and two-dimensional configurations of authority, and, indeed, in many cases it has been the limitations of the existing configuration which has provided the catalyst for the initiatives which have led towards differentiated integration. This consideration, too, should be entered in the balance sheet when assessing the emerging multi-dimensional order.

Thirdly, even if it is conceded that the generic problems of political authority loom particularly large in the context of a multi-dimensional configuration, the difficulties identified need not be insurmountable. In the final analysis, none of the problems associated with differentiated integration is intractable. This is true even of the fundamental problem of reconciling the incommensurable claims to sovereign authority of different legal orders which lies at the heart of boundary management. In one sense, reconciliation appears a logical impossibility, in that these claims to ultimate authority are bound to yield a series of different conceptions of the proper boundaries of various legal systems, and there is no basis on which any claim can be subordinated to any other. In another sense, however, we should recognise that claims to sovereign authority are simply social facts.[137] As social facts, they depend upon their articulation by key officials of the legal orders in question, and if these key officials conclude that it is not in their interest as custodians of a particular legal order to defend the exclusive version of sovereignty in an exclusionary fashion, then we have the basis for a framework of mutual accommodation. This is the space in which the MAD doctrine operates under the two-dimensional order, and what is required for the same result under a three-dimensional order is a mechanism similarly able to concentrate the minds of all strategic actors on the dangers associated with the uncompromising intra-systemic assertion of sovereignty. In the final analysis, therefore, the problem is sociological rather than logical, and so remains amenable to solution.

In addressing problems of incommensurability and, more generally, in seeking bridging mechanisms between different authority systems, the conversation between key players across legal systems is likely to continue, as it has done within a two-

---

[137] Hart, *op cit,* n 10, 116.

dimensional order, to take place within a constitutional or meta-constitutional discourse, calculated to provide solutions which are general and authoritative. Yet, this raises a fourth problem, already alluded to in our discussion of social legitimacy.[138] Even if there is no logical impediment to the mutual articulation of legal systems, from a sociological perspective it is problematical to rely upon the development of new constitutional or meta-constitutional discourse and technique in conditions where constitutional discourse itself has lost its traditional mooring in the normative apex of the sovereign state.

This objection may be answered with the aid of systems theory. In an important insight, Teubner has argued that the re-framing of law under the pressures of globalization has transformed but not diminished the role of constitutional law.[139] Under the old frame of 'rule-hierarchy'[140] constitutional law was on top, legitimating all other measures within the legal order of the state. In a context where the configurations of political authority with which legal orders are associated are multi-dimensional and thus more competitive, more fluid and more precarious, constitutional law finds itself re-situated at the periphery of a heterarchical legal order. The new legal order is framed in heterarchical, rather than hierarchical terms, because no set of legal rules other than constitutional rules has the normative force to establish an internal hierarchy. But, most importantly for the present discussion, the constitutional framework is now relocated to the periphery of the legal system because it has to engage closely and constructively with an increasingly volatile order of political authority. In other words, rather than providing the normative guardian of the traditional sovereign legal order, constitutional law is now required to be a flexible instrument managing the ever-shifting interface between law and politics. This transformation indeed represents a significant challenge to constitutional law and discourse, but one which is demanded and validated by the changing relationship between legal and political order.[141]

What is required to meet this challenge is a discourse which, like the pragmatic vocabulary associated with differentiated integration, is sensitive to the technical complexity and dynamism of a multi-dimensional order but which has a more distinctly normative edge, capable of encouraging critical debate about the underlying purpose and basic design principles of new differentiated arrangements. In this regard, it may be useful to draw upon terminology which has been applied in the wider academic conversation about the nature and justification of the developing structure of the EU in general, and differentiated integration in particular. While there is no scope within the present context to pursue the implications of this terminology,

---

[138] Cf, Section C.

[139] Teubner, 'Breaking Frames: The Global Interplay of Legal and Social Systems,' (1997) 45 *American Journal of International and Comparative Law* 150; 'Global Bukowina: Legal Pluralism in the World Society' in G Teubner (ed) *Global Law Without a State* (1996 Gower) 3. Other interesting attempts to apply Teubner and Luhmann's legal autopoiesis to the EU include Bańkowski and Christodoloudis, 'The European Union as an essentially contested project' (present volume); Bańkowski, 'Comment on Weiler,' in S Bulmer and D Scott (eds) *Economic and Political Integration in Europe* (1994 Blackwell) 161; Maher, 'Accommodating Difference: Co-evolution of Community and National Law,' (1998) 36 *Journal of Common Market Studies* .

[140] Teubner 'Breaking Frames,' *loc cit,* n 139, 158.

[141] *Ibid,* 158; Teubner broadens the analysis to argue that legislation in general is marginalised within the legal order and becomes engaged in structural coupling with politics, but he clearly views constitutional law as the most important species of the genus of legislation.

it includes concepts such as consociationalism,[142] mixed commonwealth,[143] condominium and confederation,[144] and themes such as subsidiarity,[145] political constitutionalism[146] and intercultural dialogue.[147] The aim, as with the development of contemporary constitutionalism more generally, is to develop an architecture of political authority which draws upon the constitutional traditions of the sovereign state but which is capable of capturing and evoking a more complexly configured pattern of authority.

Yet, for all that we should not succumb to the dystopian vision of differentiated integration, we must also acknowledge that the action required to address its problems demands a set of attitudes and commitments which, on account of the very political dynamics which have brought us to this point, are largely absent. If contingency, ambiguity and disagreement remain the key motifs of the emergent order of differentiation, then they may continue to frustrate efforts to tackle its most fundamental problems.

For example, a large element of the problem of political efficacy and democratic accountability was traced to the lack of trust and understanding between national and supranational institutions, yet given the circumstances of recent initiatives in differentiated integration, and, in particular, the drive towards a more permissive system, it is difficult to see how this distrust may be overcome. The proliferation of initiatives makes for greater institutional diversity, while the increasing willingness to receive into the EU order pre-established institutional frameworks—Schengen being the obvious example—may exacerbate rivalry and extend the cultural distance between institutions required to co-operate. Further, the development of general enabling clauses for enhanced co-operation under the Treaty of Amsterdam, with only limited scope for opposition from those not willing to participate,[148] provides a mandate for more extensive fragmentation. Crucially, the inclusion of open-ended enabling clauses amounts to a declaration that differentiated integration is no longer a sufficiently serious departure from the institutional norm to merit the preparation of a pre-determined package in the Treaty itself or to require close case-by-case consideration. And in this process of normalisation and casualisation of differentiation there is the risk that the bonds of solidarity which continue to unite the fragmented institutional structure around the common purposes of the Union will gradually be weakened.

Another example of the dynamics of structural change militating against successful treatment of problem areas revisits the issue of the prospects for the development of an effective new constitutional or meta-constitutional discourse around the subject of

---

[142] Cf, Chryssochou, 'New Challenges to the Study of European Integration: Implications for Theory-Building,' (1997) 35 *Journal of Common Market Studies* 521.

[143] Cf, MacCormick, *loc cit,* n 135.

[144] Cf, Schmitter, 'Imagining the Future of the Euro-Polity With The Help of New Concepts,' in G Marks, F W Scharpf, P C Schmitter and W Streeck (eds) *Governance in the European Union* (1996 Sage) 121.

[145] Cf, Scott, Peterson and Millar, 'Subsidiarity: A 'Europe of the Regions v. the British Constitution,' (1994) 32 *Journal of Common Market Studies* 32.

[146] Cf, Bellamy and Castiglione, *loc cit,* n 135; 'The Communitarian Ghost in the Cosmopolitan Machine: Constitutionalism, Democracy and the Reconfiguration of Politics in the New Europe,' in R Bellamy (ed) *Constitutionalism, Democracy and Sovereignty; American and European Perspectives* (1996 Aldershot) 111.

[147] Cf, J Tully, *Strange Multiplicity: Constitutionalism in an Age of Diversity* (1995 Cambridge University Press).

[148] Cf, new Arts K15(1), K12(1)-(2) TEU, new Art 5a(1)-(2) EC Treaty.

differentiation. As argued above, such a discourse faces formidable problems in combining and transcending the older language of one and two-dimensional constitutionalism and the new, and essentially pragmatic, understanding of differentiation in a novel form of constitutional conversation between legal systems. Quite apart from the content of such a discourse, there is the prior difficulty of devising an agreed procedure for generating or for ascribing constitutional authority to this new form of dialogue. Constitutional discourse originates within the framework of the sovereign state and, even within the context of a two-dimensional configuration of authority, constitutional discourse typically remains tied to particular legal orders.[149] Against such a backdrop, agreeing a new constitution-making procedure which stands above the various orders requires the representatives of the various orders to sacrifice interpretative autonomy and to trust their constitutional fate to an independent constitutional authority. And if this seems unlikely,[150] the alternative solution of ascribing constitutional authority to a site within one of the existing constitutional orders (whether national, EU or within a differentiated arrangement) is just as problematic. Such an ascription of authority tends to beg, rather than resolve, the question of the appropriate structural relationship between different legal orders. In these circumstances, indeed, it is difficult to escape the circular conclusion that in order to establish its authority to address the relevant structural questions from a particular site, any particular constitutional 'authority' must purport to have already resolved them, at least provisionally—a claim which cannot guarantee acceptance and recognition at other, rival constitutional sites.

Finally, we may note that alongside this large paradox concerning the provision of an authoritative method for generating or identifying constitutional discourse, the underlying lack of political agreement about the ultimate destination of differentiated integration also undercuts the solution, by way of new bridging mechanisms, to more specific co-ordination problems posed by its operation. Two examples will suffice. Take, for instance, the principles of non-interference with the *acquis communautaire* or with 'the competences, rights, obligations and interests' of the non-participating states which qualify the right to enhanced co-operation under the general enabling clause of the Treaty of Amsterdam.[151] Given the dynamic nature of the relationship between the economic core and other concerted activities of Member States, and given the close interdependence and mutual vulnerability of Member States, it is hard to see how non-participating states will not invariably be prejudiced to some extent by closer co-operation amongst the others.[152] And given that the objective of the principle of non-interference cannot be to forbid all initiatives, and that non-participating states are under a reciprocal duty not to impede the implementation of closer forms of co-operation by others,[153] the real question must be whether the benefits of close co-operation outweigh the prejudice caused. But this is a question which can only be answered from the point of view of the perspective of either group. There is no common reference point of interests or values and so no neutral point of adjudication between these groups. In other words, the fundamental disagreement about the appropriate terms and limits of collective action which initially drove the open-ended initiative in flexibility at Amsterdam ensures that there can be no objective basis for

---

[149] Cf, ns 23–27 above. Cf, also Walker, *loc cit*, n 132, 278–281.
[150] Cf, Walker, *loc cit*, n 132, 278–283.
[151] New Art K15(1)(e)-(f).
[152] Cf, Edwards and Philippart, *op cit*, n 1, 14–15.
[153] New Art K15(2).

adjudicating between the concerns of the different groupings of states thereby established.

If it may be expected that states involved in differentiated arrangements which reflect such significant differences in political world-view are unable to agree on the substantive standards or values which inform new meta-constitutional rules, rules which instead concentrate on decision-making structures might appear better equipped to attract consensus.[154] However, that is perhaps to overestimate the propensity of divergent interests to view decision-making structures in other than instrumental terms. The more sceptical view may be illustrated by returning to Weiler's suggestion of a Constitutional Council for Europe as a forum to resolve the meta-constitutional question of the boundaries between legal orders.[155] Whether applied to a two-dimensional configuration or a three-dimensional configuration, the solution again begs the question: on what basis would parties in fundamental disagreement about the location of inter-systemic boundaries agree upon the structure and operating criteria of any dispute-resolution device? The acute danger exists that they would each assess any such device purely in terms of its likely consequences for their preferred view of the proper balance of constitutional authority, and on that basis fail to establish lasting agreement.

In the early, tentative attempts to find substantive or structural rules to avoid or adjudicate boundary disputes within a multi-dimensional order, there are echoes of the idea, suggested by some commentators,[156] that *supraconstitutional* norms may provide a solution. This gains weight from the EU's own flirtation with the idea of 'supra-constitutionality' in the decision of the ECJ on the legality of the draft EEA Agreement in 1991.[157] In determining that the proposal for an EEA Court with a jurisdiction overlapping that of the ECJ was unconstitutional in that it threatened the autonomy and integrity of the Community legal system, the ECJ suggested that the idea of autonomy and integrity was a logically prior constitutional principle which somehow stood above, yet helped to validate and secure, the positive constitutional order of the Community. But while the idea of a trumping supraconstitutional norm may be appropriate in a context, such as that of the EEA decision, where one legal order is in a clear position of superiority over the other and is seeking to validate the other in its own terms, it is difficult to see how supraconstitutionality has a coherent and authoritative role in the context of a dispute between legal orders neither of which will concede the superiority of the other. Again the difficulty lies in discovering an objective basis for a legal norm to prevail over the preferred and conflicting solutions of the actors internal to each legal order, and this question is not avoided by the mere invocation of the language of supraconstitutionality.

In summary, the 'non-project' of differentiated integration cannot effectively address its own profound problems in terms recognisable within traditional paradigms of constitutional thought, yet its principal players are reluctant to seek to address them in any other terms. This is not to say, however, that differentiated integration is doomed to follow a corrosive dynamic of increased fragmentation, legal inde-terminacy, declining democracy and political failure. If the political will is sufficiently mobilised, an adequate framework of meta-constitutional institutions, rules and

---

[154] Cf, Walker, *loc cit*, n 132, 275 *et seq.*

[155] Weiler, 'The Reformation of European Constitutionalism,' *loc cit*, n 25, 127

[156] Cf, Harmsen, *loc cit*, n 1, 131–133.

[157] *Re The Draft Treaty on a European Economic Area* Opinion 1/91 [1992]1 CMLR 245.

conventions to manage a multi-dimensional configuration of authority may emerge. Yet the unequivocal message of this article is that no such reassuring conclusion is guaranteed, and that just as the conceptualisation of multi-dimensionality demands a radical departure from existing analytical schemes, so, too, the delivery of a normative solution to its novel stresses and tensions requires the fashioning of a regulatory framework every bit as distinctive from the frameworks used to manage less complex political orders.[158]

---

[158] For a provisional attempt to develop a new analytical and normative framework adequate to multi-dimensionality, see N. Walker, 'Flexibility within a Metaconstitutional Frame: Reflections on the Future of Legal Authority in Europe' in de Burca and Scott, *loc cit*, n 1, 9; also published as Harvard University Jean Monnet Paper no. 12/1999.

4

The Problem of Membership in European Union Citizenship

Jo Shaw

I Introduction

This paper develops a constructive and critical approach to the concept of Union citizenship, formally enshrined in the EU Treaties only since the Treaty on European Union entered into force in 1993, but possessing also a deeper heritage within the framework of the EU legal and political orders.[1] It focuses specifically on the 'membership' issue, starting from a legal formalist perspective under which the members are defined by reference to the outer boundaries of the EU polity, as those who are nationals or citizens of the constituent Member States. However, it critiques and goes beyond such a perspective, suggesting that it is internal boundaries which represent the limits of citizenship as membership of a polity, as much as external borders and legal categories based on nationality. Using a frame of analysis in which citizenship is envisioned as relational rather than singular, and as dynamic rather than static, the paper develops a case study of the use of legal concepts of equality and non-discrimination by the Court of Justice in its case law. The manipulation of 'equality' de-constructs and re-constructs the boundaries of membership in quite radical ways. Yet this determination of the scope of membership is one which is outside the immediate control of the Member States, even though they, as the formal 'masters' of the Treaties, have set the formal limits upon the category 'Union citizen' in provisions of primary Community law. The case study reveals a complex conjunction of identity politics, individual legal rights and claims, and interacting judicial and legislative roles in the evolution of the relational and dynamic concept of membership used in this paper. Setting the scene for this discussion, the introductory sections of the paper very briefly review the concept of Union citizenship in the law of the European Union, and then situate it within an understanding of citizenship which draws upon both theoretical understandings of the EU as an emergent polity, and contemporary citizenship theory. As we shall see from the theoretical turn taken in Sections IV and V of this essay, the formal citizenship provisions of the EU are used here as essential scene-setting material, not as the starting point of the analysis.

As a legal formality, citizenship of the European Union was institutionalised by the Treaty of Maastricht amending the EC Treaty. A new Part Two was included in the Treaty establishing the European Community, with Article 8(1) EC proclaiming:

---

[1] See generally A. Wiener, *'European' Citizenship Practice – Building Instituitons of a Non-State*, Boulder, Col.: Westview (1998); J. Shaw, 'Citizenship of the Union: Towards Post-national Membership?', in Academy of European Law (ed.), *Collected Courses of the Academy of European Law*, vol. VI, Book 1, The Hague: Kluwer Law International (1998), pp. 237–347 [also published as Harvard Jean Monnet Working Paper No. 6/97].

'Citizenship of the Union is hereby established. Every person holding the nationality of a Member State shall be a citizen of the Union.'

Simple words; and, perhaps, empty gestures also. The formal rights and duties which Article 17(2)[2] then goes on to 'attach to' citizenship in the provisions which follow are few, and they are primarily linked to residence in a Member State other than the one of which the citizen is a national. They comprise a right of residence in other Member States (which is not absolute and may be – and has been – limited by Council legislation) (Article 18), voting rights based on residence in local and European parliamentary elections (Article 19), consular and diplomatic protection in third countries (Article 20), and the rights to make petitions to the European Parliament and to make complaints to the European Ombudsman (Article 21). Only the last two are not directly linked to free movement within the EU or at least movement away from the home state to a third country. This emphasis highlights the primary heritage of Union citizenship, which lies in a conception – fostered principally by the Commission and the Court of Justice[3] – that the free movement of persons within the EU implies more than merely economic rights under the Treaties and secondary legislation. The predominant emphasis of the citizenship rights is to constitute the strong transnational citizen who holds and exercises rights *vis-à-vis* the Member States which are set up as the obstructive parties. It does nothing, on the face of it, to constitute either a vertical relationship between the EU and 'its' citizens, or a horizontal relationship between the citizens *inter se*. It suggests little or nothing about the essentially reciprocal nature of citizenship, or about the problem of 'duty'.

Remaining still within the paradigms of legal formality, a different sort of picture of the Union citizen emerges from a broader 'audit' of rights and duties of citizens under European Community law and within the emerging EU polity. It is perhaps useful to conduct such an audit by reference to some sort of ideal type of citizen with 'full membership' of the EU as polity, following many standard definitions of the concept of citizen.[4] To assess EU citizenship against this standard involves ranging across substantially the whole body of EC law – an ambitious exercise. Paradoxically, the message to be derived from such an exercise in EC law is that the 'conventional' journey (described in the terms of TH Marshall[5]) from civil, to political and thence to social rights is to a large extent flipped on its head in the EU context. The legacy of market citizenship embedded in the Treaty provisions on free movement of commodities and factors of production strongly marks the present status quo of EU citizenship rights.[6] Thus what emerges is less a purely 'social' status, than a broader

---

[2] On ratification of the Treaty of Amsterdam (May 1999) a consolidated and renumbered version of the EC and EU Treaties entered into force. Hereafter, in this essay, the new numbering will be used. Articles 8a-8e EC on Union citizenship were renumbered as Articles 17-22 EC, with small but nonetheless significant amendments.

[3] See in particular Case C-168/91 *Konstantinides* v. *Stadt Altensteig* [1993] ECR I-1191, Case 186/87 *Cowan* v. *Le Trésor public* [1989] ECR 195, and Case 293/83 *Gravier* v. *City of Liège* [1985] ECR 593.

[4] I have developed my understanding of Union citizenship more fully elsewhere. See, in particular, the following: 'Citizenship of the Union', above n. 1; 'The Interpretation of European Union Citizenship', (1998) 61 *Modern Law Review* pp293-317; 'Constitutional Settlements and the Citizen after Amsterdam', in K-H. Neunreither and A. Wiener (eds.), *Amsterdam and Beyond: Institutional Dynamics and Prospects for Democracy in the EU*, Oxford: Oxford University Press, 2000 [also published as Harvard Jean Monnet Working Paper No. 7/98].

[5] TH Marshall, *Citizenship and Social Class*, Cambridge: Cambridge University Press, 1950.

[6] M. Everson, 'The Legacy of the Market Citizen', in J. Shaw and G. More (eds.), *New Legal Dynamics of European Union*, Oxford: Oxford University Press, 1995.

socio-economic status combining elements of market, industrial and welfare citizenship. Above all, however, the whole edifice is anchored through the general principle of non-discrimination on the grounds of nationality in Article 12 EC (not part of the citizenship provisions as such), and the specific expressions of that principle in the free movement provisions such as Articles 39, 43, and 49 and relevant secondary legislation on the free movement of workers and the coordination of the social security rights of migrants. In comparison, the other elements of the rights of citizenship remain starkly underdeveloped: EU citizens are largely alienated from the enjoyment of political sovereignty in relation to the European Union, and there is no meaningful public space within which they can operate as political actors. Furthermore, their civil status (i.e. their enjoyment of classical liberties) is largely constituted by reference to rights anchored in national constitutions or in a different type of 'European' frame of reference – the European Convention of Human Rights and Fundamental Freedoms. The scope and nature of Community fundamental rights themselves remains meanwhile profoundly problematic and a contested terrain.

On the basis of such reviews – whether narrower or wider in scope – one might well conclude pessimistically that Union citizenship appears marginal, from both legal and political perspectives. Indeed, harking back to Raymond Aron's classic dictum of the 1970s,[7] many might still assert that there can be no European citizens, most frequently citing the argument that without a *demos* there cannot be a citizenship.[8] There is, of course, a strong normative argument that attention *should* be paid to the broader affective dimension of European integration, in order to seek answers to the widely perceived legitimacy deficit in the supranational 'Monnet' method of decision-making which has marked much of the first forty years of Community and Union history not to mention the parliamentary deficits at national and supranational level which appear when decision-making power is concentrated ever more in the hands of governments and executives.[9] A stronger argument lies, in my view, in the conceptual sphere. It is now widely held that while citizenship may be historically closely linked to the vocation of the nation state, it is not (or no longer) inextricably bound to notions of nationalism or indeed attempts in the state context to distinguish between citizen insiders and alien outsiders. Citizenship remains a means for setting the parameters of inclusion and exclusion of any given community, as well as postulating the ideal type for participation in that community as both governor and governed. But identity, loyalty and community-based fellow-feeling can operate in different ways and to different degrees at many levels, including the local, the regional, the national and the supranational. Identity is not a zero-sum game. There are no *a priori* reasons why a form of 'community' could not emerge at the EU level, based on more than simply the holding of a set of legal rights, although so far any such 'community' has proven to be more imaginary than most. Moreover, there are equally no *a priori* reasons why the boundaries of formal legal membership must be set by reference to the category of nationals of the Member States as they are at present, although political realism might suggest that it will be some time before that national reference point is abandoned – if it ever is – to include, for example, lawfully resident third country nationals as Union citizens.

---

[7] R. Aron, 'Is Multinational Citizenship Possible?', (1974) 41 *Social Research* 638

[8] E.g. D. Grimm, 'Does Europe Need a Constitution?', (1995) 1 *ELJ* 282; R. Axtmann, *Liberal Democracy into the twenty-first century*, Manchester: Manchester University Press, (1996) pp166-167.

[9] B. Laffan, 'The Politics of Identity and Political Order in Europe', (1996) 34 *JCMS* 81.

To move towards this understanding of Union citizenship, it is essential to draw widely and deeply on the rich intellectual heritage of citizenship studies. At one level, David Held's description of citizenship simply as 'membership of a community' involving a reciprocity of rights against and duties towards that community is evocative.[10] But we need to interrogate more closely its individual elements. So we must also focus on the political element of citizenship, where citizenship constitutes the political community, or indeed vice versa. Citizenship, on this view, constitutes a 'community of concern and engagement',[11] and offers the space in which political claims can be articulated and resolved.[12] Another possibility is to focus more on personal rather than purely political identities, and on the competing claims of individuals and groups. For example, Charles Tilly identifies 'citizenship as a set of mutual, contested claims between agents of states and members of socially-constructed categories: genders, races, nationalities and others'.[13] One might conclude that citizenship comprises not only the well established dual elements of identity and rights, but also elements of access, experience and practice.[14] These emerge both through individual experience and institutional practice. The negotiation of these elements is a historical, dynamic and geographically contingent process. When read in the context of the emergence of the 'new EU polity', we begin to see that citizenship can be not just an object of study in itself, but also a frame of reference for making sense of other aspects of what might be termed the 'European condition.'

In this paper I shall examine the 'membership' element of EU citizenship. The paper concentrates upon the definition and delineation of those persons or groups who constitute the community of EU citizens. It critiques conventional approaches based on legal formalism which draw directly upon the text of the Treaty (Sections II and III). It suggests an alternative relational approach derived from the continuing interaction of the boundaries of community (i.e. issues of identity and belonging) and the boundaries of the substantive content of citizenship (i.e. the rights and duties of citizens) (Sections IV and V). It argues that within EC law a much more complex frame of reference for determining those who are 'in' and those who are 'out' is in fact operating, and draws a link between the issues of membership and equality. 'Equality' remains perhaps the most complex challenge for a citizenship project.[15] Formal rights conferred passively upon citizens are meaningless without access to political and legal processes, and without the economic means for self-sustenance. Formally empowered citizens cannot be 'full' members of the community without a minimum guarantee of participation and access provided by the state or public authorities. In Section VI of the paper, a case study is presented which examines the interaction between individuals, groups and rights in the context of the evolution of the EU as a non-state polity. It focuses upon three groups of EU citizens: economically marginal migrants;

---

[10] D. Held, 'Between State and Civil Society: Citizenship', in Andrews (ed.), *Citizenship*, London: Lawrence and Wishart, 1991 at p. 20.

[11] D. Kostakopoulou, 'Towards a Theory of Constructive Citizenship in Europe', (1996) 4 *Journal of Political Philosophy* 337.

[12] M. Everson, 'Women and Citizenship of the European Union', in T. Hervey and D. O'Keeffe (eds.), *Sex Equality Law in the European Union*, Chichester: Chancery Wiley.

[13] C. Tilly, 'Citizenship, Identity and Social History', in C. Tilly (ed.), *Citizenship, Identity and Social History*, Supplement 3, *International Review of Social History*, Cambridge: Cambridge University Press, 1996, at p. 6.

[14] See Wiener, above n. 1, Ch. 2.

[15] S. Benhabib, 'Democracy and Identity. Dilemmas of Citizenship in Contemporary Europe', in M. Greven, *Demokratie – eine Kultur des Westens?*, Opladen: Leske and Budrich, 1998.

women in employment; and gay, lesbian and transgendered citizens. The case study is intended to show how the model which is developed in the earlier sections can actually operate in practice, in the light of EC law before the Court of Justice, in order to permit refinements to that model. It is not intended to test out a hypothesis.

II Membership: the prevailing legal formalism

In legal formalist terms, the 'membership' element of EU citizenship can be understood quite simply. Again, we must return to Article 8 [17] EC in order to set the scene. It proclaims that:

'Every person holding the nationality of a Member State shall be a citizen of the Union.'[16]

Once this qualifying hurdle has been surmounted by any individual, the rights and duties incumbent upon EU citizens under EC law will automatically follow.

Critique of this membership criterion has hitherto concentrated upon the implications of the importation of a *national* element of determination into determining the scope of enjoyment of an *EU-level* status.[17] Nationality is a variably defined category based upon a combination of national and international rules, converging upon, but not always wholly coterminous with, citizenship at the national level. Subject only to restrictions on denying the benefit of dual EU nationality to persons also with third country nationality, this is a matter within the definitional sovereignty of the Member States.[18] In that sense, the nationality criterion is, without doubt, a 'statist' concept, perhaps illsuited to an evolutionary postnational concept such as Union citizenship. It is also a criterion where there is little evidence of convergence between the widely diverging systems of law of the Member States; these divergences result in forms of 'inequality' regarding the legal conditions governing the holding or acquisition of Union citizenship since a person must first have or acquire the nationality or citizenship of one of the Member States (e.g. by naturalisation or registration under the conditions laid down under national law, by descent in a country applying *jus sanguinis* or by birth in a country which still applies *jus soli*).[19]

Moreover, the exclusion of all legally resident third country nationals from Union citizenship, *including* those already benefitting indirectly from free movement by virtue of their membership of the family of a Community national taking advantage of one of the free movement rights under the Treaties and secondary legislation, and those enjoying limited free movement rights *into* the Union under an Association Agreement such as that between the EU and Turkey, as well as nationals of the EEA countries who enjoy full free movement rights within the EU, has been the subject of sustained discussion and criticism. This exclusion gives rise to a number of paradoxes. On the

---

[16] In some language versions, e.g. the Italian, where a concept of nationality is not recognised at national level, the term 'citizenship' (*cittadanza*) is used.

[17] C. Closa, 'Citizenship of the Union and Nationality of the Member States', in D. O'Keeffe and P. Twomey (eds.), *Legal Issues of the Maastricht Treaty*, Chichester: Chancery/Wiley, 1994; S. Hall, *Nationality, Migration Rights and Citizenship of the Union*, Dordrecht: Martinus Nijhoff, 1995; S. O'Leary, 'Nationality Law and Community Citizenship: a tale of two uneasy bedfellows', (1992) 12 *Yearbook of European Law* 353.

[18] Case C-369/90 *Micheletti* v. *Delegación del Gobierno en Cantabria* [1992] ECR I-4329.

[19] R. Koslowski, 'Intra-EU Migration, Citizenship and Political Union', (1994) 32 *Journal of Common Market Studies* 369.

one hand, such legally resident third country nationals may already enjoy within the Member State where they reside the informal status of so-called 'denizen' by virtue of stable residence. The acquisition of this status follows a pattern of evolution in the enjoyment of many citizenship rights which has seen more and more rights of a 'basic' or 'fundamental' nature conferred on a universalistic and individualistic basis on all those subject to the laws of a particular country, rather than merely its citizens, in a manner which some have termed 'postnational membership'. This pays less account to the satisfaction of a formal nationality test and attaches more readily to the incidence of lawful settlement or residence.[20] Only a narrow category of rights where a 'loyalty' element is truly intrinsic to the right are, on this model, reserved for the limited category of 'national' or 'citizen'.[21] This would typically include electoral rights especially those in national elections, and certain duties including forms of jury or other public service such as military service. On the other hand, third countries nationals are not excluded from all citizenship-like rights. First, they will benefit from some rights of a fundamental nature, such as the right to non-discrimination on grounds of sex in the employment context, where no differentiation is made as to the nationality of the beneficiary. Likewise, a claim for breach of fundamental rights such as an interference in property interests brought against the EU legislature in areas such as the customs union, the common commercial policy or the common agricultural policy will not fail because the claimant is a third country legal or natural person, provided they can show the relevant legal standing in the Court of Justice or national court. Second, the distinction loses sight of one of the strong ironies of the EU citizenship provisions, namely that a number of 'rights' included in the list in Part Two of the EC Treaty as 'citizenship rights' – when reiterated in the context of the institutional provisions relating to the European Parliament – are given to third country nationals as well. Thus the rights to petition the European Parliament and to apply to the Ombudsman are extended to any natural or legal person established in the EU.[22]

Overall, therefore, the blanket exclusion of third country nationals from the *status* of EU citizenship (if not from all *rights* of a citizenship-type nature) tends to reinforce a perception that the formal definition of EU citizenship on the basis of Member State nationality may result in outcomes which are excessively narrow from the standpoint of the politics of immigration and the demands of justice.[23]

III   The problems of legal formalism

So much for the political and normative problems raised. This section sets out, in brief terms, a number of problems of a more conceptual nature to which the application of a legal formalistic approach to the issue of 'membership' as underlying the ascription of Union citizenship gives rise.

First, understood in the legal formalistic terms of nationality, the membership element of EU citizenship appears above all to be a passive and rather static status. It is 'given' and 'received'. It is essentially a product of a unilateral declaration on the

---

[20] Y. Soysal, *Limits of Citizenship. Migrants and Postnational Membership in Europe*, Chicago/London: University of Chicago Press (1994).

[21] R. Bauböck, 'Cultural Minority Rights for Immigrants', (1996) 30 *International Migration Review* 203.

[22] Compare Article 21 with Articles 194 and 195 of the EC Treaty.

[23] See *inter alia* T. Kostakopoulou, 'European Citizenship and Immigration after Amsterdam: openings, silences, paradoxes', (1998) 24 *Journal of Ethnic and Migration Studies* 639.

part of the drafters of the Treaty of Maastricht that 'Europe' was 'ready' for a concept of citizenship, but without any real evidence as to why this might be so other than that it might somehow reinforce the glue which seeks to hold the EU together. EU citizenship, seen in those terms, responds, therefore, only to one side of one of the classic dualisms of citizenship theory, those of 'active' and 'passive' citizenship and of the citizen as both 'governor' and 'governed'. It provides no critical purchase on the nature of the 'glue' itself. It does not immediately encompass the idea that the citizens may have – even as a fictional construct – banded together, or consented voluntarily, to being a political community.

Second, it is very much part of a tradition of a 'documentary' approach to citizenship. On this view, citizenship 'comes alive' at border crossings, when passports – the indicia of membership – must be shown. Without denying the significance of the external dimension of membership, it is important that other dimensions are revealed by analysis. The legal formalism of the approach also means that important elements of the third country national dilemma are lost sight of. In particular, there is the question raised by normative political theory – confronted by Seyla Benhabib amongst others – as to whether a democratic society can be a complete and closed system with non-porous borders which people enter by birth and exit on death.[24] Allowing entry and exit is, she would argue, a precondition of an open democratic society. Hence the conceptualisation of issues such as alienage, immigration and the treatment of foreigners is crucial to the conceptualisation of the polity as a whole.

Third – and in this context the criticism is a much wider one – citizenship of the Union must be understood as an open-textured concept, and not within a frame of legal formalism. This point emerges already from the brief discussion in the introduction to the paper and is developed further in Section IV as a prelude to the reconceptualisation of membership.

Fourth – and this is the point which will be picked up throughout this paper – the use of the nationality criterion in Article 17(1) seems to indicate that the *only relevant* distinction in relation to Union citizenship is between those with and those without the nationality of the Member States. This reifies the internal/external borders issue (which is unfortunate – important though the debate on the status of third country nationals undoubtedly is) and constructs one dominant meaning for concepts of 'inclusion' and 'exclusion' based on that distinction. Conversely, it creates an impression of equality *within* the Union which is not borne out on closer examination – either in relation to those exercising the paradigmatic Union citizenship rights (free movement *between* the Member States) where the economically marginal have typically been treated as legally marginal also, or in relation to groups *within* the Member States themselves, especially those whose legal, political or economic status has classically been marginal within liberal legal, political and economic orders, such as women, gays, lesbians, transsexuals, and people of colour.[25] It ignores the excluded within the boundaries.

Finally, the formalist approach to the issue of membership suggests also that there is a simple progression from determining 'who are the members?' to deciding 'what are the rights?'. Membership, citizenship and citizenship rights are seen as a linear progression, rather than a circular process of mutual reinforcement between com-

---

[24] Benhabib, above n. 15.
[25] H.L. Ackers, *Shifting Spaces: Women, Citizenship and Migration within the European Union*, Bristol: The Policy Press (1998), Ch. 3.

munities and evolving systems of rights and duties, or a set of overlapping circles of entitlements for and responsibilities upon individuals and groups, based on multi-faceted identities of gender, race, ethnic origin, religion, family status, sexual orient-ation, class, and so on. The important point is to recognise the close link between conceptualising membership and conceptualising citizenship itself.

IV   Reconceptualising membership

The first step towards reconceptualising membership involves adopting a construc-tivist approach to Union citizenship in general. Hence, the first part of this section is concerned with more general questions, and the discussion moves only later to the specific issue of membership. So far relatively little work has been done on Union citizenship within the emerging constructivist tradition of EU governance studies.[26] Two exceptions are provided by the work of Theodora Kostakopoulou and Antje Wiener, both of whom acknowledge a degree of indeterminacy in political and social relationships generated by the increasingly uncertain coupling of nation, state and nationalism.

From within the domain of political philosophy, Kostakopoulou[27] suggests seven propositions which uphold her theory of constructive citizenship; of these, perhaps the most important is the one which rejects an essentialist concept of individual identity or foundational communities as the basis for citizenship but suggests instead that the European Union might evolve as a 'community of concern and engagement'.[28] Set alongside this underlying precept are propositions about the need for a problematized politics of 'belonging' or membership, a critical reinvention of the language of rights, the acceptance of a public domain for decision-making and participatory democracy, the upholding of values of social justice, and the awareness of multiple commitments and shifting identities which affect people's abilities to be 'full' and active citizens. The paper concludes with a call for an open concept of political life which allows constant contestation to be a way of life rather than a deviant practice.

Similarly, Wiener[29] examines the constructive potential of Union citizenship, but from a perspective which uses a socio-historical frame of analysis drawn from critical social history, critical international relations and EU new governance scholarship, in

---

[26] K. Jørgensen (ed.), *Reflective Approaches to European Governance*, Basingstoke: Macmillan, 1997; K. Jørgensen (ed.), *The Aarhus-Norsminde Papers: Constructivism, International Relations and European Studies*, Aarhus, Denmark, 1997; T. Christiansen *et al.* (eds.) *The Social Construction of Europe*, Special Issue, *Journal of European Public Policy*, Vol. 6, No. 4, 1999.

[27] Above, n. 11; see also ibid, 'European Union Citizenship as a model of citizenship beyond the nation state: possibilities and limits', in A. Weale and M. Nentwich (eds.), *Political theory and the European Union. Legitimacy, Constitutional Choice and Citizenship*, London: Routledge, 1998.

[28] Kostakopoulou, above, n. 11 at 346; compare the different approaches of Jürgen Habermas ('Citizenship and National Identity', in B. van Steenbergen (ed.), *The Condition of Citizenship*, London: Sage, 1994 – 'constitutional patriotism'), Joseph Weiler ('Does Europe need a Constitution?', (1995) 1 *European Law Journal* 219 – 'supranationalism'), and Etienne Tassin ('Europe: A Political Community', in C. Mouffe (ed.), *Dimensions of Radical Democracy*, London: Verso, 1992 – 'public spaces of fellow-citizenship') to non-ethnic notions of a 'community' of Europeans. So far, as each of these (and indeed other) models lack empirical detail, the choice between them seems largely an abstract one at this stage.

[29] See above n. 1; see also A. Wiener, 'Assessing the Constructive Potential of Union Citizenship – A Socio-Historical Perspective', (1997) 1 *European Integration online Papers* No. 017; http://eiop.or.at.eiop).

order to set out the creeping development and concretisation of the 'resources' of citizenship from ideas into practical policies. The detailed presentation of empirical evidence concerning these policies from the inception of the European Community onwards through the Treaties of Maastricht and Amsterdam demonstrates the point at which this approach diverges from the more abstract approach of Kostakopoulou. Wiener's work is grounded in the process of interpreting and explaining the evolution of European integration, from a broad institutionalist perspective on how those policies are made and with a focus on the governance processes and institutions of a non-state polity-in-the-making.

Following closely this methodological and theoretical approach, I would argue that it is important to adopt an approach to interpreting and using a construct of Union citizenship which draws not only on the critical theories of citizenship, but also upon the contribution of regional integration theory to understanding how and why policies emerge in the EU context and to identifying the crucial actors and interests within different policy fields and at different levels of policy-making. It is an approach which takes full advantage of the rich theoretical canvasses offered by both citizenship theory and integration theory at the present time. Thus, in previous work,[30] drawing on critical, socio-historical and institutionalist literature, I have sought to harness the contestability inherent in the concept of citizenship by characterising EU citizenship as having a dynamic, relational and negotiated nature which emerges most clearly through the juxtaposition of the different primary elements of the citizenship figure (identity/belonging/membership and rights) within a space carved out within the framework of EU integration processes. This is a space in which the practices of citizenship are constantly negotiated and re-negotiated between different agents of integration, or actors involved in processes of integration. At the same time, the structural conditions for the exercise of individual and group autonomy in the EU context are thereby transformed. In the specific context of the EU, these practices need to be seen against the continually shifting backdrop of a polity-in-formation of a fragmentary nature. Above all, this is an approach to EU citizenship which rejects, or at least transcends, the boundaries of legal formalism.

Yet to many, it is not at all obvious that there can be forms of supra-state or supranational citizenship, including EU citizenship. What if national identity is seen as a single fixed notion, with identity itself conceived of as a zero-sum game (national-or-supranational) running parallel to conceptions of sovereignty posed in similar terms? As with plural conceptions of sovereignty, which have come more often (and certainly more realistically) to portray the holding of political power through the interlocking of separate normative orders,[31] numerous alternatives to a single fixed notion of identity based on varieties of concentric or interlocking circles have been proposed and discussed. Many such alternatives share, however, a single normative assumption (albeit not necessarily an explicitly stated assumption): that the *fixing* of a constituency or pool of potential citizens is a preliminary step necessarily prior to the task of determining the status of those citizens once defined (or 'bounded'). In stark contrast, Zenon Bańkowski and Emilios Christodoulidis have recently argued for the continuous 'contestation of constituency', and for the fluidity of the definition of

---

[30] See above n. 4.

[31] See for example N. MacCormick, 'Beyond the Sovereign State', (1993) 56 *Modern Law Review* 1; see also ibid, 'Democracy, Subsidiarity, and Citizenship in the 'European Commonwealth'', (1997) 16 *Law and Philosophy* 331.

'home' and identity.[32] They mount an argument which speaks to many of the criticisms of legal formalism outlined above.

> 'Our argument is . . . about participation, not received membership. It is from participation that the community may draw its empowerment. We will argue this by resisting any form of a priori circumscription of the relevant community. We will argue that a community's constituency should not be taken as a given as when membership is its precondition. That a community not only can and should contest its own political space, but in fact, in a significant way is generated (and re-generated) in treating its political space as contestable. Thus, not only is membership not a pre-condition for political community, but any fixing whatsoever of the contours of the relevant community is detrimental to it. We will argue that a community can only come about in contesting its very constituency and thus forever postponing its fixity.'

Citizenship predicated on such contestation is a form of 'citizenship unbound', and it is suggested that this is one means of identifying an adequate normative form for EU citizenship which suffers from neither the particularism of a restricted statist conception of citizenship *à la* David Miller,[33] nor the universalism and lack of specificity of global or cosmopolitan citizenship (e.g. the work of Andrew Linklater[34]). Above all, it incorporates the vital insight that contrary to studies such as those by Michael Mann[35] or Bryan Turner[36] which concentrate on 'moments' of state formation or constitutionalisation, the evolution of citizenship should be seen in terms of 'process':

> 'citizenship did not arrive at one moment for all people; rather different groups gained different aspects of this in different periods'.[37]

Aside from the fluidity of the categories of membership at any given moment in history, the contestation of constituency itself is also an effective reminder of the deep-rooted contestability which resides within each and every theory, concept or account of citizenship.

We reach now the core of this paper's presentation of an alternative non-formalist and non-linear account of membership. As Bańkowski and Christodoulidis, Kostakopoulou and Wiener have all shown in different ways, it is the issues of participation and access emerging from the conjunction of membership and rights which offer the key to both theory-building and empirical observation of the existing phenomena of European Union citizenship. In fact, on one reading, Bańkowski and Christodoulidis appear to go so far as to reject a notion of membership altogether. Instead, citizenship is seen – in a parallel to an understanding of European legal orders as interlocking normative orders – as a set of interlocking identities where one element can only be understood by reference to the other. They use the example of 'Scotland in Europe' and its impact upon Scottish identity to develop this point. This paper will not go so far as to deny altogether the possibility of defining membership, but will articulate instead a relational approach to membership.

---

[32] 'Citizenship Bound and Citizenship Unbound', in K. Hutchings and R. Dannreuther (eds.), *Cosmopolitan Citizenship*, Basingstoke: Macmillan, (1999).

[33] D. Miller, *On Nationality*, Oxford: Clarendon Press, 1995.

[34] E.g. 'Citizenship and Sovereignty in the Post-Westphalian State', (1996) 2 *European Journal of International Relations* 77.

[35] M. Mann, 'Ruling class strategies and citizenship', (1987) 21 *Sociology* 339.

[36] B. Turner, 'Outline of a Theory of Citizenship', (1990) 24 *Sociology* 189.

[37] S. Walby, 'Is Citizenship Gendered?', (1994) *Sociology* 379 at p. 384.

V   Identifying a new approach to membership

The first step in developing this approach involves rejecting the simple criteria-based approach to definition which Article 17(1) EC adopts. That is not to say that nationality of a Member State somehow ceases to be a necessary condition of EU citizenship. Clearly, legally this is so. But it cannot be a sufficient condition. It is also essential to find the tools to go beyond the veneer of formal equality amongst EU citizens that this statement generates. In order to develop an alternative and non-criteria-based definition of membership, we must ask a number of additional questions about membership beyond the 'who?' and the 'what?'. These questions and the answers which are given reveal multiple and not always internally consistent outcomes. We are challenged to determine 'how did an individual or group of individuals become members?' (i.e. the process issue), 'why are some people members and not others?' (i.e. the explication of the criteria of membership), 'what does it mean to be a member?' (i.e. rights *and* responsibilities) and 'to what extent are there direct links between the acquisition of membership and those consequential benefits?' (i.e. the relational and negotiated nature of membership). Behind these questions are further vital qualitative enquiries: are some people 'better' citizens than others (e.g. because of access to political processes or even - to be flippant for a moment - because they have taken advantage of EU free movement rights or buy more 'European' goods)? As this paper seeks to show both theoretically and empirically, there are constant interactions between the 'meaning' of EU citizenship (what does it offer the EU and the body of putative citizens? does it have a crucial legitimating function in terms of democracy and governance? how far does or should it go in replacing or supplementing national citizenships?) and the ever evolving (at least in terms of political and economic sophistication if not in geo-political range) community of members. A rather similar idea is suggested by Bauböck when he claims that

> 'the dynamic of citizenship results from the cross-application of norms so that membership becomes more inclusive by extending rights, and rights become instrumental for securing equal membership.'[38]

On this basis one might suggest a useful working definition of membership: 'the ongoing process of constructing the community of Union citizens as an open, democratic, just and equal society'.

Second, we require appropriate methods of study which allow us to apply and elaborate this reformed definition in an empirical context. In this context, the study of the case law of the Court of Justice has been chosen as a means of re-constructing a relational understanding of the membership element of Union citizenship. Case law offers an historically-sensitive tool of analysis: the acquisition (and indeed loss) of citizenship is a long term temporal relation and it affects different groups and different individuals in different socio-economic circumstances very differently, often as a function of struggles for social change. Law has frequently been one such site of struggle in relation to social change, and it is therefore possible to link the ebbs and flows of a right such as that of equality in the case law of the Court of Justice to evolving social concepts of membership and hence to a constructive understanding of Union citizenship in general. In particular, to give substance to the often amorphous

---

[38] R. Bauböck, *Transnational Citizenship: Membership and Rights in International Migration*, Aldershot: Edward Elgar, 1994, at p. 207.

concept of 'equality', courts in general and the Court of Justice in particular have used more precisely formulated legal concepts such as non-discrimination, especially in the Aristotelian guise of 'treating like things alike and unlike things differently'. Yet the concepts of 'equality' and 'non-discrimination' used in the judicial context have not always remained steady.[39]

Moreover, as a site of social change, law – and the judicial process in particular – acquires a particular meaning in the context of European Union integration, since in that context social change has also necessarily implicated processes of political, economic and legal integration and disintegration.[40] The contestation of equality before the Court of Justice, therefore, not only raises the questions about rights, duties and relationships which it would raise in a national judicial context, but also a set of questions about the *locus* of political and legal power. From where do the rights emanate? The national or the EU legal order? And what 'state' power is restricting or upholding those rights?

Combining these questions of definition and methodology, in Section VI, I develop a case study which addresses specifically the issue of 'equality', and leaves aside the other elements of openness, democracy and justice. Justice implies a normative project which this paper eschews. The issue of openness demands a perspective upon the self/other and citizen/alien distinction, and the question of democracy demands that we look carefully at the political rights of Union citizens. What is their capacity to form and be formed by a political community which is itself an ongoing and dynamic process of interaction between government, the governed and those who govern? Yet while, in many ways, political rights continue to mark out sharply the 'we' from the 'they' at the boundaries of the polity (especially in relation to the franchise which is still overwhelmingly granted at national level on the basis of citizenship not residence), *within* the polity the question of membership turns more towards the question of social rights and equality. Do all citizens in practice enjoy full membership? Is the formal enjoyment of the status of citizenship undermined by exclusion in practice from enjoyment of the benefits which are distributed in the name of the polity? In this context, the existence of rights guaranteed by law and problems of access to judicial mechanisms of protection are crucial. Hence, it is possible and moreover useful to tease out the implications of the dynamic notion of membership adopted here in the context of the evolution of the case law of the Court of Justice specifically on the question of rights. In that context, the focus is not on the question of the *content* of those rights, so much as the questions: 'to whom are they already ascribed?' and 'who else claims them and how?'. It may in fact sometimes be less with individuals that the site of struggle is located, than with groups and social movements. In part, the case study is concerned with the articulation of rights claims in the context of the politics of identity. The EU has offered an interesting forum within which rights-claims can be formulated, since it has become strongly attached – since the early years of the evolving legal order – to a form of constitutionalism which is highly rights-based. But if one goes beyond the veneer of the constitutionalisation of the Treaty – namely that the Treaty and secondary legislation can give rise to rights which individuals may rely

---

[39] C. Barnard, 'The principle of equality in the Community context: *P, Grant, Kalanke* and *Marschall*: four uneasy bedfellows?', (1998) 57 *CLJ* 352; G. More, '"Equal Treatment" of the Sexes in European Community Law: What does "Equal" Mean?', (1993) 1 *Feminist Legal Studies* 45.

[40] K. Armstrong, 'Legal Integration: Theorizing the Legal Dimension of European Integration', (1998) 36 *Journal of Common Market Studies* 155; J. Shaw, 'European Union Legal Studies in Crisis?', (1996) 16 *Oxford Journal of Legal Studies* 231.

upon in national courts – the precise allocation of public goods on the basis of these rights is deserving of closer attention.

Social rights encompass a wide range of different matters. Some are close to classic civil liberties, such as the right to sex equality especially in its more formal manifestations. But others are closer to the entitlements characteristic of the modern welfare state, such as the rights to education, basic needs, health care, etc. In relation to these, of course, the Community has limited competence in the sense of its ability to grant or withhold such entitlements in relation to individuals or groups. But it can force the Member States to accord those rights which they do grant to a wider range of persons, in other words to make the relevant community of concern and engagement in relation to social rights *all* EU citizens and not just citizens or nationals of any given Member State. Likewise, the right to substantive sex equality – the right to benefit from measures intended to correct the effects of *past* inequalities – is further away from the liberal promise of formal equality and the *leitmotiv* of protection from state interference which structures the idea of civil rights. In addition to these two well recognised categories of rights, also to be found within the EU legal order are rights which many German scholars have termed '*derivative Leistungspflichten*'.[41] These 'derived' rights constitute a halfway house between civil liberties and social rights; for example, the right to non-discrimination on grounds of nationality, which is in itself a classic civil liberty, represents the formal basis for the acquisition of welfare and social rights by migrant EU citizens in other Member States.

Although this paper uses concepts of social rights as a frame of reference, and especially the manner in which they can be translated into legal claims in the EU context through the means of *derivative Leistungspflichten*, this should not be taken to suggest that social rights are unproblematic.[42] It does not deny that there are problems with attempts to distribute public goods through the legal structures of 'rights claims', or that difficult issues are raised by the allocation of the burdens, duties and costs to social groups and individuals as well as to the state, which are the converse side of successful rights claims. In the case of EU social rights those burdens typically fall upon the Member States or upon other individuals such as employers. They rarely if ever fall upon the non-state public body which provides the legal system which generates those claims, the EU itself. Hence rights talk for the EU is 'cheap talk', and may in fact be calculated to undermine a sense of a community of fate between EU citizens from different Member States because of perceived unfairnesses in access to public goods. The interaction with the principles of majoritarianism and democratic politics may also undermine the nature of social rights – but that claim has to be tempered in the context of the EU which has no meaningful system of majoritarianism

---

[41] This is an idea developed in the context of constitutionally protected rights under German law; see B. Pieroth and B. Schlink, *Grundrechte-Staatsrecht II*, Heidelberg: Müller Juristischer Verlag, 10th edition, 1994, p. 20 *et seq.* Gersdorf applies the idea in discussing the evolution of fundamental rights protection within EC law beyond the classic civil liberties: H. Gersdorf, 'Funktionen der Gemeinschaftsgrundrechte im Lichte des Solange II-Beschlusses des Bundesverfassungsgerichts', *Archiv des öffentlichen Rechts* 1994, Vol. 119, p400. See also R. Alexy, *Theorie der Grundrechte*, Frankfurt/Main: Suhrkamp Verlag, 3rd Edition, 1996, p. 391. I owe these points to Sybilla Fries.

[42] For more details on problems of social rights and social citizenship in the EU see Shaw, 'Citizenship of the Union', above n. 4 at pp. 329-340 and J. Shaw, 'Social Policy ad Citizenship in the European Union', Paper presented to a panel on *Legal and Political Perspectives on the Governance of the Social Dimension*, at the European Community Studies Association Biennial International Conference: Seattle, USA, June 1997.

and a very weak concept of democracy in relation to legislative decision-making. However, if we are prepared to accept at least the basic precepts underlying criticisms of liberal approaches to citizenship, which doubt the veracity of claims to universalism and universal protection of the individual inherent in liberalism, then there must be some foundation to the intuition that in the allocation of public goods some groups do fare badly.[43] In our case, we shall examine only non-economic migrants within the EU, women in employment and gays, lesbians and transsexuals.

VI   Individuals, groups, and their rights in the EU: a case study

The objective behind this case study is not to test a hypothesis, but to tease out more empirical detail in relation to the account presented in the earlier sections of the paper, to assist its refinement as a theoretically informed understanding of EU citizenship as more than a formal legal concept. In each part of the case study, I shall discuss a number of Court of Justice cases, highlighting the way in which the individuals and groups are constructed and re-constructed under EC law and identifying the different groups and interests involved (e.g. social movements, national legislatures, national administrations, other institutions). It uses developments in relation to criteria of inclusion and exclusion where the boundaries of the 'Community' are constantly contested and negotiated as a function of the legal concepts of discrimination and equal treatment. In EC law, discrimination and equal treatment are pervasive tools of legal analysis.[44] They are generally applied with a view to securing one or more underlying policy objectives of the EU polity in relation to integration. In observing shifts in the status of three marginal categories under EC law through the ascription and denial of rights, we can learn more about how those groups are defined.

The case study charts changes in the ascription of rights in relation to a number of aspects of social citizenship. These changes result from variety of causes: changes in the EU's own constitutional frame, interactions between national and EU citizenships, the interlocking normative orders of EC law and national law, the granting of new legislative responsibilities to the EU's own political institutions, developments in national law and politics, and the evolution of distinctive politics of identity and the politics of welfare within the EU and its Member States. In each case, different institutions, actors, interests and structures are implicated by the rights claims made and the adjudications reached. In each case, the ebbs and flows of Court of Justice case law have carried the individuals and groups concerned closer to or further away from the enjoyment of 'full membership' as equal members of the society in which they live their lives. The fact that this occurs through the medium of EC law as well as (or as an alternative to: it may vary from case to case) national law, is not mere historical accident, but evidence of the emergence of Union citizenship as a relevant political and socio-economic category. This is the case notwithstanding the fact that only the first part of the case study bears a strong formal link to the publicly prominent part of Union citizenship, namely the internal migration or free movement

---

[43] J.H. Ely, *Democracy and Distrust: A Theory of Judicial Review*, Cambridge, MA: Harvard University Press, 1980, p. 164.

[44] G. de Búrca, 'The Role of Equality in European Community Law', in A. Dashwood and S. O'Leary (eds.), *The Principle of Equal Treatment in EC Law*, London: Sweet and Maxwell, 1997; G. More, 'The Principle of Equal Treatment: From Market Unifier to Fundamental Right?', in G. de Búrca and P. Craig (eds.), *European Union Law: An Evolutionary Perspective*, Oxford: Oxford University Press (1999); Barnard, above n. 39.

aspect. This indeed reinforces the argument that many of the most important distinctions in relation to Union citizenship arise in situations apparently *internal* to the Member States. Accordingly, the other instances of social rights development through case law charted in this paper are no less constitutive of (or evidence of the lack of) social citizenship Union-style.

A   Non-economic migrants [45]

EC law has traditionally drawn relatively rigid distinctions between economically active categories of migrants (and their dependent family members) protected by the Treaty's core provisions and long-established secondary legislation, and those who fall into more marginal categories such as tourists, students, pensioners and the independently wealthy. These distinctions give rise to layers of entitlement.[46] That division in entitlements has been instrumentalised by a distinction between the *lex specialis* of Articles 39-42, 43 and 49 EC, in tandem with important implementing legislation such as Regulations 1612/68 and 1408/71 and the *lex generalis* of Article 12 EC. This provision establishes the general and residual right to non-discrimination on grounds of nationality and the Court has held it to be directly effective on a number of occasions[47] although its precise scope remains unclear. Thus, for example, the existence of differing layers of entitlement based on whether the claimant is economically active or not is particularly clear in relation to vocational training rights: the migrant worker and his or her children are entitled not only to equality in the conditions of educational access (e.g. the same fees and grants towards fees as nationals), but also to equal access to grants and/or preferential loans given to domestic students. They will rely upon provisions such as Articles 7(2) and 12 of Regulation 1612/68. Migrant students with no other connection with the host Member State must rely upon Article 12, read in conjunction with Article 150 EC (or, in earlier years, Article 128 EEC) and have been restricted only to the former group of rights.[48]

But above all, it has long appeared that those who were entirely dependent upon the public purse for support could not rely upon free movement rights such as the right of entry and residence since they fell outside both the Treaty provisions and the three residence directives of 1990/1993 on the free movement and residence rights of those of independent means, retired persons, and students.[49] In the latter cases, the host Member State has been empowered to look for those wanting free movement rights to have adequate sickness insurance and to be able to show that they will not become a burden upon the state with sufficient resources to maintain themselves above the basic social assistance level in the host state. It appeared moreover that those dependent on welfare could not rely upon the right to non-discrimination on grounds of nationality

---

[45] This section of the paper draws heavily upon S. Fries and J. Shaw, 'Citizenship of the Union: First Steps in the Court of Justice', (1998) 4 *European Public Law* 533.

[46] See Ackers, above n. 25.

[47] E.g. Cases C-92 & 326/92 *Phil Collins and Others* [1993] ECR I-5145; see generally S. O'Leary, 'The Principle of Equal Treatment on Grounds of Nationality in Article 6 EC. A lucrative source of rights for Member State nationals?', in Dashwood and O'Leary, above n. 44.

[48] See for example the contrast between Case 9/74 *Casangrande* v. *Landeshauptstadt München* [1974] ECR 773 (child of a migrant worker) and Case 197/86 *Brown* v. *Secretary of State for Scotland* [1988] ECR 3205; T. Hervey, *European Social Law and Policy*, London/New York: Longman, 1998, Ch. 6.

[49] Council Directives 90/364, 90/365, and 93/96; OJ 1990 L180/26 and 28; OJ 1993 L317/59.

in order to gain access to benefits, unless they were the family members of migrant workers or the self employed, or were retired migrant workers/self employed persons themselves. It had always been assumed, for example, that EC law had set its face against allowing or condoning 'welfare tourism' – i.e. equal access to welfare benefits in all Member States regardless of nationality – in the name of 'free movement'. This appears to be the logic of the case of *Lebon* in which the Court stated that the child of a migrant worker who was over 21 years and no longer dependent, and who did not herself qualify as a migrant worker, fell outside the scope of protection of the equal treatment principle as regards welfare entitlements even though she definitely had a right of residence under EC law, acquired through her father who was a retired migrant worker.[50] It has also been assumed since the case of *Antonissen* that, while workseekers might have a limited right of residence and are entitled to equal treatment in relation to access to employment, they have no benefit rights as such apart from those available under particular rules governing unemployment coordinated by Regulation 1408/71.[51]

The Court's recent judgment in *Martínez Sala*[52] opens an important new chapter in the development of Union citizenship in the specific context of intra-Community migration. The Court held that a Spanish national who was longterm resident in Germany – although on what precise basis her lawful residence in that country could be deduced was not entirely clear – could rely upon the non-discrimination principle in Article 12 EC as the basis for claiming equal access to a Germany child-raising benefit for her new born child. She could not be obliged to produce a residence permit, when nationals merely had to prove that they were permanently settled in Germany. The Court concluded in effect that it would make no difference to her entitlement whether or not she might eventually be found by the national court to be either a worker[53] or an 'employed person' under Community social security regulations.[54] She could claim equality of treatment, the Court found, even if she was solely dependent upon welfare and could bring herself within the personal scope of Community law by no other means than that she is a Union citizen resident in another Member State. The only material condition was that the benefit which she claimed must fall within the scope of Community law. The Court of Justice found that it was within that scope using its own earlier interpretation of a legislative measure which had expressly conferred social advantages on migrants and their families (Article 7(2) of Regulation 1612/68). Despite that apparent legislative limitation, it would now appear after the Court's reinterpretation of the intersection of the material and personal scope of Community law, in combination with the non-discrimination principle, that something close to universal right of access to all manner of welfare benefits for all those who are Union citizens and who are lawfully resident in a Member State has now taken root in EC law.

---

[50] Case 316/85 *Lebon* [1987] ECR 2811.

[51] Case C-292/89 *Antonissen* [1991] ECR I-745.

[52] Case C-85/96 *Martínez Sala* v. *Freistaat Bayern* [1998] ECR I-2691.

[53] This would be on the grounds that she had worked in the past, although hardly at all for more than 10 years since when she had been drawing social welfare.

[54] Under German social welfare rules the claiming of benefits automatically protects the recipient with sickness insurance, thus bringing her under the Community social security coordination regulations as a person covered in respect of one of the risks included in the governing Regulation 1408/71; see generally Hervey, above n. 48, Ch. 5.

There has undoubtedly been a partial disintegration of the policy logic behind the distinctions drawn between different categories of Union citizen, and this will have very serious repercussions for the Member States. In principle, the Member States can (so far at least) still rely upon their immigration sovereignty in order to cause the removal from their territory of those unable to support themselves (i.e. by focusing on the criterion of lawful residence, because strictly speaking many of those who are dependent upon welfare will not have a residence right under EC law). However, there are practical reasons why many Member States do not seek to avail themselves of this opportunity. Any procedures for removing those on welfare would be long, cumbersome and costly, and could easily be circumvented by the target obtaining the offer of even part-time below-subsistence-level employment which would be sufficient to qualify her instantly as a 'worker' under EC law.[55] As a matter of EC law, the procedures would also have to incorporate an appeals process. They might also give rise to adverse publicity and tensions between the Member States especially if they involved vulnerable categories such as single parents with young children. In any event, such persons may have residence rights under national or even international law (for example, the European Convention on medical and social assistance restricts the possibilities for contracting parties to remove foreigners on welfare from their territory *solely* because they are on welfare). But as a supplement to these restrictions, it would now appear that the welfare sovereignty of the Member States has been severely encroached upon in the name of Union citizenship by the *Martínez Sala* judgment, which breaks down the stark distinction hitherto drawn between economically active and inactive migrants. Significantly, this has occurred with the Court appearing to embrace ever more enthusiastically one of the so-called *derivative Leistungspflichten*, in the shape of the universalisation of Article 12 EC.[56]

In asserting the link between migration and citizenship along these lines, the Court is coming close to the approach of the US Supreme Court in its 'interstate travel' jurisprudence where it drew the link between citizenship and the acquisition of certain central welfare rights within the different States. In *Shapiro* v. *Thompson*,[57] the Court applied a strict standard of scrutiny to the constitutionality of State statutes restricting the welfare rights of new residents by subjecting them to qualifying residence periods. This is seen as a necessary element of the right to travel interstate – so basic within the US constitutional system that it is not specifically included in the US Constitution;[58] instead it is regarded as implicit. Implicit exactly where is never clear: it may be in provisions such as the Privileges and Immunities Clause of Article IV, it may be an incident of national citizenship, or indeed it might derive from the Interstate Commerce Clause. More recent case law has read the right to travel into either the (substantive) Due Process Clause or the Equal Protection Clause, allowing the Court to invalidate indirect burdens which 'penalize' travel such as restrictions on welfare rights, or residence requirements imposed as a condition of receiving nonemergency

---

[55] This is because of the Court's broad interpretation of what is a 'worker' for the purposes of Article 48 [39] EC: see for example Case 139/85 *Kempf* v. *Staatsecretaris van Justitie* [1986] ECR 1035.

[56] See above n. 41. This is particularly apparent in the Opinions of Advocate General Jacobs; see, most recently, Opinion of March 19 1998 in Case C-274/96 *Criminal Proceedings against Bickel and Franz*, [1998] ECR I-7637.

[57] 394 U.S. 618 (1969).

[58] Although it was included in Article IV of the Articles of Confederation: 'the people of each State shall have free ingress and regress to and from any other State . . .'

hospitalization or medical care at the expense of a public authority.[59] In such cases, the Court has concluded that the States have not proferred sufficiently compelling interests for burdening the right to travel by restricting basic 'necessities' of life. The case law has, from time to time, been heavily criticised especially for the uncertainty it gives rise to because of the different bases on which the cases have been decided. Moreover, the underlying protective doctrine in *Shapiro* v. *Thompson* has been accused of promoting a 'race to the bottom' amongst the States in the context welfare provision,[60] when read against the background of radical Federal level reforms in the framework of welfare, the cutting of programmes such as Aid to Families with Dependent Children under President Clinton's second-term campaign pledge to 'end welfare as we know it', and the decentralization of many responsibilities to the states.[61]

The parallel is limited, of course, because the European Union has never known, and is never likely to know, the type of federal-level welfare responsibilities which emerged in the United States primarily as one of the progeny of the New Deal. The raising of revenue for the welfare state, and its distribution amongst those with entitlements and needs, is a matter for the Member States, with the EU limited in policy terms to coordinating functions in relation to migrants and the encouragement of convergence. However, this understates the vital constitutive role of the equal treatment guarantee as it currently operates in EC law, which profoundly influences the instrumentalisation of both the immigration and employment/social/welfare elements of the EU's undoubtedly 'fundamental' free movement rights. But that equal treatment guarantee is not a universal guarantee of equal protection: rather it is strictly limited to the scope of the EU's concerns, because it protects only against discrimination *on grounds of Community nationality*. Those who are third country nationals have no such non-discrimination guarantee.

If revenue for welfare state distribution is limited – and it will be increasingly limited not only by the changing demographics of the Member States but also as a result of the disciplines of monetary union – then the increasingly broad-based application of this non-discrimination principle will lead to two possible consequences. Either it will lead to a restructuring of the accepted 'community of concern and engagement' in relation to welfare because the right to migrate and the consequent burdens which might then fall upon public authorities will be regarded as a normal incident of EU citizenship, just as many argue that the right to travel and the consequences including those in relation to public goods which flow from that is an incident of US national citizenship. That needs to be accompanied by mechanisms for transfer payments in appropriate circumstances. Alternatively, it may lead to a radical rethink of the *scope* of welfare entitlements by the Member States. Notwithstanding rhetorical commitments in the Preamble to the EC Treaty and Article 2 EC to higher standards of living and economic and social cohesion, nothing in the equal treatment principle will be able to arrest an inexorable race to the bottom. Indeed, it is possible the Member States have recently written for themselves the ideal justification for such a development by adding the new sentence to Article 17 EC at the Amsterdam

---

[59] *Memorial Hospital* v. *Maricopa County* 415 U.S. 250 (1974).

[66] See T. Zubler, 'The Right to Migrate and Welfare Reform: Time for *Shapiro* v. *Thompson* to take a Hike', (1997) 31 *Valparaiso University Law Review* 893.

[61] The Personal Responsibility and Work Opportunity Reconciliation Act 1996. On how this policy change took root in the US, see T. Banchoff, 'Historical Institutionalism and Welfare Reform in the United States', Centre for European Studies, Harvard University, Seminar on State and Capitalism since 1800, May 19 1998.

Intergovernmental Conference to the effect that 'Citizenship of the Union shall complement and not replace national citizenship.' This reassertion of national sovereignty in relation to citizenship could justify a parallel reassertion of national welfare sovereignty.

B   Sex equality and the status of affirmative action

In two recent cases, the Court of Justice has had to respond to one of the most pressing dilemmas of the equality/citizenship debate: the possibilities of affirmative action on behalf of groups suffering longterm disadvantage in the labour market. In the EU context, this has so far been limited to a debate about affirmative action for women workers. This debate is structured by two key factors: the nature of the norms under consideration and the challenge of 'equality' in the workplace in the context of a multi-level system of governance involving interactions between power residing at the regional, national and supranational levels.

Until the agreement upon the Treaty of Amsterdam – on which more later – the relevant legal framework was limited to a directive guaranteeing equal treatment on grounds of sex in matters of employment.[62] Thus far, the only Treaty-based guarantee of sex equality has been what was, hitherto Article 119 EC, which provides for equal pay, and is therefore largely irrelevant to the affirmative action debate so far as it pertains to access to employment, training and promotion. However, of more general relevance is Article 2(4) of the Equal Treatment Directive which provides that the Directive shall be 'without prejudice to measures which promote equal opportunity for men and women, in particular by removing existing inequalities which affect women's opportunities.' The 'federal' complexity results from the interaction between the EU-level guarantee of equality contained in the Equal Treatment Directive, read in the light of this saving clause, and possible conflicts with national and regional legislative frameworks which seek to establish, for example, quota systems to promote women's employment in areas where they have been underrepresented. These are particularly common in the Germany, where each of the *Länder* has some form of legislative framework for using the *Land* public service as a laboratory for equal opportunities.[63] The emerging conflict seems to be between programmes for substantive equality agreed on a majoritarian basis at national or regional level, and what has hitherto been a rather formal guarantee of sex equality operating at EU level.

From the perspective of feminists and others campaigning for affirmative action programmes, the worst case scenario appeared to be happening when the Court of Justice was faced with its first challenge by a disappointed man to the refusal of appointment under the Bremen *Land* positive action law. The applicant in *Kalanke* argued that his (EC) right to equality was infringed when he and a female co-worker applied for a promotion to the post of section manager within the public service of the City of Bremen.[64] A tiebreak situation emerged, because it was decided that the two applicants were equally qualified for the post, and accordingly the female applicant was given preference in accordance with the Bremen law. This provided that 'in the

---

[62] Directive 76/207 OJ 1976 L39/40.

[63] C. Barnard and T. Hervey, 'Softening the approach to quotas: Positive action after *Marschall*', (1998) 20 *Journal of Social Welfare and Family Law* 333; D. Schiek, 'Sex Equality Law after Kalanke and Marschall,' (1998) 4 *European Law Journal* 148.

[64] Case C-450/93 *Kalanke* v. *Freie Hansestadt Bremen* [1995] ECR I-3051.

case of an assignment to a position in a higher pay, remuneration and salary bracket, women who have the same qualifications as men applying for the same post are to be given priority if they are underrepresented.' This was a radical variant of the tiebreak and preference rule, firstly because underrepresentation was defined at 50 per cent or less and secondly, because it did not contain an *explicit* hardship clause allowing the balance to be tipped back in favour of men where circumstances required this.

In answer to questions posed by the national court about the relationship between this rule and the EC equal treatment guarantee, the Court found that applying the strict quota rule would be unlawful discrimination against the man because it was incompatible with the EC guarantee of equal treatment. It reached this conclusion notwithstanding the strong majoritarian and (national) constitutional legitimacy of the measure (agreed within regional and national legislatures, accepted as lawful under the German constitution). The Court was unable – or unwilling – to bring the Bremen clause within the scope of the limited Article 2(4) exception for equal opportunity measures.

There was a strong negative reaction to the Court's judgment in Germany (and indeed elsewhere[65]) – where affirmative action measures have become very much an accepted part of equal opportunity policies, and many public and private interests and groups including local and regional women's bureaux, trades unions, and other groups have invested considerable energy in attempts to enshrine positive action into national and regional laws. The Court's ruling was felt to be insufficiently respecting of national and regional policy choices, and difficult to reconcile with the principle of subsidiarity (Article 5 EC) which should precisely protect the autonomy in such matters of sub-units of the European Union. Measures were proposed to change the Equal Treatment Directive to ensure that at least the softer variants of national affirmative action programmes were safe from the scrutiny of the Court of Justice (perceived now to be a negative influence, after so many years of being held up as the great hope of liberal rights-based feminism).[66] More dramatically, agreement was reached in the Amsterdam Intergovernmental Conference to amend the Treaties themselves to protect equal opportunities measures. A new paragraph 4 was added to what is now Article 141, extending its reach into equal treatment generally, and apparently elevating the status of equality of result or outcome, at the expense of 'mere' equality of opportunity:

'With a view to ensuring full equality in practice between men and women in working life, the principle of equal treatment shall not prevent any Member State from maintaining or adopting measures providing for specific advantages in order to make it easier for the underrepresented sex to pursue a vocational activity or to prevent or compensate for disadvantages in professional careers.'

In a Declaration attached to the EC Treaty, the Conference directed the Member States in taking such positive action measures to 'aim at improving the situation of

---

[65] The academic comment was predominantly negative: for examples, see E. Szyszczak, 'Positive Action after *Kalanke*', (1996) 59 *Modern Law Review* 876, S. Prechal, 'Case note on Case C-450/93 *Kalanke* v. *Freie Hansestadt Bremen*,' (1996) 33 *Common Market Law Review* 1245, S. Moore, 'Nothing Positive from the Court of Justice,' (1996) 21 *European Law Review* 156, H. Fenwick, 'Perpetuating Inequality in the Name of Equal Treatment', (1996) 18 *Journal of Social Welfare and Family Law* 263. In an interesting example of academic-judicial interaction, Advocate General Jacobs' Opinion in *Marschall* is heavily laced with negative reactions to those criticisms by academic feminists.
[66] Proposal for a Council Directive amending Directive 76/207 COM(96) 93; OJ 1996 C179/8.

women in working life.' These new developments are backed up by a more general change, namely the inclusion of a new paragraph 2 in Article 3 [3] EC which lists the activities of the Community effectively mainstreaming gender equality policies:

> 'In all the activities referred to in this Article, the Community shall aim to eliminate inequalities, and to promote equality, between men and women.'

Of course, the 'women's lobby' is noticeably more organised and more closely keyed into the decision-making centres at national and supranational levels than almost any other social movement within the EU.[67] Certainly, it demonstrated an enviable capacity to translate its objections to the *Kalanke* judgment (and one should note, of course, the extent to which the debate on affirmative action has divided rather than unified feminist and anti-racist movements in the United States) into concrete proposals then adopted at the highest level in the EU.[68] Perhaps it was in response to these types of reactions that when the Court was faced shortly after the Amsterdam agreement with another affirmative action case – but this time involving the more common variant of affirmative action legislation which included a hardship clause to protect the interests of men finding themselves in specific problematic circumstances – it concluded that such a measure *did not* conflict with the EC guarantee of equal treatment. Thus, in contrast to the negatively worded Opinion of Advocate General Jacobs in the *Marschall* case, the Court's rhetoric in its judgment was markedly changed from the formalism of *Kalanke*. It reminded its readers that:

> '. . . even where male and female candidates are equally qualified, male candidates tend to be promoted in preference to female candidates particularly because of prejudices and stereotypes concerning the role and capacities of women in working life and the fear, for example, that women will interrupt their careers more frequently, that owing to household and family duties they will be less flexible in their working hours, or that they will be absent from work more frequently because of pregnancy, childbirth and breastfeeding.
>
> For these reasons, the mere fact that a male candidate and a female candidate are equally qualified does not mean that they have the same chance.'[69]

So, in deference to a sense of the exclusion of female citizens from the full enjoyment of membership within the polity, the Court concluded in favour of a *restriction* in the scope and reach of EC law and the EC constitutional guarantee of formal equality. It did not transmute that guarantee at EU level into a guarantee of substantive equality. Rather, it pulled back the reach of EC law, in order to allow *German* women (or, better, women employed in Germany) to enjoy the benefit of their struggles for equality at *national* and *regional* level and therefore their enjoyment of the benefits of membership

---

[67] On the many successes in relation to the politics of women's rights, see generally C. Hoskyns, *Integrating Gender. Women, Law and Politics in the European Union*, London: Verso, 1996.

[68] U. Liebert, 'Gender politics in the European Union: the return of the public', paper presented to the 1998 Annual Meeting of the American Political Science Association, Boston, September 1998, identifies lobby politics of one of a number of linked answers to the puzzle of why gender policies should have been advanced in the Treaty of Amsterdam. She cites also the influence of small Nordic states who placed this issue on their IGC agenda, the responsiveness of the Commission as a strategic actor to changes in public opinion which include approval of equal opportunities policies alongside a growing gender gap in approval ratings for the EU, the role of the European Parliament and more general cultural changes in values and attitudes towards gender and equality issues. See also S. Mazey, 'The European Union and women's rights: from the Europeanization of national agendas to the nationalization of a European agenda?', (1998) 5 *Journal of European Public Policy* 131.

[69] Case C-409/95 *Marschall* v. *Land Nordrhein-Westfalen* [1997] ECR I-6363 at paras. 29-30.

at that level. The *Marschall* case, therefore, provides nothing positive in the sense of delivering the promise of equality through EU citizenship for those arguing in favour of affirmative action in *other* Member States, although together with *Kalanke* the saga of positive action in the Court of Justice must be seen as an indirect contributor to the strengthening of a concept of substantive equality in the EC Treaty through the Amsterdam Intergovernmental Conference.[70] This presents an interesting contrast to the Court's direct approach to citizenship in *Martínez Sala* which immediately implicates the welfare systems of every Member State in the process of integration through judicial interpretation.

C   Sex, sexual orientation and transsexualism: the evolving concept of 'discrimination'

The final part of the case study addresses attempts made, particularly by interest groups arguing for the extension of equality guarantees to cover sexual orientation discrimination, to extend the reach of EC *sex* equality law. In the case of *P* v. *S and Cornwall County Council*,[71] the Court accepted an argument derived from its earlier case law on pregnancy discrimination to the effect that discrimination against a male to female transsexual was discrimination based 'essentially if not exclusively, on the sex of the person concerned.' Having undergone gender reassignment, P was dismissed from her post in Cornwall County Council. She was found to have been discriminated against in comparison with a person of the sex P was deemed by the authorities still to belong to (i.e. a male). The judgment contains strong language on such discrimination, saying that 'to tolerate such discrimination would be tantamount, as regards such a person, to a failure to respect the dignity and freedom to which he or she is entitled, and which the Court has a duty to safeguard.'

Unsurprisingly, in view of such language, some commentators suggested that this marked the emergence of a general constitutional principle of equality in EC law, based on essential moral and ethical groundrules about the treatment of one person by another.[72] Might such a principle then give rise to the inclusion of sexual orientation discrimination within the ambit of EC sex equality law? In fact, this liberal promise was very shortlived. The next attempt to rely upon *P* v. *S* came in a case which did indeed seek to extend sex equality protection to cover sexual orientation discrimination. The applicant in *Grant* was a lesbian employee of a railway company in the United Kingdom, who had been denied travel benefits for her same sex partner, where such benefits had been given to her predecessor in the job, a man with an opposite sex partner.[73] The Court refused to accept the logic of a 'but for' test ('but for' her sex, Grant would not have been discriminated against); instead it compared her situation to that of a man with a same-sex partner. He too would have been denied benefits, and there was nothing in that denial which fell within the scope of EC law as presently constituted. Pointing to the agreement, in the Treaty of Amsterdam, of a new legislative power giving the Community legislature the competence to enact measures to combat discrimination based, *inter alia*, on sexual orientation (Article 13 EC), the Court declined to extend its judicial role in this respect to offer an inclusionary jurisprudence. It recognised, perhaps, that at this stage the extension of Community

---

[70] See Barnard, above n. 39 at p. 371.

[71] Case C-13/94 [1996] ECR I-2143.

[72] C. Barnard, '*P* v. *S*: Kite Flying or a New Constitutional Approach?', in Dashwood and O'Leary, above n. 44.

[73] Case C-249/96 *Grant* v. *South West Trains Ltd* [1998] ECR I-621.

sex discrimination law to cover sexual orientation would not receive the unanimous approval of the Member States.[74] In so doing, it went against the Opinion of Advocate General Elmer, who applied the *P* v. *S* reasoning of 'essentially but not exclusively based on sex' to the sexual orientation question as well.

The reason for attempting to change the scope of EC sex equality law by including sexual orientation essentially derives from questions of legal strategy pursued by interest groups mobilising around the issue of sexual orientation and campaigning for equality and human rights. Grant's case was supported by Stonewall, a UK organisation which campaigns for precisely these goals on behalf of gays and lesbians; it does so essentially within the confines of conventional political and legal processes. The use of activist resources for strategies of rights-based equality has always been controversial within organisations representing oppressed or minority groups and their members. Sometimes – wrongly – these debates are conflated with a simple opposition between being 'pro-rights' or 'anti-rights'. In fact, as Carl Stychin reminds us, 'rights struggles around equality are both complex and multifaceted'[75] – testimony to the sophistication of arguments around both 'equality' and 'rights' themselves. Moreover, the strategy of support for 'equality through legal rights' must be regarded as all the more controversial in circumstances where, as Kenneth Armstrong points out, Grant could only win her case if her identity as a lesbian was covered in favour of focusing upon her identity as a woman.[76] The resolution of the case through the 'but for' test would not disturb or trouble a legal classificatory system which continued to hide the identities of gay and lesbian citizens, treating them primarily as a function of their sex, not their sexual orientation or sexual practices. The cost, in terms of legal strategy, then, is to accept that rights claims brought within an unchanged legal framework must result in those who bring them accepting that classificatory schemes will be applied which are the result of the logic of the law, not necessarily either the logic of recognising oppression and discrimination or the logic of a positive self-image constructed in the context of an identity politics which has driven forward both the legal and political claims of gays and lesbians. So, at the present time, gays and lesbians are excluded from the type of 'equality protection' afforded in respect of discrimination between men and women, which lends some protection to women as a disadvantaged category notwithstanding its predominantly formalist frame of analysis. In terms of the development of membership, gays and lesbians are still an 'out' category.

As to the ebbs and flows of Union citizenship, in this case the Court is explicitly pointing to the EU legislature to take up the challenge of 'who are the members?'. This may prove a more fruitful route than the judicial process has been so far. Whether this will occur, even after the new Treaty of Amsterdam has been ratified, must be a matter of considerable doubt.

D Reviewing the case study

What of the status of the emerging Union citizen in the context of these three elements of the case study? What of the reconceptualisation of membership as the ongoing and

---

[74] T. Connor, 'Community Discrimination Law: No Right to Equal Treatment in Employment in Respect of Same Sex Partner', (1998) 23 *ELRev.* 378.

[75] 'Troubling Genders', (1997) 2 *International Journal of Discrimination and the Law* 217 at p218; see also D. Herman, *Rights of Passage: Struggles for Lesbian and Gay Legal Equality*, Toronto: University of Toronto Press, 1994.

[76] Armstrong, above n. 40 at p. 166; see also K. Armstrong, 'Tales of the Community: Sexual Orientation Discrimination and EC Law', (1998) 20 *Journal of Social Welfare and Family Law* 455.

dynamic construction of community identified in the previous sections? We have used the case study to examine evidence of the interaction between the boundaries of community and the boundaries of the substantive content of citizenship. It is apparent that the situation has changed most clearly in recent times in relation to the migrating citizen, a strong transnational actor asserting his or her rights *vis-à-vis* the Member States. Here Union citizenship stands explicitly on the cusp between the classic paradigm of integration as market-making and a political future of integration as polity-formation and the construction of political and social communities.[77] To this person has been attached, by virtue of Article 17(2) EC, certain rights fundamental to the EU legal and economic order, in particular the right to non-discrimination in Article 12 EC. Membership, on this view, is seen primarily as a function of having a status in relation to the Community integration project – however marginal in economic terms. What remains incompletely defined is the nature of that integration project: market-making or polity-formation. In practical terms, the concept of non-discrimination has been enlisted as a legal instrument. The situation in relation to the non-economic migrant and Union citizenship is that *Martínez Sala* has moved the *real* boundaries of citizenship much closer to the *formal* boundaries of citizenship precisely by making non-discrimination on grounds of EU nationality and the link to EU citizenship the prime determinant of access to welfare benefits throughout the EU.

But the case study shows the continuing contrast between elements of Union citizenship which are linked to the progress of integration, and those which not so connected. The link is made between citizenship and migration and not between citizenship and equality. For, when pressed on the margins of 'equality', the Court has not shown a equal degree of sensitivity to inequalities deriving from the limits of membership as presently set, even despite the pressures brought to bear through the politics of identity and the strategic efforts of effective national and transnational social movements. It has returned certain matters to the national, regional and EU legislatures, highlighting the limits which subsidiarity and respect for the distinction between legislative and judicial roles currently and perhaps rightly places upon the possibility of harnessing the cohesive force of Union citizenship. The case study reinforces an impression of the incomplete nature of EU citizenship, operating within an incomplete legal order. It is not simply the fact that the EU has had an economic vocation, and that this has structured much of its legal and political evolution. Rather, in so far as rights claims go beyond the vocation of the single internal market, the presence of some (sex) and the absence of others (race, sexual orientation) is not always wholly capable of rational explanation and may as much be the product of historical accident.

VII   Conclusion: beyond legal formalism in EU citizenship studies

The starting point for this paper was a critique of formalism in EU citizenship studies which locates the interpretation of Union citizenship in the formal definitions and distinctions to be found in the Treaty. Going beyond legal formalism and adopting a constructivist interpretation of Union citizenship does not mean, however, abandoning legal methods or assigning a subordinate role to law in relation to politics. On the contrary, we have seen through a case study based on the work of the Court of Justice

---

[77] On this distinction see Everson, above n. 6.

the link between distinctions grounded legal concepts and principles such as 'rights' and 'equality', and the evolution of social practices such as identity politics or transnational lobbying which interact with institutional processes of polity-formation.

The thesis in this paper was not, of course, that more rights – and in particular more social rights – necessarily need to be attached to the status of Union citizen before it can be regarded as a meaningful status for those who are the body of members. Perhaps more rights will be constitutive of a stronger form of EU citizenship; perhaps not. The 'more rights' thesis is always one to be treated with caution in the context of societies which are broadly liberal and democratic in character. Moreover, critiques of rights from the feminist, anti-racist and identity politics movements have themselves landed many weighty blows on the status of rights as statements of individual or collective value in a society. The contention of this paper is narrower. It is that social rights and the development of social rights in conjunction with the identification of groups who are at present often marginalised within the EU polity are vital components of the redefined relational concept of membership as the ongoing process of constructing an open, democratic, just and equal society. In that sense, it is less about the rights than about the groups and individuals who rely upon rights and their position in relation to Union citizenship. It demonstrates that the boundaries of membership in the sense defined in this paper are constantly contested, remain unfixed and are not *a priori* established. Rights struggles are dynamic and constitutive of both individual and group identity. Their ongoing character denies the fixity of membership in the sense that no struggle through law is ever 'complete'. Moreover, like any other type of citizenship, Union citizenship is not in truth a single universal status, but actually a patchwork representing overlapping interests and identities, where genders, races, nationalities, ethnic origins, religions, sexual identities and classes, etc. intersect and cut across each other. Differences and similarities are, therefore, continually in the process of contestation and negotiation. Above all, it is the internal boundaries which emerge from this analysis – and not just external borders – which define the limits of Union citizenship.

In consequence, therefore, the paper has been less concerned with the rights themselves – although the previous section has highlighted many causes for concern in relation to the uneven development of social rights in the Union – than with what the exercise of rights claims and the judicial treatment of those claims say about the type/s of society/ies European live their lives in and how such society/ies actually relates to individuals and groups as members. It does therefore seek to contribute, at least indirectly, to an emerging debate about rights within the European Union.[78] But more specifically it presents one snapshot – or perhaps better 'moving picture'[79] – of how the shifting boundaries of EU rights, and the interaction between judicial decision-making, the changing constitutional politics of the EU, and the rights claims of individuals and groups structure membership of the EU polity. To suggest that Union citizenship represents the institution which will 'rescue' the European Union from its legitimacy deficit is both banal and naïve. It is, however, a vital component in the emerging constitutional politics of the Union as a polity-in-the-making.

---

[78] See C. Stychin, *A Nation by Rights. National Cultures, Sexual Identity Politics and the Discourse of Rights*, Philadelphia: Temple University Press, 1998; I. Ward, *The Margins of European Law*, Basingstoke: Macmillan, 1996.

[79] '[W]hat one makes of the EU depends on whether one examines a photograph or a moving picture', P. Pierson, 'The Path to Eurpoean Integration. A Historical Institutionalist Analysis', (1996) 29 *Comparative Political Studies* 123 at p. 127.

5

Beyond the *Bundesverfassungsgericht*: On the Necessary Cunning of Constitutional Reasoning

Michelle Everson

It has frequently been remarked that it seems to have been reserved to the people of this country, by their conduct and example, to decide the important question, whether societies of men are really capable or not of establishing good government from reflection and choice, or whether they are forever destined to depend for their political constitutions on accident and force.

Hamilton, *Federalist Papers*

I Introduction

With his observation that European law has distinguished itself less through its normative coherence, and more by virtue of its creation of 'a constitution without constitutionalism,'[1] one authoritative commentator has taken the long-overdue step of questioning the normative foundations of European legal evolution, thus at long last firmly placing the 'integration through law' movement in a new and highly critical light.[2]

This renewed emphasis upon constitutionalism—or the political/philosophical theories of social and private ordering underlying the law of the constitution—above formal law, thus not only heralds a possible withdrawal from the over-eager, and sometimes arrogant, substitution of juridification for politicisation which marked much of European governance in the 1980s. Rather, it is also indicative of a recent and subtle re-assessment of contemporary notions of 'good' government; a movement which has seen the rationalising concept of 'functionalism,' or outcome-driven legitimacy, heavily qualified and re-evaluated in the light of more traditional and subjective governmental/constitutional values. Accordingly, where once the judicial extrapolation of putative constitutional concepts such as 'direct effect' or 'supremacy' from the Rome Treaties was simply celebrated as triumph of legal reasoning over lack of political intent, and was deemed further, to be an exemplary instrument of 'good' administration by simple virtue of its successful operationalisation of the stated goal of European integration. Today, the measure of the constitutionality of European law is to be found, not merely in its efficient pursuit of substantive integrationist outcomes, but rather in its equal ability to secure 'good' government, both through the safeguarding of the democratic nature of the integration process and through the maintenance of on-going and universal respect for personal autonomy.

---

[1] Weiler, 'Does Europe Need a Constitution,' (1995) 1:3 *ELJ* 259.

[2] Interestingly, this represents an attack—or better formulated a re-assessment—from within, for the most powerful and detailed exposition of the movement's work, M. Cappalletti/M. Secombe and J.H.H. Weiler (eds), *Integration Through Law* (1986 De Gruyter).

Undoubtedly prompted by the political uproar and judicial reserve which greeted the integration-augmentative TEU at national level, the drive to constitutionalise European law has nevertheless not been without difficulties all of its own. The problems are twofold and inexorably interrelated. The first—a paradoxical side effect of the earlier functionally driven, and in its effects at least, distinctly neo-liberal approach to legal integration—arises simply because the evolving European polity is highly atypical and fragmented in nature. The dynamic European polity is thus not only characterised by an intricate scheme of multiple and formally sovereign national collectivities on the one hand, and (*de facto*) autonomous European institutions on the other; but is likewise further complicated by the powerful presence within it of Europe-wide private values and interests which have been liberated by, and which are still forming in response to, personal and enabling European rights. In other words, the polity is an evolving political environment of integration which plays host to a still emerging, yet decidedly plural, maelstrom of national, private and community interests, each seeking to promote their views at European level.

To the natural difficulties of capturing this indeterminate polity in a constitution-alist format, however, must also be added the simple fact that even in their most liberal of manifestations, existing constitutions or formal expressions of constitutionalist orders—and vitally, practice here almost universally parts with theory[3]—have proven to be unwieldy beasts; unwelcoming of plural polities and tending instead to tackle the most fundamental of all questions of private and social ordering—that of the balancing of 'naturally diverse'[4] interests—by postulating an idealised aggregative interest or 'common good;' famously established in the founding or constitutive act, and subsequently continuously re-affirmed by, and given expression through, the assertion of the decisional sovereignty of a single and representative political body.[5] As a consequence, the formulation of a European Constitution—or the constitutionalis-ation of the integration process—would necessarily appear to be a step into the unknown: a highly novel attempt to establish a constitutionalist order, not only with no anchor in aggregative thinking, but also with an explicit eye to the problem of structured mediation between diverse plural interests.

This paper accordingly takes a three-step approach to the problem of constitution-alising European law. First, it risks adding to an already overflowing debate by highlighting the *Bundesverfassungsgericht's* by now infamous *Brunner* judgment:[6] a danger which is nonetheless courted in a dual endeavour both to illustrate the normative failings of the integration through law movement, and to demonstrate the subsequent shortcomings in national constitutionalist thinking. Secondly, it vitally turns its attention away from traditional constitutional analyses to investigate various interdisciplinary models (non-majoritarian, supranational and heterarchical) of the nature of the evolving European polity, as well as its underlying constitutional character. That is, normatively-flavoured, yet pragmatic, approaches to 'real-world' conditions within the evolving European polity, which may also be read as an implicit critique of the *Bundesverfassungsgericht's* atrophied constitutional stance. And thirdly, it concludes by more closely considering the introduction of interdisciplinarity to the

---

[3] *Infra*, II C 2.

[4] Cohen/Sabel, 'Directly-Deliberative Polyarchy,' (1997) 3:4 *ELJ* 313–342; the notion of natural diversity capturing the very simple fact that different individuals and groups of individuals within a society will invariably hold varying opinions and pursue divergent interests.

[5] Or a Parliament, cf, Gerstenberg, 'A Comment on Cohen and Sabel' (1997) 3:4 *ELJ* 343.

[6] All citations from the English translation [1994] CMLR 57.

European constitutional debate, and begins, albeit sketchily, to tackle the technical issue of the explicitly pluralist and proceduralised constitutionalisation of European law and the integration process.

II   The Brunner Paradox: Constitutional Atrophy vs Europe's Dynamic Polity

The putative Treaty on European Union drawn up by the intergovernmentalist Maastricht summit and, more particularly, its endeavour to speed up the pace of European political union, was greeted with judicial and political disquiet throughout Europe. Nonetheless, no other national, political or judicial forum has provided so comprehensive and normative an account of the underlying reasons for national resistance to augmented integration than the *Bundesverfassungsgericht* in its *Brunner* judgment on the compatibility of the TEU with the German Constitution. Given the exceptionally detailed nature of its considerations, it is therefore unsurprising that this particular instance of 'integration-denial' was not only to attract the greatest degree of post-Maastricht academic comment,[7] but was also—as the sometimes contradictory bones of the judgment were slowly picked over—sometimes to come to be seen and disapproved of as an isolated and peculiarly German 'happening.'[8] As a consequence, critique was subsequently to range from the somewhat curious—especially in view of the constitutional Court's explicit preparedness to recognise the ECJ's jurisdiction over human and even civic rights[9]—suggestion that *Brunner* was little more than a product of a deep historical strand of pre-political illiberality within German constitutional thinking;[10] to the more measured assertion that its paradoxical final acceptance of the TEU—in stark contrast to its own reasoning—was prompted by the German constitutional order's 'mistaken' but unshakeable faith in teutonic *ordo-liberal* thought.[11]

Such accusations of parochial constitutional thinking apart, however, *Brunner* may nonetheless be argued to have been reflective of more universal constitutionalist concerns and difficulties. First, as it expressed an overarching legal concern, clearly exposing the paucity of existing attempts to theorise Europe and its law both outside the framework of national constitutionalism and with insufficient regard to the 'disintegrative' as well as 'evolutionary' properties of a living body of European law. But secondly, since the Court's subsequent efforts to tame European legal development and to tailor its continuing evolution to certain of the underlying normative demands

---

[7] Contrast simply the vast number of 'Maastricht responses' with the almost total lack of comment on the infinitely less revealing—UK parliamentary debates and judicial review proceedings.

[8] For one among many notable exceptions, R.Bellamy/D. Castiglione (eds) 'The Constitution in Transformation,' Special Issue, (1996) *Political Science Studies* (Autumn).

[9] *Loc cit*, n 1, and n 6 at 12–13 and 24. More precisely, to share this jurisdiction. But the partial internationalisation of the civic jurisdiction nonetheless implying that the *Bundesverfassungsgericht* subscribe to a liberal view of constitutionalism predicated upon personal moral autonomy rather than any crass form of pre-political communitarianism.

[10] *Loc cit* n 1; here the comment seems, with a notable degree of rhetorical skill, to have placed far too great a degree of emphasis upon the views of Judge Kirchhof—whose writings admittedly do seem to betray a predilection both for Carl Schmitt and Herder—and too little on competing elements within the judgment, *infra* II B 2, seemingly more reflective of modern German constitutional thought, and its position upon more general constitutionalist problems.

[11] Or the (mythological) notion that 'money' can in some way be isolated from the exercise of political power, cf, Joerges 'Taking the Law Seriously: On Political Science and the Role of Law in the Process of European Integration' (1996) 2:2 *ELJ* 105.

of the German Constitution, it similarly exposed the shortcomings within all traditional (national) constitutional orders. In short, though recognising the dynamic nature both of European legal development and of a corollary process of post-national polity-building—and likewise demanding that these interrelated *teloi* be subject to some form of strict and on-going normative review—the German Justices were nonetheless unable to identify a suitably flexible and evolutionary European constitutionalist framework within which such an evaluation might meaningfully take place. Rather, in a move which might be labelled the 'Brunner paradox,' the *Bundesverfassungsgericht* sought instead to assess a dynamic and plural European polity through a re-assertion of the static demands of aggregative national constitutional thinking.

A   Sovereignty Now?

1   Doctrinal Inadequacy and Systemic Dichotomy

Remaining initially within the realm of formal law—and foreshadowing the constitutionalist paradox—it is immediately noteworthy that the *Brunner* judgment turned first and foremost on doctrinal deliberations which exposed the inability of formal legal methodology to categorise coherently either the specific character of evolving European governmental organisation, or the status of its law.[12] Called upon to assess whether the Federal Government's blanket commitment of Germany to the detailed provisions of economic and monetary union had alienated too great a degree of the *Bundestag's* decisional autonomy,[13] the Court had perforce to consider the legal relationship established between the *Bundesrepublik* and the evolving European Union. As a simple matter of methodological logic, the character of this relationship would itself depend upon the legal status of the Union and would likewise determine whether European policy and law-making might take place without direct reference to the democratic institutions of the Member States. In other words, the German Justices were faced with the thorny question of whether the Union disposed of some form of autonomous, or 'quasi-constituted,' authority of its own, or whether it was still ultimately dependent upon the 'transmitted' sovereignty of its 'constituent' parts, the Member States: the latter option having the notable consequence that the EU might never be allowed to infringe too greatly on the final expression of national sovereignty, the unfettered decisional autonomy of the German Parliament.[14]

In European legal circles, these questions had, quite naturally, long been the subject of debate. Interestingly, however, while European discussion had been quite openly 'fact-driven'—taking the apparently widely-accepted supremacy of European law as its starting point[15]—the *Bundesverfassungsgericht* nonetheless chose to tackle the issue

---

[12] *Ipsen*, 'Zehn Glossen zum Maastricht-Urteil,' (1994) 29 Europarecht 1.

[13] Interestingly, though this complaint did lead the Court to consider the issue of 'democracy,' or the ability of the German electorate to influence the policy and law-making of the European Union, it did so in an indirect manner. The direct challenge—that the whole of integration had alienated the democratic legitimation element within the *Grundgesetz* per Article 97(3)—as posed by the Green Faction within the *Bundestag* was deemed to be inadmissible by virtue of lacking *locus standi*. here the Court may have—for political reasons—been engaging in a process of damage limitation: the sight of a higher national Court directly questioning the legitimacy of all facets of European integration, perhaps being too much for Europe to bear.

[14] More precisely, a decisional autonomy fettered *only* by the German Constitution.

[15] That is, the preparedness of national Judges throughout the community to apply European law in preference to national law, Weiler, 'Journey to an Unknown Destination: A Retrospective and Prospective on the ECJ in the Arena of Political Integration,' (1993) 31 *JCMS* 416.

with the aid of the established, though manifestly outdated, doctrinal norms of constitutional and international law. Declining to trace a brief span of 30 years of novel European legal evolution, it sought instead to locate the Union methodo-logically within historically entrenched legal disciplines. As a natural consequence, where European lawyers had been freed from the constraints of inflexible doctrinal thought and had been able to take note of the 'real-world' developments which had seen the European institutions, and most importantly European law, attain a conceptually indistinct but factually verifiable measure of autonomy from their international treaty bases,[16] the German judges were left with a clear choice: the Union was either a simple treaty organisation established under international law, or had somehow elevated itself to the status of a 'constituted' and sovereign (federal) state.

Where European law was able to accommodate (and, on occasions, obscure the difficulties of) the grey area of legal and institutional development which the evolving European Union had opened up, and could accordingly simply designate itself and the Union *sui generis*, the Federal Court had chosen to tie its own hands. Both constitutional and international law being rooted in the notion of the fully sovereign constituted state, neither contained the norms to allow for the doctrinal capture of newer theoretical, and sovereignty-limiting, corollaries of *sui generis* European development such as, for a recent example, supranationalism.[17] As a simple matter of dogmatic course, left hanging between a rock and a hard place, the German Justices additionally underscored their refusal to locate the EU in the doctrinal 'never-never' regions between international organisations and state; expressing their preference for formal legal certainty above descriptive accuracy by veering explicitly towards an 'internationalist' solution—designating the Union a *Staatenverbund* (association of states) and the Member States the *Herren der Verträge* (masters of the treaties).[18]

The primary adherence to established doctrine, the additional preference for an internationally flavoured solution, and above all, the uncompromising legal picture drawn of sovereign states contracting amongst themselves, all brought with them an undeniable and unpalatable whiff of 19th Century statal organisation, and predictably attracted a mass of criticism which highlighted the seemingly retrograde return to legal rhetorics of the sovereign state.[19] More specifically, however, the German Court's emphasis upon the associational or contractual nature of the European treaties was also to draw critical fire, since, quite contrary to their apparent aim of establishing a clear legal scheme of sovereign authority, the Justices were argued to have, in fact, laid the foundations for a fundamental clash between national and European law, with conflict focusing on the now hotly-disputed issue of European legal supremacy.

In other words, the judgment had opened up a dichotomy between a body of European law which—driven simply by the normative power of factual develop-ments—was wholly and irrevocably committed to maintaining the hard won supremacy of a legal system which had been secured through a wearisome process of dialogue with national courts, and a traditional constitutional order which was equally determined to view European law as a simple derivation from international treaty law. This is, as a body of law having legitimacy only to the extent that it is compatible with

---

[16] *Ibid*, see the sheer number of successful 177 references.

[17] Joerges/Neyer, 'From Intergovernmental Bargaining to deliberative Political Processes: The Constitutionalisation of Comitology,' (1997) *ELJ*, 273–299; also, *infra*, III B.

[18] *Loc cit*, n at 43 *et seq*; note, however that the CMLR prefers 'federation' to 'association.'

[19] *Loc cit*, n 1.

sovereign national legal orders. This dichotomy appeared, in turn, inevitably to raise the question of which legal system would from now on determine the limits to the European jurisdiction. Viewed from the perspective of European law, the European treaties constituted an autonomous legal order with primary law and long-standing judicial practice both legitimising the European institutions and logically extending to them and, in particular, to the ECJ, the final measure of legal supremacy: the competence to identify their own jurisdictional boundaries. In strong contrast to this, however, stood the *Brunner* judgment and the logical consequence of notions such as the *Staatenverbund* and *Herren der Verträge*: the apparent confirmation by the *Bundesverfassungsgericht* that it would seek to internalise European law within the German constitutional order—denying its supremacy and regarding it as little more than a series of limited powers delegated by the *Bundesregierung*—and would accordingly reserve to itself the final power of adjudication over its extent.

2   The Unsettled Question of Supremacy

By contrast, and to move away formal legal methodology, it is nonetheless possible to view the dichotomy between European and national orders in less than final terms. Thus, on the one hand, the German Court's exhortation to the Member States to decline the temptation to use Article 235 EC as an *ersatz* means to overcome the EU's lack of a competence—as well as its thinly-veiled warning to the ECJ that any further attempt to widen its jurisdiction through too extensive an interpretation of provisions such as Article 30 EC, would not be greeted too favourably within German constitutional circles[20]—might seem to herald an inevitable and damaging conflict. On the other hand, however, one (positivist) commentator has welcomed the potential battle between national and European legal orders, less as a fatal clash between judicial titans, and more as an indication of the novel evolution of 'plural legal sovereignties.'[21] In this view, one clearly coloured by the Anglo-Saxon predilection for the persuasive (if not normative) power of 'rules of recognition,' the attempt made by the German constitutional order to hierarchisize supremacy and place European law in a position of dependency was, in the terms of 'real-world' legal relationships, an irrelevancy: at best a mere methodological oxymoron, and at worst a distinction germane only within the limited confines of German constitutional law. Outside this stylised world, the legal stage was instead, and was still, host to a variety of legal orders, each equipped with their own internal and coherent body of rules and doctrines to govern the establishment and validity of substantive norms. Seen in this light, any legal act complying with the cognitive strictures of one system would in all cases be imbued with legality under that order; with the notable implication[22] that the subsequent matter of wider legal acceptance, or jurisdictional supremacy, would simply boil down to a prosaic, judicial-led, process of forum-shopping, with individual Courts (or indeed any other legal authority) deciding which legal order to give preference to and when.

On a first reading, the scenario of plural legal sovereignties—one celebrating of legal difference and admitting of possible incoherence—seems remarkably well-adapted to the post- (and even pre-) *Brunner* legal environment. Thus, on the one hand, the judicial forum-shopping connotation, or the significance of the systemic

---

[20] *Loc cit*, n 6 at 64 and 65.

[21] MacCormick, 'The Maastricht Urteil: Sovereignty Now,' (1995) 1:3 *ELJ* 286.

[22] Though note, not one explicitly drawn by the author.

choices made by individual courts, would seem accurately to capture the unusually practical and predatory nature of European law; placing the origins of its claim to supremacy, not merely within its own normative framework, but rather, and vitally so, in the highly conditional process of dialogue whereby the ECJ secured for itself individual national judges as addressees of its norms. On the other hand, however, legal pluralism would equally seem to explain, or at least follow on from, the notable degree of incoherence within the German Court's reasoning. Thus, as an initial explanatory aside, the Federal Court's stubborn preference for constitutional and international law doctrines, despite the readily apparent mismatch between facts and norms, would accordingly seem—in a faint echo of systems theory—to be less an instance of wilful judicial oblivion,[23] and more a simple result of that Court's natural adherence to its own internal cognitive rules. Far more importantly, however, and from a solely descriptive point of view, a complex pattern of plural legal sovereignty would likewise appear to be the inescapable consequence: first, of both the *Bundesver-fassungsgericht's* substantive conclusion that a blanket delegation of Federal monetary powers was in fact constitutionally admissible, and of its decision to share its competence over civic rights with the ECJ; but secondly, also of its failure to provide lower national courts with clear guidelines on the exact nature of the supposed limits to the European jurisdiction.

Alternatively, in determining that a European institution (the future ECB) might dispose of a breadth of executive powers undreamed of in the German constitutional setting,[24] the *Bundesverfassungsgericht* had not only made a mockery of its claim to be establishing a clear link between European policy and law-making and the German democratic process,[25] but had also extended to European law—more particularly, that deriving from the TEU provisions on the EMU—an autonomous sphere of operation so large as to make German constitutional law's assumption of final sovereignty at best, very much a residual one.[26] Similarly, though reserving to itself the power to apply civic rights within the German jurisdiction, the Court's decision that the ECJ might lay down the general principles underlying those rights, nevertheless alienated certain of its own primary—and once exclusively held—constitutional functions. Equally, however, the judgment's distinctly discursive rather than prescriptive style, together with its purely public law terminology, similarly seemed to determine that lower courts, and more particularly, different legal disciplines within the national order—and here one should highlight private law[27]—would continue to maintain their own peculiar relations with the European legal system. In other words, in the absence of an authoritative and comprehensive delineation of jurisdiction framed in terms comprehensible to all the varied segments of the national legal order, it was probable that European law, with its multifarious and subtle connections to national legal

---

[23] As implied by European lawyers, *loc cit* n 11.

[24] And here note that the 'independence' of the *Bundesbank* is *not* derived from constitutional provisions, but is instead based upon a political-legal concordat, and is in any case tempered by the personal political relations maintained between the *Bundesregierung* and the staff of the Bank.

[25] *Loc cit*, n 11.

[26] An impression confirmed by its recent refusal to offer any judicial opinion on the matter of whether the EU has correctly observed its own convergence criteria, *The Four Professors*, Decision 2.4.1998, nyr.

[27] Presumably having a very complex relationship with European law all of its own; while likewise, not being fully cognisant of public law methodology, and thus less likely to take the *Bundesverfassungsgericht's* considerations into account when applying/interpreting European law.

systems, would continue to find many willing interlocutors (and thus practical supporters for its supremacy) within the highways and byways of the German legal arena.

Seen from a solely analytical point of view, the final considerations would thus appear to be determinative. In short, academic uproar notwithstanding, the Federal constitutional Court had not placed an immutable barrier in the path of the legal integration process. Instead, whilst formally re-asserting its own sovereignty,[28] it had nonetheless, and at a very practical level, also set the scene for a new 'contest of legal disciplines,' with the European legal stage now being characterised by complex processes of inter-jurisdictional dialogue; the substantive outcomes of which would be the sole arbiter in establishing which legal order take precedence and when.

3   *The Normative Limit to* Sui Generis *European Legal Evolution?*

Finally, however, though accepting the analytical and descriptive power of the plural legal sovereignties scenario, it might nonetheless also be argued that—with its roots firmly planted in stony positivist soil—it fails to capture fully the subtle normative flavour of the post-*Brunner* legal environment. In other words, by relegating the *Bundesverfassungsgericht's* considerations to the status of internal cognitive deliberations relevant only to and within the German legal order, the analysis pays inadequate attention to the German Court's underlying endeavour to place normative limits on *sui generis* European legal development by postulating its genesis in national constitutional orders, and thus vitally demanding that its further evolution—by virtue of judicial dialogue or otherwise—be subject to the normative values established within those orders.

More commonly identified as an endeavour by the Court to address the Union's supposed 'democracy deficit,' such an attempted subordination of the European legal system to national constitutional orders has potentially complex ramifications—formally (if not practically) limiting the ability of the Union and its law to encroach upon national political sovereignty, at least to the degree that it has not established a democratic equivalent of its own—but nonetheless also addresses the pressing question of European law's increasingly weak normative foundations.

B   *From the Autonomised Market to the Dynamic Market Polity*

In other words, and three decades on from its foundation, the European Communities and Union have been radically—though almost incidentally—transformed from simple customs union into a post-national and politically-flavoured joint economic enterprise which nonetheless largely remains uncertain as to its governmental nature. Under such circumstances, the basis of European law's legitimacy would necessarily seem to be ripe for extensive overhaul. In vital addition, however, the question of exactly what form of polity Europe is involving into, would also appear to be determinative for the identification of a meaningful manner in which to approach the issue of how European law's normative foundations are to be re-established. As the following section seeks to argue, the intricate and uncertain transformation of the European economic sphere from a simple and limited zone of (non-political)

---

[28] *Loc cit*, n 21.

commercial interchange into a complex and 'socialised'[29] market polity, dictates that traditional views—among them those of the *Bundesverfassungsgericht*—on the acceptably normative, or 'constitutional,' nature of social orders and their legal structures, prove inadequate in the face of Europe's novel, still evolving and uncertain plurality of national, supranational and private interests.

1   Functionalism vs Ordo-liberalism: European Law's Failing Normativity
The process of European integration is undoubtedly paradox-laden, and perhaps nowhere more so than in the matter of European legal evolution: European law's meteoric rise from international treaty backwater to the legal *corpus* of the moment, being matched only by the increasing intensity of its *totentanz* with its own legitimising bases. The measure of the success of European law having lain in its remarkable ability to further the course of integration in the face of political atrophy, this functionalist triumph has nonetheless fatally rebounded. The forceful promulgation of European personal economic rights[30] and the aggressive application of jurisdiction widening provisions, such as Article 30 EC,[31] have both cut swathes through the politically-legitimated regulatory economic arrangements of the Member States and have likewise necessitated a process of substantive—that is politically-led and socially-moulding[32]—re-regulation at European level.[33]

In economic and political terms—and deploying the German academic vernacular—this process has accordingly signalled a transformation of the EC/U from the Member States' private *Zweckverband*, or 'special purpose association,' designed and rigidly limited to the pursuit of the Community's common 'economic' good,[34] to a more wide-ranging and indistinct body with various political powers of its own. As a consequence, it has met with a degree of disdain in those 'conservative' academic circles dedicated to maintaining the economic purity of a European Union, lying alongside, instead of above, the 'strong' rather than politically dependent Member States.[35] In legal terms, however, the far-reaching transformation of the 'European

---

[29] Note, however, the notion of a 'socialised' market does not entail, at least in this analysis, any notion of social policy regulation. Rather, 'socialisation' (the German term is more accurate: *Vergesellschaftlichung*) encompasses the post-national attempt to create new 'non-hierarchical' links between politics, society and the market place—that is a new mode of ensuring that the market-place embodies the politically-determined social and ethical values of its clients and addresses. Direction no longer being provided for by simple legislative processes. But, rather, through the more diverse series of institutional arrangements (*eg*, committees, agencies, networks) and private and legal forces (consumer power and consumer rights) which the EU has established.

[30] Articles 48,52,59,63 EC Treaty.

[31] For an excellent analysis of the ECJ's extension of its jurisdiction, M. Poires Mauduro, *We the Court* (Hart 1998).

[32] Cf, n 29.

[33] Cf, Ch. Joerges, *Markt ohne Staat*, Working Paper of the European University Institute, No. 91/15 (1991 EUI). This process and its results are by now well-known—to briefly recap, however, it rests upon the unfortunate fact that, for example, a decision to knock down a national regulatory arrangement under the 'pure' (non-political) auspices of European competition policy (85 EC), is often necessarily followed by the political establishment of positive European rules, regulative of competition (85 (3)). In other words, a solely legal act is inevitably followed by political intervention at the European level,

[34] For the most detailed exposition, cf, H. P. Ipsen, *Europäisches Gemeinschaftsrecht* (1972 J.C.B. Mohr).

[35] E. J. Mestmäcker, *Risse im Europäischen Sozial Kontrakt* (1997 Hans Martin Schleyer Stiftung), for the most recent re-assertion of the long-standing notion that the EU and its law is legitimate only to the extent that is remains an organisation without political competences of its own, and rigidly limited to serving the pre-determined political goals of its Member States.

market space' has likewise had deep ramifications, placing the legitimacy of the integration through law movement in doubt as European law has at length sprung the confines of the *ordo-liberal* economic constitution,[36] admittedly continuing to serve its primary function of entrenching personal economic rights (and safeguarding them from unwarranted political manipulation), but at the same time increasingly taking on substantive regulatory functions.

In other words, in a curious dualistic paradigm, the neo-liberal and disintegrative character inevitably ascribed to primary Community law during its functionalist pursuit of integrationist goals,[37] has likewise resulted in a demand for compensatory regulation, with the similarly functionalist requirement for European regulative homogeneity,[38] dictating that unravelled national regulatory provision must be re-established at Community level by secondary and substantive European law. With this inexorable passage from negative to positive integration, Europe's law has consequently moved far beyond the simple codification of economic liberties, has acquired political overtones, and has begun actively to shape market relations. In so doing, however, it has similarly jeopardised any claim that it may once have had to being a *corpus* of law legitimated outside the politicised constitutional orders of the Member States. Where once the normative foundations of the European legal order might have been identified in its politically-neutral juridification and autonomisation of private market forces,[39] the slow evolution of a European market with substantive regulation of its own—together with the role played by law in the shaping of economic enterprise—has taken the European legal order from the sphere of the 'private' economy to that of the 'public' political realm, thus necessarily raising the question of exactly 'where' its normative genesis now lies.

2 The Climate of Integration: an Uncertain and 'Socialised' Market Polity

Leaving aside its somewhat curious confirmation that 'juridified' European Monetary Union might take effect without prejudice to the *Grundgesetz*,[40] the *Brunner* judgment then appears, as a whole, to be a response to the pressing problem of an increasing lack of normativity within the *sui generis* European legal system. First, since it seeks to stem the disintegrative effects of neo-liberally flavoured primary European law at the Member State level: re-asserting the formal sovereignty of the national constitution and vitally reserving the competence to assess the limits to integrative-disintegrative European Treaty provisions to the *Bundesverfassungsgericht*. But secondly, and very significantly so, since it also reminds the *sui generis* European legal order that since its roots lie within national constitutions—this perhaps being the real significance of the term, *Herren der Verträge*—its possible future development needs also to take note of the normative values which those orders embody.

---

[36] For the Grandfather of ordo-liberal thought at his most theoretically detailed, cf, Mestmäcker 'On the Legitimacy of European Law,' (1994) *Rabels Zeitschrift für ausländisches und internationales Privatrecht*, 615–635.

[37] Everson, 'The Legacy of the Market Citizen,' in J. Shaw/G. Moore (eds) *New Legal Dynamics of European Union* (1995 Clarendon).

[38] Falke, 'The Post Market Control of Goods in the European Communities,' in H.-W Micklitz *et al* (eds) Federalism and Responsibility (1994 Graham &Trotmann).

[39] *Supra*, n 36.

[40] In effect, designating this portion of Treaty law a 'private affair' requiring no anchor in Germany's political constitutional order.

This second—both 'realist' and 'evolutionary' strand—within the judgment, was concretised in the Court's explicitly expressed preparedness to withdraw from the full execution of formal German constitutional sovereignty, in step with the evolution of the concept of European 'political' citizenship and the increasing powers of the European Parliament.[41] As such, the recognition that a democratised European law might one day supersede national constitutional order, seems primarily to belie the impression that the Court was wedded hopelessly to international and constitutional law doctrine, and, in particular, was irrevocably committed to the dogma of the immutably sovereign state. On a similarly positive note, it likewise indicates that the *Bundesverfassungsgericht* could itself conceive of a role for *sui generis* European law beyond the narrow confines of the autonomised and private market sphere, or the 'European Economic Constitution.' However, the specific demand for parliamentary democratisation—without which the national order would not withdraw[42]—also betrayed a deep ambivalence on the part of the Justices towards the indistinct characteristics of the fragmented and dynamic European market polity to which the European legal order had given birth.

In brief explanation, however, the matter of substantive European re-regulation, and with it the creation of a 'socialised' European market polity, has been very much an *ad hoc* affair. Thus, though on the one hand the European legal order was once again to demonstrate its extraordinarily innovative flair, creating regulatory tools and arrangements where none had been envisaged by black-letter treaty law. On the other hand, the complex and multi-level structure of European governance[43]—together with an on-going tension between the originally neo-liberal nature of the internal market and its evolving political regulation or 'socialisation'—has nonetheless determined that European regulatory mechanisms and policy-making processes are characterised by a high degree of uncertainty, both with regard to nature of their substantive outcomes, and in view of the pressing question of which social and political interests— as well as 'private' market values—are most legitimately represented and by whom.[44]

In other words—and as an exemplary scenario—the functionalist drive for harmonised market re-regulation, which has seen a diverse set of European regulatory institutions established at Community level in order to set the 'common' norms by which the internal market should be administered,[45] has been marked by two fundamental dichotomies. First, the on-going tension between 'rationalising' thought which seeks to further the economic liberty component inherent within the European treaties through technocratic governance[46] and a more traditional, politically-interventionist, attempt to imbue European regulatory policy with social and ethical values.[47] And secondly, the increasing conflict as to who might be best placed to represent these competing interests-values: with the apparently natural division of representative labour between a technocratically-oriented Commission and a series of Member States heedful of the social and ethical concerns of their polities, not

---

[41] *Loc cit* n 6.

[42] *Ibid.*

[43] Or, the decisional dualism inherent to the Member State-autonomous EC institutions divide.

[44] Everson, 'Administering Europe?' (1998) 36:2 *JCMS* 195.

[45] Notably, committees, agencies and regulatory networks, *ibid,* for details.

[46] Largely through minimalist and technocratic-expertocratic regulation. A rationalising view most cogently represented by Giandomenico Majone, cf, 'Europe's Democracy Deficit: the Question of Standards,' (1998) 4:1 *ELJ* 5–28.

[47] Joerges/Neyer, *loc cit* n as a counterweight to technocracy, cf, also, *infra*, III C.

only being complicated by 'socialising' tendencies within the increasingly political Commission,[48] but also being further fragmented by the direct demand of European citizens personally to represent their economic interests as well as their social-ethical values at European level.[49]

The evolving political climate of European integration, and thus the 'socialised' internal market polity, is highly indeterminate, both as to its guiding *raison d'être* and its personal characteristics. Should it simply be constructing and securing a 'private' sphere of economic relationships, or need it evolve a social and thus public market order? Equally, are the Member States and Community institutions appropriate representatives of social-ethical values and Community ideals? Alternatively, should an evolving European public—possibly having interests divergent from those of the national political collectivities or the Community institutions—be given greater access to the European decision-making process? In the language of the academic constitutional lawyer, this climate amounts to an evolving, fragmented and pluralist polity, giving rise to concomitant constitutional difficulties entailing the identification of mechanisms which might secure democracy by balancing naturally diverse and—as an added complicating factor—still developing interests. In the mind of a living constitutional Court, however—to whit, the *Bundesverfassungsgericht*—it similarly amounted to a serious abuse of a traditionally democratic German polity: an abuse which could only be corrected at European, rather than national level, through the evolution of a parliamentary democracy, or an aggregative European constitutional order.

C   Constitutional Atrophy: the Constitutional Postulation of the Common Good

1   An Analytical Reformulation

To date, the *Brunner* judgment has largely been viewed from one of two perspectives. The first—an inevitable result of the Court's somewhat injudicious ruminations upon cultural, linguistic and social homogeneity as a pre-condition for democratic discourse—dwelling famously upon the seemingly pre-political predilections of the German Justices,[50] and in a more positive light, locating the decision at the communal end of the great communitarian-liberal philosophical divide.[51] The second—concerning itself less with the formal re-assertion of German constitutional sovereignty and more with the evolution of a European polity—highlighting the Court's apparent inability to conceive of democratic processes outside a traditional nation, or federal nation state.[52]

---

[48] Landfried, 'Beyond Technocratic Governance,' (1997) 3:3 *ELJ* 255.

[49] This movement not only being apparent in the evolution of interest-group committees, with the Commission being advised by various pan-European social interest groupings, but likewise being noticeable in the presence of European commercial interests within agency networks. And perhaps most interestingly for lawyers, also playing its part in attempts to increase the catalogue of 'substantive' European rights, cf, Reich 'A European Constitution for Citizens: Reflections on the rethinking of Union and Community Law,' (1997) 3:2 *ELJ*, 131–164, for a latter day manifestation of the ever present tendency towards the substitution of juridification for politicisation—with lawyers strangely (and perhaps somewhat foolishly) seeking to 'codify' the political concerns of individual Europeans to give them standing at the European level.

[50] *Loc cit*, n 1.

[51] *Loc cit*, n 8.

[52] Mancini, 'Europe: the Case for Statehood,' (1988) 4:1 *ELJ* 29.

Not denying the relevance of either of these analytical approaches—and in effect considering issues raised by both—it might nonetheless be argued that if viewed from the perspective of traditional concrete constitutional orders, the major stumbling block within the judgment instead becomes the Court's inability to theorise a constitutionalist model to balance pluralist, diverse and evolving Member State, Community and private interests without the aid of an idealised, constitutionally-postulated and secured 'aggregative interest' as the final adjudicative expression of the 'common good:'[53] the 'finite' constitution[54]—established by the constitutive act, and further secured by and securing of representative majoritarian democracy—standing in the path of an overarching European constitutional order, or the evolution of a higher legal framework, sensitive to 'reality.' Or, and more particularly, a legal order capable of submitting the 'real-world' processes of plural legal development and the evolution of a pluralist post-national polity, to effective normative control.

2   Constitutionalism and the Mastery of Social Schism

Lying between 'law and politics,'[55] it has thus become common to conceive of constitutionalism in terms of two extremes: the liberal and the communitarian constitutional order. This apparent and stark dichotomy between higher legal orders established in the exclusive service of one pre-political polity, or cultural-linguistic-religious entity, and those based upon a universal recognition of individual moral capacity, however, has nonetheless tended to detract attention from the common cause of all constitutions—and here a modern reformulation of Schmittian views may be used without fear of approbation—that is the mastery of the inevitable social and political schisms and centrifugal conflicts which pose a constant threat to any society's continued existence.[56] Picking up this common cause within liberal constitutional thought, such a purpose thus translates into the claim that, far from being based upon the unrestrained and destructive individualism which personal autonomy might imply, the liberal constitution likewise serves the goal of social cohesion: constitutionally secured and universal individual moral capacity (*Handlungsfähigkeit*), simply acting as a vital pre-condition for civic, deliberative and 'healing' political interaction between diverse and competing individuals and interests.[57]

Given this essentially proceduralist element within liberal constitutional thought—that is, the emphasis placed on the discursive or deliberative justice which flows from interaction between individuals whose autonomy is constitutionally guaranteed—the final decisive faith which existing liberal constitutional orders nonetheless place in the substantive, conflict-regulating mechanism of constitutionally-secured majoritarian democracy, or a 'postulated aggregative interest,' may appear somewhat incongruous: the notion of aggregation similarly implying the practical closure of the liberal polity both to external justice claims and to internal minority (though possibly rational)

---

[53] For the origins of this argument, phrased as the problem of the 'unitary sub-strata' of the nation state, cf, 'Towards a Legal Theory of Supranationality: The Viability of the Network Concept,' (1997) 3:1 *ELJ*, 33–54.

[54] Or the 'closed' constitution.

[55] U.K. Preuß, 'Der Begriff der Verfassung und ihre Beziehung zur Politik,' in *idem Zum Begriff der Verfassung* (1994 Fischer), at 7.

[56] *Ibid*, at 8.

[57] Holmes, 'Verfassungsförmige Vorentscheidungen und das Paradox der Demokratie,' in U.K.Preuß, *op cit* n 55.

interests. Certainly, a few strands within liberal constitutional circles do appear to find common cause with Rousseau, deeming the retrospective creation of the sharply-delineated 'nation' through the voluntary constitutive act and its subsequent crystal-lisation in a unitary and representative system of national parliamentary democracy to be somehow necessary for the 'quasi-spiritual' purpose of social cohesion.[58] However, as recent authoritative critique has forcefully reminded us (and these commentators), such conjectured unitarianism is, in modern terms at least, more generally seen as liberalism's problem, rather than its natural outcome.[59] In other words, whilst the postulation of a substantive 'common constitutional good'—with representative majoritarian politics having the final say in matters of conflict between naturally diverse interests—may in practice form the core of liberal constitutions, reifying the unitary political process and giving it the status of the on-going expression of the constitutive will, such an aggregative constitutional interest does not form an inevitable or integral part of liberal constitutional thought; a conceptual body more fundamentally committed to the establishment of 'deliberative rationality' than a representative outcome.

In view of this conclusion, one is naturally drawn to ask why existing constitutions seem never to have sought to move beyond a substantive formulation of the common good which places the unitary national democratic process at the heart of its higher normative order. Alternatively, why has the law of the liberal constitution never sought to take liberal thought to its logical conclusion, constructing civic deliberation outside the limited, and—in effect, if not in theory—'exclusionary' notion of aggregative democracy with its necessary corollary of the 'finite' constituted polity? One possible and partially-convincing answer is provided by the critical, and ever deconstructivist post-modern suggestion that this constitutional atrophy has very little to do with the internal methodological struggles of normative law *per se*, and is more a simple result of the evolving industrial nation state's historical and functional (law-external) demand for social, economic and political homogeneity.[60] At the normative level, however, it might, and will likewise, be argued that the source of this liberal atrophy may in fact lie in the very real difficulties which law faces in its efforts to establish the concrete procedural norms of adjudication which could complement more modern liberal approaches to the balancing of naturally diverse interests without the aid of parliamentary aggregation.[61]

3   *Aggregative Interest and the European 'Common Good'?*

Accepting the analytical reformulation of the issues tackled in the *Brunner* judgment, and imputing to the *Bundesverfassungsgericht* less a desire either to preserve pre-political German homogeneity or contradictorily to impose a communitarian character on a heterogeneous European polity, and more a will constitutionally to master the social and disintegrative schisms which mark the process of European integration, the real failing in the judgment becomes readily apparent. Trapped in a

---

[58] Preuß, 'Two Challenges to Modern Citizenship,' (1996) *Political Science Studies* (Autumn).

[59] A thought-provoking exchange, J. Habermas, *Die Einbeziehung des Anderen* (Suhrkamp 1996), 278–281.

[60] Ladeur, *loc cit* n 53.

[61] Instructive in this regard, Cohen/Sabel, *loc cit* n 4, who, while long-since having theoretically refined a directly-deliberative alternative to majoritarian democracy, nonetheless have only just begun, tentatively to identify the concrete legal and governmental within which a directly-deliberative democracy might be made operational.

mode of thinking which placed majoritarian political processes at the heart of the constitutional order, and further sought to balance naturally diverse interests through the postulation of a substantive European common good, the Court was left with two finite possibilities and no intermediate normative tools to govern conflict between interests during the possible, though not inevitable, passage from one to the other. The European Union was either a conglomerate of diverse unitary national polities each with their own aggregative political interest, thus determining that autonomous European law need restrict itself to the sphere of private market relations. Or, it was in possession of a substantive common good of its own—expressed through the majoritarian will of the European Parliament—and might as a consequence extend its 'constitutionalised' legal operations into all spheres of society.

Alternatively, in a legal paradox of extraordinary proportions, the Court failed abjectly to address the most pressing problem of European legal development: the means of dampening social schism, or the identification of a normative order which might adjudicate between, rather than simple aggregate, competing interests and thus 'justly' guide an on-going rather than static process of European integration, as well as, the dynamic and uncertain establishment of a post-national polity. With the substantive outcome of integration in doubt, and the character of the evolving European polity likewise uncertain, the immediate demand would seem to be for some form of proceduralised European common good. Europe requires an overarching normative/constitutional order dedicated to mediating between diverse and still evolving interests and values, and similarly adjudicating in the process of dialogue between plural legal sovereignties.

III   Three Models of the European Constitutional Order?

With sections of European law—more particularly the personal economic freedoms—still irrevocably committed to the functionalist pursuit of European integration, there appears to be an inevitable and awkward paradox inherent to the notion of creating a European constitutional order, or perhaps better phrased, constitutionalising *sui generis* European law by ascribing to it a procedural mediating function. In short, as an instrument of integration, the European legal system would inevitably seem to be an actor within the evolving European polity, adding to its complexity through its integrative-disintegrative effects. The assumption of an additional procedural role of mediation between diverse Member State, Community and private—and even its own—interests would thus appear to embroil European lawyers in Janus-like machinations, requiring them to tailor their activities in the light of the immediate political and social circumstances. Given the necessary delicacy of such an activity, it is thus tempting to refrain from any attempt to specify too closely the constitutional principles of mediatory proceduralism; instead placing regulatory faith in the Kantian sentiment that our higher courts, as repositories of our full democratic and legal respect, are perhaps better left to go about this task in peace and unfettered by any theoretical baggage or stilted academic requirements.[62]

This said, however—and retaining a similar respect for law's true genius or technical ability to adapt facts to norms—the analysis nonetheless moves on in an attempt to identify at least certain of the guiding principles which might aid the *sui generis* European legal order to constitutionalise itself through the establishment and

---

[62] *Loc cit*, n 1.

policing of a procedural European common good. It does so, however, not by engaging in any form of traditional—politically or philosophically motivated—constitutionalist analysis; but rather, through an investigation of three inter-disciplinary models of the emerging and 'socialised' internal market polity, together with their implicit and explicit characterisations of the legitimate European constitutional order. In other words, in the face of an unprecedented polity, the initial task would logically appear to be one of 'real-world' polity identification. And whilst—as is readily apparent—interdisciplinarity is not in itself a guarantee of analytical objectivity, the various blends of traditional political science and modern economics (non-majoritarianism), European law, international relations theory and sociology (supranationalism), or law and post-modern theory (heterarchical analysis), nonetheless do open up new vistas upon the true nature of the integration process and the 'socialised' European market polity. Though no one model is investigated in full, their combined views upon the legitimate character of the European polity and its law provide a useful springboard for further and procedural constitutional innovation.

A   The Non-Majoritarian European Order

Though latterly much embattled, its preferred mode of European governance—the fully independent regulatory agency—having met with a certain degree of disfavour in the European arena,[63] non-majoritarian thought nonetheless proves an invaluable point of departure, being an explicit attempt to theorise and normativise the uncertain climate of integration and market 'socialisation' without the prop of majoritarian democratic processes.[64]

Though born of modern economics—more particularly, the notion that the criteria of macro-economic efficiency can guide and shape 'non-political' market governance by ensuring that regulation never stray into those redistributive social policy concerns which are ever requiring of majoritarian deliberation[65]—non-majoritarian thought nonetheless has strong roots in the political constitution. It thus forcefully claims that its isolation of market governance from political forces serves the goal of democracy[66] by safeguarding the democratically set goals of the polity from the predatory inclinations of a transitory political elite. Accordingly, the often-made comparison between non-majoritarianism and neo-liberalism is misleading: non-majoritarian thought placing less emphasis on the unrestrained pursuit of individual economic rights, and more upon the political creation of an autonomised sphere of market activity. A sphere which is guarded, on the one hand, from disruptive redistributive goals, and is regulated, on the other, by rational/expert considerations with an eye to the increase of overall economic welfare, rather than the pursuit of individual and possibly selfish, economic goals.

Translated to the sphere of the uncertain climate of European integration and market 'socialisation' this determines that non-majoritarian thought equally parts company with *ordo-liberal* conceptions of the European order.[67] On the one hand,

---

[63] Kreher, 'Agencies in the European Community: A Step Towards Administrative Integration in Europe,' (1997) 4:2 *JEPP*, 225–45.

[64] At its most theoretically detailed, G. Majone (ed) *Regulating Europe* (1996 Routledge).

[65] Majone, 'The European Community Between Social Policy and Regulation,' (1993) 31:2 *JCMS* 153–70.

[66] *Loc cit* n 46.

[67] *Loc cit* n 36.

sharing with them the desire to conceive of the European legal system outside the political constitutional orders of the Member States. But on the other, arguing that the regulation of the 'autonomised' European market sphere is not a simple matter of legal codification—with European rights simply and neutrally securing the boundaries of the market—and is instead a substantive matter of regulatory policy-making, with expert epistemic and technocratic communities actively shaping the market in the pursuit of aggregate rather than individual economic welfare.

Characterising the European Communities as a non-political 'fourth branch of government,'[68] the non-majoritarian strand of thought thus appears to retain faith in the political constitutional orders of the Member States, but at the same time seems to serve the economically rationalising elements within the Rome Treaties. Thus, the autonomised European market could only come into being following the majoritarian decision of the national political collectivities that this be an acceptable goal. Equally, it can only remain in being insofar as it is restricted to the macro-economically efficient pursuit of aggregate welfare and does not stray into social or political issues which remain the exclusive concern of Member State constitutional orders. Similarly, however, the scheme of expert and technocratic governance should aid in ensuring that economic activities in Europe no longer be perverted to transient welfarist or simply expedient political goals, and are instead tailored to allow for overall and sustained wealth creation.

Moving on to consider the form of legitimate European polity which this model envisages, and its underlying vision of a European constitutional order, it is at once apparent that the integration-polity which it postulates is a very limited one, whilst the measure of the constitutionality of European law, seen in this light at least, would accordingly lie in its ability to shield this polity from disruptive political concerns and selfish individual economic claims. In other words, neither the Member States nor individual Europeans—through too aggressive a pursuit of their personal economic or even social rights[69]—should be allowed to play a part in the process of market 'socialisation'. Equally, European law need, on the one hand, withdraw from its all too eager attempts to introduce extra private participants into the debate through the juridification of political-social interests,[70] and, on the other, concentrate on the establishment of the legal mechanisms which would not only protect the autonomous European institutions from national political interference, but also ensure their expertocratic-technocratic deliberative 'quality.'

In conclusion, however, non-majoritarian thought offers any attempt to develop a proceduralised European Constitution, or the constitutionalisation of the integration process, a subtle and fruitful variation upon a Madisonian theme. To be sure, economically rationalising market rights and, more particularly, the aggregate welfare which their unhampered pursuit will bring, is the final goal of internal market regulation. However, and vitally so, individual economic rights are not the governing locus for normative oversight of the 'socialised' European polity. Rather, 'politics' is to be kept at bay from the 'socialised' market polity via the securing of expert deliberation. Repellent of the disrupting vagaries of a sometimes doubtful political process and the self interest inherent to economic autonomy alike, the implicit pursuit

---

[68] G. Majone, *Independence vs Accountability*, Working Paper of the European University Institute (1994 EUI).

[69] *Supra*, n 49 for literature cataloguing such rights..

[70] *Ibid*, for an example of exactly this tendency.

of a (substantive) European common good in aggregate welfare, is instead to be based on the (proceduralist) privileging of the position of those 'who can best judge' whether particular regulatory provisions are truly suited to serving this overall aim or not.

B   Deliberative Supranationalism: The European Experiment

Interestingly, the deliberatively supranational model of European governance[71]—an explicit, rather than implicit, attempt to identify the constitutional roots of the European order—has emerged out of long-standing interaction and disagreement with non-majoritarian thought. Vitally, however, what was once merely a prosaic disagreement on the practical applicability of the macro-economic criterion of aggregate welfare, has now taken on normative dimensions with the deliberative school of thought crucially questioning whether 'expert-knowledge' be a appropriate yardstick against which the overall democratic/constitutional quality of European deliberation might be measured.

In elucidation: with its lawyerly respect for primary European law, or provisions such as Article 30 EC, the deliberative school of thought has never denied the rationalising effect of European economic rights. On the contrary, it shares with non-majoritarian thought a vision of the process of European integration as a consolidation of a sphere of private market relations, overcoming of the economically stagnatory, and quite often unjustified, legal arrangements atrophied in the 'welfarist'[72] economic orders of the Member States.[73] However, with a similarly respectful eye to Article 36 EC, and an equally pragmatic suspicion that economic regulation can never be fully isolated from social or ethical policy concerns, it likewise argues that there is a justified dualism in the European integration process: with Member States possessing a 'constitutional' right to advance their views where and when European policy-making strays into the social and ethical sphere.[74] In other words, though not necessarily concerned with social redistribution in the traditional sense, modern markets do inevitably create new and unforeseen risks, thus giving rise to a 'limited' redistributive concern in the matter of the allocation of the costs of risk-regulation:[75] are governments, consumers or the market to carry the burden of such costs? Accordingly, in the European setting, this translates into the claim that national governments must have a say in an on-going political process of market integration and regulation—identifying the limits to and allocating the cost of acceptable risk—but, similarly and crucially alters the climate of 'European deliberation:' determining that rationalising expert knowledge must always be balanced against legitimate social and ethical policy concerns.

Taking a closer look at the constitutional implications of this model, it thus transpires that the evolving European polity should similarly reflect such dualism with Member States—in an echo of aggregative thinking[76]—representing the social and

---

[71] For its now fully (or almost fully matured contours), cf, Joerges/Neyer, *loc cit* n 17.

[72] That is, the confusion of social policy with simple 'regulatory' economic oversight.

[73] Joerges/Neyer, *loc cit* n 17.

[74] E. Vos, *Institutional Frameworks of Community Health and Safety Regulation* (1998 Hart)

[75] Joerges, 'Product safety in the European Community: Market Integration, Social Regulation and Legal Structures,' (1992) 38 *Journal of Behavioural and Social Sciences*, 132–148.

[76] An aggregative tendency, deriving both from international relations theory's continuing emphasis upon the sovereignty of states within international regimes and from the normative consideration that Member States, with all their cultural and historical richness, remain the best fora in which naturally diverse interest may be balanced, Joerges/Neyer, *loc cit* n , at 293.

ethical concerns of their polities, and the Community institutions seeking to represent and further the 'rationalising' goals of European economic integration. Equally, however, the measure of the 'quality' of deliberation is not simply to be found in substantive expertise, but rather in the processes and political climate which allows expertise 'justly' to be balanced against social and ethical concerns. With this, the deliberative model of supranationalism represents a step forward in the search for a proceduralised constitutionalised European order: no longer postulating the European common good in the substantive terms of the supremacy of collective political decision-making or expert deliberations. Instead, the measure of deliberative supranational justice is to be found in the process by which political considerations are balanced against expert (rationalising) advice.[77]

To conclude, however, the deliberative model of supranationalism likewise contains a sting in the tail. Europe, it argues, is already a constitutional order.[78] The foundations for European constitutionalism were inevitably laid as the Rome Treaties—through their entrenchment of universal economic rights—solved the dilemma of the finite liberal constitution, necessarily—though in an unforeseen manner—forcing closed national polities to take the interests of non-nationals into account both within their domestic orders and in the joint effort to establish a rationalising European order. On this score then, European law has already largely played out its constitutional role: opening boundaries and creating the fora[79] in which the deliberative play off between rationalising and political interests might take place. Accordingly, beyond its role in continuing to provide judicial and institutional fora in which diverse views might be aired, there is little left for it to do. Alternatively, the civility and quality of deliberation—or the correct/convincing balancing of interests—cannot be assured by formal legal provisions, but is instead a simple 'sociological' result of the plurality and diversity of a European integration process which has forced experts and governments to ground/re-evaluate their interests and ideas through confrontation with many other views .[80]

This final point is indicative of the model's subtle understanding of the complexity of the problem of *Faktizität* and *Geltung*: clearly demonstrating the practical limits to formal law, and the grey area which sees it interact with more diffuse social movements to give it real rather than imagined force. However, it is also telling of a possible limitation to its explanatory force and efficacy: the process of integration is diffuse and civil now, but it may not always be so. Alternatively, what price deliberative civility in the face of determined, organised and homogenising interests?

C   Post-Modern Theory: the Heterarchical Liberation of the 'Private'?

Given its roots in deconstructivist critical theory, any attempt to investigate post-modern legal theory for an underlying normative characterisation of Europe's emerging polity initially appears to be a contradiction in terms: the modern pressure to assess norms in the light of facts having, in this body of thought, ultimately resulted in the death of all normativity. Nonetheless, certain post-modern formulations, do

---

[77] *Ibid.*

[78] *Ibid*, at 295

[79] Most notably, European committees with their division of labour between political representatives of the Member States and the rationalising expertise represented by epistemic communities.

[80] Joerges/Neyer, *loc cit* n 17, at 293.

bring with them a degree of normative power, at least to the extent that they argue that the famous, though idealised public/private constitutional divide, need be re-evaluated not merely in pursuit of descriptive real-world accuracy, but also and (vitally so) in an endeavour to secure the socially-integrative efficacy of the law.[81]

In explanation, and immediately translating the post-modern theory to the European level, this view becomes crucial. First, since it underlines the 'real-world' fact that European integration has sprung the confines of the 'public' national collectivity,[82] with certain private interests outgrowing national political processes and instead pursuing their goals[83] in the private sphere through an attempt directly to influence market forces and decentralised administrative nodes of market regulation. And secondly, since it demonstrates that law—more particularly, regulatory law—has established a 'heterarchical,' or direct, rather than politically mediated relationship, with such 'privatised' interests, mostly through a direct exchange of information on issues such as emerging risks and the best modes of their regulation.[84] Such direct exchange subsequently serves the efficacy of law through the evolution of immediate and workable regulatory solutions.

Accordingly, though irrevocably committed simply to describe the factual process of European (economic) integration and the evolution of a dynamic (market-driven) polity, post-modern thought—and, in particular, its observation that law need retain some hold on reality to ensure its efficacy and thus power to integrate society—contains lessons for the evolution of a European constitutional order. First, though having no vision of a 'legitimate' polity of its own, reminding both non-majoritarian and supranational thought that the national collectivities in which they place so much of their faith are only one element within the European polity, since much political-social development now takes place at the level of the private. And secondly, highlighting law's increasingly direct, rather than parliamentarily mediated, interaction with political and social forces.

Abstracting to the question of constitutional design, this would appear to have two consequences. First, as politics has spread into the realm of the private, so too must a constitutional order dedicated to 'controlling the political.' Secondly, however, with its direct connection to a politicised private sphere, law—and this must be an element within the 'privatised' constitutional order—need develop mechanisms to ensure that the process of law-interest interaction serves universal rather than selfish aims.

IV   Conclusion: Constitutional Interdisciplinarity and Proceduralism?

There is a growing tendency among lawyers seeking to constitutionalise the European legal and social order to revert to traditional comparative tools of constitutional analysis, trawling through existing 'black-letter' constitutions in an endeavour to identify the formal constitutional mechanisms which might aid them in overcoming the immediately apparent problems of European integration such as the postulated

---

[81] Ladeur, 'Postmoderne Verfassungstheorie,' in U.K. Preuß (ed), *op cit* n 55.

[82] Ladeur, *loc cit* n 53.

[83] Mostly economic but also social-political, and environmental interest is telling here, cf, Ladeur, 'The Integration of Scientific and Technological Expertise into the Process of Standard-Setting According to German Law,' in Ch. Joerges *et al*, *Integrating Scientific Expertise into Regulatory Decision-making* (1996 Nomos).

[84] *Ibid.*

'democracy-deficit,' or the unwillingness of Member States to cede to augmented demands for a transfer of their sovereign powers.[85]

Explicit within this paper, however, is a critique of such traditional approaches within the European setting. Europe, it would seem, is as ever at the very limits of experimental governance: a largely unforeseen integration dynamic giving rise to an ever-changing, and ever novel, climate of market 'socialisation' and post-national polity-building. On the one hand, this experimental European development has clearly exposed the limits to 'discipline-internal' constitutional thought: the *Bundesverfassungsgericht* being normatively unable to capture the 'real-world' process of European governmental evolution within its established doctrine. On the other hand, however, it has also seen a qualitative change in academic discourse; the plurality and innovation of the integration process being mirrored by the increasing diversity and inventiveness of social science debates. Just as Europe has opened up once 'closed' national political orders and policy-making to scrutiny through exposure to the views of other national systems and individual interests liberated by the integration dynamic, so too has it forced individual academic subjects to re-assess their fundamental premises and beliefs, searching for new analytical tools which are better suited to an evolving 'reality,' by such long-standing concepts to the rationalities and tenets of other disciplines.

Constitutional law—with its roots in social and political foundations and its specific function of promoting and defending democratic governance and individual liberty—was ever the most 'open' of bodies of legal study. Indeed, not one of its formal instruments is without a 'discipline external' element, all deriving from underlying conceptualisations of how societies should be organised. However, within Europe, just as the foundations of social organisation have been radically overhauled, so too must constitutional law engage in an identification of the rationalities which underlie its formal provisions; and furthermore, critically submit such bedrock conceptualisations to a test of their continued compatibility with 'real-world' conditions. Europe is an evolving and uncertain polity. In this confusing atmosphere, economics, political science, international relations theory, sociology and even post-modern theory, may help to show how Europe's social, market and political foundations might be recast, similarly laying the framework for a re-working of constitutional thought dedicated to the dampening of social and political schism during the integration process. This paper has taken three 'extra-disciplinary' models of the uncertain climate of European integration. In so doing, it has sought to move its basis for analysis far beyond the formal constitutional arena with all its traditional political and social pre-conceptions. The aim is take the European constitutional debate beyond both the *Bundesverfassungsgericht's* fixed doctrinal and conceptual stance and European law's outmoded lack of normative self-reflection and 'accidental' constitutional design.

With its conclusion that a European constitutional order must be based on legal principles and mechanism designed to foster rational and respectful deliberation between diverse and evolving interests, instead of foolish legal attempt to create a substantive European common good, it is left with certain pressing problems. First, the normativisation of 'fora' of deliberative civility, or the identification of legal mechanisms to ensure the on-going diversity and rationality of European debate.

---

[85] As a recent example, the attempt to show that existing conceptions of 'federal' constitutional orders might prove appropriate within the European order; so allowing for the constitutional capture of a linguistically and culturally diverse rather than homogeneous polity, Mancini *loc cit* n 52.

Secondly, the pinpointing of a mode to introduce the constitutional order into the private sphere, shaping both private and regulatory law, to ensure that liberated private interest is also 'civic' and prepared to accept and, importantly, serve deliberative outcomes. And thirdly, the evolution of principles to govern judicial deliberation, ensuring that the clash between plural legal sovereignties is not simply characterised by whimsical court-room behaviour.

At this very practical level, the attempt to normativise European law, or proceduralise a European constitutional order, is nothing if not demanding. How can such idealistic aims possibly be secured? Strangely, however, it is also at exactly this level that established mechanisms and doctrines of formal law may establish their worth. As concluding and very concrete examples. First, the rigid application of rules of reason provisions, forcing participants in putatively deliberative debate to ground their arguments and interests in generally accepted rationalities.[86] And secondly, the Europe-wide judicial adaptation to the Anglo-Saxon world of precedents; or, the means by which Courts themselves become neutral guardians of 'civility' by establishing, securing and promulgating a coherent and legitimate body of technical, ethical, social and political rationalities to guide post-aggregative debate both between plural legal order and between naturally diverse interests.

---

[86] Everson, *loc cit* n 44.

6

Does the European Union Pervert Democracy? Questions of Democracy in New Constitutionalist Thought on the Future of Europe

Daniel Wincott

I   Introduction: Questioning Statism: The Normative Turn in EU Studies

Recently discussion of the process of European integration and the character of the European Union has taken a theoretical and particularly a normative turn. Questions of constitutionalism have bulked particularly large in this discussion. These questions have taken new forms. Rather than being concerned with the technical merits of constitutions, particularly when understood as limiting devices on public power, they are characterised, first, by a focus on the politics of constitutions and constitutionalism and, second, a consideration of the law and constitutionalism outside of the conceptual framework within which they are conventionally located—that of state sovereignty. Both aspects place legal and political theory (back) at the centre of imagining or conceptualising the future European political and legal architecture.

In this article, I review some recent normative evaluations of the European Union.[1] Developing the analysis in this way risks distorting the arguments of those whose work I discuss, but allows me to welcome them, while suggesting that their balance should be modified somewhat. My concern is that the problems of 'democracy' associated with the European Union may be underplayed in some of this literature. I argue that the European Union may not simply have a democratic deficit, but that the question

---

[1] MacCormick, 'Democracy, Subsidiarity and Citizenship in the Context of European Union,' (1997) 16 *Law and Philosophy*, 331–356 citations from a manuscript version of the paper; Weiler *et al* 'European Democracy and its Critique,' in J. Hayward (ed) *The Crisis of Representation in Europe* (1995 Frank Cass), 4–39: especially at 28. Important recent articles in the *European Law Journal* have discussed these issues in ways which bear on my theme powerfully—see Majone, 'Europe's 'Democratic Deficit': The Question of Standards,' (1998) 4 *European Law Journal*, 5–28; Mancini, 'Europe: The Case for Statehood,' (1998) 4 *European Law Journal*, 29–42 and Weiler, 'Europe: The Case Against the Case for Statehood,' (1998) 4 *European Law Journal*, 43–62. I have attempted to take account of the arguments developed in these articles, which appeared after the initial draft of this paper was written, in my final version here. I fear that I have done so in a preliminary manner only. For a different view of the democratic problem see A. Weale 'Democratic Legitimacy and the Constitution of Europe' in R. Bellamy *et al* (eds), *Democracy and Constitutional Culture in the Union of Europe* (1995 Lothian Foundation).

of the 'perversion' of democracy within Europe should be taken more seriously.[2] The EU 'perverts' democracy if it allows national governments to escape domestic mechanisms of democratic accountability. To the extent that domestic politics is perverted, it also weakens or breaks the 'indirect' democracy of the Council of Ministers. My objective is not to establish that the 'perversion' of democracy is a ubiquitous feature of the European Union, although I do want to argue that it appears persistently in a variety of EU governance arenas, and that it may play an especially important role in determining the arena within which particular issues are considered. Instead, it is to propose that the EU's democratic problems may be somewhat deeper than much of the new constitutionalist literature suggests. While I accept the thrust of its critique of the mainstream view of the 'democratic deficit,' I believe that the new constitutionalism can learn from a number of strands of political analysis which address the issue of the perversion of democracy in Europe.

If the 'perversion' thesis has some truth to it, then my fear is that the European Union may be very difficult to 'reform' so as to render it appropriately 'democratic,' unless a basic re-organisation and re-form occurs, probably in the context of considerable popular pressure for change. After reviewing literature relevant to the 'perversion' thesis, I argue that we need more 'political' or 'historical sociological' analysis of European integration and disintegration, and analysis of the interplay and conflict between political projects which animate these processes. Perhaps in a reflection of the elitist and technocratic character of the Union itself, relatively little EU scholarship has been concerned with the 'political' in this sense. It seems to me that if the Union is to be 'democratised,' it will be as an element of the broad political project of European integration. Without wanting to disregard changes in the role of the European Parliament wholly, I do not discern much of an appetite for 'democratisation' within any currently influential political projects. Nor can I see much evidence of substantial pressure for such a change bubbling up from below.[3]

I do not wish to be misunderstood here. First, the democratic qualities of politics within nation states should not be exaggerated. Second, some of the most forceful proponents of the position that the EU empowers state elites in relation to their domestic systems develop arguments which are explicitly statist[4]—they suggest that states retain fundamental control over the process of integration. This is not a position

---

[2] The notion of perversion is borrowed from Weiler *et al*, *loc cit*, n 1—I would like to make it clear that the criticism of this article that I develop later is of the impression which I think is given by the overall balance of the argument—my use of the idea of democratic 'perversion' expression illustrates the extent to which I have borrowed from him. On the issue of perversion see also, Scharpf, 'The Joint-Decision Trap: Lessons from German Federalism and European integration,' (1988) 66 *Public Administration*, 239–278; Scharpf, 'Community and Autonomy: multi-level policy-making in the European Union,' (1994) 1 *JEPP*, 219–242; Moravcsik, 'Why the European Community Strengthens the State: Domestic Politics and International Co-operation' Paper presented at the Conference of Europeanists, Chicago, IL, USA (April 1994); P. Taylor, *The European Union in the 1990s* (1996 OUP); Dunleavy, 'The Allocation of Governance Functions in the European Union: Explaining the 'Drift to Brussels,' Paper to the Forschungsgespracht 'Creating Countervailing Institutions in Europe' University of St Gallen, Switzerland, (September 1996); Mancini, *loc cit*, n 1, at 40–41

[3] J. H. H. Weiler suggests that the Danish referendum was a watershed in the battle for democracy, indeed, by describing it as a 'well aimed shot over the bows' he almost seems to suggest that it had this purpose—*loc cit*, n 1, at 53. I remain concerned about this episode, with worries similar to those expressed by Mancini, *loc cit*, n 1, at 41, despite not endorsing his argument for the construction of a European state.

[4] A. Moravcsik, *op cit*, n 2.

I want to endorse. Paradoxically, at times, those in positions of power within states using 'Europe' to increase their autonomy from domestic interests, may risk losing control of some issues. Although these issues may be 'controlled' by various complex means, they need not be controlled or accountable at all, once removed to a murky world of committees and expertise.

After these introductory remarks, the article is organised into four sections. In Section II, I am concerned with the conventional view of the democratic deficit. Section III reviews the treatment of the democratic issue in the context literature which adopts a broadly 'post statist' image of European governance. Often, work of this sort emphasises the complexity of the Union and seeks to locate democratic elements within the overall balance of the polity.[5] Section IV introduces a series of analyses pertinent to the theme of the 'perversion' of democracy, and considers them with the issue of whether and how it might be deployed in a non 'statist' framework. By way of conclusion, in Section V I argue that the task of imagining a more democratic union may be helped if, alongside the more familiar forms of policy and legal analysis, the history of the Union and the developmental paths currently open to it (to us!) are conceptualised more politically, taking account of the role of competition between political projects.

II   Statism, the Democratic Deficit and the Limited Scope of Normative Discussion Concerning European Integration

An important strand in the 'new constitutionalist' thought on the European Union develops a critique of much of the existing discussion of the 'democratic deficit.'[6] The basis for the critique of mainstream accounts of the democratic deficit is that they view the European Union from a statist perspective. Weiler suggests that 'democratic theory and democratic sensibilities have developed almost exclusively in statal contexts.'[7] Recent work on the European Union in legal and political theory, not least by members of the Edinburgh Seminar, suggests that statist models may obscure rather than illuminate the present character of, and future possibilities for, the European Union. In effect, a good deal of the new 'normative' literature suggests or implies that statist notions have created misleading, and arguably impossible, standards against which to judge the character of the European Union's 'democratic deficit.' These difficulties may be exacerbated because the 'democratic deficit' expression is often used to bundle together a number of different themes including; 'technocratic decision-making, lack of transparency, insufficient public participation, excessive use of administrative discretion, inadequate mechanisms of control and accountability'[8] as well as issues of popular participation and representation. While these issues might be better analysed individually for many purposes, to the extent that we are interested in an overall evaluation of the character of the Union, ideas of 'democracy' are likely to remain important.

---

[5] As MacCormick does explicitly, *loc cit*, n 1; and I believe is at least implicit in some of Weiler's work, see Weiler *et al*, *loc cit*, n 1

[6] MacCormick, *loc cit*, n 1; Weiler *et al*, *loc cit*, n 1

[7] Weiler *et al*, *loc cit*, n 1, at 28—given this genealogy, the reconceptualisation of democracy may to prove difficult.

[8] Majone, *loc cit*, n 1 at 14–15.

Of particular interest for me here is the manner in which statist models contribute to the mis-diagnosis of the European Union's democratic disorder and therefore provide a flawed basis for prescribing a cure. Much writing on this issue disparagingly compares the European reality with an idealised version, rather than the messy and imperfect historical realisations, of state democracy in Europe. It is all too easy to develop a critique of the European Community from a purist democratic point of view.[9] The myths which have grown up with and around the putatively sovereign state disguise both its own flaws and the potential alternatives to it. Although it is by now well established that state democracy does not live up to its ideal, it remains difficult to free our minds of inappropriate aspects of its influence. In my view the core of the statist image projected onto the European Union is a particular view of the democratic deficit, associated with the position of the European Parliament. There is a long standing argument that the powers of the European Parliament are too few and too weak and most critics of the democratic deficit advocate an extension of its powers.[10] Moreover, the underlying aspiration that the Community should become a state writ large may be regarded as neither attractive nor viable.

The statism of the conventional view of the democratic deficit also provides a rather formalistic view of the problem. It suggests that the democratic difficulties of the Union could be resolved by creating an organ which had the characteristics of a democratic legislature. As we have already seen, it is not at all clear that the legislatures of democratic states live up to the ideal image which is often presented of them. It is far from certain, for instance, that the widespread sense of unease about the Union's democratic credentials would be resolved by such a move.[11] Moreover, arguments of this sort have a certain naive quality about them. They seem to suggest that the Union's democratic problems are accidental, rather than essential (or at least deeply ingrained), institutional features of the Union. They do not address the concern that powerful actors may have created, or re-shaped, the Union's institutions in ways which entrench the 'democratic deficit' in order to serve their own interests.

In this context, it is worth paying serious attention to the conventional metaphor used to describe the Union's democratic problems. The notion of a democratic deficit immediately suggests that there is too *little* democracy. It seems to me that this image dovetails nicely with the political agenda of the European Parliament, implying that giving *more* power to it would solve the problem. The notion of a deficit might also suggest that Europe has overdrawn its democratic account, that it was 'borrowing' to finance current projects, against future legitimacy. This echoes the approach of Jean Monnet, who used explicitly non-democratic techniques to make concrete achievements in limited areas. It has been particularly associated with the Commission.[12] In addition, it seems to me that the 'deficit' metaphor suits the interests of the European Parliament. Although (elements within) the Parliament has sought to claim the role of a 'constitutive assembly' from time to time (notably in the early and mid 1980s), it has

---

[9] Ironically, a similar purism, although attached to an opposing set of political objectives, is characteristic of many Euro-sceptics, whose objection to integration rests on an idealised image of states.

[10] See for example, some of the discussion in J. Lodge (ed) *The European Community and the Challenge of the Future* (1989 Francis Pinter).

[11] Weiler *et al*, *loc cit*, n 1; A. Weale, *loc cit*, n 1

[12] Featherstone, 'Jean Monnet and the 'Democratic Deficit' in the European Union,' (1994) 32 *Journal of Common Market Studies*, 149–170.

for the most part, sought to gain more power broadly within the existing institutional framework.[13]

Taken together these features of the debate lead to a profound impoverishment of the normative discussion of European integration. Presenting the solution to the democratic and popular problems of the Union in terms of changes in the formal powers of the Parliament has tended to impose a statist straitjacket on the discussion. Non-statist conceptions of federalism[14] currently seem to play only a marginal role in discussions about European integration, as 'federalism' is associated with statism even by many of those who do not to use it to describe the creation of a centralised European state.[15] Of course, other factors have also contributed to the poverty of the normative discussion about Europe until recently, as well shall see. However, in the context of a European project developed in largely technocratic, that is non-normative, terms, the fact that a rather narrow, formalistic and statist discourse on the democratic deficit has tended to dominate what normative discussion has occurred has served only to worsen the situation.

Other factors which have contributed to the impoverishment of the normative element in the European debate include the emphasis on practical achievements in Monnet's 'method,' and, especially, the restricted nature of the debate concerning the potential 'terminus' of the Union (*ie*, how its potential 'end-states' might be characterised), perhaps to avoid offending the sensibilities of those in positions of power in existing states. In addition, it seems to me that the idea that the European Community/Union has maintained peace in Europe has sometimes been deployed in ways which have contributed to the restriction of debate about alternatives for Europe. I do not want to be mis-understood here. The avoidance of war, and particularly of wars as devastating and brutal as those between 1914–18 and 1939–1945, is profoundly important. Moreover, I think that the European Community probably did make a contribution to the maintenance of peace. However, other factors also contributed to this 'peace'—it is at least arguable that France, the UK, Germany and Italy did not fight another war among themselves largely because of the development of the Cold War and the East-West division of Europe. My difficulty is with the use of the issue as a kind of normative 'trump' of extraordinary power (historical analysis in support of the proposition that European integration has prevented war is rarely offered). The claim that the European Community/Union has provided peace has and can effectively foreclose normative discussion about its current character and future form.

It is worth pointing out that the strong association of the democratic deficit with a statist conception of the potential role of the European Parliament represents a rather more 'stripped down' account of the core of the conventional understanding of the problem than is sometimes presented. For example, Weiler's 'Standard Version' of the democratic deficit is rather more varied than the version I present here.[16] His conception of 'Inverted Regionalism,' the first (and by implication, most important) element in the 'Standard Version,' is the aspect which is most compatible with my

---

[13] Weale, *loc cit*, n 1 provides an extended account of the 'democratic baptism' which he believes is now required. Majone, *loc cit*, n 1, at 7–14 provides a critical analysis of the assumptions behind many prescriptions for addressing the democratic deficit.

[14] See, for example, some of the discussion in M. Forsyth *Unions of States* (1981 Leicester University Press); D. Elazar (ed) *New Trends in Federalism* (1996) 17 *International Political Science Review*, 349–429.

[15] See, for example, F Mancini, *loc cit*, n 1 at 39–40

[16] Weiler *et al*, *loc cit*, n 1

image of the conventional view of the democratic deficit here. In fact, I believe that many elements of Weiler's 'Standard Version' are actually reproduced in his alternative models of governance and democracy, or in the problems they contain. Thus, the discussion of the perversion of democracy has a strong affinity to what he calls the international or consociational model and comitology may have some affinity with infranationalism. Sometimes, he uses the same terminology in both contexts—he discusses corporatism in the context of both the standard version and 'infranationalism.' In addition, Weiler's three models of governance may share features, or at least have affinities, which make their separate treatment potentially problematic. Nevertheless, it is worth pointing out that Weiler's discussion of 'Inverted Regionalism' suggests that the problems of the democratic deficit may be fairly intractable, particularly for reasons of the lesser 'specific gravity' of each individual and the greater 'remoteness' of its institutions, especially the Parliament.[17]

III New Constitutionalism and Democracy

Recently, the task of imagining the future form of the European Union has begun (again) in earnest.[18] Much of this work operates at the margins of the (sovereign) statist framework, or even explicitly outside of it. In a similar vein, the quantity of self-consciously normative theorising about the integration process has increased while its quality has improved. A variety of sources, contemporary, historical and conceptual, have been used in the attempt to generate a language in which to discuss a non-statist future for Europe. As well as the notions of federalism, confederalism and subsidiarity, which are more familiar in the European context, and therefore, perhaps tainted by their association with existing political positions, the concepts of consociation, condominium, consortium and commonwealth[19] have been suggested as providing fruitful ways of thinking about Europe and its future.

These conceptions of the Europe Union generally conjure images in which 'democracy,' while having an important place, is not the only element in its 'constitution.' Moreover, the notions of 'democratic' representation and accountability they imply are pluralistic, while the conventional understanding of democracy, at least as it seems to have featured in debates about the European Union, has a monolithic quality about it. All of this seems to me to shift the terms of the debate about Europe onto more helpful ground. If purist notions of democracy, based on the notion of the representation of a unified collective will do not describe the most ethnically homogeneous of nation states accurately, then they can hardly be expected to prove a fruitful guide to understanding the huge scale, enormous complexity and vast diversity of the European Union. Yet, a doubt remains in my mind about the 'democratic' character of the European Union, even re-imagined in these terms. I will attempt to articulate this doubt by engaging with some of the most important and influential

---

[17] Weiler *et al*, *loc cit*, n 1, at 6 and 7—8

[18] Weiler *et al*, *loc cit*, n 1; MacCormick 1990, 'Beyond the Sovereign State,' (1993) 56 *Modern Law Review*, 1—18; MacCormick 'Sovereignty, Democracy and Subsidiarity' in R. Bellamy *et al, op cit*, n ; N MacCormick, 'The Maastricht-Urteil: Sovereignty Now,' (1995) 1 *European Law Journal*, 259; N MacCormick, 'Liberalism, Nationalism and the Post-sovereign State,' (1996) 44 *Political Studies*, 553–567; N MacCormick, *loc cit*, n 1; P. Schmitter 'Representation in the Euro-Polity' 1992/3

[19] Cf, Walker, 'European Constitutionalism and European Integration,' *Public Law* (1996), 266–290; MacCormick, *loc cit*, n 1; Schmitter 1992/3; Weiler *et al, loc cit*, n 1.

versions of the new constitutionalism. At this stage, it is worth stating clearly that I will not be engaging with the so-called 'non-demos' problem.

Three recent analyses of the problem of democracy in the European Union—by MacCormick, Majone and Weiler and his collaborators—seem to me to be particularly important.[20] The studies by MacCormick and Weiler both have an empirical or analytical aspect which emphasises the complex, multi-dimensional character of the European Union.[21] However, each treatment of this complexity or multi-dimensionality is distinctive. It seems to me that MacCormick makes claims about the characteristics of different institutions within the Union, and different phases of processes of making and enforcing European rules. He is particularly concerned with the *overall* balance between these different aspects. By contrast, although Weiler does seem to have particular institutions and actors in mind as he describes three facets of the complexity of the European Union (the international, supranational and infranational), the boundaries between his 'models'—or at least between their empirical referents—are left rather fuzzy.

In normative terms, MacCormick makes important claims about what is legitimate or appropriate—what the Union ought to be—as well as describing or analysing what it is. With Majone, MacCormick seems to subscribe to the view that the European Union is—in general terms—legitimate, that the methods of law and policy-making or enforcement are basically appropriate. Weiler's normative agenda is rather less clear. On the one hand his account can be read as suggesting that the problems of democracy in Europe are much more complex—and thus more difficult to solve—than had generally been believed previously. On the other hand, by treating the problems of the three modes of governance within the Union as particular, Weiler's account may inadvertently disguise their systematic character.

MacCormick's vision of the European Union as a 'mixed Commonwealth,' one of the best developed 'new constitutionalist' works, is concerned to defend the broad appropriateness of the form and, to a lesser extent, the level of its 'democracy.' His account rightly provides 'a salutary reminder that merely to point to some un- or non-democratic element in a given constitutional set-up is *eo ipso* to damn it' and develops the powerful argument that 'discussion of the democratic deficit in Europe needs to take due account of the complexity of the democratic ideal applied to a commonwealth on this scale that brings together so many and such diverse parts, peoples and traditions'[22]. Rather than damning the EU for its un- or non-democratic elements, it is important that all its elements, which MacCormick envisions as oligo-bueaucratic and indirectly democratic, are in some sort of 'rough' or 'reasonable balance.'[23] It is important to note that 'democratic' elements remains central to this vision of the current and future operation of the European Union, albeit mainly in the indirect form of the individual accountability of ministers to domestic legislatures for their activities in Europe.

My concern is not that the democratic element in this vision is too tenuous or 'remote' from the people, although there may be some validity in such arguments. Instead, it is that aspects of the organisation of the European Union, particularly the

---

[20] MacCormick, *loc cit*, n 1; Majone, *loc cit*, n 1; J. H. H. Weiler *et al*, *loc cit*, n 1.

[21] Patrick Dunleavy's account, *op cit*, n 2, in which formal models of four different facets of integration are developed could also be read as concerned with the issue of complexity.

[22] MacCormick, *loc cit*, n 1, at 21 and 33 respectively.

[23] *Ibid*, at 21.

Council of Ministers and 'Comitology,' allow actors within national executives to escape those democratic controls that still exist domestically. At a stroke, this 'perverts'[24] democracy within the states and destroys the key link for indirect democracy at European level. If there is some validity in this reading of the European Union, then the mixed Commonwealth loses its 'reasonable balance.'

If the operation of the European Union does create a problem of 'perverted democracy,' the difficulty may not be simply associated with its 'day-to-day' operation, it might also seriously call into question the prospects for reform. I share a good deal of MacCormick's scepticism about the constructivist rationalism implied by the attempts at 'grand re-design and comprehensive constitution-making'[25] that has been proposed on a number of occasions in the recent past. The notion that the 'correct' European constitution could be dispassionately designed and put in place to solve the problem of democracy seems to me to be misplaced. On the other hand, if the notion that the European Union perverts democracy has some validity, then the scope for gradual amelioration of the democratic problem seems likely to be limited. In particular, the prospects for the changes in the operation of the Council of Ministers seem slim, especially as they would generally have to be agreed by the Council itself, acting under the current procedures, or by the European Council or an Intergovernmental Conference, both of which are structures which share many of the key democracy-perverting features of the Council of Ministers. Although there may well be competing—if you like, balancing—tendencies within the European system which lend support or pressure for reform of the Council of Ministers, if there is truth in the 'perversion' thesis, then such a change might go against the grain of its current *modus operandi*, rather than with it. At best, we might be able to describe this situation as one in which basically opposed principles struggled with one another. This is not the same as balance.

Clearly, it is not unheard of for political actors to change structures which seem to serve their own interests (particularly if these structures are implicated in the production of collectively 'sub-optimal' or problematic results). For example, the overall package of constitutional reform in the UK (including devolution—and proportional representation—in Scotland and Wales, decentralisation in England whether by means of directly elected Mayors for major cities or Regional Assemblies or some combination of the two, Freedom of Information, and Proportional Representation) seems to have limited the state power which the Labour Government can wield. This may be the reason why Prime Minister Blair appeared uneasy about the package. Constitutional reform was made possible by the experience of eighteen years of Conservative rule followed by a general election remarkable both for its overall result and the commitment to constitutional reform of many new Members of Parliament. It is hard to imagine how an equivalent mood for change might be engendered in the European Union.

Although it is not presented as a contribution to the 'New Constitutionalism', Majone's work on regulation and democracy is both relevant and sufficiently important to be considered here, albeit briefly. Vision of 'democracy' and accountability in the European Community is particularly sanguine. It develops out of a powerful critique of statist and majoritarian 'solutions' for the democratic deficit, and

---

[24] Weiler *et al*, *loc cit*, n 1, at 7.
[25] MacCormick, *loc cit*, n 1, at 32—33.

suggests that the current arrangement of the EC is broadly acceptable, at least in terms of accountability. I believe that there may be justification for looking again at two core elements of the analysis—the accountability of independent agencies and the separation of economics and politics.

The argument that independent agencies can be held to account through non-majoritian techniques is central to this analysis. It seems to me that the application of this argument in the EC context relies on an analogy with the national institutions of the USA which may be inappropriate. Their relationships to domestic legislatures and other political 'constituencies' seems to me to be significantly different from the position of members of national governments when they act as political 'principals' or as *ex post* monitors of the actions of independent agencies in the EC context. In the setting of broad objectives and the co-ordination of regulation, it seems to me that the position of the Council and the Commission (even taking the role of the European Parliament into account), is not analogous to that of the US Congress and president.[26] Even allowing that the 'democratic' is only one element in the system—the balance— by which independent agencies are held in check, it remains an important one, which may have an attenuated—or even 'perverted'—character within the EC.

The idea that it is strictly limited in scope is an important factor in visions of a 'balanced' Community, within which mechanisms of accountability can operate effectively. Since Maastricht, the scope of EC powers has not expanded in the way it did in the 1970s and 1980s. Whether or not this change is one in the 'deep structure' of the Community (introducing a system of limited powers) and attributable to the subsidiarity principle[27] remains an open question. It is possible, at least, that this change is more conjunctural and has an episodic character. In any event, the part played by national leaders acting in the European arena in the earlier phase of expanding competences (seemingly 'without limits') should make us pause for a moment, especially as many of the basic expansions took place during the 1970s, a period still widely viewed as one of stasis in European policy-making.

The separation of economics from politics is an important theme of Majone's argument. Majone's interpretation of the evidence suggests that the people(s) of Europe show a preference for ongoing economic integration, separate from political integration. This can only be achieved if integration is concerned with efficiency and economics rather than redistribution and politics (or, viewed at the level of relationships between Member States, at least that efficiency maximisation occurs before redistribution).[28] Independent agencies are the appropriate institutional form for keeping politics out of regulation. Similar arguments underpin the normative justification for the weak development of redistributive social policy at European level. The question of whether politics and economics can be kept separate should also address the impact of European regulation on national patterns of governance in general, and of social policy in particular. Without wishing to ignore the impact of the evolution of the world economy on the policy configurations of Member States, far from being wholly separate, policies seemingly based on efficiency at the European level have had substantial impacts on the sustainability of traditional patterns of redistributive politics nationally. Although they do not necessarily justify the development of a supranational 'welfare state,' the impact of European 'regulation' on

---

[26] Majone, *loc cit*, n 1, at 20 mentions the significant roles of Congress and the president.

[27] Majone, *loc cit*, n 1, at 8–10.

[28] Majone, *loc cit*, n 1, at 28.

national redistribution may be an important source of popular opposition to further integration. The interweaving of politics and economics in this way represents a significant dilemma for 'Europe'; both the *status quo* and the likely paths from it may be problematic.

Weiler's normative position on the Union's democratic credentials is more ambivalent, it seems to me. The use of the word 'perversion' to describe the impact of the European Union on balance of executive and legislative power within the Member States—and, by extension, their 'democratic balance'—is drawn from Weiler's work.[29] Even if something of a defence of the EU's democratic credentials *is* part of his purpose, it is embedded in a deep critique of accountability and representation in the European Union. Each of the three facets of the Union, or the integration process, with which Weiler is concerned seems to have its own—fairly intractable—democratic problems. The discussion of these models is modest in tone, including an explicit acknowledgement that it will not 'in and of itself, point to "democratic" deficiencies or solutions.'[30] Nevertheless, there are two ways in which Weiler's analysis may, perhaps inadvertently, disguise the democratic problems of the Union. First, by separating out the supranational, international and infranational levels of governance, his analysis may downplay their interaction and the features that they share, in a way which distracts our attention from possible systematic aspects of the democratic deficit. Second, too much may be claimed for the 'models of democracy' with which each of these modes of governance is associated. Each has significant democratic problems of its own, especially when applied to the EU.

Weiler is concerned to treat the international, supranational and infranational modes of EU governance as distinct, and not to provide an account which resolves the relationship of the various facets of the Union's democratic deficit to one another, whether in general theoretical terms, or in a particular narrative account of episodes or phases of the integration process.[31] In other words, in terms of what international relations scholars understand as the 'levels of analysis' problem, Weiler seems to be arguing that a variety of theories can be legitimately or successfully run alongside one another so long as they each deal with a different 'level.'[32] Without wanting to be drawn into the detail of this debate, it seems to me that the theories used at different levels of analysis should not be mutually exclusive.[33] If they are compatible, then the best that can be said is that the use of different theories at various levels of analysis is incomplete.[34] In fact, I think that a more integrated account of the various facets of

---

[29] Weiler *et al, loc cit*, n 1, for example at 7.

[30] Weiler *et al, loc cit*, n 1, at 28.

[31] Recent remarks suggest that Weiler himself still wishes to keep the various models separate, see, Weiler, *loc cit*, n 1, at 52 as well as Weiler *et al, loc cit*, n 1. I believe that an analysis of the development of the democratic deficit might be integrated fruitfully into Weiler's magisterial historical account of the 'legal' and 'political' development of the European Community 1991 The Transformation of Europe (1991) 100 *Yale Law Journal*, 2403–2473

[32] Cf, J. Peterson, 'Decision-making in the European Union: towards a framework for analysis,' (1995) 4 *Journal of European Public Policy*, 69–94 for a clear application of the influential 'levels of analysis' approach to the study of decision-making in Europe.

[33] That is, unless an argument that the EU 'contains' its own negation is being run explicitly.

[34] Cf, L. Cram 'Integration Theory and the study of the European policy process' in J. Richardson (ed) *European Union: Power and Policy-making* (1996 Routledge) and L. Cram *Policy-making in the EU: Conceptual Lenses and the integration process* (1997 Routledge) as well as, Wincott, 'Institutional Interaction and European Integration: Towards an Everyday Critique of Liberal Intergovernmentalism' (1995) 5 *Journal of Common Market Studies*, 597–609, for discussions which state or imply a certain caution about the separation of these 'levels'

the Union described in Weiler's account can be achieved. Indeed, it seems to me that the inclusion of features of each of the three 'models' in the 'Standard Version' of the democratic deficit suggests that the basis of an integrated account of this sort might be present in the article itself.

I have already argued that Weiler's account of the 'Standard Version' of the democratic deficit includes features which correspond to characteristics of the other two 'Models of Democracy.' Thus the general discussion of the perversion of democracy, the issue of neo-corporatism and the issues of transparency associated with 'Comitology,'[35] all seem to me to be defining features of consociationalism and infranationalism, the two alternative, putatively non-statist models discussed later in the essay. I am tempted to treat the existence of these features within the 'Standard Version' as an invitation to seek out commonalities[36] among the various modes of governance discussed by Weiler. These commonalities might provide the basis for an integrated account of modes of governance. Interesting similarities may exist, for example, in the non-majoritarian qualities of the putatively 'consociational' features of the international mode and the independent agencies characteristic of the infranational sphere. Moreover, if there is mileage in the 'perversion' thesis, then the interplay or movement between these different levels or modes of governance is likely to play an important role. National elites may be in an especially strong position to shift issues from one arena to another, particularly in order to shield an issue from popular scrutiny. In doing so they may, of course, lose control of particular issues to some extent. Blame-shifting and blame-avoidance have probably made a significant contribution to the growth of infranational governance.

Although Weiler is distinguished as a critic of the European Union on democratic grounds, it seems to me that his discussion 'European Democracy—International, Supranational, Infranational' and 'Models of Democracy,'[37] give too strong an impression that European democracy is well developed and entrenched. They suggest that the various 'forms of governance' discussed are associated with particular (normative) democratic logics. This, it seems to me, claims too much—as an examination of the models will indicate. Weiler explicitly argues that the 'Standard Version' of the democratic deficit 'captures most of' the supranational model's 'actual or potential shortcomings.'[38] In Weiler's account these shortcomings are numerous and wide-ranging. They imply that democracy must be 'diluted' and perhaps even 'perverted' in the integration process. While it might be suggested that neo-corporatism and consociationalism are each concerned with the representation of interests, at least in the European Union context (and possibly also in principle), it is debatable whether this representation should be regarded as democratic.

There are difficulties in describing either of these models individually as 'democratic.' The case is clearer with respect to neo-corporatism than consociationalism. Generally, it is discussed as a way of organising a polity (in statist contexts

---

[35] Weiler *et al, loc cit*, n 1, at 7–9.

[36] For example, while it might not be regarded as controversial to assert that the 'infranational' is concerned with functional specialisation and 'efficiency,' it would seem more odd when made about the operation of the 'international,' which is general rather than specialised, and political or bargained rather than 'efficient,' however, as we shall see in Section IV below, the most influential exponent of the 'international' perspective on European integration proposes that involvement in the EU not only 'strengthens the state' but also promotes efficiency—see A. Moravcsik, *op cit*, n 2

[37] Weiler *et al, loc cit*, n 1, at 24 and 28.

[38] Weiler *et al, loc cit*, n 1, at 32.

a state form or state regime) rather than a model of democracy.[39] We are much more accustomed to talking of a neo-corporatist state than a neo-corporatist democracy. The question is somewhat more complicated in the case of consociationalism, where the notion of 'consociational democracy' has a greater resonance. Nevertheless, the notion that consociationalism is a form of democracy has been subject to powerful critique.[40] Even if consociationalism is accepted as a model of democracy, it is not at all clear that the supposedly 'consociational' characteristics displayed by the EU are those which would grant consociationalism its democratic character. In particular, as we shall see in more detail below, it involves the 'representation' of internally homogenous and largely hermetic social segments. This is hardly an adequate description of the populations of the Member States. One of the features of consociationalism which *is* apt in the EU context is 'cartelisation of elites'[41] which hardly suggests democratic accountability.

IV   Does the European Union 'Pervert' Democracy?

The key issue for the present account, then, is what mileage there is in the notion of the perversion of democracy. The particular form in which this issue has been expressed so far—the perversion of democracy—has been borrowed from Joseph Weiler and his colleagues, for whom it was a theme in 'The Standard Version' of the democratic deficit, albeit after what I regard as the central theme of 'Inverted Regionalism.' However, despite methodological and theoretical differences, I believe that a similar idea has been expressed by other authors, including Scharpf (in his analysis of *Politikverflechtung*), Moravcsik (who argues that the European Community strengthens the state), Taylor (whose work includes an application of consociational theory to the European Union) and Dunleavy (in his rational choice models of the 'drift' to Brussels).[42] I will compare the notions of the perversion of democracy present in these analyses.

   Weiler's recent work is in a 'new constitutionalist' vein. It explicitly raises the issue of the appropriateness of statist concepts in the analysis of European integration. This marks him out from the other accounts here, although they vary both in the degree to which they treat the issue of statehood as explicitly problematic and in their (explicit or implicit) analytical use of the categories associated with state sovereignty. At one extreme, Moravcsik treats the state as unproblematic and uses the issue of the perversion of democracy to bolster a strictly statist position, treating the EU as a conventional international organisation posing no essential threat to the sovereignty of existing states. While his discussion of the perversion of democracy is interesting, in my view, it is embedded in a basically flawed grand narrative of integration. Although Dunleavy's discussion of transaction costs and the 'drift to Brussels' shares many similarities with Moravcsik's analysis, he explicitly distances himself from discussions of integration which are concerned with the 'forms and aspects of statehood' and 'the

---

[39] Although it might be associated with functional representation and functional democracy.

[40] Barry, 'The Consociational Model and its Dangers,' (1975) 3 *European Journal of Political Research*, 393–412.

[41] P. Taylor, *op cit*, n 2.

[42] Weiler *et al*, *loc cit*, n 1; Scharpf, *loc cit*, n 2 (1988); Scharpf, *loc cit*, n 2 (1996); A. Moravcsik, *op cit*, n 2 and Moravcsik 'Preferences and Power in the European Community: A Liberal Intergovernmentalist Approach,' (1993) 31 *Journal of Common Market Studies*, 473–524; P. Taylor, *op cit*, n 2; P. Dunleavy, *op cit*, n 2; Judge Mancini has also touched on this issue in a recent paper, *loc cit*, n 1.

lineaments of "sovereignty".'[43] Indeed, the flexibility and multidimensionality of Dunleavy's models serve as an interesting corrective to Moravcsik's implicit tendency to employ a *telos* of the (nation) state.[44] Taylor, who is particularly associated with the application of consociational theory to the EU, suggests that the states and the institutions of the Union are in a symbiotic relationship, although this idea borrowed from biology, seems to be used metaphorically rather than conceptually, and its diachronic implications are not drawn out. Scharpf's position on these issues is also complex. His application of the logic of *Politikverflechtung* to European integration was grounded on the understanding that the Member States controlled the European policy process and used a unanimity decision-rule (it was based on research conducted in the early and mid-1980s). On the other hand, his concern was not directly with issues of sovereignty, but rather with the implications of specific institutional forms whether found at national or supra-national level.

Arguably, Moravcsik makes the key claim most forcefully.[45] He asserts that the democratic deficit is an inherent characteristic of the operation of the European Community/Union system. The democratic deficit is squarely located in the operation of the intergovernmental fora, including Treaty negotiations, Intergovernmental Conferences and the Council of Ministers. It is tied to the 'intergovernmental' character, or at least to intergovernmentalist explanations of the Community. Secretive deliberations and binding decisions insulate members of government from domestic scrutiny and become a means by which (members of) national governments manage to take decisions which they would have been unable to take within an autonomous national context. To use English constitutional language to make Moravcsik's point, the undemocratic character of the Council of Ministers is the EU's 'efficient secret.'

Unfortunately, Moravcsik rather spoils his argument by chaining this claim to an essentialism of the state. The entire account is motivated by a concern to demonstrate that European integration strengthens the state. In this context, 'the state' is defined rather trivially and instrumentally as those who hold the few most important positions in national executives. In an attempt to lend credence to this approach, he concentrates on those decisions over which Heads of Government or Heads of State, and perhaps also Foreign Ministers, have maximum control. In effect, then, the strengthening of the state is thus conceptualised as the strengthening of elements of the national executive against domestic interests.

One difficulty with this approach is that it ignores the extent to which the organisation of the Council of Ministers may actually fragment the national executive, giving functional office holders the greater autonomy *vis-à-vis* their colleagues, and creating problems of the internal co-ordination of government and policy. He does discuss the Common Agricultural Policy, which could be regarded as the most acute example of a policy of this sort, but he accounts for it as a problem of the power of domestic interests, rather than one of the autonomy of Agricultural Ministers at European level. Moreover, he seems to think that even here a comparison with EFTA might show that the state had been strengthened *vis-à-vis* domestic groups by EC membership.[46] It seems to me that a degree of concern about the functional

---

[43] P. Dunleavy, *op cit*, n 2, at 7.

[44] This teleological quality of Moravcsik's analysis is discussed in D. Wincott, *loc cit*, n 34, especially at 607.

[45] Albeit, unfortunately in a paper which although widely read is not as accessible as it might be, having been circulated as a conference paper and a working paper.

[46] A. Moravcisk, *op cit*, n 2, at 14.

specialisation and the degree of autonomy for (certain) special interests within the Community framework might be appropriate.

A second difficulty with this approach, which again raises a broader issue, concerns its roots in synchronic analysis or 'comparative statistics.' An analytic approach which treats particular dramatic 'moments' in the integration process, is likely to 'discover' that the Member States bulked large—dominated—the decision-taking process. If moments at different points in time are compared, then their 'essential' similarity—the importance of the representatives of states—may appear to shine through. However, diachronic accounts seem to show first, that actors other than the representatives of states make a contribution and, second, that what Moravcsik calls the 'preferences' of states are re-shaped in the process of integration.[47]

A further problem is created by an inconsistency in the view of the domestic politics with which Moravcsik is operating. His general agenda for Liberal Intergovern-mentalist theory is to show how European integration serves domestic interests, because domestic interests constrain governments. The image of domestic politics here is liberal and pluralist.[48] At times, however, Moravcsik wants to argue that (liberal pluralist) democracy at domestic level is ultimately self-defeating. Particular domestic interests effectively control sectors of activity which they then operate to their narrow advantage. Collectively sub-optimal outcomes result. It is hard to see how he can sustain a generally liberal pluralist view of domestic politics while developing arguments of this sort.[49] The key question, which Moravcsik does not answer directly, concerns the source of state 'preferences' when not driven by domestic interests—in other words, when governments have 'slack' from domestic democratic pressures.[50] Despite his comments on functionalist regime theory,[51] the answer to this question which can be uncovered in Moravcsik's work has a functionalist quality. Free of pressure, governments do things in the common interest that promote efficiency, which rent-seekers would prevent them from doing domestically.[52] In addition to the smuggling in of functionalism, a substantive/normative element is introduced into an approach which generally seems to aspire to formalism and positivism. Moravcsik makes the general claim that efficiency is served by 'market liberalisation and stabilisation policies'—and the common interest is served by this sort of subversion of democracy.[53] It seems that alongside the strong state the free market is the destination of Moravcsik's functional telos.

Although many of them share elements of his account, none of the other authors subscribe to Moravcsik's oddly one-sided view of intergovernmentalism. For example, while Scharpf stresses the importance of ('intergovernmental') unanimity decision-rules, his analysis allows for the possibility of change. Indeed, his account of policy-making in the Federal Republic of Germany emphasises how dis-satisfaction with

---

[47] Wincott, *loc cit*, n 34; Pierson, 'The Path to European integration: A Historical Institutionalist Analysis,' (1996) 29 *Comparative Political Studies*, 123–163; Cram, 'Calling the Tune Without Paying the Piper? Social Policy Regulation: The Role of the Commission in European Union Social Policy,' (1993) 21 *Policy and Politics*, 195–217; Cram, 'The European Commission as a Multi-Organization: Social Policy and IT in the EU,' (1994) 1 *Journal of European Public Policy*, 383–402; and in some detail in L Cram, *op cit*, n 19.

[48] Moravcsik, *loc cit*, n 42.

[49] Compare the analyses in Moravcsik, *loc cit*, n 42 and A. Moravcsik, *op cit*, n 2.

[50] Wincott, *loc cit*, n 34; L. Cram, *op cit*, n 34 for earlier statements of this critique.

[51] A. Moravcisk, *op cit*, n 2, at 43–44.

[52] A. Moravcisk, *op cit*, n 2, at 5.

[53] A. Moravcisk, *op cit*, n 2, at 5.

Politikverflechtung changed the context and eventually the forms of decision-making, a theme which comes out still more clearly in his subsequent work.[54] Scharpf's account places considerable emphasis on the Common Agricultural Policy, in which, directly contrasting with Moravcsik's view, he regards as a product of the form of decision-making in the Community, rather than the strength of domestic pressures. Too often, the CAP does not get the attention it deserves, given its absorption of the resources of the Community. Nevertheless, a model which requires large-scale 'overspending' on Community projects does not provide an appropriate image of the decision or policy processes more generally, characterised, as they often are, by 'regulatory' policies, which do not make heavy demands of the Community budget. Of course, there may be deeper features which the 'regulatory' approach shares with analyses of *Politikverflechtung*. Indeed, in his more recent work, Scharpf has concentrated directly on the issue of technical regulation.[55] Here, he also emphasises the potentially positive-sum nature of European or joint-decision making, even were no 'European public' or common institutions of political culture to develop.

Another approach—the application of consociational theory to the European Union—modifies the strong intergovernmentalism associated with Moravcsik's approach more decisively, while retaining some of the sense that the EU might 'pervert' democracy. Clearly, intergovernmentalism and consociationalism have a family resemblance; both emphasise 'cartelistic' characteristics of elite behaviour in the Union. This resemblance may provide the basis for Weiler's association of the international (intergovernmental) with the consociational.[56] However, their relationship is open to dispute. Paul Taylor, who is particularly associated with consociational models of the EU, explicitly distinguishes it from intergovernmentalism, of which he discerns hard and soft varieties.[57] Nevertheless, the differences between some forms of intergovernmentalism and Taylor's own approach may be smaller than he implies. Indeed, his characterisations of intergovernmentalism (in each of its forms) seem to imply a 'zero-sum' opposition between 'Europe' or 'integration' and the states, whereas Moravcsik's 'Liberal' form of intergovernmentalism attempts to explain why Member States may have incentives to turn to 'Europe,' a position which resembles Taylor's notion of 'symbiosis' to some extent.

A question about the applicability of consociationalism to the EU should be addressed. This question can be asked equally about the versions of the approach provided by Taylor and Weiler. The crucial issue here concerns what—who—is represented. Consociational theory suggests that various 'sectors' of society are represented. Known in the argot as 'pillars,' they are culturally distinct (based on religion and perhaps language, but not necessarily spatially/territorially separated) and *homogenous*. Each pillar is a powerful social unity, which constitutes individual identities and provides an entire social world. It is the claim that these social worlds can be effectively *represented* as unities that allows consociationalism to claim democratic (or perhaps 'popular') credentials, for all it requires is a substantial degree of elite autonomy to facilitate compromise. Whatever we think of this claim as applied to, say, the Netherlands in the 1950s, it is much more difficult to make it in relation the relationship between Member States and their entire populations. The claim to a

---

[54] Compare Scharpf *loc cit,* n 2 (1988) and *loc cit,* n 2 (1994).

[55] Scharpf, *loc cit*, n 2 (1994).

[56] Weiler *et al, loc cit*, n 1, at 24, 28.

[57] P. Taylor, *op cit*, n 2, at 78–79.

'representational' democracy made in consociational theory cannot be extended fully to the EU.

The skewed ('domestic') distribution of costs and benefits of European integration within the Member States, which is precisely associated with internal divisions or fragmentation, are disguised by this approach. We are left with a series of (important) similarities between the patterns of elite activity in the EU and consociational 'democracies,' but with the former polity deficient in the key balancing element of popular representation. Some of these characteristics may not be the same as those provided by intergovernmentalism, even in a liberal form. First, Taylor does not make it wholly clear who is in the elite cartel. If states are equivalent to social pillars, the analogy with 'domestic' consocationalism suggests that they are made up of state elites. On the other hand, the notion of symbiosis might suggest that other groups could be in the cartel. The idea of symbiosis between European and Member State levels faces a difficulty similar to that faced by liberal intergovernmentalism, of the accretion of competences at the European level. While the notion of symbiosis may help to direct our attention towards the discovery of positive rather than zero-sum games, can we expect the balance between these two levels to alter systematically over time? Unlike Moravcsik, Taylor seems open to the idea that the states that have been 'strengthened' by Europe have also been caught in a process of *engrenage* and substantially reshaped by integration.[58]

A number of different approaches seem to suggest that a primary reason that administrative and political elites might shift policy-making to Brussels is that they can enhance their autonomy *vis-à-vis* domestic political constituencies.[59] However, the account here suggests that this is not the whole story. If it is not, we need some sort of analysis of other pressures that might exist. Some accounts which start from the (broadly historically justifiable) basis of state sovereignty, couch the explanation in terms of the strategic errors made by state elites. Thus, Pierson argues that state 'actors ... in a strong initial position' who 'seek to maximise their interests' end up 'fundamentally transform[ing] their own positions (or those of their successors) in ways that are unanticipated and/or undesired.'[60] In general, however, I would argue that other influential actors need to be identified, such as European institutions or (European) business or 'capital' and their objectives specified, in order to make sense of the process.[61]

However, the other actors usually identified in this context do not seem to have much incentive to 'democratise' the European Union. For example, although the Commission may have a rather abstract and long term concern about the overall 'success' and sustainability of the Union which might militate in favour of democracy, its more immediate and concrete interests point in a different direction. Dunleavy's account of the European bureaucracy suggests that it is at best neutral on the question of democracy, instead being concerned to concentrate on control/regulatory functions rather than delivery functions.[62] This account is rather formal, in the sense that it (deliberately) does not involve consideration of the Commission's substantive

---

[58] P. Taylor, *op cit*, n 2, at 20–21.

[59] A. Moravcsik, *op cit*, n 2; P. Taylor, *op cit*, n 2; P. Dunleavy, *op cit*, n 2; Weiler *et al*, *loc cit*, n 1.

[60] Pierson, *loc cit*, n 47, at 126.

[61] For analysis of institutions Cram's work is exemplary, see *loc cit*, n 47; and *op cit*, n 34, on the role of business see M. Green-Cowles, 'Setting the Agenda for a New Europe: The ERT and EC 1992,' (1995) 33 *Journal of Common Market Studies*, 501–526.

[62] P. Dunleavy *op cit*, n 2, at 17–22.

objectives, its 'mission,' and concentrates on its bureaucracy to the exclusion of its political dimension. In general, it seems better suited to the explanation of the manner in which the Commission is involved in the policy process, rather than strongly suggesting that it has the ability to accumulate competences. However, analyses with more of a 'substantive' element, including Cram's,[63] which engage explicitly with the strategic concerns of the Commission and its Directorates-General in fostering integration and accumulating competences, suggest a broadly similar perspective on their attitude to democracy.

In some of the foregoing analyses, the loosening of the domestic constraints on national governments is depicted as being in the common interest. However, there may be reasons to doubt the view that pressure at European level is more balanced than it is at the national one. Turning to the role of business, which has been increasingly recognised as a key force in the integration process,[64] the prospects are not promising. Indeed, some scholars, primarily attribute the intractable nature of the European Union's democratic problem to 'capital,' as well as analysing blame-shifting and blame-avoidance by members of nation-state governments.[65] Dunleavy's account concentrates on the interests of European capital as a whole, in an intentionally abstract manner. He suggests that 'capital' has an interest in concentrating on those areas of policy-making with which it is most concerned at levels of governance over which it has greatest control and where popular control is weakest. In other words, they have incentives to develop the European Union in order to isolate certain policies from potential popular control.

In general, then, the notion that the democratic deficit is an inherent and immutable feature of the European Union *is* associated with a statist and formalistic version of intergovernmental theory. However, a weaker, but nonetheless deeply pessimistic, version of this view does seem sustainable, even outwith a statist vision of the European Union. An assessment of the prospects for change in this situation requires an analysis of the competing political projects which vivify the contemporary politics of the Union. It is to a brief outline of these 'projects' that I now turn, by way of conclusion.

V   Conclusion

It seems hard to dispute the notion that the best way of understanding the European Union is to emphasise its complex and multi-faceted character. The foregoing account also suggests, I hope, that the 'democratic deficit' may be deeply ingrained in the structure of the Union. It seems likely that this situation can change only in the face of substantial pressure of some sort. It is, however, less than clear what the sources of such pressure might be. In order to evaluate the prospects for change of this sort, it is worth exploring the nature of the political projects that have developed—or may develop—around the European Union. There has been surprisingly little academic analysis of the European Union couched in terms of competing political projects. What—mainly journalistic—discussion there has been of this sort has tended to associate particular (dis)integration projects with nations or groups of nations within

---

[63] Cram, *loc cit*, n 47 and *op cit*, n 34.

[64] Cf, especially M. Green-Cowles, *loc cit*, n 61.

[65] P. Dunleavy, *op cit*, n 2.

the Community, perhaps for good reasons. However, there are signs that this form of analysis may be becoming more popular.[66]

Hooghe and Marks identify five 'projects' around the European Union which, while some may overlap to an extent, are also partly incompatible—even hostile to one another. Four of these 'projects' are 'current' in the Union, following on from the broadly successful 'market unification' project. These projects are neoliberal, democratic, 'organised space' and 'national.' Two of these 'projects'—the neoliberal and national—are actively hostile to the further democratisation of the Union, on grounds of the likely consequent interference in the economy, and the diminution of national power. The project of creating a European 'organised space' seems to offer qualified—and largely instrumental—support for democratisation. It might help proponents of the project to achieve their other objectives. Hooghe and Marks depict this support largely as a mirror image of the reasons for the neoliberal opposition to it.

The final project is directly concerned with democracy, which Hooghe and Marks view as being concerned with the European Parliament, the (upgrading of a) European regional chamber, European citizenship and conceptions of democratic rights. According to their account, the democratic project seems to be associated with extending a conventionally statist vision of liberal democracy to European level. Moreover, it faces powerful opponents, of the sort described earlier in the present account. Its proponents are the Parliament itself, certain Member State governments— or better, parts of state elites—(most notably Germany) and, more equivocally, the Commission. In the end, Hooghe and Marks point to the unidirectional or rachet-like character of the process of 'increasing democracy,' which they attribute to a general legitimacy of liberal democracy. This diffuse legitimacy, they argue, makes it extremely difficult to reverse concessions made to the European Parliament.

More work focusing on political project in the process of European integration would be of value. In particular, assessing the future evolution of the Community and especially the prospects for its democratisation, whether in the form of increasing the influence or power of the Parliament or, more generally, in changing patterns of accountability and representation, requires an assessment in these terms which accurately assess both the existing structures of and around the Union and the character and power of the actors and forces associated with each project for change. However, considering the European Union in terms of political projects does underline the limited extent to which European people(s) have engaged with the integration of Europe politically. While Europe may provide economic opportunities for some, in popular politics it seems to be regarded as a threat and resisted, for the most part. The images of the political movements which helped to secure civil, political and social rights over the last two or three centuries seem out of place in the European Union context. Of course, these images may well be fundamentally tainted by statism, given their place in its genealogy. These movements also had a violent and exclusionary side to them, which we would wish to avoid repeating, if possible. Nevertheless, in my view without a new sort of popular involvement in Europe, elements of the structure of the European Union which tend to pervert democracy are unlikely to change.

---

[66] L. Hooghe and G. Marks, 'Birth of a Polity: The Struggle over European Integration.' Paper presented to the Conference on 'The Politics and Political Economy of Contemporary Capitalism,' Humbolt University and the Wissenschaftszentrum Berlin, May 1995 and at the American Political Science Association meeting, Chicago, September 1995. The authors concentrate on two 'projects' in their 'The Making of a Polity: The Struggle over European Integration: in H. Kitschelt *et al* (eds) *Continuity and Change in Contemporary Capitalism* (1998; Cambridge University Press).

7

Legitimacy and Governance Beyond the European Nation State: Conceptualising Governance in the European Union

Caitríona Carter and Andrew Scott

I   Introduction

In this paper, we examine a number of related themes that have emerged in the literature concerning the legitimacy problems confronting the European Union as it evolves as an arrangement for governance that resides at a level 'beyond' the nation state. We take as our starting point the legitimacy crisis that became such a prominent feature of the EU in the aftermath of the signing of the TEU, and which continues to obstruct moves towards closer European integration. We locate this crisis within a broader constitutional deficit in the arrangements that mediate relations between each of the EU, the Member State and the individual citizen. We argue that to understand the emergence of the legitimacy crisis—manifest in a dramatic shift in popular opinion *vis-à-vis* the construction of 'an ever closer Union' at the end of the 1980s, signalling the onset of a legitimacy crisis within (and of) the EU—it is necessary to reflect not only on the evolving constitutional architecture of the EU and associated policy developments, but also the modalities whereby such changes are transposed to Member State constitutional and political arenas, and to the policy processes within those states impacted upon by European integration. For it is still the case that, despite the Treaty reforms of the 1980s and 1990s, it is the Member State which remains the dominant participant in European integration; a situation that is unlikely to change over the foreseeable future. And while it has been the leadership of Member States which has given European integration its principal driving force, equally, the centrality of the Member State to the enterprise has restricted the capacity of the EU to adjust or police common policies, or respond to emerging problems in ways which satisfy the explicit and implicit objectives of European integration. In this paper we develop an approach in which constitutionalism is regarded as being more than simply the constitutional architecture of the EU Treaties. We augment the orthodox approach by focusing on the (legitimating) modalities which are necessary to facilitate the constitutional development of the EU, and argue that the legitimacy crisis reflects a failure in the operation of these modalities.

The remainder of this paper is organised into five sections. In the next section we identify the core problematic of the EU as the legitimacy crisis, and consider some of the responses that have been proposed to deal with this. In section III we consider the role of the individual in the EU political and constitutional architecture, and discuss the problems for legitimacy that arise from approaches that regard the individual from a nationalist perspective only. In section IV we elaborate a three-level approach to the question of EU legitimacy, and argue that the legitimacy crisis is the result of a deep-seated constitutional—and thus political—deficit within the European Union. We discuss a number of potential mechanisms for closing this constitutional deficit. Our conclusions are presented in the final section.

II   The Origins and Nature of the Legitimacy Crisis

The literature on the EU 'legitimacy' crisis emerged in the wake of the adverse popular reaction to the signing of the EU. The political intensity of the ratification debate in a number of key Member States (particularly Germany, France, and the UK) was interpreted as evidence that the EU, both as a constitutional arrangement and as a policy-making (or decision-making) process, no longer commanded the uncritical support of its citizens. The force of the opposition to the TEU proposals demonstrated that the period of 'popular consent,'[1] which had facilitated an elite-driven and ultimately successful period of European economic integration (involving intensive trans-national co-operation, joint decision-making and common institution building) across post-war Western Europe, had come to an end. It appeared that British Prime Minister Thatcher had caught the general mood of publics across the EU when she labelled the TEU as 'a Treaty too far.' Popular opposition appeared to focus principally on the implications of the TEU for the rather ill-defined notions of national sovereignty and national identity, or symbols thereof (such as the national currency). So intense was the debate that many seasoned observers came to doubt that the Treaty would be ratified. In the event the TEU was ratified, but the internal disharmony created in the process provided little comfort for the integration maximalists that the European enterprise was back on the rails.

In the aftermath of the TEU ratification, analyses of EU legitimacy continued to dominate the academic debate. This can be explained partly as a consequence of the far-reaching implications for the EU if it its governance arrangements and common policies failed to command broad public support. Indeed, it was this concern that persuaded the designers of the 1996 Inter-Governmental Conference (IGC) that any review of the TEU must consider measures that would enhance the EU's popular legitimacy. In part too, however, the legitimacy crisis commanded attention because it posed difficult theoretical issues for students of European integration. Why had European integration become contested at this juncture, given the comparatively uncontested progress in the construction of common governance arrangements recorded hitherto? And if the crisis reflected a general mood that some fundamental limit of integration had been reached, in the sense that any further integration is possible only through an appropriation (at the EU level) of the essentially foundational functions of the nation state, not only would this jeopardise further integrative initiatives it might well also render problematic the effective delivery of prevailing policies. It is the interpretation of the legitimacy question in this latter sense—as reflecting the non-existence of a narrative that yields both a theoretical defence of, and practical handbook for, the construction of a governance beyond the nation state—which will be considered in this article.

---

[1]   Wallace/Smith, 'Democracy or Technocracy? European integration and the Problem of Popular Consent,' (1995) 18:3 *West European Politics*, at 144.

In broad terms, governance at national level can be conceived of as the panoply of institutions, rules and political conventions which together are regarded as an acceptable set of arrangements for the making, dispensing and enforcement of law and policy on the part of the governing authority.[2] Acceptability is assured first so long as the governing body—operating through the appropriate institutions—adheres to these rules and conventions (which reflect the foundational normative order of the polity) and, second, in so far as the underlying values and aspirations of the society (democratically gauged) continue to be met within that particular governance framework. Weiler has described the first condition as the requirement of formal legitimacy, while the second is consistent with his representation of a parallel need for the social legitimacy of governance).[3] Both are necessary for legitimacy of governance, but neither in isolation is sufficient. And, as Weiler demonstrates, these twin elements need not be in harmony; what is formally legitimate may be contested by the polity, and what is socially accepted may be abhorrent by reference to any rational normative value system by which formal governance systems are constructed. Moreover, it is unlikely that, within each and every occasion of disharmony, a meta-rule can be found to mediate this situation. Consequently, the political process itself will be engaged directly, with the aim either of amending formal rules in the interests of securing greater social legitimacy or modifying societal values to maintain the integrity of the formal system. The working assumption is that governance within EU nation states corresponds, generally, to these requirements; that formal and social legitimacy are in harmony or that, where this isn't the case, modalities exist either in the form of meta-rules or political processes that are capable of effecting a reconciliation between these elements. Hence, governance in the nation state is presented as the 'ideal type' constitutional arrangement.

However, when we look to the governance of the EU we find a different situation. The legitimacy of Union governance formally construed (as a constitutional authority) was, from the outset, derived *exclusively* from the legitimacy of its core constitutive elements—the nation states—and *not* directly from the citizens within those Member States.[4] Thus, the EU as a constitutional arrangement originated as an extension of the nation state with no attention, understandably, being given to dynamics which would facilitate the nation state becoming a 'subset' of the EU, nor the issues that would raise. The popular appeal of European integration on the other hand—its legitimacy in the social sense—rested principally on the material (political, social and economic) benefits it promised to deliver directly to individual citizens, benefits that were not available if nation states continued to operate as independent entities within the orthodox structures of international diplomacy. The weakness inherent in this particular hierarchical ordering between the nation state and the EU governance levels would become apparent should disharmony arise between the legitimacy of EU governance in the formal sense, as a constitutional arrangement, and its acceptability as an arrangement capable of delivering identifiable benefits to the

---

[2] Cf, for example, K. Armstrong and S. Bulmer, *The Governance of the Single European Market* (1998 Manchester University Press), at 256–260.

[3] Weiler, 'After Maastricht: Community Legitimacy in Post-1992 Europe,' in W.J. Adams (ed) *Singular Europe: Economic and Polity of the EC After 1992* (1992 University of Michigan Press), at 19–20.

[4] While it is the case that the EU as a decision-making system did provide for an involvement of the citizens, a provision that has intensified since direct elections and the growing powers of the European Parliament, no enhanced provision for the direct legitimation of common policies was (or has been) established with respect to the EU as a supranational constitutional arrangement.

publics involved. In such a situation, neither a meta rule nor a direct political process involving individual citizens was available for effecting a resolution between these elements of the legitimacy of this governance level beyond the nation state. It is straightforward to demonstrate how such a disharmony could arise.

For the material benefits deriving from the initial phase of economic integration to be realised, the establishment of a powerful supranational governance level was required. Rather than being an inevitable aspect of economic integration *per se*, this was a consequence of the comparatively high degree of state intervention in economic affairs within the founding Member States. In part, this was a product of the peculiarly West European (social) system of governance that had emerged post-1945 and which involved the collective provision of a wide range of public services. As a result, the scope for integration to be achieved through 'negative' (market liberalisation) measures was relatively small, and pointed instead to a significant degree of policy harmonisation between Member States (*ie* 'positive' integration) and, subsequently, a comparatively high degree of common policy-making. The concomitance of this, of course, was the emergence of an independent and constitutionally powerful supranational governance structure (including enforcement).[5] Given that a regime in which common policies supplanted national policies (made binding by Article 100), it was inevitable that 'winners' and 'losers' would emerge in terms of the Member State distribution of the costs and benefits of economic integration.[6] However, the constitutional separation of EU citizen from EU governance meant that public support for integration was linked directly to the economic and political benefits it delivered at the level of the individual Member State. If integration no longer was (seen to be) providing benefit, or if integration costs appeared that outweighed these benefits, popularity for the project as a whole would be likely to diminish, and its legitimacy in social terms become tarnished. The upshot would be disharmony between legitimacy in the formal sense and in the social sense, and the scene would be set for a struggle between the national and supranational levels of governance. Member State governments would then face a political conundrum. Continued support for seemingly 'costly' integration would damage their domestic political standing, but appeasing domestic constituents would require Member States to deliberately breach the authority of the supranational level of governance, thereby undermining its claim to legitimacy. This latter course was made possible solely because the legitimacy of the supranational governance in the formal sense was derived from that of the constitutive nation states. Notwithstanding later reforms which enforced and extended the rule of qualified majority voting, the supranational element in decision-making, as a constitutional arrangement the evolution of the EU has remained firmly in the hands of its Member States.

In this argument, the dynamics of the present legitimacy crisis emanate from an approach to economic and political integration which involved, necessarily, the transfer of significant competencies and authority to a supranational governance level which, although deriving public support through the prospective material gains on

---

[5] In the absence of this, individual Member States would be able to act, or threaten to act, opportunistically in order to acquire a greater share of the material gains from integration and the arrangement would collapse. This accounts, in large measure, for the radical jurisprudence developed by the ECJ during the 1960s as documented by Weiler, 'Fin-de-Siècle Europe,' in R. Dehousse (ed), *Europe after Maastricht: An Ever Closer Union?* (1994 Becks).

[6] Cf, for a discussion of this, Scott, 'Theories of International and Regional Economic Integration in a Global Economy,' in P. Barbour (ed) *The European Union Handbook* (1996 Fitzroy Dearborn).

offer, was characterised by a constitutional deficit in terms of direct public participation in constructing or amending the rules and procedures governing the decision-making system of the EU. Instead, relations between citizens and EU governance were mediated through national governments, part of whose objective was to buttress their domestic position by maximising the gains and minimising the losses from economic (and political) integration. The result was that a symbiotic, though inherently unstable, relationship between the national and supranational governance levels within the EU was a quintessential feature of the constitutional arrangement that gave direction to, and determined the pace of, European integration.

In large measure, the foregoing account of the origin and character of the EU's legitimacy crisis is a particular account of what has been referred to as a crisis of the 'Monnet method' in European integration. In general terms, that account presents the crisis of legitimacy as a consequence of a breakdown in the mechanisms through which integration is being achieved, rather than as a collapse of popular support for the objectives of, and means for securing, the 'ever closer Union.' At the heart of the breakdown are the nation states that comprise the EU, and the intergovernmental bargaining arrangements that permitted the progressive—though not uncontested— development of common policies and collective governance until the early 1990s. Crucially, the Monnet method involved national elites and had little scope for the popular involvement of the publics over which the new governance arrangements were to preside.[7] In the wake of the legitimacy crisis, integration can no longer proceed without the direct, and potentially obstructive, involvement of these publics. Laffan argues:[8]

> The politicisation of integration and its expansion into sensitive political space necessitates renewed attention to questions of community-building and the affective dimension of integration . . . The legitimacy crisis in the Union demonstrates the limits of the Monnet method at a time when national governance structures are challenged . . .

Laffan argues that, hitherto, the European project itself acted as a vehicle for the development and validation of the nation state. This has now ended. The European project, among other developments, has unlocked a number of forces inimical to its further development as these forces collide with the national identity that previously was buttressed by integration. Laffan identifies three factors which explain the crisis of the nation state as an integrative vehicle—political nationalism in the face of unpopular aspects of further integration (immigration, loss of identity, policy developments); the revival of territorial politics at a sub-national level;[9] and the collapse of communism and the consequent 'search for an overarching European identity.' The difficulty for the European project is that each of these influences fundamentally challenges the prevailing notion of the nation state and, consequently, jeopardise an integrationist dynamic which has thus far depended upon a particular conception of the nation state.

A similar treatment of the nature of the crisis of legitimacy can be found in Hirst.[10] He argues that the EU is currently experiencing a number of centrifugal forces that are

---

[7] Laffan, 'The Politics of Identity,' (1996) 34:1 *Journal of Common Market Studies* 81–102.

[8] *Ibid*, at 83.

[9] Cf, also, A. Scott/J. Peterson/D. Millar: 'Subsidiarity: A 'Europe of the Regions' *v* the British Constitution,' (1994) 32:1 *Journal of Common Market Studies* 47–67.

[10] Hirst, 'The European Union at the Crossroads: Integration or Decline?,' in R. Bellamy *et al* (eds) *Democracy and Constitutional Culture in the Union of Europe* (1995 Lothian Foundation Press).

threatening the cohesion of the integration process itself. He identifies three such forces. The first is the collapse of a unifying adversary with the demise of the Soviet empire. The second is the decline of political homogeneity and the emergence of alternative and radical politics, chief amongst which is the rise of sub-national political parties and the rise of the right in response to perceived threats from immigration. Third is the faltering in the rate of growth of material prosperity and the concomitant increase in numbers unemployed. This places before the EU a challenge to which it has failed to respond adequately. Against this, Hirst sees the internationalisation of the global economy and the associated decline in effective national sovereignty as representing the key centripetal force in the EU at present.

Weiler, meanwhile, paints on an even larger canvass, locating the crisis that occurred over the ratification of the Treaty on European Union as indicative of a fundamental break in the history of post-war Western Europe. Weiler suggests that the difficulties encountered in ratifying the TEU reflect a profound crisis in the entire European (integration) project. His fin-de-siècle thesis indicates that the overriding *ideals* upon which European integration is founded—peace, prosperity and supranationalism—have, in the main, been satisfied.[11] This leaves further integration with no real raison d'être:

> The Europe of Maastricht is devoid of ideals. The Member States of the European Community are being swept by an electorate which, not unlike its American counterpart, is increasingly frustrated, alienated and angry with politics as usual. Sadly, 'Europe' has become just that—politics as usual . . . 'Europe' is an ideal which has lost its mobilising force, it is a force which has lost its mobilising ideals.[12]

While it is the case that each of these accounts of the EU legitimacy crisis of the EU explain the timing of that crisis, none explicitly locate its underlying cause in the constitutional process whereby the EU was constructed. Moreover, the implication in each is that a resolution of the legitimacy crisis for the EU will involve reforms which permit either a fusion to occur between legitimacy in the formal and social sense as is (held to be) the case in nation state governance, or actions to be undertaken which ensure that each Member State, on balance, gains in the material sense from further integration thereby re-asserting the relevance of the arrangement to national citizens. In our view, neither outcome is realistic in the foreseeable future. Moreover, we contend that the conceptualisation of legitimacy implicit in these analyses in misconstrued. In our view, the legitimacy deficit of EU supranational governance is a feature *inherent to* the 'Monnet method' of integration *given* the particular features of West European nation state governance as it developed immediately after 1945.[13] As a consequence, and assuming that the nation state will remain at the core of EU governance, we must consider, as an alternative, modalities by which the outcomes from European integration might be reconciled with the interests of the EU polity. A critical aspect in this consideration is an interpretation of 'legitimacy' not only as being a static feature inherent to, and indistinct from, a particular constitutional arrangement, but rather as an on-going formal and social outcome that must be

---

[11] Weiler, *loc cit* n 5.

[12] *Ibid*, at 204.

[13] Thus it may not be a feature inherent to integration arrangements between economies where there is minimal government regulation of the economy and/or society.

continually renewed or re-asserted by that constitutional arrangement.[14] Any failure of the constitutional arrangement so to do is likely to trigger a political crisis whose resolution may require change to that constitutional arrangement. Consequently, the defect in the Monnet method arguably lies in the inability of the constitutional arrangements of integration under that procedure to renew the legitimacy of the undertaking over time, particularly in the event of integration reaching the stage in which a level of governance beyond the nation state is required.

III   Nationhood Versus Citizenship

Thus far, we have addressed the dynamics of EU legitimacy from a constitutional and statist perspective, and presented a version of the legitimacy crisis in which it is the challenge that further integration poses to the material interests and constitutional position of the nation state which may account for current doubts over the path that European integration is taking. At this juncture it is necessary to focus attention on the prospective position of individual citizens in the EU constitutional process. The centrality of the nation state in determining the pace and direction of European integration inevitably produces a situation in which the individual citizen enjoys maximum power when operating as a national of a Member State, rather than as a citizen of the EU. This would appear to strengthen greatly the position of those who argue that because nationalism plays a central role in legitimising political power, only by acquiring all the trappings of classical nationalism can European governance hope to achieve legitimacy.[15]

In a more recent contribution, Joseph Weiler has skilfully brought together a number of the various strands common to this account of the contemporary legitimacy debate in a powerful critique of the *no demos* thesis.[16] In that work, he demonstrates that a potent—though unconvincing—account of the emerging legitimacy crisis in EU governance can be provided by pointing to the absence of a European *Volk* over which this governance prevails—that is, a people bound together by a common set of ethno-cultural features such as language, history, cultural habits, religion and ethnic origin. According to that view, peoplehood and nationhood are simultaneously determined as the joint outcome of a shared history and common culture, and together these elements form the basis of the modern democratic state. Consequently, any arrangement that severs this direct link between *Volk* and state governance has, by definition, a lack of legitimacy. Quite apart from the historical defects that can be pointed to, this argument has a seductive tidiness in that it posits a coincidence between the political boundary of current European nation states and the ethno-cultural boundaries that divide the (many) peoples of Europe. The gravity of the legitimacy crisis which confronts the EU as a governance regime is then made clear:[17]

> Turning to Europe, it is argued as a matter of empirical observation, based on these ethno-cultural criteria, that there is no European *demos*—not a people not a nation. Neither the subjective element (the sense of shared collective identity and loyalty) nor the objective

---

[14] This is to view legitimacy as a 'flow' rather than a 'stock' variable.

[15] Laffan, *loc cit*, n 7; Smith, 'National Identity and the Idea of European Unity,' (1992) 68 *International Affairs* 55–76.

[16] Weiler, 'Legitimacy and Democracy of Union Governance,' in G. Edwards/A. Pijpers, (eds) *The Politics of European Treaty Reform: The 1996 Intergovernmental Conference and Beyond* (1997 Pinter)

[17] *Ibid*, at 257.

conditions which could produce these (the kind of homogeneity of the ethno-national conditions on which peoplehood depend) exist. Long-term peaceful relations with thickening economic and social intercourse should not be confused with the bonds of peoplehood and nationality forged by language, history, ethnicity and all the rest.

The implications for European integration that flow from this reasoning are both stark and incontrovertible. There can be no legitimacy of governance unless there is a pre-existing *demos* defined in ethno-cultural terms: the nation is the pre-requisite of the state. As Weiler notes:[18]

> . . . to insist on the emergence of a pre-existing European *demos* defined in ethno-cultural terms as a precondition for constitutional unification or, more minimally, a re-drawing of political boundaries, is to ensure that this will never happen.

Weiler then proceeds to demolish this essentially impoverished interpretation of the governance—past, present and future—of the European continent, and the 'no *demos*—no legitimacy' proposition derived from it. From the perspective of our argument, the striking aspect of Weiler's analysis, and refutation, is its concentration on the role of the individual within the legitimation of governance arrangements. For what Weiler identifies as a crucial flaw in the 'no *demos*' account is its inability to de-couple nationality from citizenship, a flaw that is sufficient to preclude the emergence of a legitimate governance arrangement that is constructed on other than ethno-cultural foundations—as, for instance, the case of a civic society in which individuals are bound together by, *inter alia*, '. . . shared values, a shared understanding of rights and societal duties . . .'[19] By switching the unit of our analysis away from the individual as a 'national' to the individual as 'citizen,' Weiler establishes a framework which allows the subject of legitimacy of (EU) governance to be de-linked from the much narrower politics of (Member State) nationalism, and which is consistent with a fluid constitutional architecture. At the very least we are now able to acknowledge the possibility that a model of pan-national governance can be construed that *does* enjoy popular legitimacy, although it does not answer the question of how this might be achieved. However, what clearly is *not* being envisaged in all of this is a situation in which one 'state' simply supplants another 'state,' or the constitution of a supra-national governance emerges to trump the constitution of old nation state governance. For those who continue to explain the EU legitimacy crisis in terms of the absence of European 'nationhood,' this indeed remains the crucial issue. However, within the context of an evolving governance founded upon the dynamics of modern civic society, the choice need not be so stark. Instead, the constitutional architecture could accommodate a range of overlapping normative orders nested within it, each of which reflected an alternative—though not necessarily competitive—composite group of social activity. In practice, of course, precisely such a situation prevails within nation states. Individuals may be members of many societal arrangements, each of which has a specific structure and contains operating rules and norms (constitutions).[20]

As we will now discuss, by de-coupling 'nationality' from 'citizenship,' Weiler essentially establishes a position for the individual in which she may make a key

---

[18] *Ibid*, at 261.

[19] *Ibid*, at 263.

[20] Membership of incompatible societal units (regarding objectives and/or constitutions) is generally ruled out by the principle of transitivity.

contribution to the construction of a supranational governance arrangement that is capable of accommodating nation states but which does not derive its legitimacy in the formal sense exclusively from national governments.

IV Securing Legitimacy: A Three-Level Model of Europeanisation

Our argument is that the Monnet method of integrating the separate economies and polities of (thus far) Western Europe lacked a mechanism for establishing (and constantly renewing) the legitimacy of the process, in so far as this involved a reconciliation between the aspirations of individual citizens on the one hand, and the performance and direction of supranational governance on the other. Indeed, it might be claimed that under the Monnet method tension between the nation state and supranational levels of governance was unavoidable, and that, inevitably, this would trigger a nationalistic response on the part of individual citizens. In this section we draw on the 'Europeanisation' theme that has been developed in the EU public policy literature to augment our critique of the legitimacy crisis and to indicate modalities through which this crisis may be managed without altering the fundamental architecture of the EU.

The concept of Europeanisation has far-ranging interpretations in the literature. At its most extreme, Europeanisation is used to describe a process whereby new models of policy formulation and decision-making are emerging in domestic politics. A key proposition implicit to this approach is that systemic properties and outcomes of domestic governance structures[21] are subject to modification as a direct response to political and economic considerations arising at the supranational level. Consequently, we can conceptualise the process of Europeanisation as involving changes in domestic governance arising from the economic and political imperatives of EU membership, and impacting upon both procedural and substantive aspects of domestic politics and policies. Ladrech defines Europeanisation as:[22]

> . . . an incremental process of reorienting the shape of politics to the degree that EC political and economic dynamics become part of the organisational logic of national politics and policy-making.

In a similar vein, Goetz poses the central research question within the Europeanisation literature as being:[23]

> [T]o what extent [are] national politics, governmental-administrative structures, policy-making procedures and the substance of public policies changing in reaction to the political and economic imperatives arising out of EU membership?

The significance of Europeanisation to the legitimacy debate is clear in that it offers an account in which national governance *systems* are subject to external influence and may be modified in response to those influences. In orthodox integration theory we are familiar with approaches depicting the process of EU governance as being influenced

---

[21] Outcomes from which are assumed to satisfy the 'legitimacy' requirements.

[22] Ladrech, 'Europeanisation of Domestic Politics and Institutions: The Case of France,' (1994) 34:1 *Journal of Common Market Studies* 68.

[23] Goetz, 'National Governance and European Integration: Intergovernmental Relations in Germany,' (1995) 33:1 *Journal of Common Market Studies* 91–116, at 92.

—exclusively or predominately—by national actors and interest groups.[24] The flow of influence is primarily from the nation state to the common EU theatre. Whilst there may be some room for mediation and influence on the part of other EU actors and institutions, as is emphasised in supranational accounts of integration, these tend to be weak and/or only influential at the margin.[25] In the Europeanisation approach, on the other hand, it is conjectured that the EU governance process involves a two-way arrangement whereby national actors and interest groups themselves are subject to a reverse process: as 'EC political and economic dynamics become part of the organisational logic of national politics and policy-making.' This is altogether stronger in that it is suggestive of a change in the nature of national politics and policy-making as *systems of governance* capable of incorporating a common EU public policy dimension which, subsequently, effects an adaptation of the domestic political culture.[26] It is, therefore, suggestive of a domestic political culture adapting to 'European' values and underlying principles of modus operandi. This need not challenge the intergovernmental nature of bargaining within the EU. What it is likely to do, however, is to influence or modify the highly complex and country-specific modalities whereby domestic policies are made, the mechanisms through which disputes between different national constituencies are resolved, and the outcomes that these national arrangements are capable of generating. If valid, this Europeanisation process may, at one and the same time, result in a situation in which there are fewer intergovernmental conflicts to be resolved at the EU level, and accelerate the resolution of those that do arise. Not only does this imply a shift away from 'lowest common denominator bargaining' within the EU, it also promises to make less complex the 'bargains' that are struck between national administrations.

The Europeanisation thesis as applied to national governance systems is clearly significant from the perspective of the legitimacy debate. It points to adaptation in governance at the level of the nation state which reduces the likelihood of conflict between national and supranational levels. At the same time, it increases the role of the nation state as the legitimating agent between those aspects of public policy determined by the supranational governance level and a polity which continues to function through principally national channels. But it is an approach that has its critics, one of whom concludes from his study of German governance as follows:[27]

> It can . . . be shown that European integration *has not* seriously challenged the defining principles of the German federal system. In other words, from the perspective of German intergovernmental relations, the European integration process has not raised serious problems of systemic incompatibility. *On the contrary, integration has tended to support and, in some instances, reinforce, those defining characteristics.*

---

[24] Bulmer, 'Domestic Politics and EC Policy-Making,' (1984) 24:4 *Journal of Common Market Studies* 349–63: Moravscik, 'Preferences and Power in the European Community: A Liberal Intergovernmentalist Approach,' (1993) 31:4 *Journal of Common Market Studies*.

[25] It is the case that in orthodox intergovernmental analysis that 'feedback loops' are recognised whereby national positions are modified in response to unfolding negotiations. However, this is best construed in game-theoretic terms rather than as a consequence of the structural adaptation of national governance systems.

[26] The theoretical validity of 'Europeanisation' as a phenomenon within national governance systems derives principally from the preponderance of measures of 'positive' rather than 'negative' integration associated with the development of the EU.

[27] Goetz, *loc cit* n 23, at 93 (our emphasis).

It is worth noting that here Goetz is addressing the organisation of the domestic polity from the perspective of German governance as a constitutional arrangement. Not only has this remained unaltered, it has been reinforced. Finally, he concludes that the lesson from the German experience is that

> . . . the Europeanisation of national governance is compatible with the maintenance of very distinct national institutional arrangements.[28]

At the level of formal, constitutional governance, therefore, Goetz is unconvinced. However, this conclusion may not necessarily compromise the argument that, despite the maintenance of intact national constitutional arrangements, nonetheless there is a gradual development of modalities that facilitate an easier decision-making process at the supranational level as a consequence of a process of 'Europeanisation' of domestic politics. For instance, one can interpret the agreement to revert to qualified majority voting (QMV) for the purposes of implementing most of the 1992 programme, in precisely this manner. The imperative to complete the internal market required the resurrection of QMV in order to avoid an inter-state conflict over the distribution of the subsequent sectoral costs and benefits. In that case the collective interests of the EU prevailed over national interests, a situation which Member States endorsed by surrendering the veto power in the Council of Ministers with respect to Commission proposals. Although the attraction of the '1992 programme' to Member States lay in the material benefits it promised, and thus resonates with the original integration bargain from the perspective of Member States, the lack of populist opposition to the Single European Act along nationalistic lines testifies to the readiness of Member State governments to adapt domestic systems to the imperatives of integration. This does not necessarily imply that we disagree with Goetz's observations with respect to Germany. However, what it does suggest is that convergence between independent governance *systems* need not manifest itself—at least in its early stages—in a change to national constitutional arrangements. Instead, it may begin by adjustments to informal (non-constitutional) governance arrangements. Therefore, although there may be limited evidence of Europeanisation impacting upon constitutional arrangements of governance in particular Member States, we do not find this surprising. Indeed, we would expect constitutional change within Member States to be the final event in a process of Europeanisation. Before the consequences of the Europeanisation of governance systems can become entrenched in (amended) national constitutions, the systemic convergence of national governance must possess legitimacy not only in the formal sense, but also in the social sense.

It is clear that the concept of Europeanisation can be applied meaningfully when examining the adaptation of nation states' governance systems to European integration at the level of national governance systems. Now we extend the application of the concept in two ways. First, by considering the implications of Europeanisation with respect to the content and delivery of specific common policies (rather than systems of governance) and second, by focusing on Europeanisation at the level of the polity by considering the relationship between individual and governance. Clearly there is an interaction between the Europeanisation process operating at both these levels. The content of EU public policy is determined by the decision-making arrangements at the supranational level. At the same time, the impact of this policy on

---

[28] *Ibid*, at 93

individuals will shape public opinion concerning the legitimacy—in the social sense—of the integration process. This shaping may be conducive to further integration—where the individual benefits from the process—or inimical to it—where individuals consider that the costs exceed the benefits.

First, in the public policy domain, Europeanisation is a necessary (although not sufficient) mechanism for facilitating integration by adapting the design and delivery of national public policy as required to ensure the efficient implementation of common EU policies. In that sense it is simply a mechanism for promoting those changes in domestic public policy arenas that are necessary to ensure that EU public policy achieves its objectives. The concept is thus stripped of any normative element: instead it adopts a positivistic content and represents an instrument for securing progress towards an agreed end. It is, therefore, Europeanisation in the sense of Article 100 of the Treaty of Rome; the adaptation of domestic policy in the face of higher, EU level, rule-making technocracies. We can think of many examples of this type of Europeanisation; one being, the regulations governing the Structural Funds where collective benefits are expected to accrue to the EU as a result of a harmonisation of national policies. Otherwise, national policies may undermine the collective objective of policy, with non-compliance weakening joint attempts to secure progress in achieving stated objectives. The Europeanisation of public policy in this sense differs little from 'positive' integration.

The difficulty for European integration arises because public policy not only shapes public opinion and political allegiances, it also constitutes an output from political interaction between the individual and the governance system. This is because the governance system in modern pluralistic democracies is a construction based upon, and continually legitimised by, the individual. All policies reflect this relationship. If not, then the policy is susceptible to challenge. At the heart of the policy system lies the state, and the instrument of the state in enforcing the policy is the rule of law: the legal order. The state derives its authority to enact and enforce laws from the individual—the citizens. The rule of law maintains the existence of the state. At the same time, the existence of the democratic state legitimises the rule of law. Should either element change, then the policy process will lack legitimacy. Accordingly, one interpretation of the core problematic of European integration is that precisely this interaction between the individual and (supranational) EU governance is absent. Under EU arrangements, there is no self-reinforcing and symbiotic relationship between the individual, the supranational state and the (EU) policy (legal) order. The dysfunctional nature of the individual-system and, from there to law-policy, interaction at the EU level may well be sufficiently acute to explain the crisis of EU legitimacy.

On one reading, the solution would appear obvious—namely a change in the institutional architecture of the EU legislative arrangements such that policy is developed in a manner that does respect the standard tenets of democratic governance—viz. transparency and accountability—along with a legislative process that conforms to the standard practice in the EU Member States. In short, this would result in enhanced powers being granted to the European Parliament at the expense of Member State governments. Although appealing, a reconfiguration of the institutional architecture of EU decision-making arrangements itself is unlikely to resolve the current malaise in the integration process. First, given that any change in the arrangements of governance would be undertaken under the prevailing arrangements that themselves lack social legitimacy, is it possible for a revised set of procedures to enjoy greater social legitimacy? Second, it is not necessarily the case that by altering the institutional arrangements at the EU level a greater degree of legitimacy will accrue to the policies enacted at that level. The separation of the individual from the EU polity remains; nothing that has been done to modify the institutional architecture of EU governance has necessarily altered the dysfunctional position of the individual as a citizen of a Member State versus a citizen of the EU. Finally, although increasing the authority of the European Parliament at the expense of the nation state may (although may not) produce a more acceptable policy process, it will at the same time profoundly alter the dynamic of European integration through the resultant weakening of the authority of the Member State. There is nothing self-evident about the proposition that the EP is better equipped than Member States to reflect the aspirations of the individuals that together comprise the European Union. In our view the decision-making arrangements that prescribe the EU policy process represent the least problematic aspect of European integration at the present time. At the same time there is little realistic scope of reforms being implemented which elevate the role of the EU's supranational institutions to a position above that of its constituent nation states.

Second, we must consider the scope for Europeanisation occurring at the level of the individual. This is a considerably more complex matter, involving as it does the active engagement of the individual in something we would wish to define as the 'European political process' in a manner similar to the engagement of the individual in national politics. It is at this point that the 'individual-as-citizen' enters the arena, and supranational politics as a process for defining an essentially normative European order replaces a version of supranational politics whose primary purpose is to maximise the national gains from international integration. It requires the development of modalities that animate, and institutions that facilitate, individual political behaviour that extends beyond the nation state and which engages the European political and policy arena. Moreover, it implies a role of the individual in supranational governance which extends well beyond the essentially limited role provided for under the Monnet method of integration. However, as we discussed earlier, it is the foundational fragmentation of the EU along national lines (and which defines the Monnet method) that constitutes an obstacle to the development of genuinely representative politics at the EU level. Consequently, '"Europeanisation" is far more pronounced at the level of public policy-making than of politics.'[29]

Europeanisation at the level of the individual, should this occur, does not imply that integration will necessarily become smoother, or less problematic. However, it is suggestive of the development of a European political community in which the governance process (the fusion between politics, policy and law) is firmly rooted in the society over which it prevails. One must regard this as a necessary—and perhaps sufficient—condition for the integration project in the EU. Indeed, unless this transpires it is ever more likely that integration will increasingly develop in a fragmented manner, characterised by a 'variable geometry' whereby Member States that do not have a domestic mandate to enter into particular elements of European integration will be prevented—by domestic considerations—from doing so. Instead countries may be members of individual 'policy communities,' but need not be members of all. Such an arrangement is problematic from the perspective of the institutional unity of integration and the operating procedures of the Union. These difficulties become especially acute in the event of policy spillover—*ie* where

---

[29] Laffan, *loc cit* n 7.

developments in one policy arena spillover and affect outcomes and conditions in another policy arena. Consequently, whilst appealing in the sense that it permits integration to proceed wherever and whenever it may be reconciled with (a subset of) national interests, a variable geometry solution would appear to be unstable as an institutionalised compromise.

If we rule out the variable geometry outcome as a possible solution to the problem of Europeanisation, then, to what arrangement are we to look to resolve the legitimacy crisis, on the basis that the emergence of a pan-national European identity is deemed neither practicable nor desirable? Two possibilities suggest themselves as potential mechanisms for mediating in the difficulties in developing Europeanisation at the level of the individual. Both implicitly utilise the notion of 'individual-as-citizen' rather than 'individual-as-national.'

The first, which we have commented upon elsewhere,[30] involves the notion of overlapping normative orders. That is to say, individuals may be members of different normative structures in so far as the central elements of each are consistent. Thus an individual can at one and the same time be a parent, a medical practitioner, and a member of a religious order. There may be tensions between the day-to-day requirements of each order, but in essence there is no necessary fundamental contradiction between these roles. Being a parent carries with it no activities that necessarily conflict with the roles required of a medical practitioner or a member of a religious order—although it is possible to envisage situations where a fundamental conflict may arise. Equally it is possible to consider these as mutually supportive roles where the participation in one activity strengthens the capacity to participate in the others. Transferring the analogy to the EU theatre, one might conceptualise being at one and the same time a Scot, a Briton and a European. There is no necessary contradiction between these roles, although there may be. Being a Scot need not be incompatible with being British which, in turn, need carry no conflict with being a European. It all depends upon the obligations associated with each role. The situation we are describing is not one where 'orders' are conceived as distinct entities—as Santos expresses it, they are not to be seen as separate activities which might co-exist in the same political space. Rather these are 'different . . . spaces superimposed, inter-penetrated and mixed in our minds as much as in our actions. . . .'[31] No single role takes precedent over any other in the hierarchical sense. Instead, these are different perspectives and viewpoints that coexist in identical space. Mutual support from contemporaneous interaction is as likely a consequence as mutual antagonism. The concept of overlapping normative orders carries with it, therefore, an assumption that sovereignty—the source of hierarchies in the world of the nation state—need not enter the picture at all. We must conceptualise beyond the boundaries of the nation state if we are to 'Europeanise' the individual. As Weale reminds us,[32] the foundation of federalism as an organisational form involves the ability of each citizen to belong to at least two communities—the community of the Member State and the community of the union. It is a mechanism for fostering this development that appears to be absent in the case of Europe.

---

[30] Bańkowski/Scott, 'The European Union?,' in R. Bellamy (ed) *Constitutionalism, Democracy and Sovereignty: American and European Perspectives* (1996 Avebury).

[31] Santos, 'Law: a Map of Misreading,' (1987) 14 *Journal of Law and Society* 279–99.

[32] Weale, 'Democratic Legitimacy and the Constitution of Europe,' in R. Bellamy *et al* (eds) *op cit* n 10.

The second avenue worthy of exploration, and one that is consistent with the preceding viewpoint, is subsidiarity. By subsidiarity we are referring to the dictum that policy should be made as closely as possible to the citizen: what we have called elsewhere 'substantive' subsidiarity.[33] The significance of subsidiarity is that not only does it offer a mechanism for developing European public policy which is more likely to be acceptable to the individual—as the individual is more closely involved in its articulation—it also serves to address the national legitimacy crisis as well. This is to recognise that there is a crisis of public policy at the level of the nation state as well as at the EU level. Two factors stand out in this respect: the revival or reassertion of territorial politics at the sub-national level, and the increasing globalisation of the international community. In both instances we have support for Daniel Bell's famous dictum that the nation state is too large to deal with the small issues, and too small to deal with the large issues. The revival, or reassertion, of territorial politics at the sub-national level undoubtedly is related to the growth of the EU level of governance. For instance, in Scotland we find the slogan 'independence in Europe' becoming ever more potent as a rallying cry for a nationalist party for whom constitutional change previously understood to imply fundamental political and economic separatism and not harmonious co-existence within a framework of supranational policy-making. The politics of Scottish independence today, on the other hand, while still being presented as a legitimate expression of an arguably suppressed national identity, no longer invoke connotations that independence equals isolationism. One might go even further and suggest that the resolution of a number of historical sub-national political and territorial disputes are finding new energy from the emergence of a governance structure that does not depend for its integrity or legitimacy on the sanctity or inviolability of the nation state. The nation state becomes unnecessary: the large issues are handled by the EU governance, leaving local communities to develop policies that suit local conditions and aspirations. Heterogeneity can thus be accommodated within a single entity in a way which the nation state has failed to achieve.

To a limited extent the EU has moved to foster the growth of subsidiarity. The Treaty on European Union provided for a Committee of the Regions (CoR) as a first step in addressing the increasing aspirations on the part of a number of Member States for representation at the EU on the part of sub-national groupings. Naturally these demands emanated principally from Member States that had reasonably powerful sub-national groups in the first instance—especially Germany where the Laender were concerned lest their constitutional position be undermined as a result of the growth of European policy competencies. However, the CoR undoubtedly falls far short of the type of institutional arrangement that is necessary if we are to move towards a further Europeanisation of the individual. It might be argued that unless real progress is being made to enhance the constitutional power of the individual as a European citizen (there is no reason why she might not be entrusted with this responsibility), the individual is unlikely to support the further development of the EU.

V   Concluding Comments

The argument advanced in this paper is that the legitimacy debate in European integration is best conceptualised as involving three distinct levels of analysis—system

---

[33]   Scott *et al, loc cit* n 9.

of governance, public policy, and the individual. We have argued that at the heart of the current legitimacy crisis lies the inappropriateness of the original method of integration which was driven by, and attained legitimacy from, the position occupied by the nation state. This resulted in a situation in which the broader social legitimacy of European integration was inextricably bound to the share of net gains from integration that accrued directly to individual nation states. The challenge now confronting the EU is to devise and introduce modalities which enable the legitimacy of supranational governance to be enhanced other than through the mediation of the nation state. Otherwise, it will be necessary to reconcile the legitimacy of a governance structure that lies 'beyond the nation state,' with a constitutional arrangement in which the nation state continues to represent the predominant and superior level of governance. This latter course is, we suggest, unlikely to be forthcoming.

There is evidence that the Europeanisation process is effecting a change in national political arrangements, and that EU political and economic dynamics indeed are becoming part of the logic of domestic policy-making at the level of the system of governance. This implies that conflict resolution at the EU level should become easier as Member States progressively come to terms with the impracticability of 'going it alone.' If we can loosely depict the EU-level negotiating options at the disposal of a Member State government as 'exit' (by exclusion or exercising a national veto), 'voice' (constructive engagement) and 'loyalty' (acceptance of supranational decision-making rules), Europeanisation at this level should result in the 'exit' option being used less often, and 'voice' and 'loyalty' increasingly being used to resolve disputes. But although this might result in more efficient policy-making at the EU level, it will not in itself enhance the social legitimacy of EU governance. This will require a Europeanisation process to be engaged with respect both to the content of public policy, and with regard to the polity directly. Otherwise there is a risk that not only will the momentum for further integration be interrupted, but that current arrangements could begin to unravel. However, we must interpret Europeanisation in the proper manner. There is no short-cut to achieving a European political community. On the other hand we do not consider it need await the development of a European identity. A middle route can be plotted, one that involves the development of alternative government arrangements at both domestic and EU level. In our view such alternative arrangements must give considerable weight to the active involvement of the individual—the citizen—in the process of policy making and implementation. Perhaps only such a 'bottom-up' approach will be sufficient to ensure the cohesion of the EU as it becomes ever more diverse and, possibly, divergent.

In the final instance we would conclude that unless the arrangements for EU governance are reformed in this vein, the EU as an international arrangement will be unable to achieve even the minimal objectives of delivering gains from economic integration. There are two reasons for this. The first relates to the global economic challenges that require a collective response at the EU level if the gains from a unified internal market are to continue. Two economic challenges are pressing: the stability of EU currencies and enhancing the competitiveness of EU industry in an ever more contested globalised economy. Intra-EU currency stability almost certainly requires the successful transition to a single currency. But this raises profound problems of national economic management, as is evident from the intense debate surrounding the practical and institutional consequences of monetary union. Competitiveness in the global economy raises quite different political and economic questions that focus on the continued viability of the European Social Model that developed post-1945.[34] At a minimum it would seem that an enhanced degree of EU policy harmonisation is required in this area if prevailing national policies are to be prevented from seriously distorting the pattern of competition between firms located in different EU Member States. The second reason which compels reforms in the legitimacy of EU governance involves the need to construct a normative political project for the EU as a collective entity which reflects the ideals and goals of societies across the Union. Otherwise it is likely that public policy, the means of delivering outcomes that reflect these normative principles, will retreat as inter-EU nation state conflicts undermine the entire public policy nexus. The construction of a framework to formulate and implement an EU-wide public policy which genuinely reflects the ideals and aspirations of the EU polity must, in our view, urgently be addressed. Failure to do so may result in market forces simply driving out public policy with the loss of the cohesive aspect that such policy plays in society in general.

---

[34] For a discussion of this, cf, Carter, 'The European Social Model: Framework or Fallacy', in J. Usher (ed) *The State of the European Union: Structure, Enlargement and Economic Union* (forthcoming 1999, Longman).

8

The Limits of
European Union Citizenship

Carole Lyons

Introduction

'Citizenship of the Union is hereby established. Every person holding the nationality of a Member State shall be a citizen of the Union. Citizenship of the Union shall complement and not replace national citizenship.'[1]

Imagine reading those words twenty years ago, let alone fifty or a hundred years before. European Union citizenship is a dramatic and palpably potent, original outcome of European integration. It is a testament to power of and yet also a test of the limits of supranationality. It is the epitome of the non-negotiated nether regions in the relationship between nation state law and supranational law; by definition, it is supranational in form but lives only on the basis of a nationally determined body of laws. This symbiotic character of Union citizenship renders it complex and confusing, as attempts to understand it or give it meaning based on its origins in national law are bound to be insufficient, yet to resort to the same exercise from a supranational perspective is impossible. So much is, rightly, expected of citizenship of the European Union; by citizens in a concrete manner in the general facilitation and betterment of our lives as Europeans; and, theoretically, in providing the scope to analyse the nature of the vertical (citizen/Union) and horizontal (citizen/citizen) relationships which are being formed in contemporary Europe. In this chapter I argue that European Union Citizenship is fundamentally and intrinsically limited while, at the same time, it is inherently unlimited as a political and legal concept and could be developed beyond anything which might be anticipated given its nation state based conceptual origins. This seemingly contrary observation is based on exploiting the ambiguity currently surrounding the meaning and interpretation of Union Citizenship but suggesting that this be done very much in the acknowledgement of the context of the political and judicial reality in which any substantial development is likely to occur. For this purpose, it is useful to consider European Union citizenship as a hybrid example of 'functional citizenship',[2] instrumentally related to material benefits and rights, as opposed to non-functional or affective citizenship, rooted in nationality centred emotions and conditions. In order to see more clearly where the borders of Union citizenship lie it is necessary to maintain a coherent distinction between the functional and non-functional dimensions. In the nation state paradigm there is a conflation of

---

[1] Article 17 European Community Treaty (ECT) (previously Article 8.1 ECT using the pre Amsterdam Treaty numbering. The Amsterdam Treaty entered into force on May 1 1999)

[2] Fleming, M., The Functionality of Citizenship, (1997) Harvard Jean Monnet Working Paper, *http://www.law.harvard.edu/Progams/JeanMonnet/papers/97/97-10.html*

these,[3] with access to the material benefits of membership of a polity normally linked to the cultural and political affinity underlying nationality laws. The 'decoupling' of the functional dimension of citizenship from its non-functional base seems possible as well as necessary in the European Union as there is no 'Union nationality'. It may be only a matter of time before this artificial link (Union citizenship/fifteen nationality laws) cedes to favour the enhancement of the vertical (functional) and horizontal ('new' non-functional) relationships mentioned above. But this desirable severance will have to be mediated through the existing procedures for review and reform of the EC/EU, namely Member State treaty change and European Court of Justice treaty interpretation. In this chapter, I look at the latter in particular and what the ECJ *has done* already for Union Citizenship and suggest some directions for what *might be* achieved in the future.

The structure of the chapter is as follows: Part 1. briefly looks at the EC Treaty provisions where Union Citizenship is located. In Part 2., there is an examination of ECJ reaction to Article 8 (now Articles 17–22) to date, an analysis which does not immediately hint at future dynamism. The institutional positions thus grasped, the remainder of the paper is devoted to the exploration of how the full scope of an historicised, contextualised citizenship might legitimately be read into Articles 17–22 EC. The function of these arguments is not to test citizenship, to condemn its weaknesses and failure to satisfy legal and political aspirations. Its scope is both more confined and more optimistic; it rests on an analysis of Articles 17–22 EC framed within Europe's "capacity to develop the conditions of emancipatory politics"[4] and laws.

I   A brief overview of Union Citizenship

European Union Citizenship is defined in Articles 17–22 (previously Article 8 of the European Community Treaty (ECT). These Articles are, at one and the same time, awesome in the chutzpah of their declaratory character, and yet they dwindle into detail and ambiguity and are thus rendered limited and bland. Union Citizenship has been deliberately detached from the legacy of judicial development which preceded it and these provisions are drafted in arrogant neglect of the entire history of citizenship in Europe.[5] The embarrassment of these intellectually antiseptic Treaty provisions was born out of IGC compromise rather than the kind of studied research which normally precedes a such a momentous creation. Articles 17–22 seem to command a low key, restrained and theoretically confined reaction. They, deceptively quietly, declare that EU Citizenship shall exist henceforth and proceed to root the concept in a bundle of previously existing EC law provisions mixed with some new benefits for the nationals of the Member States. Unlike its historical antecedents, for example citizenship in revolutionary France, Union Citizenship was not launched onto the political and legal map of the EU with fanfare, debate or even great enthusiasm. It seems so much like an unfortunate combination of (Member State and institutional) vanity and (substantive) banality. At one level, it might have appeared that Articles 17–22 were no more than a

---

[3] See Fleming, though, where the 1992 new Dutch Citizenship and nationality laws achieve some degree of 'decoupling'. Supra n. 2, p.6

[4] U. Vogel, 'Emancipatory politics between universalism and difference: gender perspectives on European Citizenship' in P. B. Lehning and A. Weale, *Citizenship, Democracy and Justice in the New Europe* (London, 1997) p. 142 at p. 157

[5] On the general position of history in EC Law see further, P. Allott, 'The crisis of European Constitutionalism: reflections on the revolution in Europe' 34 *CMLRev* 439 (1997)

consolidation of previously existing, if imprecisely determined, Treaty based rights. Viewed from this perspective, Citizenship seems to be a disappointing constitutional development, tied to the economically determined free movement right, suggesting little more than a cutting and pasting of other rights from elsewhere in the Treaty to add ballast to the weak democratic element of the EC/EU, and significant only in the political rights granted under Article 19.

The Amsterdam Treaty did not make a substantial change to EC Treaty provisions on Citizenship. The following wording is added to Article 17.1: 'Citizenship of the Union shall complement and not replace national citizenship'. This wording reflects the cautious perspective of the Danish government after Maastricht.[6] It may also have been introduced by the Member State governments mindful of the ECJ casting over-eager interpretative eyes on Articles 17–22 in the future. The question is what is the nature of this complementarity? In principle, it does not necessarily have to be construed negatively because it suggests that, once the essence of citizenship of the Union has been discerned, then it is not inferior but equal in status to national citizenship. This wording also can be said to concretise Union citizenship to some extent, for even though it cannot replace another form of citizenship, acknowledging it as some form of alternative citizenship in this manner has the effect of underlining it's potential impact. Interestingly, the proposed new wording does not refer to *Member State* national citizenship, suggesting the possibility (given wide judicial interpretation) of citizenship of the Union being open to those not in possession of EC Member State nationality (for example, long term resident non-nationals).[7] So the position on Citizenship after Amsterdam is that the *status quo* has more or less been maintained and the definition remains largely unaltered. Ultimately, this was not to prove to be the IGC for serious, intellectual and theoretical input into the real meaning of citizenship, preferring, as it did, to deal with its decoration rather than its foundations.

The criticisms of Union Citizenship are well known and extensively documented.[8] It

---

[6] "The provisions of Part Two . . . do not in any way take the place of national citizenship" Decision of the Heads of State and Heads of Government. Edinburgh 12 December 1992.

[7] See Kostakopoulou, T., 'Towards a theory of Constructive Citizenship in Europe' (1996) *The Journal of Political Philosophy*, Vol. 4, No. 4, pp. 337-358

[8] See, for example, C. Closa, 'The concept of citizenship in the Treaty on European Union' 29 *CMLRev* 1137 (1992); ibid. 'Citizenship of the Union and Nationality of the Member States' 32 *CMLRev* 487 (1995); H.U.J. d'Oliveira, 'European Citizenship: its meaning, its potential' in R.Dehousse (ed.) *Europe After Maastricht. An Ever Closer Union*, (Munich, 1994); M. Everson, 'The Legacy of the Market Citizen' in J. Shaw and G More (eds.) *New Legal Dynamics of the European Union* (Oxford, 1995) p 73; M. Everson and U. K. Preuß, *Concepts, Foundations and Limits of European Citizenship* (Bremen 1995); R. Kovar et D. Simon, 'La citoyenneté européenne' *CDE* 285 (1994); E. Meehan, 'Citizenship and the European Community', 63 Political *Quarterly*, (1993), p. 172; ibid. Citizenship *and the European Community*, (London, 1993); D.O'Keeffe, 'Union Citizenship' in D. O'Keeffe and P. Twomey (eds.) *Legal Issues of the Maastricht Treaty* (London 1994);S.O'Leary, 'Nationality Law and Community Citizenship: a case of two uneasy bedfellows' 12 *YEL* 353 (1992); ibid. 'The Relationship between Community Citizenship and the Protection of Fundamental Rights' 32 *CMLRev* 529 (1995); ibid. *The Evolving Concept of Community Citizenship*, (The Hague, 1996); U. K. Preuß, 'Problems of a Concept of European Citizenship' 1 *ELJ* 267 (1995); ibid. 'Two challenges to European Citizenship', 44 *Pol.Studs* 543 (1996); J. Shaw, 'The many pasts and futures of Citizenship in the European Union' 22 *ELRev* 554 (1997a); ibid. 'Citizenship of the Union: towards post-national membership' in *Collected Courses of the Academy of European Law* (The Hague, 1998a); ibid. 'The interpretation of European Union Citizenship' (1998b) *Modern Law Review*, Vol. 62, No. 3 p. 293, J.H.H. Weiler, 'European Citizenship and Human Rights' in *Reforming the Treaty on European Union, The Legal Debate*, J. A. Winter *et al* (eds.) (The Hague, 1996) at p. 57, ibid. To be a European Citizen: Eros and Civilization' (1999) in J. H. H Weiler, *The Constitution of Europe* (CUP, 1999) A. Wiener, *'European' Citizenship Practice, Building Institutions of a Non-State* (Boulder, 1998)

is a 'conferred',[9] non-consensual, unique new status bearing little relation to the traditional meanings of the word, and was ill suited to creation by international treaty making methodology. Nonetheless, Articles 17–22 have been inserted into the Treaties and will not escape the attention of the ECJ interpretative machinery.[10] This chapter firstly undertakes a location of Union Citizenship in its historical space and secondly, a consideration of its constitutional scope in a comparative context. The argument focuses not on 'alternative' approaches to citizenship but rather on forecasting how a judicially shaped future might fill the constitutional vacuum that Articles 17–22 EC have created. The argument is that an acknowledgement of the historical substance of the relationship between individuals in Europe (the precise history of citizenship itself), an intrinsic part of the EU's inheritance, as well as an incorporation of comparative influences from other constitutional domains which can be absorbed into the thinking on and judicial evaluation of Articles 17–22, may allow citizenship to escape from its stark, textual confines.[11]

II   Citizenship before the European Court of Justice

To date, Union citizenship, still residing in constitutional infancy, has not been subjected to a very lengthy form of EC level judicial examination or interpretation.[12] The cases in which Citizenship has been considered have arisen largely in the context of free movement of persons law, and therefore of Article 18.[13] Given the ambiguity of this provision and its potential effect on the exercise of free movement by individuals under EC law it is unsurprising that the Court should have been faced with arguments centred on this dimension of citizenship.[14] The Opinions of the Advocates General have been significant in most of these cases. In *Skanavi*,[15] AG Léger adopts a cautious

---

[9] *Second Report from the Commission on Citizenship of the Union* COM (97) 230

[10] This is not to suggest that the fate of citizenship of and in the EU rests entirely with ECJ interpretation. See further Weiner (1998), *supra.* n. 8.

[11] For wider perspectives on the subject, see, for example, J. Habermas, 'Citizenship and National Identity: Some Reflections on the Future of Europe', 12 Praxis *International* (1992); R. de Lange, 'Paradoxes of European Citizenship' in Fitzpatrick P ed. *Nationalism, Racism and the Rule of Law*, (Aldershot 1995), P.B. Lehning, 'European Citizenship: a mirage?' in Lehning, P. B. & Weale A., *Citizenship, Democracy and Justice in the New Europe* (London, 1997); L. Nauta, 'Changing conceptions of citizenship' 12 Praxis *International* (1992) p 20; U. K Preuß, 'Citizenship and Identity: Aspects of a Political Theory of Citizenship' in R.Bellamy *et al* (eds.) *Democracy and Constitutional Culture in the Union of Europe* (London, 1995) at p. 107; V. della Sala and A. Weiner, 'Constitution making and citizenship practice - Bridging the Democracy Gap in the EU?' SEI Working Paper No 18, Sussex European Institute (1996)

[12] See Shaw (1997a) (*Supra.* 8) at pp. 558-9 on the Court's reluctance in this matter which is in stark contrast to interpretations by the Court of, for example, Articles 5, 6 and 119

[13] Article 18 (ex Article 8a): Every citizen of the Union shall have the right to move and reside freely within the territory of the Member States, subject to the conditions and limitations laid down in this Treaty and by the measures adopted to give it effect.

[14] This issue was the subject of an abortive reference to the ECJ in the *Adams* case. (C-229/94, *R v Secretary of State for the Home Department, ex parte Adams*, [1995] AER **EC** 177). This case concerned the possibility of interpreting Article 8a. 1 as bringing intra-state restrictions on free movement within the scope of the Treaty. A subsequent ruling held however that such restrictions would still be seen as wholly internal - Case C-299/95, *Kremezow v Austria*, 1997 ECR I-2629. See further, Craig P and de Búrca G, *EC Law, Text, Cases and Materials*, 2nd ed. (Oxford, 1998), Chapter 15 and Craig P and de Búrca G (eds.) *The Evolution of EU Law* (Oxford, 1999), Chapter 14

[15] Case C-193/94 *Criminal Proceedings against Sofia Skanavi and Konstantin Chryssanthakopoulos*, [1996] ECR I-929

approach towards the application of the citizenship provisions in stressing that the right of residence in another EU Member State derives not from Article 8a (now Article 18) but from Article 52 (now Article 43).[16] The Court finds Article 8a to be a general expression of the rights provided under Article 52, and therefore secondary in importance to specific free movement provisions and as a consequence 'it is not necessary to rule on the interpretation of Article 8a.'[17]

After that blunt dismissal of Article 8's significance, the ECJ again overlooked an opportunity to examine the provision in *Boukhalfa*.[18] Here, the position of Advocate General Léger demonstrates a different level of appreciation of Article 8 and his Opinion includes strong support for the possible hidden qualities of that Article. Ms Boukhalfa was attempting to assert non-discrimination rights based on the policy of the German embassy in Algiers to discriminate between locally employed German nationals and other nationals (including EU nationals). The case, in a similar way to *Skanavi*, did not call into play any of the newly conferred benefits of Article 8 but raised questions of the relationship with Article 6 EC (now Article 12). The Advocate General, in his discussion of the fundamentality of free movement of persons law argues that it promotes "a feeling of belonging to a common entity', a feeling further enshrined by citizenship.[19] He questions here both the very reason for citizenship and implicitly its character as a defining status by asking "What would be the effects of such a feeling of belonging or such citizenship if they disappeared once the geographical borders of the Union were crossed?."[20] The interesting dimension of this argument is the manner in which inchoate and more generalised qualities are attributed to the bland and sparse face of Article 8a.1. It is also very significant that the emphasis is on this sense of 'belonging' which ought to flow from Union citizenship, a concept close to the absent 'membership' dimension claimed by critics of Article 8.[21] Remarking upon the responsibility of the ECJ to take this citizenship from the constitutional twilight zone, AG Léger reminds us that this article "is of considerable symbolic value" and that "it is for the Court to ensure that its full scope is attained".[22] "The concept should lead to citizens of the Union being treated absolutely equally, irrespective of their nationality". In order words, the implication is that Article 8 has changed the nature of the relationship between Member State nationals and the rights deriving to them from the Treaty. The Court ignores these significant arguments and does not mention Article 8 in its judgment.[23]

Advocate General Pergola subsequently delivered an Opinion which considerably reinforced the hints at expansive interpretation by his colleague. The case, *Sala*,[24] concerned the payment of a child-raising allowance to a Spanish national living, but

---

[16] Paragraph 21 of his Opinion.

[17] Paragraph 22 of the Judgment.

[18] Case C-214/94 *Ingrid Boukhalfa v Bundesrepublik Deutschland* [1996] ECR I-2253.

[19] Paragraph 31 of the Opinion.

[20] *ibid.*

[21] For example Weiner (1998) *Supra.* note 8

[22] Paragraph 63 of the Opinion.

[23] The ruling was given in April 96, perhaps a sensitive timing given the IGC context.

[24] Case C-85/96 *Maria Martinez Sala v Freistaat Bayern*, judgment of 12 May 1998. For detailed analysis see Fries S and Shaw J, 'Citizenship of the Union: First Steps in the European Court of Justice' (1998) *European Public Law*, Vol.4, No. 4, p. 533, More, G., 'The Principle of Equal Treatment' in Craig and de Búrca (1999) supra n. 14, Chapter 14, p. 536-540, O'Leary S., 'Putting flesh on the bones of European Union Citizenship' (1999) 24 *European Law Review*, p 68 and Toner, H. 'Union Citizenship caselaw: transformation or consolidation' (1999, forthcoming)

not working in Germany. This particular benefit was payable to EC nationals who were in possession of a residence permit which Ms Sala was not. The Advocate General engages in a broad interpretation of Ms Sala's status so as to allow her to be recognised as a migrant worker under the relevant secondary legislation. However, despite these interpretations of worker status law, he suggests that if her status as a worker cannot be confirmed, then the question of her entitlement remains to be answered and he poses the following question: "If it turns out that the claimant is not a worker, the question which, *residually*, remains to be answered is: what *other* provision is offered by the Union's legal order to prevent a community national in these circumstances, residing in Germany being discriminated against by comparison with German citizens?"[25] This is a question which could not have been asked before the TEU changes and demonstrates an inventive use of Article 8, which is the provision he suggests may provide a solution. The ECJ went on to hold that Sala, even though a non-economically active Member State national, was lawfully resident in Germany and was entitled to be protected from discrimination on grounds of nationality and therefore entitled to receive the child benefit. This decision is interesting as it extends the right to equal treatment to a Member State national who was not economically active and for whom the source of lawful residence in another Member state was not EC law.[26] The extension of this right to Ms Sala was facilitated by the interpretation of Union Citizenship provisions.

What can one conclude from the above cases?[27] This initial testing ground for citizenship cases has demonstrated a willingness on the part of the Advocate Generals to endorse a recognition of an independent significance for Article 8 EC. The cases all have a free movement dimension and testify to the well known weaknesses and limitations in this area of law. Arguably the drive for reform and advancement suggested in the Opinions is motivated more by the need to reform this law. However, there are more than strong indications of a recognition of the potential that the Treaty citizenship provisions offer given wide interpretation. Thus far, however, the reticence of the Court has been matched only by the idealism of the Advocate Generals. But there are suggestions that Article 8 may not remain the staid, restricted, contained measure that its textual reality implies if it continues to be subjected to the kind of reasoning here especially evident in *Sala*. As Fries and Shaw say '. . . it would appear that something close to a universal non-discrimination right, including access to all manner of welfare benefits has now taken root in Community law as a consequence of the creation of the figure of the Union citizen'.[28] It may require a case disconnected from free movement and involving another of the Article 17–22 rights for the Court to develop a more expansive perspective on the meaning and status of citizenship. In linking citizenship to free movement, one of the most sensitively controlled dimensions of integration, in this obvious way in Article 18, the Member States have rendered the Court gagged and bound in any case concerning the two. For, if the end result of an expansive interpretation of Article 18 would have an effect on free movement rights, then the Court might understandably be cautious in the face of Member State positions.

---

[25] Paragraph 14 of the Advocate General's Opinion, emphasis original

[26] It was instead an international agreement, the European Convention on Social and Medical Assistance.

[27] Other cases where Article 8 arisen included Cases C-4 &5/95 *Stöber and Periera v. Bundesantstalt für Arbeit*, 1997 ECR I-511 and Cases C-64 & 65/96 *Land Nordrhein-Westfalen v Uecker and Jacquet*, 1997 ECR I-3171 where the Court ruled that Article 8A does not cover free movement within a Member State. See, generally, Shaw (1997a) at p. 559, .

[28] Fries and Shaw (1998), *supra* n. 24

III   Citizenship beyond the Treaty?

In the Introduction I mentioned the contrary character of Citizenship; an unimaginative, limited concept at one level, this being most obviously manifested in the Treaty provisions themselves which prioritise and embody its 'functional' nature. But, on the other hand, Citizenship does not have to be confined to the seeming banalities of Articles 17–22, partly because elements of Citizenship existed before these provisions were drafted and partly because the entire essence and reality of European Citizens and their dreams for the concept cannot be captured by the Treaties. In this Part, I suggest a multi-layered conceptual perspective on Citizenship.

The emergence of citizenship at Maastricht had a well established lineage of directly relevant ECJ pronouncements but also an ancestry which proliferated at different levels which can be said to have contributed to the past of Articles 17–22. Citizenship is rooted in an EC history of its own which the Court can legitimately build upon in future interpretations and this Part is devoted to an attempt to locate and classify the identifiable elements of citizenship's past in the Union. Having examined above the current institutional perspectives, this Part of the paper forms a short bridge between the institutional reality and the historical and comparative aspirational material to follow. It outlines a framework designed to facilitate the emergence of citizenship *of* the Union in full recognition of the unexplored depth of citizenship *in* the Union. The phases or layers identified below overlap, chronologically and substantively, and the purpose of this categorisation is to suggest an holistic perspective of the framework within which the future scope and meaning of citizenship would necessarily be determined. This loose classification essentially constitutes an attempt to grasp intellectually both the core and the spirit of citizenship in the Union as an alternative to opting for the location of its essence either simply (and superficially) in Article 17–22 alone or, in ignoring the Treaty, searching for it in the everyday reality of the relationship between the governed and governors in the Union or between citizens themselves. Citizenship is an, as yet, unworked out composite of both of these elements, which means that the Court will never have complete control over the full meaning of citizenship and neither will the practice of citizenship in the Union be able to divorce itself from judicial appreciation. The main purpose in this categorisation is to allow the diverse sources of citizenship to be recognised and integrated with each other. If this discussion implies the lack of a role for the citizen it is because it is a classification directed towards future expansive interpretation rather than being focused on the actual, limited extent of the citizenship relationship within and with the Union. It is proposed as a framework for deeper comprehension and appreciation, rather than a detailed analysis or serious critique of all the elements which would rightly be considered in these contexts.

Judicial Citizenship

Some of the essence of EU citizenship rights emanating from the Court hail from an era characterised by what can be termed a 'revolutionary' perspective towards the Treaty. This layer or phase of citizenship development did not see the word citizenship actually uttered by the Court but evidenced a radically expansive interpretation of EC rights deriving to individuals.[29] It can be loosely understood as the coming of age of

---

[29] An example would be C-159/90 *Society for the protection of Unborn Children v Grogan* [1991] ECR I-4685 which brought abortion law into the fabric of citizenship. "European law this provides an arena for normative debates which may not exist in domestic legal systems.. ' Vogel (1997) at p. 148

citizenship in the EC without the actual vocalisation of the concept. The case which most strongly characterises this phase is that of *Cowan*.[30] The latent possibilities inherent in this case have been identified in an Article 8 context when Advocate General Pergola attempted a *mélange* of *Cowan* and Article 8 to attempt an EC law based classification of the status of a non-worker, single-mother resident in Germany in *Sala*.[31] But the right to receive services pronounced in *Cowan* has yet to have its full scope examined and used by the Court. If the Court persists in the reticent reflections on Article 8 discussed above, jurisprudence such as *Cowan*, from this juridically located layer of citizenship, offers the potential for a more radical development of the role of the individual under EC law than do Articles 17–22. Consider, for example, whether the right to enter another Member State to receive services would encompass the right of an indigent to stay and beg in that State.[32] EC free movement law has a well-established economic hierarchy which would exclude the poorest of EC nationals from benefiting from the so called 'fundamental' freedom. Article 17 confers citizenship on EC nationals, impliedly regardless of economic status, but its primary constituent element is embedded in free movement. This, as was discussed above in relation to the cases concerning Article 8, is the limiting factor in any attempt at an independent definition of citizenship. But, *Cowan*, unlike free movement is not predicated upon the economic status of the national claiming to benefit from its provisions, so its wording could in the future allow for rights to flow in favour of those who could not claim a similar right under the restrictive provisions of Articles18. This fossilises certain important citizenship related rights which may mean that judicially inspired citizenship could continue to develop more broadly outwith the framework of that provision. 'Belonging' and 'membership', fundamental elements of any form of citizenship, ought not to be available only to those wealthy enough to participate in the benefits. Article 18 ties future membership to the 'market' based view of integration. Not to be a viable market participant removes you therefore from the realm of citizenship.[33] This is a market which would exclude indigents and others trapped in poverty despite their citizenship status and rendering its primary component meaningless for them.

Constitutional citizenship

This layer of citizenship is the Treaty based one, that is, Articles 17–22 EC.[34] It formally attaches a political dimension to the erstwhile market citizens, though in a weak and diluted form only. This constitutional citizenship has its origins in Member State Treaty making fora and negotiations; it springs from the drafting table directly to the 'fundamental' without passing the Court. It now exists alongside the judicial layer

---

[30] Case 186/87 *Cowan v Le Trésor Public* [1989] ECR 195.

[31] Opinion p. 27.

[32] See P. Rosanvollan, 'Citoyenneté politique et citoyenneté sociale au XIXe siècle ' 171 *Le Mouvement Social* (1995) p 9 at p. 20 for a brief suggestion about the relationship between the right to beg and fundamental rights. US constitutional law has been use to argue the rights of indigents and others in similar positions. EC law, because of its economic focus and limited fundamental rights dimension, has not yet been tested in this subject.

[33] See further, Everson(1995) *Supra*. n. 8 and *ibid*. 'Economic rights within the European Union' in R. Bellamy *et al* (eds.) *Democracy and Constitutional Culture in the Union of Europe* (London, 1995) p. 137.

[34] As will be discussed below, the distinction between revolutionary (real, open) citizenship and constitutional (formal, closed) citizenship was well recognised.

of citizenship, waiting for inspiration and substance. It post-dates the Court's wider perspective on the role of the individual in integration and may therefore suffer from a come lately position with the judicial layer or dimension of citizenship being perceived as the more flexible and more suitable for expansion. To date, there has not been, as explained above, any extensive development of constitutional citizenship but future evolutions will necessarily occur in the context of co-existing layers and not in splendid isolation. It will not be allowed the luxury of the timing and uncritical space which surrounded the Court's interpretations in the early years. A form of politicised subject has been created under Articles 17–22 but even in the movement from Article 17 to Article 18 there has already been a diminution in the importance of that status; from nationality as entry requirement to the citizenship club to the implication that entry has its price and that is pre-determined by the exclusionary 'economic activity' requirement. The next layer is a suggested antidote to the impoverishment of this constitutional layer.

Participatory Citizenship

This layer giving life and presence to Union citizenship, has a wider breadth than the previous two layers. This level of belonging or membership is not directly dependant upon judicial interpretation or renegotiation of the Treaties. If it is less tangible in origin it is the most concrete layer in terms of encapsulating the reality of citizenship in the EU for EC nationals. It represents levels of inclusion and participation in the integrative process of many who do not directly come within the market based Treaty framework. EU integration, regulation, harmonisation and law and policy making have a bearing upon many who are prevented from any direct form of involvement; in other words, legal obligations filter through to those who have no reciprocal rights. Such excluded categories of people include children, refugees, illegal entrants and other non-economic actors amongst others. This stratum of citizenship does not always imply or involve a positive or active level of participation as many nationals and residents are involved in the sphere colonised by Union law and politics involuntarity or at least without active support and consent. This does not necessarily just refer to the over-familiar dearth of legitimacy which characterises the relationship between the Union and those who have at least limited political access to its processes.[35] Identifying and recognising the significance of the participatory dimension of Union citizenship also entails acknowledging the enforced involvement or entanglement which integration has propagated. Children, for example, are the 'subjects' of EC regulation in the field of employment and immigration but without any corresponding mechanism for ensuring the representation of their position. This may not be entirely divorced from the situation under domestic law. However, the position of those affected by Union immigration and asylum provisions constitutes a more marked degree of negative participation. The remedy gap engendered by the influence of EU level mechanisms to control asylum and immigration starkly represents the meaning of involuntary participatory citizenship.

This layer of citizenship does not only relate to the inclusion of those conceived as being outside the realm of active involvement in integration but defines and encompasses the less direct way in which many people relate and communicate in an active way within spheres of integration which are 'close' to them in the real sense,

---

[35] de Búrca G., 'The Quest for legitimacy in the European Union' (1996) 59 MLR 349

rather than the ordained, IGC enforced closeness. It is participatory in terms of *who* is included (in both positive and negative ways) and *what* type of relationship with the Union it refers to. At this level, citizenship involves a direct connection with aspects of integration not mediated through Member States or institutions. Participation can arise in many different forms, positive here rather than negative as described above; the farmers who regularly collect subsidy pay-outs and whose livelihood is determined by the EC; grass roots, cross-border gatherings of women excluded from the more formal layers of citizenship;[36] the Erasmus/Socrates funded students; the factory workers actively resorting to EC social policy legislation. Some of these are obvious; what is less obvious is the sense in which connections between citizens themselves (horizontal citizenship) and citizens and the Union in a global, non-vocalised manner (vertical citizenship) are both being animated at this level,[37] creating a positive and active communication space for those who might be marginalised or who lack access to power within the confines of national law and politics.

Citizenship conceived from this participatory perspective exists outwith Articles 17–22 and beyond and disconnected from the full scope of the Court's jurisdiction. Vogel speaks of an 'imagined community' and the diffusion of citizen activity into everyday practices of family life[38] allowing minority (and other) interests to find a resonance which is usually denied to them in national politics.[39] This layer encompasses a wider, more active conceptualisation of citizenship identifying the diffusion of EU related citizenship activity into everyday contexts which have proved effective in breaking the singular, one way, link between citizenship and the state. It captures the sense in which there is something beyond the grasp of both judicial and constitutional citizenship which has not been articulated at a politically powerful level. It is at this level that the borders of EU citizenship are blurred and vague. There can be restriction of this participation by Member States when they select an IGC 'opt-out' for their citizens thus demonstrating that these ill-defined connections require recognition, institutional guarantees and unifying principles in order to protect this level of real political empowerment (as opposed to the constitutional conception of political citizenship of Article 19).

IV Citizenship without a past?

Much of the mood of this chapter is forward looking, attempting to anticipate a positive future for Citizenship. But in this Part, I argue that the past is as important as the future. This is something which has been overlooked in the functional formulation of Union Citizenship, reflecting a general ahistoricised tendency in European integration. This Part then is about the need for Citizenship to be located in an inventive context which fully acknowledges its historical roots. The significance of Europe's past, both immediate and more distant, is overtly denied in the Treaties and the instruments and policies which shape and influence integration. There are obvious reasons why the more recent historical elements would be ignored; the Franco-German alliance which dictated the direction of integration would not have been

---

[36] See, further, Vogel (1997)

[37] Vogel (1997) refers to Tassin's 'European fellow-citizenship' "which evolves less from the legal and administrative consolidation of citizen status than from the multiple sites and communicative processes of citizen activity" (at p. 157)

[38] At p. 145

[39] ibid. at p. 156 She gives the example of pensioners demanding a pensioners parliament in Europe.

served by too much remembrance of the past. But institutions and policies devoid of recognition of their historical debts are bound to be eventually found lacking. This level of lack of awareness of the significance of history and the subsequent need to historicise the innovations spawned by integration is particularly marked in the case of citizenship. Article 17, in creating a constitutional citizenship for the Union, is the direct descendant of citizenships formed in European nation state constitutions since the eighteenth century. Their legacy and influence have fed through to the TEU introduced provision via Member State conceptions and uses of citizenship. Any future interpretation of Articles 17–22 has an obligation to acknowledge this long-term influence and learn from it in order to fully comprehend and construct that provision in a meaningful manner. The entire constitutional heritage of Europe is replete with rich lessons for what is being invented in the name of Union.[40] It is as much part of the identity of the polity and the individuals as are political, social and cultural influences. But within the realm of judicial interpretation and constitutional invention this is not sufficiently acknowledged. The members of the ECJ hardly need a lesson in the use and integration of history but there may be specific reasons why this Court, which so ably accompanied institutionally driven integration, may not readily have historicised its decisions in the past; no doctrine of precedent and the influence of civil law systems may explain the relatively confined approach to historically influenced analysis by the Court.

Citizenship in revolutionary France during the period 1789 -1804 is one of best examples of the inheritance underlying Article 17 which can be evoked in order to increase understanding of this provision. There are particular and especially instructive influences to be gleaned from the recognition of the influence of citizenship developments during that period of time for the more bland version which is its direct legacy two hundred years later. The timing is apt as the period 1989–2004, though unlikely to witness the same cataclysmic events and dramatic constitutional developments of that era, is bound to witness Articles 17–22 undergoing an important evolution. The suggestion is that the starting point for an understanding of the history of citizenship in the EU is not Paris of 1974 but Paris of 1794 (the height of the Republican, revolutionary period), for, while the lead up to Maastricht is important in appreciating how Article 17 could have emerged in the first place, the significance of the provision lies rooted far more deeply than institutional manipulation of the concept.

There are many dimensions of French revolutionary citizenship which are especially apt in the historicising of Union citizenship.[41] Those highlighted here revolve around the exclusion of women from citizenship status in this period.[42] This raises questions of the understanding of the nature of duties and gender related dimensions of citizenship which remain controversial and unsolved today in modern formulations of citizenship including the EU version. The primary parameters and functions of

---

[40] See further Allott (1997) supra. note 5.

[41] See, generally, K M Baker, *The French Revolution and the creation of Modern Political Culture* (Oxford, 1997), F. Fehér, *The French Revolution and the Birth of Modernity* (Berkeley, 1990); A Forrest and P Jones (eds.), *Reshaping France* (Manchester, 1991); H Mason and W Doyle (eds.) *The Impact of the French Revolution on European Consciousness* (Gloucester, 1989); S Melzer and L Rabine, *Rebel Daughters: Women and the French Revolution* (Oxford 1992); S Schama, *Citizens – A Chronicle of the French Revolution* (London, 1989).

[42] See further D Godineau, 'Femmes en Citoyenneté: pratiques et politiques' *Annales Historiques de la Révolution Française* p. 197 (1995).

citizenship have not radically evolved since that period of time to the extent that it remains, as in its EU incarnation, economically dictated and therefore, implicitly, gender biased. Much has rightly been made of the failure to connect citizenship with fundamental rights[43] in the EU and of the inherent discriminatory effects of the built-in link with free movement, but the neglect of the socially inspired element of citizenship is equally if not more significant.[44]

Women were not classed as citizens in the early states of the revolutionary period. There was, instead, a "self-reinforcing triangle of manhood, military duties and political rights"[45] which influenced the definition and conception of citizenship thus ensuring the exclusion of women. Many of the early constitutional definitions of citizenship during this period of time incorporated the duty to bear arms as an inherent dimension of citizenship.[46] The ingrained discriminatory 'Soldier/Citizen' formulation inevitably excluded women from the citizenship status; if the primary duty of the *citoyen* was to bear arms to defend the Republic, then those conceived as not having the ability to bear arms would of necessity be prevented from benefiting from citizenship. Framed as a duty, it could be constructed as a privileged right serving to preserve citizenship for men only and acting as a pre-determined exclusion operating against women.[47]

It was this dimension of citizenship, and as a reaction against the gendered nature of politics during the revolutionary era, which brought about a response from women in revolutionary France and led to their claims for empowerment and involvement in the political process.[48] Without formally possessing citizenship rights (and duties), women began to argue for their participation in the public and political life of France. In 1792 there began demands from women for the right to form a female national guard.[49] In 1793, women began increasingly relying on the *Declaration des Droits de l'Homme* to claim that citizenship rights, including the right to vote, were natural rights which could not be denied them. The arguments were based on the concept that the Republic constituted an ' *espace de réciprocité*'[50] which ensured, or ought to ensure, that the exercise of citizenship, and therefore participation in public and political life, was not limited to its constitutional definition.[51] Demands for involvement and empowerment were derived initially from exclusion from the duties of citizenship and widened to form claims for access to the rights also.

---

43 For example, O'Leary (1995) *supra*. n. 8

44 See, for example, L Ackers, *Shifting Spaces: Women, Citizesnhip and Migration within the European Union* (Bristol, 1998), R A Elman (ed.), Sexual Politics and the European Union (Oxford, 1996), M Everson 'Women and Citizenship of the European Union' in T Hervey and D. O'Keeffe (eds.), *Sex Equality Law in the European Union* (Chichester, 1996) and Shaw (1997a) *supra*. n. 8

45 M. P Johnson, 'Citizenship and gender: the Légion des Fédérées in the Paris Commune of 1871' 8 *French History* 276 (1994) 276 at p. 277

46 Godineau (1995) at p. 198

47 "Armed women in paramilitary formation undermined one of the central assumptions justifying the denial of the political rights to women, that only men could be warriors, and therefore citizens' Johnson (1994) at p. 276

48 Godineau (1995) at p. 200

49 ibid.

50 ". . . dans lequel tous les membres du corps social doive coopéerer au bien de tous, à la chose pubic, la *Res Publica*" ibid.

51 Herein resides the recognition of the significance of the difference between constitutional (formal) citizenship and what was then termed revolutionary citizenship (which would accord more closely with participatory citizenship) discussed above.

While, obviously, the position of women under Union citizenship is far removed from the blatant discrimination of the 1790's in France, this historically influential era does allow for some parallels to be drawn with Europe of the 1990's and, consequently, for didactic analysis to feed into the understanding of Articles 17–22. For 'Soldier/ Citizen' read 'Consumer/Citizen' as the exclusionary element of our modern citizenship; Article 18 and 19 rights are largely exercisable only upon work based residence in another EU Member State by the financially empowered potential consumer (as opposed to the economically disabled who might draw upon the State's resources rather than contributing to them). This formulation has both direct and indirect exclusionary effects barring the non-consumer from the political rights which ought to flow from citizenship (in the same way that the duty to bear arms did so). Furthermore, the Article 17 definition of citizenship clearly excludes non-EC nationals; this limitation ought not to be taken for granted as seeming as natural as the exclusion of women must have seemed to constitution drafters in the 1790's. A revival of the gender based inclusionary concept of *'espace de réciprocité'* perspective of the political domain could be used to construct a framework for EU citizenship which breaks the nationality/citizenship mould. Finally, even this cursory examination of Article 17's constitutional ancestry offers insights into the use of citizenship duties. So far, this element of the provision has attracted little attention and the duties which were imposed at the same time as the conferral of rights lie dormant and untouched.[52] But future definitions of such duties could result in possible indirectly gender based and other forms of discrimination preventing full participation in citizenship just as the duty to bear arms did.

There are many wider, less focused lessons from this age of citizenship which could constructively be used to justify a deeper conception of citizenship than the superficial creation offered under Article 17, and the powerful story of women's struggle for inclusion is just one element of this relevant, deeply embedded history. The concept of the public space allowing participation and the exercise of rights which do not fall within formal, constitutional definitions of citizenship could be claimed by many detached from the political and economic processes determined by integration. Not for the first time in history has citizenship been used as the artificial tool of legitimacy, then and now, but the examples above suggest a heritage for citizenship which cannot be ignored by an enlightened and open-minded judiciary.

V   The constitutional limits?

Seven years after its 'invention' it as yet unclear what the future direction of Union Citizenship will be. The previous section argued the need for a judicial glance 'backwards' towards the EU's constitutional heritage. Here, the proposition is extended in recommending that judicial interpretation of Articles 17–22 embrace a glance 'outwards' towards influences from constitutional determinations in other jurisdictions in order to adopt an expansive perspective on the potential of EU citizenship. In *P v S and Cornwall County Council*,[53] Advocate General Tesauro examined legal developments in other jurisdictions in order to evaluate the possible position of transsexuals under EC equal treatment law.[54] The Court heeded the advice

---

[52] Article 17 (2) (ex 8 (2)) 'Citizens of the Union shall . . . be subject to the duties imposed [by the EC Treaty]'

[53] Case C-13/94 [1996] ECR I-2143

[54] Directive 76/207 EEC.

of the Advocate General to make a 'courageous decision' in order to pronounce one of its most liberal decisions on the scope of a piece of secondary legislation.[55] The possibility of other such external jurisprudential influences is the subject of this section using a very selective example only of the kind of comparative caselaw related to citizenship which could conceivably be brought to bear in an analysis of Articles 17–22. There is an abundance of comparative material which the Court could draw upon in this regard in the recognition of other sources of law.[56] The following two potential influences on the unfolding of Citizenship are examined: A. the Australian High Court decision in the *Mabo* case,[57] as a significant example of postcolonial constitutionalism[58] which has the potential to influence EU citizenship development and scholarship; and B. a consideration of the case of 'outsiders' within, the Amerindians of French Guyana and the boundaries of citizenship within the EU.

A   *Mabo and the Fiduciary Union?*

The *Mabo* decision is well known for having established the principle of native title to land and abolishing the doctrine of *terra nullius* insofar as it pertained to Aboriginal ancestral title.[59] This, ostensibly, may seem a momentous decision in its in own right but disconnected from issues of citizenship in Europe. The connections are however there to be made and reside primarily in the potential exploitation of the concept of the 'fiduciary duty' owed by the Crown which was discussed in the case. In the EU, nobody seems to want to claim possession, or more properly perhaps, responsibility for citizenship; ignored by citizens themselves aware of the hollowness of Article 17, its significance shunned and denied by the Court, receiving only cursory attention from the Member State governments in IGC mode, it sits awkwardly in the critical Part Two of the EC Treaty, a beacon flashing brilliantly but speaking no one.[60] An imaginative judicial decision from Australia is not going to revive the drooping spirits of EU citizenship but there are insights in the case suggestive of a modern role for the citizenship in a federal context. Apart from the concept of Fiduciary Duty, there are other dimensions of Mabo which could have a bearing on the eeking out of a form of politics and constitutionalism appropriate to European Union; considerations of sovereignty in a postcolonial federation,[61] questions of subsidiarity and the mediation of values between the various levels in a state; and the example of the overthrowing of age old, in-built assumptions by an emancipated judiciary in recognition of a new morality for a new era.[62] This enlightened decision forced consideration of what laws

---

[55] The Court itself however did not refer to the cases from other jurisdictions. Indeed it does not even make a reference to the AG Opinion

[56] See further U.K. Preuß, 'Two Challenges to European Citizenship' *Political Studies* (1996) p 534

[57] *Eddie Mabo and Others v State of Queensland* [No. 2], High Court of Australia, 3 June 1992, 66 ALJR at 408

[58] Duncan Ivison, "Decolonizing the Rule of Law: Mabo's Case and Postcolonial Constitutionalism" (1997) 17 Oxford Journal Of Legal Studies p. 253

[59] For lengthy analysis of Mabo see, for example, *Essays on the Mabo Decision* (Sydney, 1993).

[60] The Commission's 'Citizens First' campaign has had little success in altering this position.

[61] Ivison (1997) p. 277 on questions of indivisible sovereignty and 'the rather banal fact that the sovereignty of Australia is not justiciable in an Australian municipal court has been taken to rule out any consideration of the manner in which sovereignty was acquired, i.e. the consequences of that acquisition."

[62] "[The common law] 'cannot be frozen in an age of racial discrimination'" Brennan J. at p. 422 of the decision

were appropriate for contemporary Australia, concerns germane also to the Luxembourg judiciary.

The principle of racial exclusion was at the very foundation of the Australian state and permeated overtly into laws and political practice of the country until relatively recently.[63] The Aboriginal community was treated as a 'populus nullius'[64] and "there was a form of 'imperial constitutional law' which maintained this wrongful myth and 'which governed the acquisition of Crown sovereignty in settler states'.[65] The Court in *Mabo* held that the claimants retained ancestral title to their lands and rejected the long- established non-recognition of Aboriginal land rights. The principle of *terra nullius* (an international law fiction) served to uphold and substantiate racially dictated laws in supporting the notion that, on the arrival of Europeans, Australia was unoccupied territory. This resulted in the denial and negation of the very existence of the Aboriginal population as a cultural, social or legal entity[66] and condemned them to a kind of civil death. They had no legal personality accorded to them and were not entitled to protection under the law but had all the obligations of the law imposed on them.[67] Land rights have a particular importance for Aborigines; their customary law is marked by an ancient, embedded attachment to the land which sees land as a live entity.[68] *Mabo* can be considered all the more radical in inverting ingrained racist legal fictions in the recognition of the fundamental property rights of Aborigines to their ancestral lands.[69]

Part of the judgment was based on the acknowledgement that the public authorities (the Crown) had failed in the obligation to protect Aboriginal interests, i.e. in their Fiduciary Duty. Toohey J[70] puts forward the proposition based on the notion of Trust and principles of equity[71] which he suggests underlie the Crown's powers. He sees the relationship between the Crown and the claimants as giving rise to a fiduciary obligation on the part of the Crown based on the scope of the one party to exercise a discretion capable of affecting the legal position of the other. On colonisation of Australia, there was a transfer of executive power which ought to give rise to the general presumption that the rights of indigenous people would be protected.[72]

---

[63] "Until 1967 they were still excluded from the Constitution; moreover, as recently as the 1960's, some of that long standing body of horrendously racially discriminatory legislation was still on the statute books in various States. . . ." B Hocking "Human Rights and Racial discrimination after the Mabo Cases: no more racist theft?" in *Essays* (1993) (*supra*. n. 57) p. 178 at p. 185

[64] ibid.

[65] Ivison (1997) at p. 262

[66] R Lafargue, 'La 'révolution Mabo' ou les fondements constitutionnels du nouveau statut des Aborigènes d'Australie', *Revue du Droit Public* (1994) p. 1329 at p. 1332

[67] There are superficial parallels with Third Country nationals resident in the EU in terms of their position as non-recognised under EC law, or being in a zone of secondary recognition only

[68] Not dissimilar to the position of the Amerindians discussed in *B.* below

[69] The decision has however been exposed to critical examination. See, for example, M J Detmold, 'Law and Difference: Reflections on Mabo's Case' in *Essays on the Mabo Decision* (1993) at p. 39

[70] At p. 408 of the judgment.

[71] Which had been recognised and used in a similar context in US constitutional law also: *Country of Oneida v. Oneida Indian Nations*, 1985 (470 U. S. 266)

[72] "A fiduciary obligation .. does not limit the legislative power of .. Parliament but legislation will be a breach of that obligation if its effect is adverse to the interest of the title holders or if the processes it establishes does not take account of those interests..' (at p 494) "Courts still struggle to isolate the essence of such relationships and it has not yet been suggested that the category of such relationships is closed." R Blowes "Governments: Can you trust them with your Traditional Title?" in *Essays* (1993) *supra* n 57at p. 134

The concept of a 'fiduciary duty' extrapolated from *Mabo* could offer insights in relation to issues of sovereignty and democracy in the EU; a relationship of trust based on transfer of political (rather than property) rights could be formulated at two levels. Member States have 'contracted out' of national level rights under the EC/EU Treaties and there is a transfer of some of the essence of the nationally determined relationship between public power and the citizen which the EC and EU now hold and exercise under a form of political trust, giving rise to responsibility and duties on its part. "Underlying such relationships is the scope for one party to exercise a discretion which is capable of affecting the legal position of the other. One party has a special opportunity to abuse the interests of the other"[73]; this sums up in an unusual but incisive manner the nature and origin of the EC/EU's power and competence. Apart from the restrictively interpreted 'access to justice rights' under Articles 230 (ex 173) and 288 (ex 215), there is little scope for nationals of the Member States to effectively (legally) enforce their relationship with the institutions of the EC/EU. As international Treaty creations, superficially it might be argued that no legal scope existed to establish a link or 'contract' sufficient to enforce the relationship. But since the pioneering days of *Van Gend en Loos*,[74] there has been Court endorsement of the special nature of individuals under EC law, which recognises the *sui generis* consequences of supranationality. However, the appropriate *loci* for exercise of this special relationship has consistently been found by the Court to be at the Member State level[75] an acknowledgement that the States have duties arising out of the transfer of rights under the Treaties but no comparably wide position as regards the Community/Union itself has been formulated. Using a 'fiduciary duty'/political trust based analysis of the nature of EC/EU powers could offer the potential to frame the relationship with nationals of the Member States in such a way as to give the EC/EU both an identity as well as a level of general responsibility not recognised in the Treaties. The mechanism for doing so might be found in the expansive interpretation of Articles 17–22 being suggested throughout this paper; EC nationals have been classed, without consent, as citizens of the Union and given both limited rights and undefined duties as a consequence. Although this classification is peremptorily dependant on the nationality relationship which the Member State controls, the status must raise questions of the nature of the relationship with the Union which citizenship has surely created or enhanced. To date, European Parliament voting rights and access to the Ombudsman are the only such indications which hint at this connection. But if citizenship is to be considered as a reciprocal relationship, the duties and responsibility of the other party (the Union) remain to be defined.[76] This 'protection' or responsibility dimension of citizenship can be supported also by a comparison with United States citizenship.[77]

---

[73] Toohey J. at p. 493 of the judgement

[74] Case 26/62 [1963] ECR 1

[75] From *Van Gend* through indirect effect (*Von Colson and Kamann* (Case 14/83 [1984] ECR 1891) and *Marleasing* (Case C-106/89 [1990] ECR I-4135)) through to the *Francovich* remedy (Cases C-6/90 and C-9/90 [1991] ECR I-5357). See further Craig and de Búrca, 2nd ed. (Oxford, 1998) Chapter 4

[76] The notion that citizenship involves reciprocal duties is implied by Preuß in his discussion of the comparison between European Citizenship and United States citizenship ". . . we may understand European citizenship as an instrument which serves to remove 'from the citizens of each state the disabilities of alienage in the other States' US Supreme Court, Paul v Virginia, 75 U.S. 168, 180 (1869), in U K Preuß, 'Two Challenges to European Citizenship' *Political Studies* (1996) p. 534 at p. 550

[77] "In the American case the establishment of national citizenship served to render the Union the protector of individual rights which were jeopardized by the Member States' Preuß (1996) at p. 550

The EC Treaties and the community *acquis* are not totally devoid of elements which might suggest a duty based reading of Article 17, which would serve to render citizenship a more real concept; the Article 226 (ex 169) and 227 (ex 170) enforcement procedures, for example, suggest some level of responsibility on the part of the institutions. The political trust or fiduciary duty interpretation of citizenship might serve also as a space to explore the remedying of the high levels of accepted democratic deficits in the EC/EU, based as it is on the concept of protection of those unilaterally deprived of rights by public powers. Questions of 'governmental' obligations and political trust or the concept of the 'trust in the higher sense' derive from colonial cases where this was distinguished from the normal form of trust.[78] In the EC/EU, this concept has potential use in a wide range of cases in the sphere of fundamental rights, environmental law cases or issues of regional policy and structural funds which have a partnership dimension.[79] This form of trust can arise because of the circumstances of the relationship in which the EC/EU might be seen as based on the transfer of the 'property' which nationals of the Member States had in the control over national level law and policy making, now partially lost because of sovereignty transfers under the Treaties.

B   The reluctant citizens? The Amerindians of French Guyana.

If "Indigenous people represent the most far reaching challenge to the modern equation among nation, state and law . . .',[80] they also represent a direct challenge to European Union Citizenship. 'It is the essential nature of law to recognise difference' (a failure to some extent rectified in *Mabo*)[81] and the EU has complex layers of difference which EC law has to deal with. While *Mabo* may seem like a distant legacy of colonialism (even though it involves a Member State), the residues of the colonial age are still very much prevalent in the EC/EU, requiring consideration of the nature of the relationship between EC law and people who are many steps removed from its legitimate sphere of application, people who indeed not Europeans. Postcolonial constitutionalism is not in fact an external, comparative source of law but one which has an application to situations which arise within the territorial boundaries of the EC/EU. The case of the Amerindian community of French Guyana is considered here to highlight the extent to which Citizenship may be considered an inappropriate inclusionary instrument for all those it assumes to class as citizens. There has, in general, been little focused opposition to EU citizenship; the Eurosceptic agenda has concentrated on EMU and other high profile issues and not Articles 17–22. Of course, Euroscepticism tends to be the voice of the relatively powerful and economically motivated and not the expression of the poor or otherwise disenfranchised and certainly rarely representative of those most distant of Europeans, residents of regions which are politically and legally part of the EU though not part of Europe.[82] Colonially determined affiliations construct artificial Europeans of the residents of

---

[78] *Kinlock v Secretary of Sate for India* (1882) 7 App Cas 619 and *Tito v Waddell* (no. 2) [1977] All ER 129 where the concept was argued unsuccessfully

[79] See, further, J Scott, 'Law, legitimacy and EC Governance: Prospects for Parternership' *JCMS* Vol. 36, No 2 Special Issue, *Integrating Law*, K. Armstrong and J. Shaw (eds.) (1998)

[80] de Sousa Santos, B., *Towards a New Common Sense: Law, Science and Politics and Paradigmatic Transition* (London, 1995) at p. 318

[81] M J Detmold 'Law and difference: reflections on Mabo's case' in *Essays* (1993)) at p. 39

[82] Article 299 EC (ex 227)

these territories and cannot ensure that citizenship will be accepted by them on the same terms as nationals resident in the EC. This section is a brief consideration of the issues which are raised by having created an all encompassing citizenship under Article 17 which makes assumptions about its universal appeal. The discussion is centred on the implications of Articles 17–22 for non-Europeans but it has wider implications in terms of the extent to which EC law can accommodate difference. There is a mounting body of literature[83] on the treatment of TCN's *within* the EU itself which highlights the gradually emerging secondary status of those excluded from the benefits of EC law even though legitimately resident in the physical space which it governs. Residents of French Guyana and of other French *departements d'outre-mer*, are naturally entitled to all the benefits of EC law in the maintenance of the legally supported fantasy that these areas of the world constitute part of Europe. The EU inherited the values and myths of a colonial era and mediates them by simple incorporation into the body of EC law without special exception. Here, as well as suggesting some potential problems for the falsely universal declarations in Article 17 EC in terms specifically of 'others within', it is also argued, as with the *Mabo* extrapolations above, that exposing EU citizenship to such challenges to its universality can allow it to develop and evolve as a more multi-faceted, substantive status. Article 17 EC, a kind of constitutional blunderbuss in its stark generality, may prove to be an especially unsuitable tool for endowing the Amerindians of Guyana with citizenship status.[84] These *de jure* Europeans were resident in the territory before the arrival of Europeans in 1604. Although not a large community (6000 approx.) their relationship with the colonial power has for some time posed problems under French law.[85] As a gradually emerging influential local political force seeking to ensure the upholding of their identity, culture and languages they have made claims to entitlement to ancestral lands not dissimilar to the Australian Aborigines. Beyond questions as to what extent French law can accommodate these claims is the issue of how EC law might impinge upon them. In French Guyana, there is a long tradition of a difference between the constitutional position of the Amerindians and partial only application of the law. Entitled to citizenship and nationality of the French Republic, they initially manifested no interest in either status, mostly because of their alternative reliance upon customary law to regulate those aspects of life which would have brought them into the sphere of application of French public law.[86] The 1960's however witnessed a concerted campaign of 'Frenchification' which resulted in a widespread take up of French nationality and citizenship. Nevertheless, certain communities refused to do so, seeking to safeguard their identity and traditions.[87] They continue to have no civil status (*état civil*) under French law with the result that they have no voting rights. This situation raises questions of the extent of application of Articles 17–22 to these reluctant citizens.

---

[83] See, for example, T Hervey, 'Migrant workers and their families in the European Union: the pervasive market ideology of Community law' in J Shaw and G More (eds.) *New Legal Dynamics of European Union* (Oxford, 1995) and T Kostakopoulou, 'Why a 'Community of Europeans' could be a Community of Exclusion' 35 *JCMS* (1997) p. 301

[84] On this community's position under French Law see I Arnoux, "Les Amérindiens dans le département de la Guyane: problèmes juridiques et politiques" *Revue du Droit Public* p. 1615 (1995)

[85] French law does not encompass the recognition of national minorities. France has not ratified the Council of Europe texts relating to the protection of the rights of national minorities

[86] Arnaux (1995) at p. 1624

[87] *ibid.* p 1625 The Wayana and the Palikur tribes refused to become citizens on the basis of preserving their identity and traditions.

However, even those Amerindians who have accepted French citizenship have only a limited relationship with this status; they may vote but are not required to pay full taxes or do military service (Article 17.2 might require some accommodation for this situation) and live generally only partly governed by the Civil and Penal Codes. Customary law serves instead to regulate family life, property and criminal law in an effort to preserve identity and take account of concepts of right, family and property which they do not share with French law on these matters. For example, some communities allow polygamy and their definition of family is very wide. This, and their concept of collective use of land without ownership amongst other traditions, would pose serious challenges for some fundamentals of EC law were such a confrontation ever to arise in a judicial setting. Meanwhile, even this summary analysis of the position of one group which resides literally at the boundaries of EC law exposes the fragility of boldly declaring 'Citizenship of the Union is hereby established'. Learning to accept the legacy of colonialism is part of the recognition that the EU has a diverse history which cannot be divorced from the face of Treaty.

Conclusion

The secret subtleties of Union Citizenship await discovery. It has been relegated to an area of secondary importance by the Member States and accepted as a given by the political institutions. Of course, there is a real, living citizenship outwith the Treaty provisions, but any concrete definition of the status for the purposes of not only exercising Union citizenship but *enforcing* it necessitates Court attention. This paper was about the need for this constitutional rejuvenation of citizenship in the Union, in the context of judicial interpretation. But the fundamental dilemma is that this process will be effective only in acknowledging that the essence of what it means to be a European citizen cannot be judicially determined. Its spirit lies elsewhere and its limits lie far beyond Articles 17–22 EC.

9

Democracy, Sovereignty and the Constitution of the Europe Union: The Republican Alternative to Liberalism*

Richard Bellamy and Dario Castiglione

The European Union (EU) has appeared to many analysts as an incoherent mix of the supranational and federal, on the one hand, and the inter-national and inter-governmental, on other. Its hybrid nature makes democratic accountability problematic. The lines of responsibility are often unclear and many decisions get made betwixt and between the established mechanisms of democratic control as matters of executive or administrative discretion. Both criticism of and remedies for this situation standardly appeal to the norms and practices of liberal democracy. Those favouring a move towards greater integration advocate removing the democratic deficit within the EU by extending liberal democratic institutions to the European level through such measures as enhancing the powers of the European Parliament, formalizing the evolving European constitution, and instituting a quasi-federal distribution of sovereign power.[1] Those who adopt a more intergovernmental perspective, by contrast, maintain political authority must largely remain with the constituent nation states, since their linking of people, territory and community provide liberal democracy's only viable context.[2]

In what follows, we shall contest this common starting point. We argue that the very global economic and social forces that have promoted European integration have

* Research for this paper was supported by an ESRC Research Grant on 'Sovereignty and Citizenship in a Mixed Polity' (R000222446). For helpful comments, we thank Tony Downes, Neil MacCormick, Jo Shaw, Jim Tully, Alex Warleigh, participants at the conference on 'Liberal Justice and Political Stability in Multinational Societies' organised by the Groupe de Recherche sur les Sociétés Plurinationales, McGill University, the TSER EURCIT Network Workshop in Reading, and seminars at the universities of Essex, Brussels, Lisbon, Leeds and Paris. Dario Castiglione acknowledges the support of the EUSSIRF Programme at the European University Institute in Florence.

[1] Cf. M. Burgess, *Federalism and the European Union*, (London: Routledge, 1989); S. Williams, 'Sovereignty and Accountability in the European Community', *Political Quarterly*, (1990) Vol. 61, No3; V. Bogdanor and G. Woodcock, 'The European Community and Sovereignty', *Parliamentary Affairs*, (1991) Vol. 44, No. 4.

[2] Cf. N. Barry, 'Sovereignty, the Rule of Recognition and Constitutional Stability in Britain', *Hume Papers on Public Policy*, (1994) Vol. 2 No. 1, pp. 10–27; D. Miller, *On Nationality*, (Oxford: OUP, 1995); A. Moravcsik, 'Preferences and Power in the European Community: A Liberal Intergovernmentalist Approach', *Journal of Common Market Studies*, (1993) Vol.31, pp. 473–524.

undermined liberal democracy at the nation state level without creating appropriate conditions for its establishment within a supranational European polity. As Schmitter and others have argued,[3] a more complex, multi-layered and hence multi-national form of governance is coming into being. As critics rightly fear, these circumstances provide ample possibilities for the self-interested bargaining and blocking that have so frequently characterised European decision making and produced measures such as the Common Agricultural Policy that are both sub-optimal and inequitable. To avoid these dangers, however, requires a quite different approach to the standard liberal democratic solution—one we dub democratic liberalism, which draws on the neo-republican tradition in politics.[4]

This analysis rests on a fuller account of the EU's democratic deficit than is usual. There are three dimensions to this phenomenon,[5] two of which are rarely addressed. First, there is the democratic deficit in the narrow sense of the relative absence of any influence by ordinary citizens over European decision-makers and the policies they enact in their name.[6] Second, there is the federal deficit. This arises from the ambiguous relationship between the central EU institutions, such as the European Court of Justice, the European Parliament and the Commission, on the one hand, which claim a federal status within their respective domains, and national governments, parliaments, courts and bureaucracies, on the other, which frequently dispute or seek to qualify such claims.[7] Finally, there is the constitutional deficit.[8] This refers to the lack of any systematic normative and popular legitimization of European political institutions due to the paucity of sustained debate about their overall shape and reach—even by the political and bureaucratic élites.[9] If the first deficit focuses on democratic accountability and representation, the second raises the issue of the distribution of sovereignty, and the third the problem of the EU's legitimacy. The three are interrelated. How one tackles the first of these deficits will largely be framed by

---

[3] Cf. Schmitter's contribution G. Marks, F. W. Scharpf, P. Schmitter and W. Streek, *Governance in the European Union*, (London: Sage, 1996); and G. Marks, L. Hooghe and K. Blank, 'European Integration from the 1980s: State-Centric v. Multi-level Governance', *Journal of Common Market Studies*, (1996) Vol. 34, pp. 341–78.

[4] P. Pettit, *Republicanism: A Theory of Freedom and Government* (Oxford: Clarendon Press, 1997); Q. Skinner, *Liberty before Liberalism* (Cambridge: Cambridge University Press, 1998)

[5] D. Castiglione, 'Contracts and Constitutions'. In R. Bellamy, V. Bufacchi and D. Castiglione (eds) *Democracy and Constitutional Culture in the Union of Europe*, (Lothian Foundation Press: London, 1995), pp. 59–79, in particular pp. 61–3.

[6] S. Williams, 'Sovereignty and Accountability in the European Community', *Political Quarterly*, (1990), Vol. 61, No 3.

[7] K. Neunreither, 'The Democratic Deficit of the European Union: Towards Closer Cooperation between the European Parliament and the National Parliaments', *Government and Opposition*, (1994) Vol 29, pp. 3–14.

[8] Cf. T. W. Pogge, 'How to create Supra-national Institutions Democratically. Some Reflections on the European Union's "Democratic Deficit"' in A. Føllesdal and P. Koslowski (eds), *Democracy and the European Union* (Berlin: Springer-Verlag, 1997), in particular pp. 160–62; and Rubio Llorente, F. 'Constitutionalism in the "Integrated" States of Europe', *Harvard Jean Monnet Chair Working Papers Series*, n. 5, 1998, in particular para. 6.1.

[9] Even Liberal Intergovernmentalists acknowledge 'Europe stands... before a series of ongoing constitutional debates,' and that 'the focus in the future... will be on the construction of a legitimate constitutional order for policy-making responsive to the desires of national governments and their citizens'. Cf. A. Moravcsik, and K. Nicolaïdis, 'Keynote Article: Federal Ideas and Constitutional Realities in the Treaty of Amsterdam', *Journal of Common Market Studies*, (1998) Vol.36, Annual Review, pp. 13–38, at p. 34.

one's thinking on the broader issues raised by the second and third. For the type and degree of democracy suitable for everyday political decisions rests to a great extent on the ways sovereignty is parcelled out and the degree to which it is regarded as legitimate for a given body to make them.[10] These dimensions define the scope, content and sphere of democracy—who makes decisions about whom, why, when and where.

This chapter elucidates the advantages of a neo-republican approach to the three deficits over more traditional liberal interpretations of democracy. Two clarifications are necessary. First, these two traditions are of course historically entwined and elements of both can be found in the political systems of most western democracies.[11] However, coexistence should not be taken for complementarity or overlap. As we shall argue below, republican justifications and conceptions of liberty, rights and the rule of law differ from the liberal's in important respects—most especially in relation to the nature and role of democracy.[12] Second, these models reflect contrasting views of the democratic ideal and hence of the norms that should inform democratic institutions.[13] Whereas liberal democratic norms provide a rationale for both majoritarian and consensual political systems, and federal and intergovernmental conceptions of the EU, we claim the emergent forms of multi-level governance call for rather different regulative norms deriving from a democratic liberal republicanism.[14]

Section 1 argues that the complexity and pluralism of modern societies has undermined the constitutional consensus, hierarchical organization of power, and

---

[10] Our main interest is the 'normative' as opposed to the 'popular' or 'social' sense of legitimacy. For these distinctions see G. De Búrca, 'The Quest for Legitimacy in the European Union', *The Modern Law Review*, (1996) Vol. 59, pp. 349–76; A. Weale 'Single Market, European Integration and Political Legitimacy'. Paper presented at the 'Evolution of Rules for a Single European Market', ESRC Conference, University of Exeter, 8–11 September, 199; 'Democratic Legitimacy and the Constitution of Europe'. In Bellamy et al. (eds.), *Democracy and Constitutional Culture*, pp. 81–94; and D. Beetham, D. and C. Lord, *Legitimacy and the EU* (London and New York: Longman ,1998).

[11] Cf. J. Isaac, 'Republicanism vs. Liberalism: A Reconsideration', *History of Political Thought*, (1988) Vol. 9, pp. 349–77; and S. Holmes, *Passions and Constraint: On the Theory of Liberal Democracy* (Chicago and London: University of Chicago Press, 1995), p. 5.

[12] See, for example, the work of Cass Sunstein, *The Partial Constitution* (Cambridge Mass: Harvard University Press, 1993) and Bruce Ackerman, *We the People: Foundations* (Cambridge, Mass: Harvard University Press, 1993) on how a republican perspective alters traditional liberal interpretations of the United States Constitution. The republican theory advocated here is more neo-Roman than 'civic humanist' (for this distinction see Skinner, *Liberty before Liberalism* and Pettit, *Republicanism*). The neo-Roman version looks to Machiavelli and has a realist edge that is more welcoming to pluralism than the rather soggy communitarianism of the neo-Aristotelian civic humanist tradition. Cf. M. Sandel, *Democracy's Discontent: America in Search of a Public Philosophy*, (Cambridge Mass., Harvard University Press, 1996); and Philip Pettit's review, 'Reworking Sandel's Republicanism', *Journal of Philosophy*, (1998) Vol. 95, pp. 73–96. While the Aristotelian view involves a politics of virtue, the neo-Roman tradition focusses on the institutional side of republicanism.

[13] Whereas A. Lijphart's famous classification, for example, looks at different ways the democratic ideal might be realised in different circumstances: see *Democracy in Plural Societies. A Comparative Exploration* (New Haven and London: Yale University Press, 1977), p. 4; and his *Democracies. Patterns of Majoritarian and Consensus Government in Twenty-One Countries* (New Haven and London: Yale University Press, 1984), pp. 21–3. Our own argument adds a further dimension and suggests that different institutional arrangements may require different normative foundations linked to different conceptions of democracy, see R. Bellamy and D. Castiglione, 'The Uses of Democracy: Reflection's on the EU's Democratic Deficit' in Erik Oddvar Eriksen and John Erik Fossum (eds) *Democracy in the European Union—Integration through Deliberation?* (London: Routledge, 2000).

[14] Cf. J. Scott, J. 'Law, Legitimacy and the EC Governance: prospects for "Partnership"', *Journal of Common Market Studies*, (1998) Vol. 36, pp. 175–93, for a parallel argument.

majoritarian decision making characterizing liberal democracy. Section 2 demonstrates that the threefold deficit within the EU arises out of these generic deficiencies of the liberal democratic model in global conditions. Strengthening liberal democracy will exacerbate rather than attenuate these problems, therefore. Section 3 introduces the concept of democratic liberalism. Of republican inspiration, this model of governance identifies the constitution with a political system that disperses power within civil society and encourages dialogue between the component parts of the body politic. Section 4 illustrates its normative and practical attractions for the EU.

I Liberal Democracy

Liberal democracy rests on a distinction between the state and civil society. Liberals see constitutionalism as a normative framework that sets limits on and goals for the exercise of state power. Traditionally, its principles are grounded in a social contract designed to legitimate the state's monopoly of violence. According to this argument, free and equal citizens would only consensually submit to a polity that removed the uncertainties of the state of nature whilst preserving the most extensive set of equal natural liberties. Interference by the state or law is only justified to reduce the mutual interference attendant upon social life so as to produce a greater liberty over all. The separation of powers supposedly fosters this aim by preventing any one from being judge in his or her own cause, thereby constraining the arbitrary and partial framing and interpretation of legislation. The rule of men is replaced by the rule of universal and equally applicable general laws.[15]

Two features of these arrangements are worth highlighting. First, as James Tully has observed, the normative consensus assumed by the 'modern' liberal conception of constitutionalism hypothesizes a degree of uniformity amongst the constitutive people.[16] It assumes that behind different beliefs and customs lies a common human nature, a natural equality of status and shared forms of reasoning sufficient to generate agreement on constitutional essentials. What divergences remain are supposedly eroded as historical progress leads to more homogeneous and less stratified societies that conform to a similar pattern of social and political organization, and stand in contrast to the ranked societies and cultural particularisms of the past. Nation building further strengthens this process. As co-nationals, the people share a corporate identity as equal citizens of the polity.

Second, the rights-based approach goes together with a conception of freedom as non-interference and of the state as a neutral ring master, unconcerned with upholding any particular set of values.[17] This understanding of the constitution encourages in its turn a purely preference-based picture of the economy and an interest-based account of democracy. In each case, what matters is the degree outcomes correspond to the uncoerced choices and express desires of those concerned. The conditions of production and the protection of public goods enter with difficulty into this view of the economy. The first are assumed to be the result of voluntary contracts, the latter left up to the invisible hand. Likewise, politics becomes a competitive market within

---

[15] See for example the French Declaration of the Rights of Man and the Citizen of 1789, especially Articles 1, 2, 4, 6, 14 and 16, and compare with J. Rawls, *A Theory of Justice* (Oxford: Clarendon Press, 1971), p. 60.

[16] J. Tully, *Strange Multiplicity: Constitutionalism in an Age of Diversity*, (Cambridge: CUP, 1995), Ch. 3.

[17] The French Declaration of the Rights of Man and the Citizen of 1789 and Rawls *A Theory of Justice* once again provide exemplary instances of this mode of thinking.

which rival interest groups bargain with each other, and involves no attempt to evaluate the interests concerned. Its purpose is purely instrumental: to protect against incompetent or tyrannous rulers by allowing their removal, and to aggregate preferences either through majoritarian voting or corporatist-style consensual politics, and encourage politicians to pursue policies that conform to such aggregate preferences.[18]

Liberals accept that economy and democracy need regulating when they threaten the constitutional structure. However, identifying when such threats occur and who possesses the authority to remedy them proves problematic. Because the economy forms part of the private sphere, there are difficulties about whether the requisite interference is either legitimate or perpetrates an even greater intrusion in people's lives than those it prevents. Such decisions cannot necessarily be left up to democratic governments, since interest groups may use the state's coercive power to further their personal goals. This dilemma raises a further source of tension between the hypothetical consent underlying the constitution and the express will of the people. Liberals try to avoid this crux by treating the constitution as a 'higher' law that provides the preconditions for the 'normal' legislation arising out of democratic politics. They see judicial review by a court buttressed by a bill of rights as the best bulwark against the democratic subversion of the constitution.[19]

Cosmopolitans extend liberal accounts of the progress of society in a post-national direction. They contend that globalisation produces overlapping communities of common fate that require and render possible global regulatory bodies, such as the EU, underpinned by uniform, equal norms.[20] However, the very forces supposed to underlie this extension of liberalism have in reality given rise to new kinds of post-modern diversity that render a liberal consensus hard to sustain. For the same processes that drive globalisation have augmented functional differentiation in the economy and society and fostered multiculturalism. The consequent pluralism of interests and values, and the growing complexity of the social and economic systems, create difficulties for the liberal model of constitutional democracy. They render majoritarian decision making more problematic, increase the difficulty of regulating

---

[18] We consider majoritarian and consensual forms of democracy to reflect the same liberal ideal, although, as we note below, certain institutional arrangements of consensual democracy may also be congruent with the neo-republican approach.

[19] Dworkin, R. 'Constitutionalism and Democracy', *European Journal of Philosophy*, (1995) Vol. 3, pp. 2–11, at p. 2.

[20] For a defence of this cosmopolitan approach, see D. Held, *Democracy and the Global Order: From the Modern State to Cosmopolitan Governance*, (Cambridge: Polity, 1995), and from a more strictly normative perspective, T. W. Pogge, 'Cosmopolitanism and Sovereignty', in C. Brow (ed.) *Political restructuring in Europe. Ethical perspectives* (London and New York: Routledge, 1994), pp. 89–122; C. R. Beitz, 'Cosmopolitan Liberalism and the States System', in Brown (ed.), *Political restructuring*, pp. 123–36; and L. Ferrajoli, L. (1996) 'Beyond Sovereignty and Citizenship: a Global Constitutionalism'. In Bellamy, R. (ed.) *Constitutionalism, Democracy and Sovereignty: American and European Perspectives* (Aldershot: Avebury, 1996), pp. 151–60. See also several of the contributions to D. Archibugi, D. Held and M. Köhler (eds.) *Re-imagining Political Community. Studies in Cosmopolitan Democracy* (Cambridge: Polity, 1998). In our own contribution to that volume and in other related essays, we have explored the pros and contras of the cosmopolitan view: cf. also 'The Normative Challenge of a European Polity: Cosmopolitan and Communitarian Models Compared, Criticised and Combined', in Føllesdal and Koslowski (eds), *Democracy and the European Union*, pp. 254–84; 'Building the Union: The Nature of Sovereignty in the Political Architecture of Europe', *Law and Philosophy*, (1997) Vol. 16, pp. 421–45. For a sceptical discussion of the effects of globalization see P. Hirst and G. Thompson *Globalisation in Question: The International Economy and the Possibilities of Governance* (Cambridge: Polity, 1996).

the unaccountable power located in civil society, and subvert the rights consensus upon which liberalism rests.

Within this new global context, liberal democracy promises more than it can deliver.[21] As a political regime it succumbs to a democratic, federal and constitutional deficit. Growing complexity and functional differentiation hinder democratic control by rendering problems more technical and less amenable to general regulations. The range and scale of decisions handled by unaccountable specialized bureaucracies, and involving considerable technocratic discretion, expands. The autonomy of many sectors of economy and society is increased. Globalisation may heighten interconnectedness but it has a highly variable impact on different classes, countries and social and economic sectors. As financial markets illustrate, this feature can weaken the ability of political institutions to impose collective decisions whilst improving the capacity for élite groups to evade and defect from them by shifting their capital around.

Having more supranational or global decision making bodies will not help. They will be too distant to regulate in a suitably differentiated manner, and are likely to lack the capacity to implement any but the most general of norms. Nor is it clear that they will be able to count on much democratic legitimacy to act in any case. Voters already feel alienated by a political system that they can influence in only the most indirect and marginal ways. It is far from clear that they will identify to any significant degree with such remote institutions or that appropriately transnational political organizations will be capable of developing—witness the low turnouts and notable absence of European political parties in elections to the European Parliament.

The difficulty of making and enforcing collective decisions is further complicated by the spread of multiculturalism. Not only are geographically separated cultures brought into greater contact with each other, but improved social mobility renders states more pluriethnic as well. Different beliefs and identities prove less amenable than divergent economic interests to the democratic horse-trading liberals standardly employ to build stable and fair majorities. As a result, the likelihood of conflict or the oppression of minorities rises. This possibility can fuel demands for self-government and the creation of multiple demoi as opposed to an enlargement of the demos.

The net effect of these processes is to suggest a fragmentation rather than an extension of the democratic public sphere, that undercuts the hierarchical organization of sovereign power. The social complexity of highly differentiated advanced industrial societies results in a proliferation of autonomous centres of power. These centres are capable of making decisions according to a variety of functionally specific criteria within their respective domains, with unpredictable knock-on effects for other parts of the social and economic system. Citizens find themselves locked into a variety of these spheres, and get pulled in opposite directions by the inner logic of each. Reconciling such clashes proves highly problematic. The various areas of social life operate with increasingly distinct and largely self-validating criteria. They become ever more taken up with their own concerns and tend to interpret the world from their own perspective, generating incommensurable and incompatible claims.[22]

Similar difficulties bedevil the constitutional entrenchment and judicial protection of the basic liberties.[23] Liberals claim the constitution can provide a neutral

---

[21] What follows draws on D. Zolo *Democracy and Complexity* (Cambridge: Polity 1992).

[22] Cf. N. Luhmann, *The Differentiation of Society* (New York: Columbia University Press 1981).

[23] Cf. R. Bellamy, *Liberalism and Pluralism: Towards a Politics of Compromise*, (London: Routledge 1999), Chs. 2 and 7.

framework for politics that rests on a separation of the right from the good. But this distinction proves practically elusive. How and when rights to privacy and to freedom of speech clash, for example, involve invoking contentious notions of the presence and absence of constraints which may be normatively and empirically evaluated from a range of reasonably different perspectives, giving divergent answers in each case. Moreover, the legitimacy and implementation gap is likely to be even greater than with the political system. Use of precedent means that legal judgement has an inbuilt tendency to self-referentiality. Legitimation comes either indirectly, via the legislature, or through a widely held normative consensus. If the influence of the former is weak, and the latter has ceased to exist, then law is forced to operate in a vacuum and be largely self-validating and practically impotent.

The deficiencies of the liberal democratic model are linked. Poor democratic accountability is fuelled by the inadequacy of a territorial and hierarchical distribution of power, and the inappropriateness of applying general, uniform constitutional norms to complex circumstances. As we shall see, the deficits of the EU are to a large extent symptomatic of this general liberal democratic malaise, and so unlikely to be cured by further doses of liberal democracy.

II   The Liberal Democratic Deficit of the EU

Analysis of the EU from a liberal democratic perspective has been especially prevalent amongst legal scholars.[24] They focus on the establishment of a common market through a process of 'negative' integration: the removal of trade barriers and restrictive practices, and the institution of the four freedoms guaranteeing the free movement of capital, goods, services and persons. As lawyers noted early on,[25] the jurisprudence of the European Court of Justice quietly, and with a remarkable degree of tacit political support, effected the constitutionalisation of the emerging body of European economic law. Through a series of landmark decisions the Court asserted European law operated with direct effect on individuals and was an independent source of obligations and rights,[26] had supremacy over the national legal systems of

---

[24] Recently, Kenneth Armstrong and Jo Shaw have remarked on the tendency to simplify the integrative role of law by considering the 'legal order as a constitutional order' and by 'overstating ... the coherence of purpose achieved by the Court of Justice', 'Legal Integration: Theorizing the Legal Dimension of European Integration', *Journal of Common Market Studies*, (1998) Vol. 36, pp. 155–74, at p. 148. We use this now familiar story not to suggest that it is true (or that it fully reflects the complexities of the legal order as an 'autonomous institution'), but as a significant example of the liberal democratic interpretation of the EU. The reservations raised by Armstrong and Shaw to such an interpretation can only add to the doubts we have on the ability of the liberal democratic model to address the three deficits. Likewise, we do not wish to underplay the tensions between federal and intergovernmental visions of integration, nor the centripetal contribution made by the latter to this process (J. H. H. Weiler, 'The Transformation of Europe', *The Yale Law Journal*, (1991) Vol. 100, pp. 2403–83). The ECJ's position is merely the most fully developed example of the liberal democratic vision of Europe. The resilience of such a view is illustrated by Judge Mancini's recent plea for European statehood; while its 'strategic' (more than simply descriptive) import is evident from Weiler's reply: 'The most interesting issue in my eyes is not the *what* of this case for statehood, but the *who* and the *how*' (both in F. Mancini and J. H. H. Weiler, 'Europe – The Case for Statehood ... and the Case Against. An Exchange', Harvard Jean Monnet Chair Working Papers Series, n. 6.1998).

[25] E. Stein, 'Lawyers, Judges and the Making of a Transnational Constitution', *American Journal of International Law*, (1981) Vol. 75, pp. 33–50.

[26] Case 26/62 *Van Gend en Loos v. Nederlandse Administratie der Belastingen* [1963] ECR 1.

member states within its domain.[27] It also described the founding Treaties as the European Community's 'constitutional charter' rather than a mere international agreement,[28] and maintained the Court's position as the competent authority to decide when European law applied and how.[29]

The Court's justification of its role in establishing and upholding the European constitution rests on impeccable liberal democratic grounds. It alleges a normative consensus exists to ensure maximal equal liberty and facilitate social interaction on terms that are the same for all. Thus, 'the preservation of the Community character of the law' requires 'ensuring that in all circumstances the law is the same in all states of the Community',[30] and has 'identical effects over the whole territory of the Community'.[31] Likewise, the Court assumes a federal organization of power, with certain aspects of state sovereignty definitively ceded to the Community.[32] Hence, EU measures derive their validity solely from European law and cannot be challenged on the basis of a conflict with national laws—even those of a constitutional status— 'without the legal basis of the Community itself being called into question'.[33] National courts must apply the rulings of the ECJ, ensure due process for the exercise of the four freedoms and uphold a general principle of non-discrimination on the basis of nationality, whilst national legislatures may become liable for failures to adequately implement EU laws.[34] Finally, the Court has regarded the European Parliament as 'an essential factor in the institutional balance intended by the treaty', reflecting 'at Community level the fundamental democratic principle that the peoples should take part in the exercise of power through the intermediary of a representative assembly.'[35]

As already suggested, this legal picture of the EU partly conflicts with the state-centric perspective commonly adopted by political scientists.[36] Moreover, tensions both between member states and between them and various European institutions have heightened recently. These strains reflect the way the liberal democratic version of constitutionalism espoused by the Court exacerbates the threefold democratic deficit described above. At the constitutional level, stress has manifested itself most clearly in conflicts over the interpretation of rights. We noted earlier how pluralism enhances incommensurable and incompatible understandings of rights and their appropriate balance. The potential clashes that result are apparent in conflicting opinions over rights protection offered by the ECJ and national constitutional courts. The ECJ has read

---

[27] Case 6/64 *Costa v. ENEL* [1964] ECR 585.

[28] *Van Gend en Loos* and Case 294/83 *Parti Ecologiste 'Les Verts' v. European Parliament* [1986] ECR 1339.

[29] The above mentioned cases, and successive interpretations of Art. 177 EC.

[30] Case 166/73 *Rheinmühlen-Düsseldorf v. Einfuhr- und Vorratstelle für Getreide und Futtermittel* [1974] ECR 33.

[31] Case 48/71 *Commission v. Italy (Art Treasures II)* [1972] ECR 527.

[32] *Commission v. Italy (Art Treasures II)*.

[33] Case 11/70 *Internationale Handelsgesellschaft* ([1970]) ECR 1125 p. 1134.

[34] Cases 6, 9/90 *Francovich v. Italian State (Francovich I)* [1991] ECR I-5357.

[35] Case 138/79 *Roquette Frères v. Council* [1980] ECR 3333.

[36] For classic statements, see S. Hoffman, 'Reflections on the Nation-State in Western Europe Today' *Journal of Common Market Studies*, (1982) Vol. 21, pp. 21–38; and A. Moravcsik, 'Preferences and Power in the European Community: A Liberal Intergovernmentalist Approach', *Journal of Common Market Studies*, (1993) Vol.31, pp. 473–524; 'Liberal Intergovernmentalism and Integration: A Rejoinder', *Journal of Common Market Studies*, (1995) Vol.33, pp. 611–28. For more recent discussions of the interplay between legal and political integration processes, cf. Weiler, 'The Transformation of Europe' and D. Wincott 'Political Theory, Law and European Union', in J. Shaw and G. More (eds), *New Legal Dynamics of European Union* (Oxford: Oxford University Press, 1995).

fundamental rights into European law to stem challenges to its competence and the supremacy of EC legislation by the German Federal and Italian constitutional courts. They argued that since their national constitutions contain bills of rights whereas the European constitution does not, they had an obligation to scrutinize EC law for conformity to German and Italian fundamental rights and to invalidate or dispense with measures that failed to meet the requisite standard.[37] The ECJ felt constrained to reassure national courts that the general principles of EC law implied rights protection. The Court contended it drew inspiration from common institutional traditions and international treaties acknowledged by the member states—most particularly the European Convention on Human Rights. Regardless of origin, however, these rights become EU rights and as such subject to interpretation 'within the framework of the structure and objectives of the community'.[38] Although Germany initially accepted the ECJ's reassurance, the Italian court has not. Outright confrontation has so far been avoided, but many doubt it can be evaded in the long run.[39]

The ECJ has espoused a narrowly economic liberal view of rights analogous to that of the US Supreme Court during the Lochner era. It has played a significant part in the privatizing of hitherto nationalized enterprises, and the weakening of welfare systems within the member states. This libertarian account of rights has produced tensions in a number of areas. The ECJ has been relatively intolerant of minority language rights, regarding them not just as restrictions on the four freedoms that can increase transaction costs by, for example, requiring multilingual labelling, but also of freedom of expression, although they could be equally interpreted as defending this latter.[40] In *Grogan* the dilemma posed by the Irish constitution's protection of the right to life of the unborn child was largely side-stepped, though the Court's definition of abortion as a 'service' clearly poses problems for the Irish state's attempts to deny its citizens' access to it.[41] These debates reveal how legitimacy cannot be based on an alleged overlapping consensus on shared liberal democratic principles and the rule of law. In spite of considerable agreement on these matters, and the amended Article F TEU notwithstanding, substantial divergences remain. Nor does an appeal to maximizing liberty help.[42] As we saw, the Court has consistently appealed to a narrowly negative and economic view of freedom in its judgements in these cases, yet this notion is often what is in dispute. The rights of national constitutions are often intended to prevent the removal of valued opportunities by the market. The boot-strapping operation of the ECJ in creating a European Constitution is a remarkable example of the self-validating nature of law. Yet this validity comes called into question when confronted by the fact of normative disagreement.[43] Significantly, the

---

[37] e.g. German Federal Constitutional Court, *Internationale Handelsgesellschaft* [1974] 2 CMLR 549.

[38] *Internationale Handelsgesellschaft* , Case 4/73 *Nold v. Commission* [1974] ECR 503; Case 374/87 *Orkem v. Commission* ECR [1989] ECR 3283.

[39] Cf. B. De Witte, 'Droit communitarie et valeurs constitutionelles nationales', *Droits*, (1991) Vol. 14, pp. 87–96; and J. Shaw, *Law of the European Union*, (London: Macmillan, 2nd ed. 1996), pp. 188–95.

[40] See Case C-260/89 *ERT v. Dimotiki Etairia Piliroforissis* [1991] ECR I-2925 for this judgement

[41] Case C-159/90 *SPUC (Ireland) Ltd v. Grogan*, [1991] ECR I-4685.

[42] On the limits of such attempts to extend rights from their original strict economic dimension to a broader constitutional meaning, see K. A. Armstrong 'Legal Integration: Theorizing the Legal Dimension of European Integration', *Journal of Common Market Studies*, (1998) Vol. 36, pp. 155–74, at pp. 167–8.

[43] Indeed, as P. Eleftheriadis notes, the Court's and its academic supporters' tendency to address the constitutional issue from a 'doctrinal' perspective simply begs the question of the 'normative justification of the new legal order', 'Begging the Constitutional Question', *Journal of Common Market Studies*, (1998) Vol. 36, pp. 255–72, at p. 269.

Court has suggested that accession by the Community to the European Convention would compromise the autonomy of EC law—exactly the problem faced by national legal orders.[44]

The Court's assertion of the supremacy of EC law suggests a federal structure based on the hierarchical ordering of sovereign power, in which the particular interpretation and implementation of general formulations can be devolved down to subordinate bodies. The same is true of the much vaunted doctrine of subsidiarity, albeit from the other end of the telescope. Recent developments within the EU suggest a very messy picture, however, with no clear division of powers between federal and lower levels. The principle of subsidiarity in the Amsterdam Protocol (and Articles A TEU, 3b EC) is masterfully vague, allowing both wide and narrow interpretations that can make almost anything or nothing the province of the Community. No criteria are offered for determining either what proximity to citizens entails, or when a matter can or cannot 'be sufficiently achieved by the Member States' on their own. Although Maastricht and Amsterdam extend qualified-majority voting by the Council of Ministers into new areas and raise the prospect of a dramatic expansion of common policies in the monetary, defence and justice spheres, these developments are hedged around with arrangements 'for derogations where warranted by problems specific to a member state' (Arts. K 15–17, 12 [formerly, K7 TEU] and 5A [formerly, K2 TEU] of the Treaty of Amsterdam, and Art. 8b EC). Thus many of the new policies allow for multiple speeds, variable geometry, and a Europe *à la carte*. The first type of variation, that accepts different rates and methods of implementation of policies such as VAT harmonization poses no great difficulty to the ideal of a homogeneous, federal Europe. The second and third are far more problematic. The former suggests a distinction between core issues that all should adhere to and peripheral ones that may be optional, the Schengen system being a plausible example of such an optional policy. The latter suggests a far more smorgasbord approach, with Britain's opt-out from stage three of EMU and the Amsterdam Protocol (Art. 73Q) on 'freedom, justice and security' being notorious instances. Perhaps most important of all, Maastricht introduced the notion of the three pillars of the European Union. The first comprises an enlarged European Community, the second and third deal with foreign and security policy and justice and home affairs respectively. The important feature of this arrangement from our perspective is that in the last two areas the mode of operation is essentially inter-governmental and the ECJ has no in-built jurisdiction. Pressure to

---

[44] Opinion 2/94 Accesion by the Community to the ECHR (28.3.1996). In this Opinion the Court put forward two separate reasons for rejecting accession. The first suggested that Article 235 EC was not an adequate ground, since it was 'part of an institutional system based on the principle of conferred powers' (i.e., from the member states). Jo Shaw (*Law of the European Union*, p. 197) argues that the court was backtracking from the high ground taken in Opinion 1/91 Re the Draft Agreement on a European Economic Area [1991] ECR I-6079, where it seemed instead to assert unequivocally the autonomy of EC law. This may be true, but such political caution on the Court's part is tempered by the second reason adduced against accession. This reinforces Opinion 1/91 and considers the Community system as an established one, whose 'entry into a distinct international institutional system' would 'entail a substantial change'. Indeed, national courts could appeal to the same argument with equal force. On the complex interaction between European and national legal orders, within a world-wide network of legal communications, see I. Maher 'Community Law in the National Legal Order: A System Analysis', *Journal of Common Market Studies*, (1998) Vol.36, pp. 237–54, who argues not only for a pluralistic analysis of their relationship, but also notes that when national systems assimilate European laws and directives, they must evaluate the latter's impact on 'the links between existing law and the social process being regulated' (pp. 246–7), if their own fundamental equilibrium as legal systems is not to be upset.

adopt uniform policies is consequently much less. As such, this system invites variation, derogations and multi-tracks.[45]

Such variability is made even more likely by the way the levels and complexity of decision making have increased, with a greater range of non-state actors being involved in the process. Thus there are not only new powers for the European Parliament (Art. 137 EC), including a highly complicated co-decision procedure (Art. 189b EC),[46] but also a new advisory Committee of the Regions involving unspecified sub-national units (Art. 198a EC) and the possibility of semi-corporatist arrangements involving the Commission in dialogue with labour and management when drafting social policy (Annex I Protocol 14 Arts. 3 and 4 EC). Such groups play an increasingly important role within the comitology process in any case. Indeed, there are now over 3000 interest groups and a 100 regional offices based in Brussels. As analysts of the EU who take a multi-level governance approach have stressed, these developments are eroding state sovereignty without creating a European super state with its own internal hierarchy.[47] Rather, function and territory have begun to pull apart, with a variety of authorities operating at different levels—from sub to supranational—in each domain. These are not hierarchically ordered with exclusive control over specific areas of policy. They overlap and are involved in continuous negotiation with each other, often in somewhat informal fora.[48]

This increasingly complex configuration of sovereign power has profound implications for the EU's democratic deficit in the strict sense of the term. The European Parliament and Court have a shared federal vocation, and tend to buttress each others claims. Thus the ECJ has seen enhanced legislative powers for the Parliament as augmenting its own democratic legitimacy and has staunchly defended its prerogatives.[49] Likewise, the Parliament has tried to take a lead in by-passing the intergovernmental process and suggesting the enactment of a European Constitution jointly with the national parliaments.[50] These attempts have not gone unchallenged, however. The amended TEC did strengthen the European Parliament in certain respects. In addition to increased powers, most notably the co-decision procedure (Art. 189b EC), member state nationals were bestowed the right to vote and stand in European elections on the basis of residence alone as part of the new status of citizen of the Union (Art. 8 b EC), and 'political parties at European level' were solemnly declared to be 'important as a factor for integration within the Union', that 'contribute to forming a European awareness and to expressing the political will of the citizens of the Union' (Art. 138a EC). Yet there has been little popular enthusiasm for these developments and some active antagonism. Far from being steps towards a pan-

---

[45] Amsterdam modified the system, removing immigration and asylum policy from the renamed third pillar to the first, suggesting the Union structure remains fluid. Britain, Ireland and Denmark in any case obtained opt outs (Article 73Q).

[46] Extended at Amsterdam, but often to areas where unanimity rather than QMV operates in the Council.

[47] Cf. Schmitter's contribution in Marks et al., *Governance in the European Union*.

[48] For a discussion of the interplay between formal and informal aspects of the decision making process, with particular reference to the role of sub national authorities, cf. E. Bomberg, and J. Peterson, 'European Union Decision Making: the Role of Sub-national Authorities', *Political Studies*, (1998) Vol. XLVI, pp. 219–235, who, on a more general note conclude that 'it is striking how *little* the EU acts to iron out national differences' (p.235).

[49] Case C-70/88 *Parliament v. Council* (Chernobyl) [1990} ECR I-2041, Art. 173 EC)

[50] OJ 1994 C61/155.

European political system,[51] uptake of European political rights remains significantly lower than in national elections. When asked in a recent poll how they describe themselves: by nationality only, nationality and European, European and nationality, or European, respondents divided 45%, 40%, 6% and 5% respectively (Eurobarometer Report No. 48, March 1998). Thus there is little evidence of a European demos or a shared political culture.

The difficulties referenda ratifying Maastricht experienced in France and Denmark have been interpreted by some as indicating a popular reaction against further European integration, although the influence of purely domestic political factors on voters makes this hard to assess. More unequivocal was the challenge thrown up by the German Federal constitutional court in its judgement in the *Brunner* case. This decision not only disputed the ECJ's competence-competence in adjudicating on the applicability of European law, it also argued that popular sovereignty within Europe was exercised primarily through national parliaments rather than the European Parliament because there was no European people.[52] The 'no demos' thesis has haunted discussion of the EU's democratic deficit ever since. A number of commentators have criticized a perceived volkish reasoning behind the German Court's argument.[53] Whilst this interpretation is open to dispute, it is certainly true that national elections give member state citizens only limited control over European developments. The consociational decision making of the Council of Ministers and IGCs manifest all the democratic shortcomings critics have levelled at that system in domestic arenas: namely, elitism, conservatism and the stifling of dissent and new voices. However, most commentators accept one cannot take a unified European demos for granted, and that European political institutions lack legitimacy as a result.[54] There is now growing agreement on the need to talk of dual or even multiple citizenship, reflecting our various political allegiances and membership of a variety of demoi—territorial, cultural and functional—with little congruence between them.[55]

The above suggests that the liberal democratic model of the EU has succumbed to all three aspects of the democratic deficit.[56] Instead of a constitutional consensus, we have a number of competing and overlapping constitutional traditions. Instead of a

---

[51] Simon Hix, for instance, suggests that the development of a transational party system at the European level is hindered by the present institutional structure of the Union, and by the poor understanding that political and other institutional actors have of the role that modern parties can play in the legitimation of the EU. His suggestions, though rather minimalist, can perhaps be better accommodated by the kind of neo-republican approach outlined below. Cf. S. Hix, 'Parties at the European Level and the Legitimacy of EU Socio-Economic Policy', *Journal of Common Market Studies*, (1995) Vol. 33, pp. 527–54.

[52] *Brunner* [1994] 1 CMLR 57 at p. 87.

[53] See the debate between Grimm and Weiler: D. Grimm, 'Does Europe need a Constitution?'. *European Law Journal*, (1995) Vol. 1, pp. 282–302; and J. H. H. Weiler, 'Does Europe Need a Constitution? Reflections on Demos, Telos, and the German Maastricht Decision'. *European Law Journal*, Vol. 1, pp. 219–58.

[54] Cf. D. N. Chryssochoou, 'Europe's Could-be Demos: Recasting the Debate'. *West European Politics*, (1996) Vol. 19, pp. 787–801.

[55] J. H. H. Weiler, 'European Neo-Constitutionalism: In Search of Foundations for the European Constitutional Order', in R. Bellamy and D. Castiglione (eds), *Constitutionalism in Transformation* (Oxford: Blackwell, 1996), pp. 105–21.

[56] Symptomatic aspects of the inability of the present model of politics to go beyond a superficial treatment of the various features of the 'democratic deficit' have been illustrated by Hix, 'Parties at the European Level', in relation to the public sphere; P. Norris, 'Representation and the Democratic Deficit', *European Journal of Political Research*, (1997) Vol. 32, pp. 273–82, in relation to representation; B. Laffan, 'The Politics of Identity and Political Order in Europe', *Journal of Common Market Studies*, (1996) Vol. 34,

federal organization of sovereignty, we have an emerging multi-level mode of governance involving a mix and dispersal of sovereign powers over a number of areas. Instead of a unified democratic system based on a uniform citizenship of the union, we have multiple demoi operating at different levels and kinds of political aggregation. So far, commentators have been inclined to regard this picture as a mess, castigating the post-Maastricht settlement for producing 'a Europe of bits and pieces',[57] that Amsterdam confirmed instead of remedying. And from a liberal democratic perspective it is messy. By contrast, a democratic liberalism finds this picture more congenial.

III Democratic Liberalism

Democratic liberalism harks back to a pre-liberal conception of constitutionalism that identified the constitution with the social composition and form of government of the polity.[58] Much as we associate a person's physical health with his or her bodily constitution and regard a fit individual as someone with a balanced diet and regimen, so a healthy body politic was attributed to a political system capable of bringing its various constituent social groups into equilibrium with each other. The aim was to disperse power so as to encourage a process of controlled political conflict and deliberation that ensured the various social classes both checked and ultimately co-operated with each other, moving them thereby to construct and pursue the public good rather than narrow sectional interests.

As Quentin Skinner and Philip Pettit have shown, the heart of the republican approach lies in a different conception of freedom to the liberal's.[59] Liberty is seen as a civic achievement rather than a natural attribute. It results from preventing arbitrary domination rather than an absence of interference *tout court*. Domination denotes a capacity to intentionally control and diminish an agent's realm of choice, either overtly through various explicit forms of restraint or obstruction, or covertly by more subtle forms of manipulation and influence. Arbitrariness rests in the power to exert domination at whim, and without reference to the interests or ideas of those over whom it is exercised. Pettit notes that an absence of interference can be consistent with the presence of domination. Those with such power may simply choose not to wield it. Social relations will be adversely affected nonetheless. Likewise, seeking to reduce interference may in given contexts be compatible with leaving certain agents or agencies with considerable power over others. For example, attempts to reduce the arbitrary hold men have traditionally exerted over women in marriage have been challenged on the grounds that they are too intrusive and themselves involve a greater degree of interference. Similar arguments have been used against laws to protect

---

pp. 81–102, in relation to the affective dimension of integration; J. Lodge, 'Transparency and Democratic Legitimacy', *Jouurnal of Common Market Studies*, (1994) Vol. 32, pp. 343–68, in relation to problems of transparency; and A. Geddes, 'Immigrant and Ethnic Mionorities and the EU's "Democratic Deficit"', *Journal of Common Market Studies*, (1995) Vol. 33, pp. 197–217, in relation to immigration and third-country nationals. Not all these authors may agree with the thrust of our critique, but their analyses aptly illustrate our reservations.

[57] Cf. D. Curtin, 'The Constitutional Structure of the Union: A Europe of Bits and Pieces'. *Common Market Law Review*, (1993) Vol. 30, pp. 17–69.

[58] Cf. R. Bellamy, 'The Political Form of the Constitution: the Separation of Powers, Rights and Representative Democracy', in Bellamy and Castiglione (eds) *Constitutionalism in Transformation*.

[59] Cf. footnote No. 5, above.

employees from unscrupulous employers. Even social liberals, such as L. T. Hobhouse,[60] accept that the onus of proof rests on the proponents of state intervention to show that less interference is thereby created overall. Republicans by contrast, see debate about the legitimacy of interference *per se* as misconceived. They concentrate on providing a non-dominating environment where citizens can lead secure lives, plan ahead, and live on a basis of mutual respect—conditions which may require intervention.[61]

This view of liberty shapes the republicans' distinctive linkage of the rule of law with the distribution of power and democracy. Instead of the constitution being a precondition for politics, political debate becomes the medium through which a polity constitutes itself. This occurs not just in exceptional, founding constitutional moments, but continuously as part of an evolving process of mutual recognition. Domination and arbitrary power involve more than an infringement of the formal rule of law espoused by liberals. It is entirely possible to promote general rules based on whim or self-interest and that entail a gross curtailment of people's freedom of action. The generality and universality requirements can also seem themselves arbitrary if employed to disqualify special rules that refer to properties that apply to only some groups—as when maternity leave for women or affirmative action policies are accused of being discriminatory, or when such considerations are used to block any form of regulation which might seek to focus on particular contexts or outcomes.[62] Such formal criteria appear particularly inadequate at tackling structural forms of domination, where discrimination and selective blindness have been built into the institutions, norms, social and economic relations, and procedures within which the rules are framed.

Contemporary liberal jurists try and get around these difficulties by adopting a more substantive view of the rule of law, identifying it with the upholding of rights by an independent judiciary. As we noted, this approach proves problematic. A political constitutionalism takes a different tack. Justice becomes identified with the process of politics. Political mechanisms not only ensure all are subject to the laws and that no one can be judge in their own case—the traditional tasks of the separation of powers—but also that the laws connect with the understandings and activities of those to whom they are to apply—the side benefit of dispersing power so that more people have a say in its enactment. *Audi alteram partem* forms the watchword of legal fairness, not the formal or substantive properties liberals associate with the law.[63]

'Hearing the other side' within a pluralist polity implies respecting that people can be reasonably led to incommensurable and incompatible understandings of values and interests, and seeing the need to engage with them in terms they can accept. This criterion places constraints on both the procedures and the outcomes of the political process.[64] It obliges people to drop purely self-referential or self-interested reasoning

---

[60] L. T. Hobhouse, *Liberalism* (Oxford: Oxford University Press, 1964 [1911]), p. 71.

[61] Cf. Sunstein, *The Partial Constitution*.

[62] Cf. F. A. Hayek, *The Constitution of Liberty* (London: Routledge, 1960).

[63] Cf. Pettit, *Republicanism*, p. 189; see also S. Hampshire, 'Justice is Strife'. *Proceedings and Addresses of the American Philosophical Association*, (1991) Vol. 65, pp. 19–27, in particular pp. 20–1.

[64] Cf. A. Gutmann and D. Thompson, *Democracy and Disagreement* (Cambridge, Mass: Harvard University Press, 1996), p. 57; J. Cohen, 'Procedure and Substance in Deliberative Democracy', in S. Benhabib (ed.) *Democracy and Difference: Contesting the Boundaries of the Political* (Princeton, NJ: Princeton University Press, 1996), pp. 95–119, in particular pp. 100–1; and S. Benhabib, 'Toward a Deliberative Model of Democratic Legitimacy', in (ed.) *Democracy and Difference*, pp. 67–94.

and to look for considerations others can find compelling, thereby ruling out arguments that fail to treat all as of equal moral worth. Political actors must strive for common ground through mutually acceptable modifications leading to a fair compromise.

Political compromise takes the place of a pre-political consensus, for the clashes of principle and preferences associated with pluralism preclude substantive consensual agreement.[65] How such compromises are to be achieved, and what counts as a fair hearing, depends on the issue and the character of the groups debating it. Where the clash concerns divergent preferences, then a fair compromise is likely to be achieved through splitting the difference or some form of barter. Here fairness makes the proportionate weighting of preferences appropriate. For the political equality espoused by democrats would be violated in cases where a majority vote meant that the preferences of a group that constituted two thirds of the population always held sway, and those of the remaining third never got a look in. But the character of the compromise is different in matters of principle. Here the object will be to ensure equal consideration of the content and intrinsic importance of different values for particular groups of people, so that they seek solutions that are acceptable to a variety of different points of view. Instead of bargaining, participants in this sort of dispute negotiate and argue. In the case of bargained compromises, preferences can be taken as exogenous to the system and democracy seen in largely instrumental terms. A negotiated compromise involves a more deliberative model of democracy, that leads to preferences being shaped and ranked endogenously through the democratic process itself as otherwise inaccessible information regarding the range and intensity of the moral and material claims involved comes to light. Achieving this result requires that groups reach a sufficient threshold to have a voice that people take seriously. With very small groups, that may involve more than proportionate voting power, with others somewhat less will suffice.

The emphasis placed by the neo-republican approach on compromise should not be confused with the consensus model of democracy as identified by Arend Lijphart.[66] There are two important differences that distinguish it from both consociationalism and other forms of corporatist politics. First, as noted above, it does not take preferences as exogenous to the system, but considers democratic deliberation as a way of filtering and changing preferences.[67] Second, whereas elites are central to consociational and standard corporatist politics,[68] they play a subordinate role in the deliberative model discussed here. As Jane Mansbridge argues, 'traditional corporatist models focus on external negotiation'. They assume elites act as mediators and brokers of compromises that can be translated into legislative measures. By contrast, 'more recent democratic corporatist models' stress 'internal negotiation, in which leaders also negotiate with members of their interest groups to reach agreements that

---

[65] What follows draws on R. Bellamy and M. Hollis 'Consensus, Neutrality and Compromise'. In I*dem* (eds), *Pluralism and Liberal Neutrality*, (London: Cass, 1999), pp. 54–78.

[66] Cf. A. Lijphart, *Democracies. Patterns of Majoritarian and Consensus Government in Twenty-One Countries* (New Haven and London: Yale University Press, 1984).

[67] Cf. on a similar line of argument, J. Mansbridge, 'A Deliberative Theory of Interest Representation', in M. P. Petracca (ed.), *The Politics of Interests. Interest Groups Transformed* (Boulder: Westview Press, 1992).), pp. 32–57.

[68] Cf. Lijphart *Democracies*; and *Democracy in Plural Societies. A Comparative Exploration* (New Haven and London: Yale University Press, 1977).

members can accept as binding'. [69] These models share the neo-republican desire to mobilize the 'moral resources' of deliberative democracy and make the 'quest for understanding' a central feature of the process of changing one's own and others' preferences in order to achieve fair compromises.[70]

Indeed, political system builders often overlook that different sorts of policies call for different kinds of compromise, and hence for a different quality of decision making. Yet these considerations prove more crucial than functional efficiency when deciding the level at which decisions are to be made, how groups should be represented, and the degree of autonomy particular bodies or sections of the community may claim. They are integral to a political constitutionalism, with its intimate linking of justice, the rule of law and the democratic dispersal and division of power. In the ancient ideal of mixed government, the favoured mechanism was to assign particular governmental functions to different social classes. In contemporary societies, the answer lies in multiplying the sites of decision making power and the forms of representation employed for different purposes.

Within a more complex and differentiated social context centralized and hierarchical ways of distributing power will be inadequate. Territorially based representation has to be supplemented by functional and cultural forms within particular sectors. Social and cultural interests are often territorially dispersed, or located below any specific territorial unit. Empowering certain groups may require their representation within a specific location, or across a given sector, or in the case of vertical cleavages, according to segment. Work place democracy and parent governors at schools are examples of the first; corporatist representation of unions, employer organizations and professional associations of the second; consociational representation for given ethnic, linguistic, religious and cultural groups of the third. Such mechanisms allow minority opinions to have both a degree of autonomy within their own sphere combined with a say in collective decision making. On the one hand, all groups (those asking for special consideration included) are obliged to consult the broader interests and concerns of society as a whole. On the other, these same mechanisms operate as checks and balances on the purely self-interested or partial exercise of power.

Democracy plays a central role in this system, protecting against arbitrary rule and enabling the educative engagement with others.[71] Interests are not simply advanced and aggregated, as in liberal accounts of the democratic process. They get related and subjected to the criticism of reasons, transforming politics into a forum of principle. In consequence, the need diminishes for a judicially monitored principled constitution to frame democracy. Judicial review can track whether reasoned debate occurs, but need not substitute for an absence of such deliberation. Democracy also

---

[69] Mansbridge, 'A Deliberative Theory of Interest', p. 42.

[70] Cf. C. Offe and U. K. Preuß, 'Democratic Institutions and Moral Resources', in D. Held (ed.), *Political Theory Today* (Cambridge: Polity, 1991); and Mansbridge, 'A Deliberative Theory of Interest', p. 42. Consociational democracies have traditionally been seen as non-homogenous societies in which the principle of unified sovereignty nonetheless applies. Our model, instead, aims to address the issue of a polity where sovereignty is dispersed both vertically and horizontally. For a brief discussion of this point, see Bellamy and Castiglione, 'Building the Union', pp. 441–45.

[71] Both Pettit, *Republicanism*, p. 30, and Skinner, *Liberty before Liberalism*, p. 74 footnote No. 38, stress the first benefit but regard the second as a civic humanist rather than a neo-Roman concern, which smacks dangerously of 'positive' liberty. Putting history to one side, substantively we do not believe a 'weak' positive appreciation of the virtues of participation can be totally excised from republicanism.

operates within civil society as well as the state. Power is not simply devolved down in a hierarchical manner to lesser levels of the state, as in a standard federal system. It is dispersed amongst semi-autonomous yet publicized private bodies. In this way, politics shapes rather than being simply shaped by social demands.

Republicanism has often been attacked for being impractical and undesirable. Critics contend the liberties of the ancients had to give way to those of the moderns as societies grew in scale and diversity, and the protection of individual rights came to override vain attempts to secure an elusive collective welfare. This picture proves historically and substantively flawed. Far from assuming homogeneity, the republican model was a response to social division and class conflict. As the American Federalists appreciated, territorial size and social differentiation are positive aids rather than blocks to republican government, since a plurality of voices and power centres is conducive to deliberation and a process of mutual checking. Although groups were excluded in the past—notably women and slaves—the same holds for liberal democracy, and the difficulties of updating republicanism are less than those confronting liberalism. For the focus on domination and the relation of social to political power makes the active inclusion of all groups far more essential to the republican model than the liberal, with its traditional distrust of state interference in civil society. Nor is republicanism inimical to the acknowledgement of the standard liberal set of individual rights to freedom of expression, association, bodily integrity and the like. On the contrary, it compels recognition of them since they are integral to the whole process of political deliberation. It also allows the democratic balancing of their relative weight in relation both to each other and to additional values and interests depending on the issue and the people involved.

Far from aiming at or assuming the achievement of a monolithic general will or common good, the purpose of such deliberation is to construct a compromise that specifically acknowledges diversity in the ethical reasoning of agents. Dispersing power helps both the appropriate mix of voices to be heard and the peculiar circumstances of particular contexts to be taken into account. Not only can general rules can be tailored to a wide variety of objects and concerns, and their implementation and monitoring enacted to meet the special requirements of a given situation and constituency, but also—and often more importantly—specific norms can be established to meet special circumstances and relevant differences, and collective decisions brokered amongst conflicting points of view.

This same quality facilitates the handling of complex problems. Complexity proves problematic for hierarchical forms of decision making whenever a gap exists between public standards and their specification and monitoring. It arises where the actors involved are highly miscellaneous and there is a large degree of cognitive indeterminacy as to the causal relationships between them, and contestability as to how the various factors might be evaluated. These features prevent the decomposition of complex issues into their component parts because there will be no clearly demarcated ends or interests to be served. Environmental regulations typically display these characteristics, with people disputing both the costs and benefits and the cause and effects of pollution. In such cases, devolved deliberation can lead to a problem-solving approach that seeks a suitably integrated solution to the issue that tries to accommodate the multifarious perspectives of those concerned.

Thus a democratic liberalism simultaneously addresses all three of the deficits we identified above. For the democratic making of decisions (democratic deficit) is linked to the dispersion and devolution of power to provide an appropriate mix of social forces and levels of governance (federal deficit), with both being part and parcel of a political constitution that unites law, efficacy and legitimacy (constitutional deficit). It remains to see how suited it is to the EU.

IV   The Democratic Constitution of Europe

The republican model offers a normatively appealing and empirically plausible response to all three dimensions of the EU's democratic deficit.[72] At the constitutional level, an institutional space needs to be created where those bodies delegated with the task of upholding national constitutional values may enter into dialogue with each other to resolve disputes over competences and clashes of values. Joseph Weiler has suggested that a European Constitutional Council comprising members of the national constitutional courts or their equivalents might serve this purpose.[73] Whilst welcoming this idea, we would modify it in two respects. First, Weiler fears challenges by constitutional courts to the supremacy of European law and the competence-competence of the ECJ threaten the legal integrity of the Union. He likens the potential stand-off between the two to one of Mutual Assured Destruction. We believe he goes too far. The absolute supremacy of Community law over domestic constitutional provisions has never been accepted by all national supreme courts. They have acknowledged the authority of Community law for reasons internal to the national legal order rather than, as the ECJ argues, because of its intrinsic Supremacy, and have distinguished between alterations to basic principles of the national constitution and the transfer of certain powers. As Neil MacCormick has observed, this analysis suggests a pluralistic and interactive picture of legal systems might be a more appropriate frame of analysis for the relationship of EC to national law than a monistic and hierarchical one.[74] From this perspective, the ECJ need not assert the Supremacy of any given set of laws over others, but merely seek mutual accommodations in areas of friction.

Examples of this approach already exist in some areas. In his examination of the effect of European integration on private law, Christian Jorges notes how European regulations give recognition to the interests and concerns of non-nationals within an interdependent economic order, but that decentralized fine tuning by national courts enables the accommodation of the different standards and safeguards provided by the legal systems of the member states.[75] For example, the ECJ's 1990 decision in *GB-Inno-BM* ,[76] when it ruled that Luxembourg's prohibition of leaflets advertising price

---

[72] In both *Between Facts and Norms* (Cambridge: Polity, 1996), esp. Ch 7 and Appendix II; and 'Three Normative Models of Democracy', in Benhabib (ed.), *Democracy and Difference*, pp. 21–30, J. Habermas claims there is a middle way between republicanism and liberalism, which he applies to the EU. However, he conflates republicanism with the contemporary communitarianism of Michael Sandel and Charles Taylor. These theories lack the emphasis on social conflict and liberty as non-domination that characterise the neo-republicanism of our account. See Pettit's review of Sandel (footnote No. 13, above). As a consequence of Habermas's failure to see this difference, the deliberative aspect of his thesis is highly idealised; whilst the increasingly prominent neo-Kantian features of his position, with their emphasis on rights-based constitutionalism, place him firmly, or so we maintain, in the liberal democratic camp.

[73] Weiler, 'European Neo-Constitutionalism', pp. 120–21.

[74] Cf. N. MacCormick, 'The Maastricht-Urteil: Sovereignty Now', *European Law Journal*, (1995) Vol. 1, pp. 255–62.

[75] Cf. C. Jorges, 'The Impact of European Integration on Private Law: Reductionist Perceptions, True Conflicts and a New Constitutional Perspective', *European Law Journal*, (1997) Vol. 3, pp. 387–406.

[76] Case 362/88 *GB-INNO—BM v. Conféderation du commerce luxembourgeois* [1990] ECR I-667.

reductions by a Belgian supermarket restricted the rights of consumers and traders, was a response to a situation in which Luxembourg citizens habitually cross-border shop rather than an assertion of the supremacy of European economic law. By contrast, the 1995 decision in *Alpine Investments*,[77] upholding Dutch prohibitions against firms in Holland marketing commodities futures by cold-calling even in member states that had no such prohibition, acknowledged that Dutch authorities had good reasons for their regulations without suggesting that states such as Belgian should adopt them too. Indeed, one might argue that the ECJ's desire to side step outright confrontations with national constitutional courts in cases such as *Grogan* indicates less a failure of nerve and more the acceptance of the pluralistic and compromising approach we advocate.

This observation brings us to our second divergence from Weiler. Our model does not insist on high levels of uniformity or normative consensus as a test of the rule of law. It demands the more substantive assurance that laws track the multifarious interests and values of those concerned. This aim is met by a dispersal of power designed to achieve an appropriate mix of voices instead of a formal separation of powers. It also suggests that democratic fora may be better than judicial ones for debating such issues, since they are likely to be more representative and possess greater popular legitimacy. Democratic procedures should nonetheless be such as to ensure that the debate is appropriate to the constitutional principles at stake. Thus, only considerations that affirm and relate to the standing of the parties as free and equal citizens should be admissible, and a supermajoritarian decision rule might be necessary to foster such argumentation. A European Constitutional Council need not be an exclusively judicial body, therefore. It could be more like the French *Conseil d'État*.

Similar reasoning leads us to reject a standard federal organization of sovereignty, whereby the residue of central power is devolved on a territorial basis from the top down to smaller units. As we noted above, certain functions are too dispersed, are carried out in highly divergent and changing circumstances, and have such complex causes and effects, as to make either the centralized monitoring or devising of general regulations inappropriate. Problems have to be solved in a more contextual and on-going manner, that brings the relevant parties together. The fora required will be as diverse as the issues under consideration: from schools and hospitals to the workplace. Membership will be similarly diverse and overlapping, including in these cases providers, customers, those with specialized knowledge, and other affected parties. As we have indicated, the guiding principle of representation should be to ensure an equitable and informed dialogue rather than equality *per se*. The result is that purely self-interested bargaining becomes more difficult.

This picture fits well with multi-level governance approaches.[78] These have stressed how public policy making within both the EU and the member states is more fragmented and decentralized than is often supposed, involving a wide range of actors. In consequence, both state-centred perspectives and supranational accounts prove inadequate. Neither the member states nor Brussels can control the policy agenda. EU organizations lack the capacity to push a European view, with the Commission having to vie with the other EU bodies whilst being split into numerous competing

---

[77] Case C-384–93 *Alpine Investments BV v. Minister van Financiën* [1995] ECR I-1141.

[78] For an overview, see Marks, et al. 'European Integration from the 1980s'. We have also drawn inspiration from Philippe Schmitter's contributions to Marks, et al., *Governance in the European Union*.

Directorates and surrounded by a variety of specialist committees. Within this set up, purely national interests also prove hard to push, partly because the complexity of the issues often makes it unclear where these lie, and partly because they have to compete for a voice with policy experts and trans-national interest groups.

There are encouraging signs of the emergence of a republican politics of compromise within this system. At the intergovernmental level, the EU has been characterised as a confederal consociation, for example. All four of Lijphart's criteria for a consociational system—grand coalition, segmental autonomy, proportionality and minority veto—have typified the deliberations of the Council of Ministers and negotiations surrounding the various treaties.[79] These consociational mechanisms have had the aim and effect of rendering the integrative process consistent with the protection and, to some degree, the enhancement of national identities and interests. Moreover, the Council and Inter Governmental Conferences (IGCs) have divided legislative authority with the European Parliament and Commission. Paul Craig and Neil MacCormick have also given a republican rationale to this arrangement.[80] They see it as embodying the notion of institutional balance typical of a mixed commonwealth, that represents the various interests and constituencies involved within the EU far better than making the EP the principal legislative body could.

At the other end of the policy process, Joanne Scott has argued that the 'partnership' principle employed within Community structural funding can also be interpreted in republican terms. Partnership demands that Community development operations:

> be established through close consultations between the Commission, the member state concerned and the competent authorities and bodies—including within the framework of each member state's national rules and current practices, the economic and social partners, designated by the member state at national, regional, local or other level with all parties acting as partners in pursuit of a common goal[81].

She argues that partnership shares power across different levels of government, with the Community recognising that member states are not single units and that actors outside the official public sphere also merit a political voice. Thus, it 'does not involve the parcelling out of limited pockets of sovereignty, but a genuine pooling of sovereignty'. In other words, it ensures the mixing of voices that is distinctive to the democratic liberal approach, promoting dialogue by dividing power. At the same time, the example shows how international solutions to global problems can build on local initiatives.

Of course, the compromises of the present system are frequently based on bargaining rather than negotiation and reflect a modus vivendi that entrenches rather than challenges current inequalities of power and wealth. They are also brokered mainly by elites with an interest in maintaining the status quo. A genuine republican scheme for Europe must look at ways of enhancing popular influence and involvement in the policy process. Proposals for the associative democratic governance of Europe

---

[79] Cf. Lijphart, *Democracy in Plural Societies.*

[80] Cf. P. Craig, 'Democracy and Rule-making Within the EC: An Empirical and Normative Assessment', *European Law Journal*, (1997) Vol. 3, pp. 105–30; and N. MacCormick Democracy, Subsidiarity, and Citizenship in the "European Commonwealth"', *Law and Philosophy*, (1997) Vol. 16, pp. 331–56.

[81] Council Regulation 2081/93 OJ 1993 L193/5, Article 4(1), cited Scott 1998: 181.

by Paul Hirst, Philippe Schmitter, and Joshua Cohen and Charles Sabel attempt just this.[82] To realise the republican device of dispersed sovereignty and the participatory ethic that goes with it, they advocate a scheme of vouchers, redeemable against public funds, that citizens can distribute to associations of their choice. These associations can constitute themselves on a variety of different bases, such as religion, ethnicity, profession or locality, and serve a range of purposes, from the provision of a particular service in a given place through to a more comprehensive range of services equivalent to a welfare system. The only limits on them are that they permit exit, are democratic in organisation, and meet certain conditions of viability. Associationalism is a reformist strategy that does not supplant but supplements, and offers an alternative to, existing bureaucratic and market mechanisms. Though often seen as mutually exclusive, these last two actually go together. For the regulative failures of the market produce the need for ever more stringent control by a central bureaucracy, be it the member states or the EU, which in turn generates allocative inefficiencies that only the market seems able to remedy, thereby leading full circle. More dispersed decision making that draws together local groups on issues such as regional development or schooling offers an alternative. The associational system publicises areas that liberalism treats as private without becoming part of a state bureaucracy or subject to centralised legislatures. Rather, knowledge is pooled within a number of confederal institutions that group associations and determine revenue raising powers.

In this model, a deliberative account of democracy focused on the removal of domination is intrinsic to the way politics resolves both the constitutional and federal deficits. At the constitutional level, this conception of democracy welcomes a heterogeneity of view points rather than shunning them as impossible to sum. It offers the best means for ensuring decisions are informed by relevant concerns and so avoid dominating those they affect. As a result, conflicts of values and interests can be confronted as problems to be resolved rather than as threats to the very nature of legal and political authority that one should try and avoid by deferring to a higher authority. At the federal level, it provides a rationale for creating multiple sites for decision making that reflect the plurality of our political identities and the complexity and diversity of the problems requiring regulation.

This scheme aids a process of positive as well as negative integration. The removal of constraints requires positive changes too, of course, but these have often proved inimical to initiatives requiring greater collective action. For example, the developing social agenda of the EU, with its focus on the problems of exclusion, uneven economic development and employment opportunities, and the rights of workers and immigrants, seems far better characterized in terms of the removal of domination rather than of interference. So too does a more collaborative policy in the realm of security and home affairs. In other words, a more devolved and flexible political structure for the EU need not inhibit greater European integration. On the contrary, while the process may be more differentiated, greater legitimacy and efficacy may well render it deeper too.

---

[82] Paul Hirst, *Associative Democracy*, (Cambridge: Polity 1994), pp.139–41; Philippe Schmitter, and Joshua Cohen and Charles Sabel attempt just this: cf. respectively *How to Democratize the Emerging Euro-polity: Citizenship, Representation, Decision-making*, (Mimeo, 1996); and 'Directly-Deliberative Polyarchy', *European Law Journal*, (1997) Vol. 3, pp. 313–42.

Conclusion

The European Union's democratic deficit has often been attributed to the absence of a fully-fledged liberal democratic and federal constitutional structure. We have challenged that analysis and argued that many of the legitimation problems within the EU stem from this very model of politics. Instead, we have advocated an alternative constitutional regime that draws inspiration from the republican tradition. We have argued that this approach fits the differentiated and non-statist character of European integration better than the liberal model can, whilst being more legitimate from a normative point of view. We do not say European constitutional development will take this path, merely that a future multinational European polity could be 'a Republic, if you can keep it'.

10

Identity and Democracy in the New Europe

Ian Ward

Europe, its common market and its political union, continues to struggle for an identity which can generate widespread support amongst its 'peoples'. It will be suggested in this article that this struggle is, in considerable part, rooted in certain fundamental failings in its political constitution. The current European project is trapped by an uncertainty as to whether to develop existing models of governance common to modern liberal political thought or to take a more adventurous course towards alternative post-modern models. In this catatonic state, each successive Treaty merely repeats rhetorical mantras of citizenship and democracy, whilst twiddling the occasional constitutional knob here or there. The idea that the Union is experiencing something of a constitutional 'crisis' is no longer shocking; it is taken as read. It will be suggested that if Europe fails to grasp the nettle of constitutional reform, more immediately the need to infuse Union political structures at all levels with alternative democratic mechanisms, then it will continue to wallow in a sea of popular indifference. The idea of a politically integrated Europe remains one of contestation, as well as apathy, because its advocates and designers make little effort to make its citizens feel a part of its construction or its government.

I The Politics of Identity

The related questions of legitimacy and identity have emerged at the centre of current debate in European studies. Yet, the European perspective is itself part of a far wider intellectual debate. Indeed, as Bernard Williams has recently suggested the 'politics of identity' is 'essential' to modern life.[1] Juergen Habermas suggests that the project of modernity is 'obsessed' with legitimacy and identity, and that contemporary Europe describes a particularly acute form of this obsession.[2] The idea of the self, rooted in Kant's morally driven individual, describes the essence of European modernity.[3] Citing himself precisely in the Kantian tradition, Jacques Derrida has affirmed that the question of self and other is a question of jurisprudence. The obsession with identity, he suggests, is entirely jurisprudential, and the essence of jurisprudence is the

---

[1] B. Williams, 'Identity and Identities', in H. Harris (ed) *Identity* (Oxford University Press, 1995), p. 10.

[2] J.Habermas, *Between Facts and Norms: Contributions to a Discourse Theory of Law and Democracy* (Cambridge: Polity Press), pp. 491–515.

[3] See H. Cixous, 'We Who are Free, are We Free?', in B.Johnson (ed) *Freedom and Interpretation: The Oxford Amnesty Lecture 1992* (New York: Basic Books, 1993), p. 18.

deconstruction of universalism and the recognition of universal particularism. In this, a deconstructive postmodernism is not set against modernism, but rather represents an evolution of the Kantian understanding of the situation of difference in the process of identifying the self.[4]

The crisis of identity is, at root, an existential crisis which requires an existential solution. Antony Giddens describes a modern world that is fragmenting, not only politically and socially, but also intellectually. Twentieth century (wo)man is faced with a life of choice and risk, whilst the empowerment of 'lifestyle' choices itself, promotes an existential anxiety. It also promotes a correspondingly frenetic ethic of competition.[5] Helene Cixous describes modern life as one of 'permanent mutation'.[6] Ultimately, as Giddens stresses, the acutely existential anxiety with regard to identity and affinity in the modern world generates a totalized 'lack of trust' in the 'other'.[7] The greater the fragmentation and destabilization, the greater the determination to assert the self against the other, and to define the self primarily as a rational economic actor dedicated to the exploitation of others. Eventually there is a world inhabited solely by rabid consumers, totally self-determinative, dedicated to competition and exploitation. This, as commentators as varied as Francis Fukuyama, Zygmunt Bauman and Frederic Jameson have suggested, is the post-industrial postmodern fate of classical liberal ideology.[8]

Against the modernist assumption that integration is an historical inevitability, postmodernism asserts the everpresent reality of political disintegration. There is no question of resisting this disintegration. The crisis of modernism describes the attempt to chart the transition from a centred identity to a postmodern politics of multiple identities. This idea, of multiple identities, has become increasingly popular as a means of providing a political bite to postmodern thinking. Bauman has suggested that 'Postmodernity is marked by a view of the human world as irreducibly and irrevocably pluralistic, split into a multiple of sovereign units and sites of authority, with no horizontal or vertical order.'[9] Duncan Kennedy has similarly suggested that a postmodern legal theory will be developed around an idea of 'positionaliy', defined by the indeterminacy of multiple identities.[10] In a such a theory, the individual is constituted by a series of identities, political and otherwise. In turn he or she identifies with various politics and affinities. Social psychologists describe a phenomenon of self-categorisation, in which individuals seek affinity, not with a particular group or individual, but with a multiplicity of different groups and ideals, forever shifting,

---

[4] J. Derrida, 'The Force of Law: The Mystical Foundations of Authority', *Cardozo Law Review* 11 (1990), pp. 920–1045.

[5] A. Giddens, *Modernity and Self-Identity: Self and Society in the Late Modern Age* (Cambridge: Polity Press, 1991). John Dunn has taken a very similar line, emphasising the extent to which individual competition enhances feelings of social insecurity. See J.Dunn, *The History of Political Thought and Other Essays* (Cambridge: Cambridge University Press, 1996), pp. 148–77.

[6] Cixous, note 3, p. 19.

[7] Giddens, note 5, pp. 50–65, 181–97.

[8] F. Fukuyama, *Trust* (London: Penguin, 1996), Z.Bauman, 'Sociology and Postmodernity', *Sociological Review* 36 (1988), p.311, and F.Jameson, *Postmodernism, or the Cultural Logic of Late Capitalism* (London: Verso, 1991).

[9] Z. Bauman, *Intimations of Postmodernity* (London: Routledge, 1992), p. 35.

[10] D. Kennedy, *Sexy Dressing Etc.* (Cambridge Mass.: Harvard University Press), pp. 49–50. This idea of positionality has already proved popular amongst a number of postmodern feminist thinkers, suggesting as it does an irreducibly unstable and particular location for gender.

forming and reforming.[11] There can be an infinity of social, cultural, sexual, economic and geo-political affinities. The 'positioned' self can be single, married, straight, gay, white, black, rich, poor and so on. To a certain extent, given that diversity enhances choice, this can be an empowering vision. Diversity and fragmentation destabilizes what Foucault termed the 'technologies' of power. It is the essential paradox of modernity that the assertion of identity as a mechanism for stability immediately generates the conditions for its dissolution. Multiple identities exist in a field of acute competition, securing particular affinities in particular situations, in a continual progress of integration and disintegration[12]

II Identifying the New Europe

It is within this wider ideological crisis of identity that we can situate the particular crisis of legitimacy which afflicts the European Union. Both Habermas and Derrida have suggested that the crisis of contemporary Europe represents an acute crisis of modernism. The error of European high modernism is the ultimately futile attempt to forget, to deny history.[13] In his *The Other Heading*, Derrida suggests that European modernism is founded on a respect for difference and a denial of homogeneity. The Europe of 'yesterday' is critically self-determinative. But the Europe of 'today' is not. It is trying to forget this conception of self-determination, and in doing so, is trying to forget itself. Europe denies itself in that it denies the mechanism for describing its own identity. Today's Europe claims seeks to determine normativity, and does so through a complementary claim to cultural and economic dominion. Derrida pursues the familiar deconstructionist mechanism of uncovering linguistic ambiguity in the word *capital(e)*. *Capitale* denotes cultural dominion, whilst *capital* denotes economic dominion. The rewriting of *capitale* has been necessitated by the emergence of *capital*. Culture and difference have been subjugated by the demands of capital and technology.[14] This politically dual idea of European identity – as cultural community and economic Community – is constituted by model normative European actors or citizens. Yet, for reasons we have just considered, the new European is not merely constitutional, cultural or economic. The new Europe(an) is multi-situated, and it is the failure to acknowledge, and thus accommodate, this reality which lies at the heart of Europe's crisis of identity. Following Derrida's lead, we can better ascertain the nature of this crisis by identifying the model European in terms of its economic and cultural characteristics.

A   Capital

First, and perhaps most obviously, the new Europe is a market and the new European a rational economic actor. Over the past decade, the European Commission has

---

[11] M. Sanches-Mazas, 'Intergroup Attitudes, Levels of Identification and Social Change', in Breakwill and Lyons (ed) *Changing European Identities: Social Pyschological Analyses of Social Change* (Oxford: Butterworth-Heinemann, 1996), p. 330.

[12] For a general discussion of identity politics, see H.Bradley, *Fractured Identities: Changing Patterns of Inequality* (Cambridge: Polity Press, 1996).

[13] This historicist critique has been most recently articulated by Phillip Allott in 'The Crisis of European Constitutionalism: Reflections on the Revolution in Europe' *Common Market Law Review* 34 (1997), pp. 439–490.

[14] J. Derrida, *The Other Heading: Reflections on Today's Europe* (Bloomington: Indiana University Press).

increasingly seen its role as one dedicated to modelling this actor. It is an impression which is certainly reinforced by its prescribed judicial capacity in the area of competition law and policy.[15] In many ways, Articles 81 and 82 can be seen as the real heartbeat of the Community. They are certainly the most litigated, and in these terms both the Commission and the European Court of Justice can be understood as Community institutions dedicated to refining the ideal European. Yet, by promoting such an aggressively competitive ideology, the new Europe immediately pays obeisance to a political philosophy which reduces the structurally disadvantaged to a necessary by-product of the market model. These are the uncompetitive Europeans, the excluded, the migrant poor, those who dedicated their lives to philanthropy, those who cannot find employment. European law is very much law for 'workers'. The most obvious structural economic disadvantage enshrined in Community law is suffered by women. As Evelyn Ellis has suggested, the Community consciously engineers a female 'economic underclass'.[16] The Community labour market promotes forms of job segregation which nourish gender discrimination. A preponderance of women in part-time employment, enjoying only limited Community legal rights, is an obvious example. The European woman's place is in the home. Welfare benefits are 'normally' directed to the male householder. Housework or carework is not recognised as proper work by the Court of Justice.[17] Community sex discrimination provisions, such as Article 141 requiring 'equal pay for equal work', subscribe to a normative image of the male worker whilst, at the same time, implicitly refusing to address the deeper social disadvantages which are experienced by women in Europe. In the notorious *Bilka-Kaufhaus* case, the Court of Justice even went so far as to permit sex discrimination if it could be shown that there were 'objectively justified factors' of benefit to the market.[18]

The situation of women describes the inadequacy of any normative economic models, and suggests the impossibility of defining a politics around an economic ideology. As Amartya Sen has repeatedly suggested, the rational economic actor is an illusory model, one which Adam Smith himself constantly advised could not be translated immediately into the practical political world. Economics is not a science, it does not exist in a rarified world apart from politics, society, ethics and so on. No one really leads their life as a classical liberal economic actor, no one really makes purely economic decisions. As Smith emphasised, a market is always part of a wider political world, and if it is not managed in this context, then the intensity of competition will merely condemn it to immanent destruction.[19] Juergen Habermas has suggested that the necessary re-definition of Europe must come about as a reaction to the challenge of capital. The ethic of capitalism is inherently destructive. Capitalism is a threat to democracy, and any democratic polity which seeks to define itself in terms of both

---

[15] See I. Ward, *A Critical Introduction to European Law* (London: Butterworths, 1996), pp. 130–1, P. Montagnon, *European Competition Policy* (London: Pinter, 1990), and T. Frazer, 'Competition Policy after 1992: The Next Step', *Modern Law Review* 53 (1990), pp. 612–14.

[16] E. Ellis, *European Sex Equality Law* (Oxford: Oxford University Press, 1991), pp. 36–7, and 'The Definition of Discrimination in European Community Sex Equality Law', *European Law Review* 19 (1994), pp.653–4.

[17] H. Cullen, 'The Subsidiary Woman', *Journal of Social Welfare and Family Law* (1994), pp. 413–7, and K. Schiewe, 'EC Law's Unequal Treatment of the Family: The Case Law of the European Court of Justice on Rules Prohibiting Discrimination on Grounds of Sex and Nationality', *Social and Legal Studies* 3 (1994), pp. 248–55.

[18] *Bilka-Kaufhaus* Case 170/84 [1986] ECR 1607.

[19] A.Sen, *On Ethics and Economics* (Oxford: Blackwell, 1987), particularly pp. 22–3.

must exist in a state of permanent tension, forever on the edge of dissolution.[20] The economic condition of Europe will determine the fate of (dis)integration. Wealth polarisation is perhaps the most immediate threat to the stability of the Union. 58 million European citizens are recognised by the Commission as being officially 'poor'. 3 million Europeans are homeless. 24% of citizens under 25 years of age are un-employed.[21] The average rate of unemployment in the Union has increased year by year for over a decade. It is small wonder that for so many Europeans there is little in the Union which seems to warrant an affinity. As Habermas concludes, in economic terms, the new Europe is already disintegrating and if the economic causes of this crisis are not addressed, then the possibility of any European affinity or identity will become ever more remote.

B   Capitale

Second, there is the Europe of *capitale*, the Europe that is culturally and geo-politically determined. The Union describes a culturally ideal European. It is an abiding truth that the new Europe is still governed by the old. The nation-states of Europe designed the Community, and they designed it to be a supra-national entity, in terms of an intensification rather than transcendence of nationalism. As Alan Milward described, the nation-states of Europe have conceded a degree of unitary sovereignty in order to preserve the ideology of nationalism and political sovereignty in the new Europe.[22] Yet, nationalism is in crisis, both in Europe and in the wider world, and the critical concessions made in the years following 1945 have merely served to establish the conditions for ever greater tension. Nationalism is not an ideology that can be easily compromised.[23] As Habermas again suggests, globalization refuses to accept compromise, and nurtures 'the expansion' of the political actor's 'consciousness and the differentiation and range of systems, networks (such as markets), or organizations'. The nation-state can no longer govern the modern political economy, and there is, thus, a crucial dissonance between the pretence of government, and its institutional mechanisms, and the reality.[24]

Globalization eats away at the heart of the nation-state and, in the vacuum of governance, according to Antony Smith, there is a return to ethnicity and 'tribalism'. Globalization thus represents both the triumph of capitalism and, by triggering an unavoidable nationalist recidivism, the potential of its own destruction.[25] Such recidivism can be monitored by the treatment of migratory movements. Migration describes the literal breaking apart of fixed geo-political communities, and in challenging the central mythology of nationalism threatens the 'essential' relation between national culture and nation-state governance. Rogers Brubaker has suggested that contemporary Europe can be described in terms of an ongoing 'unmixing of

---

[20] Habermas, note 2.

[21] C. Hadjimichalis and D.Sadler, 'Open Questions: Piecing Together the New European Mosaic', in C. Hadjimichalis and D.Sadler (eds) *Europe at the Margins: New Mosaics of Inequality* (London: Wiley Chancery 1995), p. 238.

[22] A. Milward, *The European Rescue of the Nation-State* (London: Routledge, 1992).

[23] A. Smith, *Nations and Nationalism in a Global Era* (Cambridge: Polity Press, 1995).

[24] J. Habermas, 'The European Nation State. Its Achievements and Its Limitations. On the Past and Future of Sovereignty and Citizenship', *Ratio Juris* 9 (1996), pp. 135–7.

[25] Smith, note 23, pp. 52–78.

peoples', a return to national identities.[26] Peter Fitzpatrick has similarly suggested that the whole idea of European constitutionalism is premised upon this essential 'mythology of European identity', captured in the relation of nation-state and nationalism. The nation-state represents a mythical epitome of European modernity, and the European Union, as the ultimate nation-state, is the ultimate nationalist myth.[27]

The geo-politics of the European nation-state is founded upon laws which seek to include certain ethnic and cultural models, and exclude others. It is familiar to talk of a European 'fortress', strengthened to repel the unwanted 'other'. The wanted 'other' – the rich white 'other' – can enter at will, but the unwanted 'other' – the poor black 'other', usually east European or African – encounters draconian judicial and extra-judicial measures designed to ensure his continued exclusion. The removal of internal borders was secured at the expense of strengthened external borders as well as a rigorous process of internal surveillance, best illustrated by the Schengen Convention and its Information Service established to monitor all migrant movements within the Union.[28] Of course, at root, the inadequacies in Union immigration policy are founded on the absence of human rights provisions in the Treaty framework. In the Maastricht Treaty, immigration matters were consigned to the non-justiciable third 'pillar'. Although many have now been placed in Title IV of the Community Treaty, the rhetoric of Article 61 still casts immigration as a problem of 'security', rather than an issue of human or civil rights. Union immigration policy is primarily geared to controlling, or more accurately, negating migration flows. Entrance into Europe is prevented, whilst permanent movement around Europe is restricted to workers only. In 1980, 65% of asylum seekers were granted access to the Community. In 1990 that figure had been reduced to just 10%. There are approximately 23 million refugees in the world, and another 26 million displaced. The new Europe has managed to provide sanctuary for just 6000. Recent years have witnessed a striking increase in extra-judicial deportations from member-states. The Commission has sponsored a policy for 'stimulating and facilitating' the repatriation of African nationals.[29] In 1991, it reported that immigration and migration was a 'problem', and suggested that 'floods' of migrants threatened to 'swamp' the Union, and threaten the stability of the market. The politics of xenophobia is written into the rhetoric of the new Europe.[30]

The repulsion of the 'other' is demanded by the mythology of European cultural identity. More precisely, it is determined by the nation-states, who seek to determine the new Europe in nationalistic terms. The fictive idea of the model European, empty in itself, can only exist as an antithesis of something else, the non-European. The result

---

[26] R. Brubaker, *Nationalism Reframed: Nationhood and the National Question in the New Europe* (Cambridge: Cambridge University Press, 1995), pp. 148–78.

[27] P. Fitzpatrick, *The Mythology of Modern Law* (London: Routledge, 1992), pp. 63–89, 112–18.

[28] The Meijers Commission made a series of damning observations with regard to the Convention and the procedures for surveillance of migration, concluding that many provisions are in breach of the European and Geneva Conventions on Human Rights.

[29] See M. Spencer, *States of Injustice* (London: Pluto Press, 1995), p. 76, M. Baldwin-Edwards, 'Immigration After 1992', *Policy and Politics* 19 (1991), p. 200, and D.O'Keeffe, 'The Emergence of European Immigration Policy', *European Law Review* 20 (1995), p. 31.

[30] Spencer, note 29, pp. 109–10. For a similar observation, see D.O'Keeffe, 'The Free Movement of Persons and the Single Market', *European Law Review*, 17 (1992), p. 19. Following the Community Immigration Ministers 1992 measures, all member-states are now obliged in Community law to expel without appeal any 'manifestly unfounded' application for refugee status. See D.O'Keeffe, 'The Schengen Convention: A Suitable Model for European Integration?', *Yearbook of European Law*, 11 (1991), p. 195.

of this is a modern Europe, and now European Union, the history of which is written in terms of cultural fascism and institutionalized racism. As Habermas suggests, it is a 'sad fact' that the historical idea of the European nation-state reveals a tendency, not to 'promote loyalty' to principles of liberal constitutionalism, but rather to promote an affinity with 'ethnocentric and xenophobic' alternatives. The new European Union merely intensifies this history.[31] The essential relation between the new Europe and its nation-states, upon which the Union is founded, is a crucially, indeed radically, unstable one. As Milward suggested, the Union is a concession to the global demands of the international market. But it is a concession which seeks to transfer nationalistic impulses onto a supra-national geo-political canvass. The new Europe is designed to enshrine precisely the same principles upon which nation-states are founded. Understood in these terms, it comes as no surprise that the new Europe has proved unable to fashion any alternative identity. In simple terms it does not really want to. Yet, in a schizophrenic sense, it needs to shape a new identity in order to preserve the old 'essentialist' identity of European modernity.[32] The establishment of the new European order is, thus, both a response to and a constituent of, the postmodern and post-industrial challenge of globalization. As Habermas concludes, it remains trapped by an irreducible tension endemic to the founding ideology of modernism, the inability to rationalize collective identity within the classical liberal paradigm. The relation between the Union and the nation-states is defined by the 'tension between the universalism of the egalitarian legal community and the particularism of a cultural community joined by origin and fate'.[33] In short, then, the legal and constitutional Community militates against the possibility of a Europe of multiple identies, the only possibility for future European integration.

III   Constitutional Crisis

There can be little doubting the reality of crisis in today's Europe. Politicians agonize about the effect of European integration on their domestic credibility. European citizens react with a mixture of indifference and hostility.[34] Economists argue the relative merits and demerits of common currency, the many and various theories of competition and the necessity or otherwise of an activist macro-economic policy in the Community. Lawyers complain about the perceived inadequacies of the constitutional and legal framework. One of the most concerted jurisprudential critiques has been articulated by Joseph Weiler, who has consistently argued that the present crisis is, at root, one of constitutional legitimacy. What distinguishes the European Union, what makes it different from any other comparable transnational polity, is its constitutional foundation. Yet, despite this foundation, Europe does not appear to be accountable to its citizens.[35] In a recent essay, Weiler has suggested that the constitutional failing is at once a democratic failing, and moreover one of 'colossal' proportions. Accordingly, if the vision of European integration is to be saved there will need to be a more imaginative approach to the idea of constitutional democracy, one which will

---

[31] Habermas, note 24, p. 132.

[32] For a general discussion of this paradox, see Allott, note 13.

[33] Habermas, note 24, pp. 127–31.

[34] In the aftermath of the Maastricht Treaty, Eurobarometer surveys revealed that less than 50% of Europeans actually thought that they or their nation-state benefited from the Union. See G. Breakwill, 'Identity Processes and Social Change', in Breakwill and Lyons, note 11, pp. 18–20.

[35] See J. Weiler, 'Problems of Legitimacy in Post 1992 Europe', *Aussenwissenschaft* 46 (1991), pp. 411–26.

acknowledge the political reality of 'co-existing multiple demoi'. Today's Europe, he suggests, is one which recognizes 'transnational affinities to shared values', which are themselves the product of 'reflective, deliberative rational choice', without pretending to any comprehensive theoretical foundation. Such 'shared values' can only be democratic values.[36] In another recent article, Weiler has again advocated mechanisms for more 'direct democracy', including legislative ballots and the formation of European 'public spaces'.[37] As we shall see in the next section, such suggestions are immediately resonant of those associated with the likes of John Rawls and Juergen Habermas, and echo a widespread belief that a postmodern world must describe a distinctively postmodern democratic politics.

There has long been talk of a 'democratic deficit' in the Community. The Treaty of Rome never envisaged a properly democratic Community, but there again it never envisaged the kind of Community that exists today. Monnet designed a form of administrative governance, for which democracy could only be an undesirable distraction. For the first couple of decades following 1958, the European Parliament barely functioned at all. The Council comprised the appropriate ministers of each member state, whilst the Commission was comprised of various political nominees of the same member states. To a certain extent, the situation is little changed today. But today it matters more. Whilst the Community was firmly intergovernmental, then the demands of liberal constitutional democracy could be satiated in domestic politics, even if only nominally. But as supranational integration has evolved, primarily in the jurisprudential form of 'integration through law', constitutional inadequacies have become ever more glaring. Thus in 1982, the President of the Parliament, Pieter Dankert could refer to his own institution as little more than a 'feeble cardiac patient'.[38] A decade later, Shirley Williams bemoaned the lack of progress in dealing with the 'deficit', which she termed the most 'urgent' problem facing the Community. Without a genuine democratic impulse, she perceptively noted, the Community cannot hope to establish a coherent political identity, or attract the affinity of its 'peoples'.[39] Juliet Lodge similarly founded the wider 'crisis in governance' in Europe on institutional inadequacies, concluding, in 1993, that the 1990s would be the critical decade when the Community would have to face up the demands for constitutional renewal.[40]

The Maastricht Treaty, and now the Amsterdam Treaty, have disappointed. Deirdre Curtin famously denounced the Maastricht Treaty for its failure to address the major constitutional questions, concluding that enhanced the very real danger of 'constitutional chaos'.[41] Most obvious is the continuing inadequacy of the Parliament, which

---

[36] J. Weiler, 'The Reformation of European Constitutionalism', *Journal of Common Market Studies* 35 (1997), pp. 97–131.

[37] J. Weiler, 'The European Union Belongs to its Citizens: Three Immodest Proposals', *European Law Review* 22 (1997), pp. 150–6.

[38] P. Dankert, 'The European Community - Past, Present and Future', *Journal of Common Market Studies* 21 (1982), pp. 8–9.

[39] S. Williams, 'Sovereignty and Accountability in the European Community', in R.Keohane and S.Hoffmann (eds) *The New European Community: Decisionmaking and Institutional Change* (Boulder: Westview Press, 1991).

[40] J. Lodge, 'Towards a Political Union?', in J.Lodge (ed) *The European Union and the Challenge of the Future*, (London: Pinter, 1993), pp. 383–5.

[41] D. Curtin, 'The Constitutional Structure of the Union: A Europe of Bits and Pieces', *Common Market Law Review* 30 (1993), p. 67.

is still the one institution which cannot properly draft or initiate legislation. As Philip Raworth commented, in the wake of Maastricht, it remains an 'idiosyncratic body incorporating a European identity that is still artificial'.[42] The Amsterdam Treaty offers little hope for the future. As Grainne de Burca perceptively noted, although the run up to the IGC suggested a continuing awareness of the need to address fundamental constitutional inadequacies, it was all too clear that the pressing domestic concerns of the participators would militate against any serious institutional reform. As she concluded, an 'exercise primarily in window-dressing following a negotiation process which is closed and remote, with public involvement and information largely confined to a few public relations exercises', will only serve to 'further reinforce the erosion of legitimacy'.[43] Chapter 15 of the draft graphically described the acuity of this prophesy. The reduction of Parliamentary delaying powers in order to expedite policies necessary for the establishment of the market, is accompanied by a reduction in the transparency of the co-decision procedure itself. Amsterdam will certainly not resolve the related crises of identity and legitimacy in the new Europe.

Of course, the Maastricht Treaty did introduce two democratic 'reforms' which were intended to address the constitutional failings, citizenship and subsidiarity. Article 8 of the Treaty established that every citizen of a member state is a citizen of Europe. The result of Article 8 (now 17) is a critical dissonance between alternative political and legal conceptions of European 'citizenship'. Article 8 describes a purely political citizenship with no rights enforceable in Community law. Citizenship of the Union is predicated entirely upon citizenship of a member state. Thus a German guest-worker who does not enjoy German citizenship is also denied Union citizenship, even if the Court of Justice will grant him certain legal rights as a 'citizen' of the Community. The legal 'citizen' remains the economic actor. Article 8 concedes political rights and, crucially, primary political affinities, to the member states. Union citizenship is stripped of any meaningful legal or political force, and represents a shallow concession to the still overriding demands of the nation-states.[44] The second 'reform', subsidiarity, was introduced in Article 3B (now 5) and intimated in a famously contradictory fashion in Article A (now 1 TEU). The ambition of subsidiarity was to effect Altiero Spinelli's original idea of 'federalism without federation'. Article A did indeed imply that subsidiarity must be seen as a mechanism for enhancing federal capabilities. Article 3B, however, suggested a more intergovernmental approach, where the Community can only take action if the 'objectives of the proposed action cannot by sufficiently achieved' by member states. Only in such circumstances, and if by 'reason of its scale or effects' it can be 'better achieved', does competence pass to the Community. Crucially undefined were 'scale or effects'. Some thought that 3B suggested automatic decentralization to the member states. Others thought that the decision as to competence rested with Community institutions.[45] Again, the

---

[42] P.Raworth, 'A Timid Step Forwards: Maastricht and the Democratisation of the European Community', *European Law Review* 19 (1994), pp. 22–3.

[43] G. de Burca, 'The Quest for Legitimacy in the European Union', *Modern Law Review* 59 (1996), pp. 374–6.

[44] See R. de Lange, 'Paradoxes of European Citizenship', in P.Fitzpatrick (ed) *Nationalism, Racism and the Rule of Law*, (Aldershot: Dartmouth Press, 1995), pp. 97–112, and S. O'Leary, 'The Relationship Between Community Citizenship and the Protection of Fundamental Human Rights in Community Law' *Common Market Law Review* 32 (1995), pp. 540–1.

[45] For a general discussion of the confusion surrounding subsidiarity, see R.Harmsen, 'A European Union of Variable Geometry: Problems and Perspectives', *Northern Ireland Legal Quarterly* 45 (1994), pp. 114–18.

Amsterdam Treaty does little to clarify the issue. Article 5 repeats the still undefined 'scale and effects' criteria, whilst the new Protocol on Subsidiarity merely adds the vacuous observation that subsidiarity is a 'dynamic principle' which 'should be applied in the light of the objectives set out in this Treaty'. So much for constitutional renewal, and the much-vaunted principles of 'transparency'.

IV   Rethinking Democracy

As was intimated in the first part of this essay, the crises of legitimacy and governance which presently afflict Europe are not specific. Michael Sandel has recently suggested that American 'public life is rife with discontent'.[46] So too, he notes, is European public life, citing Vaclav Havel's observation that 'Europe today lacks an ethos' and so must look to 'cultivate values from which the spirit and ethos of European integration might grow'. The European Union, according to Sandel, epitomises a polity built for 'businessmen' rather than 'citizens', and in which 'market forces, under conditions of inequality, erode those aspects of community life that bring rich and poor together in public places and pursuits. As in America, the 'civic' voice of Europe is silenced. The reinvestment of institutions of 'strong democracy' is the most immediate and pressing need, on both sides of the Atlantic. The 'spirit' of community, he continues, demands an alternative view of citizenship and democracy, one which sees the decentralization of political power to all sorts of localized institutions, to 'trade unions, reform movements and local government'. It is, ultimately, a matter of facilitating 'self-government'. A more participatory conception of democracy will promote a sense of civic responsibility which has been suppressed by the rise of liberal constitutionalism in western democracies during the previous century.[47]

The failings of liberal constitutionalism, he perceptively notes, is graphically illustrated by the experience of markets. The liberal constitution was written in order to facilitate the free market, at the cost of civic community and any concomitant sense of participation or community affinity. The need to recover a sense of community is all the more pressing in a modern world of globalization and increasing competition.[48] Such a thesis has been echoed by a number of communitarian critics who have founded a demand for democratic renewal on the need to ameliorate the destructive tendencies of the international market. In this spirit, JK.Galbraith has advocated the need to reinvest the 'good society' by privileging a community ethic.[49] Francis Fukuyama has appealed for the recovery of both 'social solidarity' and 'trust' by means of a more fluid politics of 'spontaneous sociability', within which each citizen aligns with multiple identities and affinities.[50] The essence of the 'good society', for both Fukuyama and Galbraith, is one which recognises that citizens have economic lives, social lives, political lives, and a multitude of other existences, all of which are valuable, but none of which are inherently more valuable than the others.

---

[46] M. Sandel, *Democracy's Discontent: America in Search of a Public Philosophy* (Cambridge Mass.: Harvard University Press, 1996), p. 3.

[47] Sandel, note 46, pp. 332, 339.

[48] Sandel, note 46, pp.117, 125–7, 203–5, 274.

[49] J. Galbraith, *The Good Society*, (London: Sinclair-Stevenson, 1996).

[50] F. Fukuyama, *Trust*, (London: Penguin, 1996), pp. 298–303, 311–20, 356–62.

Despite the pronounced description of the European idea as one of 'community', there has been precious little discussion of communitarian ideas in European studies. Weiler, notably, rejects the communitarian alternative, suggesting that it is a context specific idea, inappropriate to Europe. To a certain extent, the kind of communitarianism advocated by such as Sandel is indeed bound up with classical American republicanism, but as Alasdair MacIntyre has perhaps best appreciated, the idea of community enjoys a far more distant historical genesis. The origins of communitarianism lie in Europe, in the classical form of Athenian democracy and then again in the revised continental republicanism of Machiavelli, Harrington and the early modern continental humanists.[51] Sandel, indeed, concludes his book by citing Montesquieu's injunction, taken from Aristotle, that 'good citizens are made, not found'.[52] The idea of community is rooted in European public morality. No one appreciated this fact more than Hannah Arendt, who returned to the idea of community in order to offer a vision for reconstructing Europe after 1945. The preclusion of genuine participatory democracy, she noted, is a premise shared by both totalitarianism and liberal constitutionalism. If democracy is deficient, it is because too few people are given a reason to care. Like Sandel, she echoed Aristotle; politics is created, not discovered. A democratic politics in turn, is one which concentrates on facilitating participation by defining and preserving 'public spaces' as a locus for political activity and communication.[53]

Moreover, the desire to fashion an alternative to liberal constitutional democracy is not restricted to communitarian models of participatory democracy. Radical democracy also lies at the heart of reconstructive political liberalism. According to Roberto Unger, liberal legalism has preferred the 'conditions for a pervasive uniformity of desires and preconceptions' over those of 'communal solidarity... of extensive, coherent, concrete and intense moral communion'. A radical liberal democracy, he counters, can only evolve from a redetermination of 'group pluralism' as the creative constituent of democratic politics. A radical decentralization of power is the precondition for restoring a 'kernel of solidarity', being a 'concern with another person as a person rather than just . . . as a bearer of formally equal rights and duties'.[54] In his more recent work, Unger has urged the need for 'institutional imagination' to moderate the divisive tendencies of political economy. Repeating a consistent demand for a fluid 'transformative' politics, Unger appeals for an ethic of 'democratic experimentalism' premised on the recognition that, in a distinctively postmodern world, democracy must be defined in terms of difference rather than mythologies of universal humanism.[55] Another to have joined Unger in articulating the need for a reformed political liberalism is John Rawls.[56] In his more recent writings, Rawls has admitted the 'fact of reasonable pluralism'. The political individual lives in a community, and so the key political ideas are described in terms of 'reciprocity between free and equal citizens in a well-ordered society'. Such a politics is

---

[51] A. MacIntyre, *After Virtue: a study of moral theory*, (London: Duckworth, 1981), and *Whose Justice? Which Rationality?*, (London: Duckworth, 1988).

[52] Sandel, note 46, p. 319.

[53] See H. Arendt, *The Human Condition*, (Chicago: University of Chicago Press, 1958) and *On Revolution*, (London: Penguin, 1990).

[54] R. Unger, *Law in Modern Society*, (NewYork: Free Press, 1976), pp. 67–9, 127–8, 142–3, 206.

[55] R. Unger, *What Should Legal Analysis Become?*, (London: Verso, 1996), particularly pp. 1–23, 170–90.

[56] The similarity between Unger and Rawls has been noted by Richard Rorty. See R.Rorty, *Objectivity, Relativism, and Truth*, (Cambridge: Cambridge University Press, 1991), pp. 175–202.

one described by an 'overlapping consensus', and constituted by a process of 'rational political constructivism'.[57]

A third voice to have joined the communitarian and political liberal demands for a more radical idea of democracy, is that of Juergen Habermas. In his recent work, Habermas has attempted to describe a radical theory of participatory democracy, as a means to resolving the crises of legitimacy which afflict Europe. In *Between Facts and Norms*, he has refined democracy precisely in order to address the pervasive problem of constitutional legitimacy. Modernity, he suggests, is 'obsessed' with identity, the subjectivity of the self as co-determinative of and with the 'other', which makes the Union's singular failure to resolve the question of identity ever more pressing. As we have already noted, at the heart of Habermas's critique is the assertion that Europe, like the wider world, is experiencing an acute process of social fragmentation, intensified by the destructive urges of late modern capitalism. To counter this fragmentation, Habermas seeks to flesh out the political implications of his theory of communicative action as a constituent of community consciousness. Such a consciousness is created, not discovered, and can thus be determined as a form of communicative solidarity. Contemporary political theory must be located precisely between facticity and normativity, between arrant contingency and totalizing foundation, and such a location will be described by the 'common practice of associated citizens'. Radical participatory democracy, in other words, represents the only politics which can provide an alternative to the totalitarian impulses of modernism and the radically destabilizing alternatives suggested by deconstructive postmodernism.[58]

Habermas's ambition is to facilitate political legitimacy in a world of pluralism through radical democratic institutions. Legitimacy is not located in substantive morality, but in constitutional institutions, and it is this concentration on institutional democracy which focuses Habermas's critique. Ultimately, the resecuring of political legitimacy is a legal and constitutional question, the critical 'interpenetration of the discourse principle and the legal form'. A constitution properly legitimates those rules and laws which 'refer reflexively to the function of social integration'.[59] The practice of communicative action is engaged in the 'spontaneous sources of autonomous public spheres' and, echoing the communitarian thesis to a considerable degree, Habermas emphasises the extent to which the politics of multiple institutions compose our various 'lifeworlds', from family and gender politics, and the workplace, through various civic associations, and on to representative democratic institutions. Democratic politics, for Habermas, becomes all-encompassing: 'In the vertigo of this freedom, there is no longer any fixed point outside that of democratic procedure itself'. The 'success of a deliberative politics' depends 'on the institutionalization of the corresponding procedures and conditions of communication, as well as on the interplay of institutionalized deliberative processes with informally developed public opinions'. In terms of constitutions, this requires a 'dynamic understanding' of law and politics as a forever incomplete and uncompletable exercise, rendered so by the irreducible contingency of the political community. The modern individual, Habermas concludes, identifies, not with a comprehensive moral theory, but 'with democratic procedures'.[60]

---

[57] J. Rawls, *Political Liberalism*, (New York: Columbia University Press, 1993).

[58] Habermas, note 2, pp. 79, 16–7, 321.

[59] Habermas, note 2, pp. 14–16, 80–1, 91, 121, 287–8.

[60] Habermas, note 2, pp. 186, 298–9, 360–91.

In the specific context of Europe, Habermas concludes that it is the absence of such procedures which founds the related crises of legitimacy, identity and governance. The most 'disturbing' characteristic of contemporary Europe is the 'lack of constitutional controls of administrative activity'.[61] Bureaucracy has replaced the facilities of participation and, thus, the potential for political identity. Instead, there is a destructive determination to compete and to fragment. It is not surprising therefore that Europe's citizens do not identify with the Community, or at least not primarily. In order to address the 'crisis of identity', there will be a need to shape a 'shared political culture'. Moreover, such a Europe, a Europe of solidarity, determined by an ethic of multiple political affinities and participatory democracy, depends, in the final analysis, upon a reconstitution of its political institutions. It is a question of democracy. The new European may indeed want to be prosperous, but not only prosperous. The new European also wants to associate, to determine him or herself in a multitude of ways and to align with a multitude of polities. The new European wants to identify, but does not feel compelled to identify with the European Union. If ever a polity demanded the facility of mechanisms of democratic participation, it is the European Union. It is not a free market that Europe needs, but relief for an 'exhausted' and 'disintegrating' sense of 'social solidarity'. Rather than presenting a vacuous notion of political citizenship, the new Europe must invest in its peoples a genuine democratic community citizenship, supported by radical democratic institutions. If Europe fails to effect a means of generating 'solidarity between strangers', then Europe will remain in the grip of a debilitating fragmentation.[62]

V   Possibilities of Radical Democracy

The rhetoric of solidarity is not, of course, unknown in the new Europe. It is the absence of genuine political practice that is absent. There are plenty of fine words. Indeed, Article 2 declares that the 'Community shall have as its task, by establishing a common market . . .the raising of the standard of living and quality of life, and economic and social cohesion and solidarity among Member States'. If Article 2 is indeed the mission statement of the Community, then the idea of 'solidarity' is central to the future development of the European polity. Certainly, Jacques Delors was fond of referring to the idea of a 'social face' in Europe. In 1990, as he struggled to convince the nation-states that the putative Maastricht Treaty must incorporate such an aspect, he announced that a refined common market must 'extend beyond the single market to solidarity through economic and social cohesion'. Without such a vision, he warned, the Community will be a 'hollow creation, devoid of vitality and political will'.[63] To the extent that the Community has attempted to add some flesh to the rhetorical bones of solidarity, it is in the area of social policy and industrial relations, and it is here that we must look for glimpse of radical democratic potential.

The Community supported the idea of a Social Action Programme as long ago as 1974. Its rhetoric advised the desirability of full employment, an improvement in living and working conditions, and social dialogue in the workplace. The idea was resurrected at the Fontainebleau summit in 1984, which stressed the need for a 'balanced' Europe, and promoted a policy of 'economic and social cohesion' as a

---

[61] Habermas, note 2, pp. 428–31.

[62] Habermas, note 2, pp.445, 491–515, and note 24, pp. 125–37.

[63] Quoted in J. Lodge, 'Social Europe', *Journal of European Integration* 13 (1990), p. 135.

'democratic imperative'. Yet, the legal and constitutional effects of this rhetoric were limited. The Single European Act introduced, in Article 130, the desirability of social progress to complement the single market. The Community Charter for the Social Rights of Worker was only accepted by the member states in 1989, when Delors reluctantly agreed that it should have no legal force. The result of the Community's inability to establish a coherent social policy was evidenced by the Protocol on Social Policy to which was annexed the Social Policy Agreement in the Maastricht Treaty. The challenge to the Community's *acquis communautaire* was clear and widely denounced by academic commentators.[64] Despite the willingness of the UK to now accede to the Agreement, the Amsterdam Treaty offers little else by way of encouraging a sense of social solidarity. Whilst commentators such as Paul Teague have repeatedly argued that the legitimacy crises in Europe require the writing of a coherent 'social constitution' to complement the political, the Amsterdam Treaty militates more towards labour market 'flexibility' and suggests ever more the responsibility of member states to deal with social policy matters.[65]

The potential, and fate, of industrial relations in the Community is instructive. Sally Wheeler has suggested an affinity between the idea of 'social cohesion' in Europe, the communitarian ethic of civic and social responsibility, and the ideology of stake-holding. Echoing Fukuyama, she refers to stakeholding as a mechanism for restoring 'trust' in economic relations. The adoption of works councils, in large part prompted by the European Community, is a gesture towards stakeholding. However, she concludes that, in the absence of genuine rights of participation as opposed to mere rights of consultation, it remains a largely empty gesture.[66] The underlying idea of industrial partnership has gained increasing voice in Commission rhetoric. It was articulated in the 1974 Social Action Programme, and repeated again in the Commission report of the following year. The Commission suggested that industrial partnership was not merely a matter of economic efficiency, but of social democracy.[67] However the infamous failures of the Fifth Company Law and Vredeling directives signalled the reluctance of the member states to make such a political commitment. It was not until the Single European Act, over a decade later, that support for the idea of management-labour dialogue was actually incorporated into the Treaty framework. Article 118B encapsulated the Val Duchesse principle, expressed as 'dialogue between management and labour at European level which could, if the two sides consider it desirable, lead to relations based on agreement'. The desire to facilitate 'information, consultation and participation of workers' was repeated in the 1989 Charter. The incorporation of the Charter into the Treaty framework in 1992 might seem to have constitutionalized the principle of industrial democracy. But the voluntarism of the Val Duchesse principle remains decisive. Although the Commission must consult both management and labour interests with regard to any putative Community legislation in the area of industrial relations, there is no ultimate requirement for agreement. Moreover, the Amsterdam Treaty's preoccupation with 'flexible' labour strategies

---

[64] See, for example, E. Szyszczak, 'Social Policy: a Happy Ending or a Reworking of the Fairy Tale?', in D. O'Keeffe and P.Twomey (eds) *Legal Issues of the Maastricht Treaty*, (London: Wiley Chancery, 1994), p. 313.

[65] See P. Teague, *The European Community: the Social Dimension*, (London: Kogan Page, 1989), and J. Grahl and P. Teague, 'Economic Citizenship in the New Europe', *Political Quarterly* 65 (1994), pp. 395–6.

[66] S. Wheeler, 'Works Councils: Towards Stakeholding?', *Journal of Law and Society* 24 (1997), pp. 44–64.

[67] Bulletin of the European Communities, Supplement 8/75.

reinforces the impression that responsibility in this area remains with the member states.

In the absence of constitutionalised industrial democracy, we must look to the private sphere of directives and the extent of their implementation. Here the sense of voluntarism is all the greater. Directives relating to industrial democracy are uniformly restricted to rights of consultation only. Thus, even when the Court of Justice finds that a directive on collective redundancies has been inadequately implemented, as in the 1994 *UK* case, the indictment is limited purely to a failure to provide 'meaningful' procedures for consultation.[68] The same spirit of voluntarism founds directive 94/45 for the establishment of European Works Councils. Employees still only have the right to be consulted, and although such a right must not be too readily dismissed, it is still a long way short of genuine industrial democracy. It may be a step forward for the idea of participatory workplace democracy, but it is not a particularly large or a particularly convincing one.[69] Of course, the rhetoric continues, the vague arguments, the grand gestures. In June 1997, the Commission issued another 'Plan' for a regulation on worker consulation, decrying the inconsisent state of industrial relations law in the Community, and suggesting that consolidation, even constitutionalisation, would be a good idea. However, any commitment of both management and labour interests, it concedes, can only be on a 'voluntary' basis. If agreement is not reached, then the Commission makes no commitment to draft a regulation itself. It might, but there again, it might not. The Commission bulletin concludes that preliminary consultation has suggested that, whilst trade union reaction has been 'quite positive', that of management has 'tended to express misgivings about such an initiative'. Moreover, rather than merely facing down the Commission or citing arguments of economic expediency, management has responded by citing constitutional consistency. The principle of subsidiarity, it is suggested, militates against Community competence with regard to industrial democracy.[70]

The European constitution is cited as the primary authority for resisting any further arguments for participatory democracy in the workplace. It has to be admitted that the prospects of participatory democracy anywhere else seem even less likely. The crises of identity, legitimacy and governance in the new Europe are destined to remain. The Amsterdam Treaty makes no effort to address this crisis at a Union level. If anything, the references to flexibility and the apparent refinement of subsidiarity along the lines of nation-state primary competence, suggest that the prophecies of nationalist recidivism seem all too apposite. The future of Europe, as Habermas suggests, lies in the balance, and the alternative prospects of integration or disintegration remain equally possible. The European Community remains a community in name only, subjugated now to the all-encompassing notion of a Union of nation-states. It is perhaps as well that the pretence is abandoned. There is no European 'community', just as there is no real sense of democracy, no real political legitimacy, and no genuine sense of affinity or identity. As Hannah Arendt advised, as long ago as 1947, if Europe is to have a shared political future, it must be one which the peoples of Europe feel that

---

[68] Case C-382–3/92 [1994] ECR I-2435.

[69] Moreover, in practical terms it only applies to companies that employ 1000 workers or more, and do so in at least two member states, each of which must include at least 150 of that workforce. See C.McGlynn, 'European Works Councils: Towards Industrial Democracy?', *Industrial Law Journal* 24 (1995), p. 78.

[70] Europe Information Service, European Report, June 4 1997, *Worker Consultation: Commission Plan for National Framework Regulation*.

they had played a role in constructing and shaping. Affinities are not gifted, they are felt. Europeans may have been gifted citizenship, but the Europe that comes with it is not one to which we feel we belong. And it is not our Europe, in short, because it is not a Europe that we feel we have played a role in shaping. We have not participated in creating today's Europe, and if there is to be a tomorrow's Europe, this fundamental failing will need to be redressed.

Index